The Emancipation
of the Jews in Britain:
The Question of the
Admission of the Jews
to Parliament, 1828–1860

THE LITTMAN LIBRARY OF
JEWISH CIVILIZATION

EDITORS
David Goldstein
Louis Jacobs
V. D. Lipman

For the love of God
and in memory of
JOSEPH AARON LITTMAN

"Get wisdom, get understanding:
Forsake her not and she shall preserve thee"

The Emancipation
of the Jews in Britain:
The Question of the
Admission of the Jews
to Parliament,
1828–1860

M. C. N. Salbstein

Rutherford • Madison • Teaneck
Fairleigh Dickinson University Press
London and Toronto: Associated University Presses

Associated University Presses, Inc.
4 Cornwall Drive
East Brunswick, N.J. 08816

Associated University Presses Ltd
27 Chancery Lane
London WC2A 1NS, England

Associated University Presses
Toronto M5E 1A7, Canada

Library of Congress Cataloging in Publication Data

Salbstein, M. C. N.
  The emancipation of the Jews in Britain.

  (The Littman Library of Jewish civilization)
  Bibliography: p.
  Includes index.
  1. Jews—Great Britain—Emancipation. 2. Great
Britain—Politics and government—19th century.
3. Great Britain—Ethnic relations. I. Title.
II. Series.
DS135.E5S23   941'.004924   80-70901
ISBN 0-8386-3110-X   AACR2

To the memory of
George Philip Burstow
1910–1975
Fellow of the Society of Antiquaries and Senior History Master, Brighton College, 1950–1975, who taught me at a young age the value of a human approach to history.

Contents

Acknowledgements

This book is, for the most part, a revised version of a thesis, 'The Emancipation of the Jews in Britain, with particular reference to the debate concerning the admission of the Jews to Parliament, 1828–1860', written while the author was a postgraduate student at King's College, London, and accepted by the University of London for the degree of Doctor of Philosophy in 1974. The first chapter of the book, 'Emancipation: Climate and Environment', though also based on material incorporated in the thesis, is a revision of the prologue to the subject to be found in *The Emancipation of the Jews in Britain: An Essay on the Preconditions* (1977).

For the many criticisms, contributions and ideas which have made this a considerably better book than would otherwise have been the case, I wish to express my gratitude to Professor Paul Smith, formerly of King's College, London, and now of the University of Southampton, who gave invaluable assistance as supervisor of the thesis; Professor Ursula Henriques of the University of Wales at Cardiff and Professor F. M. L. Thompson, formerly of Bedford College, London, and now Director of the London Institute of Historical Research, both of whom sat with Professor Smith as examiners of the thesis; my senior in Emancipation studies, His Honour Judge Israel Finestein Q.C., who has given me the benefit of much inspiration and sagacity; Dr. Ian Machin of the University of Dundee, whose writings on politics and religion in nineteenth-century Britain have proved indispensable; Dr. E. H. Hunt of the Department of Economic History at the London School of Economics; Dr. László Péter of the School of Slavonic and East European Studies, London University; Mr. Malcolm Brown, author of three books on the David Salomons House at Broomhill; Mrs. Eva Sharp of the Central and East European Service of the B.B.C.; Dr. Petar Grujić of the University of Belgrade; and Dr. Robert Wistrich of the Institute of Contemporary History and Wiener Library.

I am greatly indebted to Mr. L. T. S. Littman for much encouragement and understanding in the undertaking of the project, to Mrs. Jane Goater who typed first the thesis, then the introductory work published in 1977 and finally the present manuscript, to Dr. Lionel Kochan of the University of Warwick who advised on and read the manuscript for the Littman Library, and to Dr. Vivian Lipman who scrutinized the text while the book was passing through the press.

In recalling the pleasures of research I wish lastly to express my gratitude to those who made available the various collections of manuscript, archive and other source materials listed in the bibliography.

Michael C. N. Salbstein

University of Turin, Italy
January 1982

A Prefatory Note

This study attempts to serve a twofold purpose by answering the related questions: 'How did the Jews in Britain come to receive their Emancipation?' and 'What type of Emancipation was it that they eventually achieved?'

The first question concerns itself with the story of how the disabilities which disqualified Jews from sitting in Parliament came to be removed; the campaign for political relief began in 1828 and lasted for three decades. The second question concerns itself with that participation in the life of a society which the term *Emancipation,* understood in its broader sense, necessarily denotes.

Empiricism has traditionally characterised the British approach to the resolution of political problems: while some accord praise to the view which avers that answers to questions must ever be sought in the light of acknowledged precedents and practical experience and must never be arrived at on the basis of abstract speculation, others have seen in the contemptuous dismissal of any *a priori* constitutional innovation nothing better than an apology for—to précis Emerson—'the cramp limitation in the British habit of thought, the sleepy routine, tortoise-like fear of change and drag of inertia which together conspire to resist reform of every description'. Be that as it may, the observer of a European cast of mind should not attach any sinister significance to the timing of the remission of Jewish disabilities in Britain. Contemporaries of that mid-nineteenth-century campaign were fully appreciative of the virtues of an Emancipation which had demanded, as the indispensable precondition of the removal of political restrictions, the creation of a climate of tolerance and toleration.

The first part of this book comprises two chapters, 'Emancipation: Climate and Environment' and 'The Legal and Juridical Position of Mid-Nineteenth-Century Anglo-Jewry', which serve by way of introducing the reader to the story of the Emancipation proper—this being considered in its two distinct phases of 'The Jewish Initiative' and 'The Gentile Response', as expressing a thematic treatment of the subject which should in due course appear self-explanatory.

The Emancipation
of the Jews in Britain:
The Question of the
Admission of the Jews
to Parliament, 1828–1860

Part I
INTRODUCTORY

1
Emancipation: Climate and Environment

SPIRIT OF THE AGE

It was as merchants that the Jews were first known to nascent Europe; in documents of the Carolingian period the words *Judaeus* and *mercator* appear almost synonymous. This trading and commercial role, so natural for a close-knit people dispersed from their homeland across the known face of the globe, soon came to be carefully delimited in law. Jews were not judged by the authorities of the lands in which they resided, for in common with other groups of ethnic strangers settled in a given region they were subject only to their own laws. Unable as infidels to subscribe the oaths of fealty and loyalty, they could not belong to any feudal or land-donation system and were excluded from the guilds of municipal corporations. Instead they were compelled to pay oppressive taxation in return for royal, baronial or ecclesiastical protection; the loathsome occupations enjoined upon the Jews, such as usury and non-productive dealings from which Christians as 'decent' men enjoyed exemption, were to lead to the permanent fulfilment of a distinct 'pariah' role.

In Christian Europe the Jews were branded as members of the God-killing nation who obstinately refused to acknowledge the truth of the Christian revelation. No Christian could be allowed to risk contamination by unnecessary contact with a Jew. In England early in the thirteenth century Jews were ordered to attach a piece of cloth of specified length to the front of their upper garment and were forbidden, as excommunicates, from trading with Christians.

In the eyes of the Jews Christ appeared damned as a bastard impostor, and thus religious hatred was reciprocated. Rabbenu Gershom's tenth-century poem sounded the traditional monotheistic and anti-idolatrous themes in Judaism in its rejection of the symbol of the crucified Christ:

> They decree upon us not to call to the Lord
> to accept the despised idol as god,
> to bow to the image, to worship before it.[1]

Fears of contamination, too, were mutual. The eucharistic-sacramental association of wine was responsible for the Jewish ban on its trade and consumption at all times of the year, whilst the explanation for the further thirteenth-century English prohibition of the nursing of Jewish children for the three days after Easter lay, paradoxically, in the fear entertained by Jewish parents that Christian nurses might smuggle into their households the leavened bread forbidden during Passover—which festival usually fell concurrently with Easter—and so by incorporation infuse the children with the Body and Blood of Christ.

The gulf of separation was widened by linguistic differences. The Latin alphabet was practically unknown among the Jews at the time when they lived in that territory designated in pre-fourteenth-century Jewish sources as *Loter,* the area from the left bank of the Middle Rhine extending towards the Franco-German language border which was inhabited by them in the centuries prior to the migration eastwards, and it was not by means of the written word but solely through oral contact that Yiddish was acquired. Indeed, the very name for the Latin alphabet in the Hebrew and Yiddish of the period betrays the reason: the word *galkes* literally signified something belonging to the *galokhim,* or 'tonsured ones', the Christian priests. The Hebrew and not the Latin alphabet was commonly used in adapting the *Shpra' khikayt,* the spoken language of the co-territorial non-Jewish population, to Jewish religious and cultural usage. For in exile the vernacular was indistinguishable from the religious, and *Yidishkayt,* the Yiddish term for Jewishness, expressed nothing less than a way of life and an outlook on life. Many Jews were as keen to be sealed off from Christians as Christians were from Jews, and the first Italian ghettos answered the Jewish need for a tangible symbol of corporate autonomy.

If the primacy of faith demanded the harshest possible treatment of the infidel so, conversely, did secular rivalries and ambitions postulate a more deft approach. It was here no accident that an early and most piquant example of the contempt for Jews being made to yield to a shrewd assessment of their worth and of the difficulty of adequately replacing them was afforded by one of the few hitherto strong economies of a city republic which was, for a brief period of little more than half a century ending around 1620, able to withstand newly adverse trading conditions whilst simultaneously resisting the spread of the inquisitorial and bureaucratic forms associated with the Counter-Reformation. In Venice the Sephardim (the Spanish and Portuguese Jews, most of whom had already been expelled under the Inquisition) and Marranos (those Sephardim whose clandestine adherence to Judaism belied their apparent conversion to Christianity) became lenders to the poor and almost controlled the Levantine and Mediterranean import and export trade, the considerable volume of which made possible the development of the Venetian commodity exchange as a clearing-house for the merchants of Europe.

This expediency of associating with a select class of indispensable Jews commended itself to many of the German rulers. The financing and supply of troops during the Thirty Years' War, the need to maintain standing armies in the years thereafter, the crippling burden of financial indebtedness incurred by the succession of eighteenth-century wars, and the growth of inflation caused by expenditure exceeding revenue were all factors which encouraged the rise of the *Hofjuden,* or court Jews. The collapse of the Spanish banking houses, the decline of a native merchant class whose failure to recover was reinforced by the fragmentation of the German lands into a large number of economic units sealed off from each other by customs barriers, and the inclination of those comparatively few Christian entrepreneurs who were able to thrive to concentrate within these circumscribed units on developing their own private concerns were all factors which afforded the *Hofjuden* unlimited scope and made them the more indispensable. Consolidation of family businesses through intermarriage and an easy resort for contacts to the networks of co-religionists based upon the leading European commercial centres led almost to a Jewish monopoly of the gem, metal and bullion markets. Jews supplied the administrative machinery for tax collection and were even sometimes made responsible for debasement of particular currencies. They also provided vital accounting, credit and interest-loan facilities, their comparatively large capital assets enabling them to procure those valuable orders with no immediate prospect of payment which their gentile rivals had perforce to decline.

Titles of nobility were conferred on the most successful of the *Hofjuden* who, loyal to their co-religionists in the ghettos, boldly assumed the role of *Shtadtlanim,* or intercessors. Of these the most important by the early nineteenth century were the Rothschilds, once the *Hofjuden* of Frankfurt; they invoked the aid of the Prussian government in cajoling the German Diet to consider the removal of civil disabilities and supported the efforts which the British made at the Congress of Vienna to achieve a universal acceptance of civil equality.

Yet the indispensability of the minority could never in itself have secured the emancipation of the majority; the realization of this goal depended on the extent to which 1) the new awareness that Providence alone could not explain human conduct, 2) the new spirit of humanity and democracy, 3) and the new command of material resources would predispose Christians and Jews to reassess their attitude towards each other.

First, changes affecting religion and thought were arguably the most profound. Reason, as a revolt inspired by scientific empiricism against accepted faith in general, inclined men to a Pelagian acceptance of human progress and a consequent disavowal of original sin; this was a languid, worldly tolerance which presented the most deadly threat to religious zeal because those who were indifferent and sceptical offered no front which might be attacked and declined to join with an issue which they did not even recognize. Reason, as relativism, believing that men must be judged according to the standards of the place and time in which they lived, jettisoned as absurd the idea that national collective guilt could still be imputed to a whole people for a crime committed by a small minority among them more than a millennium and a half before. Reason, in its revolt against the particularism of credos, held that the essence of religion did not lie in assent to preconceived dogmas: these must therefore be discarded in favour of self-evident ethics and of the universal moral law rooted in them. Whereas hitherto the precedence of faith, tied to goals of salvation in the next world, had demanded the punishment of sin in a man's soul, so now religion in a secular age, clearly subordinated to the aim of improving the conditions of human existence in the present world, demanded the correction of the whole of an individual's being: from such a reforming philanthropy and elevation in manners and morals the Jews might expect to benefit.

Secondly, the dissolution of a society based upon estates and the appeal to democracy and representation as the agents of integration were also important factors. The old Greek and Italian republics, through confinement of citizenship to a body of kindred families, had atrophied for want of vital infusions; the lesson of antiquity as applied to the *anciens régimes* of the eighteenth century required the abandonment of legally determined connotations of corporate status as a prerequisite of successfully persuading the individual to contract his loyalty to the wider community to which he now belonged in return for the concession of individual civic rights and equality before the law. Integration, not surprisingly, could be implemented at a perceptibly faster pace and wrought on a correspondingly higher level the farther west it was attempted. Where the political unit comprised a mosaic, as with the Habsburg peoples divided into speakers of more than a dozen languages, that challenge was the more daunting because even the most feverish administrative reform based on Joseph II's Germanization programme of assimilation had painfully to transcend the problems of conservative particularisms. In France the revolutionary *élan* so swept up the Jews as to enable them henceforth to share wholeheartedly in the task of revitalizing a unique cultural patrimony; subsequently the Napoleonic conquests drew to France the loyalty of the Jews of Europe. And in the lands across the North Atlantic, where in complete contrast to the European continent there was involved neither the overthrow of *native* political institutions enshrining the bitter Jewish-Christian legacy of separatism nor the seizure of power from higher social ranks, Jews were able to identify their own aspirations with a faith in the future success of a democratic experiment almost as soon as the young American republic and its constituent communities had given birth to the federal and respective state constitutions.

Thirdly, the advent of capitalism must be considered. As societies burst the confines of their mercantilist straitjackets, designed to monopolise the sources of a definable or quantifiable wealth, into a capitalist expansion animated by competition, the Industrial Revolution brought with it yet another revelation original to the history of the West: freedom conceded to the wealth producers meant profit for the wealth beneficiaries. The social bonds and values of the *ancien régime* were being forced to yield. There was now a transition from a society of rank to one of individual autonomy, from an agrarian order to an industrial order, from constraint on economic activity to the encouragement of production. The assumption that finance constituted essentially the sinews of war was giving way to an appreciation that finance could as easily and with more benefit be geared to the objectives of peace and trade. These were new freedoms and auguries of opportunity to the very people whose history had been a test of endurance, independence and enterprise.

No wonder then that Heine, arguably the foremost Jewish *déraciné* of the Romantic generation, could foresee 'the great assignation of our times' in an 'emancipation, not only of the people of Ireland, of the Greeks, the Jews of Frankfurt, the blacks of West India and similar depressed peoples, but of the whole world, especially Europe'.[2] But what of the ecological aspect of this 'emancipation'? A legally authorized *entry into* society must not be mistaken for even the least measure of *acceptance by* society; for Jews, as for the other 'depressed peoples' of Heine's thoughts, fate would be determined no less by the native features of the quite dissimilar environments in which they lived than by the changes of the age already touched upon here.

EUROPEAN/NORTH ATLANTIC BIFURCATION

The solvent of the eighteenth-century Enlightenment, the subsequent entry of Jews into European society as effected by the French Revolution and the boldly imaginative reforms of Napoleon, was causing the messianic yearnings for an ultimate redemption of the Jewish people to dissolve into the utopian universalism of messianic humanity; nowhere did the intellectual ferment of the years from 1815 to 1848 affect a significant number of Jews more than in the German-speaking lands of Europe, for during the preceding century the *Aufklärung* had found its specific Jewish expression in the movement for Reform initiated by the Berlin biblical scholar Moses Mendelssohn. Judaism was hereby transformed from a national into a universal faith and the Jews deemed to be no longer a national people but a universal people, not a nation among the nations but simply one of the religious communities of the world. The aspirations of those who sought integration, be they enlightened Jews or enlightened gentiles, converged in the desire for a linguistic uniformity, and welcome to many Jews were the linguistic definitions of identity proffered them by the liberals of 1848.

Yet throughout the German and Central European lands the stamp and structure of society and the lack of industrial development pointed to a set of obstacles which might come to jeopardize the prospects of a permanent integration of the Jews. The Roman Catholic Church, as in Pius IX's *Syllabus Errorum* of 1864, pronounced as anathema the secular, materialistic and liberal-reformist free-thinking civilization whose evolution seemed so inextricably bound up with the emergence of the Jews into European society; in the once torpid, formerly self-enclosed German communities a tradition of mystic Pietism, derived from an Augustinian Lutheranism which pessimistically dwelt upon human depravity, discounted any idea of employing secular instruments to establish God's kingdom on earth and preached instead an awesome trust and obedience to divinely sanctioned authority and the duties of man to accept the lot of the calling, invariably humble, to which God had summoned him.

As for the teachings of the classical economists in Britain, with which no figure in recent times had been more identified than the Jewish-born David Ricardo, these were often frowned upon. The Manchester School, with its implicit approbation of the individual quest for the highest possible market reward, was seen by its many detractors as imparting respectability to 'unfeeling egotistical calculators', 'glaciers' of the type commonly found at the highest strata where no 'moral vegetation' could grow;[3] in opposition to freedom of movement, freedom of trade, freedom of individual business opportunity and a factory capitalism which was stigmatized as condoning an 'unchristian' inhumane treatment of labour, there were proclaimed, not infrequently, the merits of tariff trade protection, of restrictions on choice of domicile, of a locally powerful and numerically restrictive guild corporatism and of the principle of association (Ger. *Genossenschaftswesen*) now finding renewed expression in the proliferation of communal cooperative enterprises.

The conception of the State which, in German and Austrian thought alike, dictated a consolidation of the existing dynastic-patrimonial and bureaucratic-military order, made little allowance for the Anglo-Saxon notion of a personal liberty. The earlier gains of absolutism at the expense of the Estates, most particularly in Prussia and other of the German territories, and the consequent disdain of institutional safeguards for the liberties of the subject given philosophical justification in writings such as emanated from the cameralist–Natural Law school, had prepared opinion to accept the claims advanced in favour of an organically integrated community, comprehended by civil and military institutions, in the service of which the individual might be enabled to realize his most valuable capacities. Thus liberalism to a number of Metternich conservatives, or even Hegelian nationalists, in the German-speaking lands of Europe suggested less an Anglo-Parliamentarianism dedicated to preventing arbitrary infringement of the *rules of law* than a recrudescence of the Jacobin-Babouvist threat to the *rule of law*. Rejection of the Jews who loomed so conspicuously in the van of revolutionary movements could be seen to be almost implicit in any Gallophobia based upon a rejection of 1789 and this conservatism, to the despair of such Romantics as the converted Ludwig Börne, reinforced the more general resentment against the Jews for having earlier identified themselves with the cause of Napoleon.

That little room could be found for the Jews in this ordering of society and values received impressive confirmation from the observations of two of the most percipient of British travellers. In 1843 Lord Ashley, the future seventh Earl of Shaftesbury, who as an evangelical patronised and sympathised with the Jews even if he opposed their admission to a Christian legislature, recorded of the many Jews whom he had encountered on a visit to the fashionable Bohemian spa of Carlsbad:

> They seem in comfortable circumstances, but separated from the Gentiles . . . They are not oppressed here, but manifestly avoided. The veil is upon the hearts of the Gentiles in respect of that people nearly as much as it is on their [the Jews'] hearts in respect of the Gospel.[4]

Two years later the littérateur Richard Monckton Milnes who, unlike Ashley, was a keen supporter of Emancipation, gave a rather more poignant and vivid illustration of the Jews' position, informing fellow Members of Parliament that

> he had lately witnessed in the Government of Prussia a most dangerous and immoral effect, arising from the encouragement given to those prejudices against the Jewish nation. He had there seen, in the midst of a highly civilized community, an animosity against this race, hardly surpassed in the United States by that existing between the black and white races.[5]

The problems which attended the integration of the Jews meant that correspondingly fewer impediments were encountered by those German and Austrian politicians who in the last third of the nineteenth century sought to exploit the novelty of the democratic franchise by translating into popular support a resentment of the Jews' dominance in certain sectors of business, banking and the professions, the press, politics and the arts. And where, as in those Habsburg lands which witnessed in 1848–49 the failure to realize political aspirations based upon separate linguistic identities, the heirs of an earlier liberal Romanticism were subsequently tempted to sacrifice recognition of diversity to the pursuit of a linguistically defined homogeneity, the Jews found themselves caught in the crossfire of dynastic and national rivalries. Thus their subsequent treatment at the hands of imperial government, Hungarian authority and the subject nationalities among the Slavs was to be determined by such additional factors as their record of loyalty to one or another of the political groupings, their presence in areas of irredenta and their economic identification with the largely German-speaking burgher class of the towns.

In agrarian Eastern Europe, comparatively unprepared for the transition from the religious to the secular, the import of *völkisch* thought had an even more unfortunate effect. Ideals tended to seek worldly expression not in appreciation of a cultural universalism, to be realized through a nourishing of each and every one of the literary-historical folk traditions of which the region had so recently become conscious, but in the respective inversions (exclusive particularisms intolerant of diversity) and antitheses (uncommon identities sacrificed to uniformity) of such a notion of unity in diversity. Already by the middle years of the century an ideological obsession with questions of identity, particularly in the western Polish lands earlier annexed by Prussia and in Habsburg Central Europe, could be seen traducing the available evidence of race differences, philology, history and toponymy in the interests, variously, of substantiating conflicting claims to cultural-political supremacy and territorial acquisition.

In the areas comprehended by 'The Pale' and its extension, in which the Jews as from the middle of the century were most thickly settled (Lithuania, Russian Poland, White Russia, the Ukraine, the western half of New Russia, Bessarabia, Moldavia, the Bukovina, Galicia, Ruthenia, Slovakia and the northern part of central eastern Hungary) society was still stratified. To be a gentleman, a peasant or a Jew denoted, more often than not, a language, a religion, a profession and a nationality. The continued use of Yiddish was significant: Jewish concern for national identity and group survival coincided with a vested interest in preserving the Jews as a quasi-ghetto entity. For in many of the East European lands the political nation was effectively confined to the various ranks of nobility which embodied the most entrenched resistance to change. The nobilities despised the Jewish financiers and advisers with whom they could not dispense, whilst the peasantries, painfully overcoming illiteracy and in many instances dependent upon the Jews for carrying through even the merest of transactions, resented the barterers and usurers and those who acted as tax-collecting agents for rapacious, and sometimes foreign, masters. Persistence, moreover, of the incubus of religious hatred, whether of Christian Judeophobia or of Jewish anti-Christian prejudice, vitiated attempts at mutual understanding: governmental schemes for improvement were liable to be denounced by the Jews as conversionist while repression served only to confirm the Jews in their sense of insecurity.

The forces of eighteenth-century imperialism saw large additional tracts of the Jewish Pale and its extension incorporated into multinational aggregates, whilst early-nineteenth-century change saw these aggregates beset by the mutually exclusive rivalries of various imperial and national ambitions. Two solutions affecting the Jews seemed foredoomed to failure: the assimilatory, articulated in such sentiments as 'Russia is our fatherland, and its air, its language too, shall be ours', and that of an Hebraic, ultra-orthodox Diaspora nationalism which, akin in concept to religious Slavophil anti-governmental populism, involved retention of those extensive rights of self-government as were thought would constitute a defence against antisemitism by helping to restore Jewish self-respect and national honour. And yet the status quo was equally unacceptable. Capitalism and socialism were to tear along the lines of social and political division and the Jews, as a people keen to acquire both property and rights, placed in the most exposed position in both the capitalist and socialist camps, knew that they would suffer in any social conflict.

Two choices, to some extent complementary, seemed to offer the Jews a realistic redefinition of their identity. There was Zionism which Pinsker, Herzl and its other founders envisaged as a form of 'Auto-Emancipation' to be brought about through the harnessing of modern technology to an ancient ideal, or socialism, which its exponents thought of as involving nothing less than the 'emancipation' of society itself not only from the particular legacy which divided Jew from gentile but from the whole set of prejudices of which this legacy appeared to be a concomitant.

Zionism blended East European nationalism with the biblical and geographical conception of nationality inherent in Judaism. The Jews were 'the chosen people', a nation selected from among the nations, commanded to reflect upon the Zion of ages past and to contemplate the Zion of tomorrow: now the hour of the ingathering was come. Herzl most certainly echoed the language of the hallowed prayer-books when arguing that the only true return would be to that land which had belonged to the Jews before the destruction of the Second Temple; when, however, he identified the national movement with the cause of civilization by declaiming that 'we should there [in the national home] form a portion of the rampart of Europe against Asia, an outpost of civilization as opposed to barbarism',[6] his words seemed rather to carry echoes of the respective Central and East European nationalist claims of his own day.

As for the writings of socialist philosophers, these were particularly of interest inasmuch as many of the values projected for the new socialist society were drawn from that very group, none other than the Jews, which had formerly been made to espouse the values so despised by the gentile majority. In this connection some consideration is relevant of the prominence of Jews in the development of the social and political systems of the modern world. Though the phenomenon might plausibly be ascribed to the Jews' gifts of interpretation or to the generations of training in Talmudic logic-chopping, such explanations must yield to what lies beyond conjecture. Only the Jews, as the outsiders who had never been conditioned by those social experiences and Church traditions which permeated the Christian environment, could stand naturally in a position of detachment from that environment: as Herder had stated 'the Jew is free of certain political judgements which it is very hard or impossible for us to abandon.'[7] The Jew comes forth as emancipator of the majority; when he is concerned with the

minority to which he himself belongs he has the subsequent task of emancipating it from that particular sense of identity almost inseparable from the
Jews' traditional role as an anti-group.

So emerges Marx, *deus ex machina,* with his attack upon the preconceptions of religious faith, the false consciousness which literally bound men to
what they could not know.[8] As against these religious preconceptions Marx
looked to that verification afforded by the natural and social sciences which
could facilitate a social transformation; religion was equated with ignorance,
and science with knowledge. The individual must be 'emancipated' from a
state of alienation in which he as an egoist can indulge the private rights,
including those of religion, allowed to him by civil society; the State in its
turn must be 'emancipated' from State religion and so be enabled to recognize not religion but only itself as the State: atheism would then incarnate
the State spirit.

Thus the thought of Marx removed from the forces which had shaped the
world both the *Logos* or *Christ-Logos,* the godly hand in history, and the
Ecclesia or *Synagogue* which had been its instrument. In this Marx, a Jew,
erased from history not only the relevance of the Christian tradition to the
life of man but also the tradition of Judeophobia which was inherent in it.

Yet Marx was, of course, as concerned with bringing about changes in
function as with effecting changes in identity and to him the corollary to the
secular liberation of man from religious bondage was a human emancipation
which would merge the individual citizen into a social framework. Here, in
consideration of the Jewish question, Marx resorted to a somewhat syllo-
gistic argument; by equating Jewishness with an obsessive concern for practical need, self-interest, financial gain and bargaining, he was able to present
capitalism as the essential expression of Judaism and could thus conclude
that the succumbing of Christian societies to the capitalist ethos denoted, to
a corresponding degree, the transformation of the members of these
societies into 'Jews'. Although socialists other than Marxists agreed that
capitalism thrived on the maintenance of class barriers and distinctions and
that the customary role of the Jews would endure only as long as these
continued to exist, the Marxist approach to the Jewish question was far
more direct and explicit, with its hailing of revolution as the immediate
displacement for the Rothschilds as the sixth power of Europe.

The choice which presented itself to many of the Ashkenazi and other
Jewries of a predominantly Yiddish tradition was one with which few of the
Sephardi and other of the Southern European Jewish communities had ever
been confronted. For during earlier centuries those living in the shadow of
the Inquisition had been able to look to the enemies of their Catholic and
Habsburg masters: to the Muslim Ottoman, locked in combat with Spain for
mastery of the Mediterranean, to the part-Calvinist Dutch, striving first to
win their independence from Spain and then to retain it, and to Protestant
England, competing with Spain for the supremacy of the New World.

Sensibly, as test of the truism that the enemy of one's enemy is one's friend, the Jews expelled from Spain had first looked east, to the power whose thrust into the heart of Europe seemed capable of avenging the humiliating defeat inflicted upon Islam by the success of the *Reconquista*. They found in the Ottoman Empire no difficulty in winning acceptance simply as Jews. Their economic, commercial and professional worth was here appreciated and with their international connections and cosmopolitan outlook many Jews proved valuable as the dragomen of the Mediterranean trade, the links between the Sultan and his merchants.

Many of the rich tradesmen came to be drawn from the Jewish community, and so too did a substantial number of the physicians, stewards, *hommes d'affaires* and interpreters of the great men. In the early years of the eighteenth century the remarkable traveller and literary figure Lady Mary Wortley Montagu recorded her observations of the Jews who lived at Adrianople 'in their houses in the utmost luxury and magnificence'; she concluded 'That people [the Jews] are in Incredible Power in this country. They have many privileges above the natural Turks themselves.'[9] The exiled Huguenot historian Jacques Basnage had recently given a similar impression of Jewish well-being in the Ottoman Empire; he noted that Istanbul and the neighbouring villages contained a prosperous community of more than a hundred thousand Jewish families based upon some thirty synagogues and that in the city quarter traditionally inhabited by the Jews there resided also the ambassadors of foreign countries.[10]

All was protection: but it was to be understood that this protection was synonymous with the right to seclusion, whereby security of person was enjoined to, and dependent on, the insulation of religion. How topsy-turvy were these Eastern precepts to the refugee from Christian Europe: the individual Jew was not, as in Catholic Venice, begrudged a measure of toleration *in spite of* his religion, but unreservedly accorded toleration specifically *on account of* it. He was the beneficiary not of inclusiveness but of the exclusiveness enshrined in the *millet* system. The *Sharī'a,* the Sacred Law of Islam, conceived of the world as being divided into two parts, the Domain of Islam and the Domain of War. The duty of true believers was to expand the first at the expense of the second. The Domain of War itself comprised two groups, the Idolaters and the People of Scripture; the 'scriptural' peoples, consisting of Zoroastrians, Jews and Christians, found themselves ranked more highly than the Idolaters and were to be tolerated, because Zoroaster, Moses and Christ were regarded as prophets akin to Muhammad. The People of Scripture retained their own respective religions and became subjects of the Sultan; they were however obliged to pay a special tax and if the Sultan so desired this tax could be accepted as a tribute from whole 'scriptural' populations who thereby attached themselves in a vassal capacity to the Domain of Islam.

The necessity of ensuring that the status of intermediacy as between Muslim and Idolater be given expression through a set of institutions which might be made to parallel exactly the monolith of Islam led to a consolidation of Jewish and Christian religious authority and autonomy, for the sultans recognized only the leading patriarchs and rabbis. In the *Dīvān* at Istanbul the Jewish religious leader customarily sat on the right of the *Shaikh al-Islām,* the head jurisconsular *Muftī* of the Empire, while the Orthodox Patriarch sat on his left; another Jew, responsible only for Jews, dispensed justice by giving an equivalent interpretation of the decisions which the Sultan handed down in respect of Muslims. Religion was paramount. Islam, Christianity and Judaism imparted such a fierce sense of identity to their respective adherents as to enable them to withstand the onslaught of nineteenth-century secularism; not even the Tanzimat Reforms could disturb the dichotomy of religious and civil courts.

The very separation enjoined by Islamic religion afforded to the Jews little opportunity of contributing to Ottoman culture and philosophy. The disinclination of the Sephardim to master Turkish and other of the native languages and the survival instead of the variants of Ladino, the language which the original refugees from the Inquisition had brought with them from Spain and Portugal, was bound up with the Ottoman desire that those comprising even the more acceptable segments of the Domain of War keep themselves apart from Muslim society. Thus, whereas the Sephardim were largely responsible for introducing printing to the Ottoman Empire, the rigid demarcation insisted upon by both the *Muftīs* and the other orders of the *Ulamā,* or representatives of the orthodox Islamic religious institution, meant that Jews had altogether to forsake the use of Turkish and Arabic and were permitted to print books only in Hebrew and in European languages.

The term *Emancipation* implies a change in status. But Ottoman society was inward-looking and keen on preservation for its own sake and the Jews could not but help being likewise affected. The Sephardim had realized to the fullest degree their gifts of interpretation in the centuries when Spain had been divided between Moor and Christian: though insecure from persecution they had performed amidst the vibrant clash of cultures a most vital and enriching symbiotic function. In the Ottoman Empire, by contrast, the Jews enjoyed such privileged recognition and toleration as a group that they could effect no contact with the corresponding alien Islamic civilization; here, even before the growth of Balkan nationalisms attendant on the collapse of central Turkish authority, the Ottoman ideal precluded the Jews as individuals from anticipating that degree of participation in the life of society as would have connoted an effective attempt at Emancipation from their corporate status.

Those other Sephardim who looked north to the Atlantic seaboard could assess their prospects of surviving in societies the very antitype of the Ottoman: dynamic, innovatory and competitive.

In the rising power of the United Provinces a sense of freedom, won against bitter odds, emphasised the virtues of self-assertion and individualism. The Dutch of the late-sixteenth and seventeenth centuries, as an urban, mercantile people keen to develop their prosperity but realizing how large a share of their wealth lay at the mercy of other governments, welcomed any immigrants, Sephardim and Marranos included, who could direct more capital and freight towards the United Provinces. Preoccupation with the immaterial, a probing of other men's religious consciences, was here, perforce, made to yield to the consideration that greatness lay not in the imposition of some Procrustean uniformity but in an imaginative, truly *laissez-faire*, policy which afforded to individuals and groups the opportunities to discover, quite spontaneously, their own possibilities.

The Sephardim and Marranos of the United Provinces came to be the most prominent in an international network trading in the Levant, the Mediterranean and the Atlantic. Their expertise, whether exercised through financial management or commodity dealing, saw the scale of their influence rise out of all proportion to their numbers and this was of commercial benefit most particularly to strategically located Amsterdam which had clearly by the second decade of the seventeenth century superseded Antwerp as the leading entrepôt of the divided Netherlands region. From this position of primacy Amsterdam now prepared to eclipse Venice and the other cities of Southern Europe as the financial and trading centre of the non-Islamic world, so attracting to herself the appellation of the Marrano 'New Jerusalem'.

That this pre-eminence did not redound to the Jews' disadvantage was in no small measure due to the religious bond which united them to many of the Dutch; the Calvinism, Mennonite Baptism and innumerable other expressions of radical Protestantism, which earlier had underpinned the successful revolt against Spanish authority, drew heavily for inspiration upon the Old Testament. Affinity of feeling was not, however, confined to the adherents of the most thoroughgoing Reform; there were the Arminian Protestants for whom the Calvinist teaching on predestination was too rigorous and there were the *politique* Catholics who were dismayed to find that the clerical and categorically dogmatic Catholicism which issued forth militant from the Council of Trent was far closer in spirit to the narrow, probing authoritarianism as represented by the Hispanicizing Inquisition than to the Devotionist, Erasmian humanist and mediatory tradition which they associated with their homeland.

The temper of Dutch society as a whole lay behind the growth of that rapport which came ultimately to be distinguished by the figures of Rembrandt and Spinoza. The works of Rembrandt indicated indeed the magnitude of the transformation in attitude towards the Jews, for the artist who painted *Christ after the Resurrection with His Disciples at Emmaus* and etched the scene of Christ healing the sick in the so-called Hundred Guilder Print was one of the first courageous enough to portray his Saviour with

Semitic or Jewish features.[11] Admittedly painters of before Rembrandt's day had included in scenes depicting the life of Christ some typically Jewish figures, but invariably these had been the persecutors and betrayers of Christ and rarely his apostles or disciples; as for the portrayal of Christ himself an almost sacrosanct tradition had prescribed an idealized face in accord with native conceptions of the beautiful and noble.

Yet for all the comparative advantages offered to the Jews by the United Provinces there did exist drawbacks which, when set against the attractions offered by the rival maritime trading and colonial power of England, could not but in their turn appear as decisive disadvantages. The more exiguous of these two sea powers could less withstand the strain of war and recover from its ravages. The United Provinces was severely affected by the operation of England's Navigation Acts, while the geographical position of Amsterdam was anyway less favourable than that of London, particularly in respect of trade to the New World. And although in 1657 a limited relaxation of some of the nationality laws did indeed benefit the Jewish communities of the United Provinces, in the very timing of this concession there lay acknowledgement of the dangers, to which such politico-economic writings as de la Court's *Interest van Holland* subsequently drew attention, of the Sephardim transferring their allegiance to across the Channel.

For in the previous year, 1656, Jews had for the first time since 1290 been allowed to reside in England; they were assured by certain of the feudal-territorial principles appertaining to the law that English nationality would automatically accrue to any native-born Jewish children.

The very fact that the Jews had not been permitted to live in England during this long intervening period of more than three-and-a-half centuries enabled the native-born descendants of immigrants—despite the controversies surrounding the status of certain of the foreign-born Jews themselves prior to the amending legislation of 1825—to attempt to establish a rapport with Englishmen which might not otherwise have been possible. One may conjecture that had the Jews not been expelled from England at some earlier date their development might have been retarded in like manner as it had been throughout the lands where they were to be found as a people of the ghetto. As it was the very absence of ghetto restrictions, and of the related traditions of *Yidishkayt* which moulded the mentality of many European Jews, enabled the arguments for toleration in the mid-seventeenth century to be positive and not mere begrudging negative reasons for granting toleration to a people long since settled in the country. Oliver Cromwell himself was very aware of the twin arguments which suggested that the prosperity of the United Provinces could in large measure be attributed to her policy of religious toleration, while conversely the impoverishment which had befallen other lands had been the consequence of bad treatment of the Jews; a concession to the Jews now could not be more timely in helping to damage both the traditional religious enemy and the current national enemy.

In the years after the resettlement England acted as a magnet for the Sephardi financiers and traders: her economy was more market oriented than those of other countries and the land was already permeated with small-scale industries. With the forging of the Anglo-Dutch dynastic link in 1689 the Sephardi Amsterdam banking houses of Caceres, Carvajal, Conegliano and Henriques became suppliers of credit for tonnage and importers of vast sums of bullion, both of these undertakings proving vital in the development of England's colonial trade. None more than the English realized the need to expand trade, and this perception of self-interest was appreciated throughout eighteenth-century Europe, from Voltaire and Montesquieu in France to Catherine II in Russia with her pithy observation that the English 'were first and always traders'. In 1744 judgment was sought from Lord Chief Justice Willes as to whether in a Court of Law a non-Christian witness who acknowledged a Supreme Being might be enabled to swear the required oaths in the manner which the witness himself expressly or impliedly declared to be binding on his conscience—for Jews the points at issue involved swearing on the Old Testament, covering the head according to Jewish religious practice, and omitting those parts of the oaths which included such declarations as 'upon the true faith of a Christian'. The Chief Justice gave compelling reasons for issuing a ruling in the affirmative. After remonstrating that any judgment of his to uphold the proposition that the law should treat all infidels as though they were 'perpetual enemies' would be 'contrary not only to the scripture but to common sense and common humanity', he continued 'and besides the irreligion of it, it is a most impolitic notion and would at once destroy all that trade and commerce from which this nation reaps such great benefits. . . . We are commanded by our Saviour to do good unto all men, and not only unto those who are of the household of faith . . . It is a little mean narrow notion to suppose that no one but a Christian can be an honest man.'[12]

Of the ubiquitous Marranos and Sephardim the essayist Steele had advised his readers during the early years of the century that these Jews were 'Parts of the sociable World by no Means to be neglected'. He elucidated the point with figures similar to those employed by his collaborator on *The Spectator,* the more eloquent Addison, who was moved to observe with wonderment that the Jews 'are, indeed, so disseminated through all the trading Parts of the World, that they are become the Instruments by which the most distant Nations converse with one another, and by which Mankind are knit together in a general Correspondence. They are like the Pegs and Nails in a great Building, which, though they are but little valued in themselves, are absolutely necessary to keep the whole Frame together'.[13] The traditionally fluid structure of England's society combined, as from the second quarter of the eighteenth century, with the new-found stability of her polity afforded to the mercantile-minded Jews opportunities of integration incommensurably greater than those existing in the lands from which many of them had emigrated. For in England status followed property, not vice versa as was the rule prevailing, with but few exceptions, throughout the Continent. Constitutional adaptation of 1688–89 vintage, the indeterminate result of successive conflicts between repositories of power, defended the multifarious rights of property as the hallmark of liberty.

The diffusion of wealth itself depended on the social mobility and political patronage which raised up those newcomers who practised habits traditionally associated with Jews. 'Trade is so far here from being inconsistent with a gentleman,' confirmed Defoe, 'that, in short, trade in England makes gentlemen, and has peopled this nation with gentlemen.'[14] This diffusion of propertied power maintained by means of an open society was the liberty so singular to seafaring and trading peoples which the philosopher Tocqueville perceived in the 1830s to be maturing in England; the price which he attached to that liberty or freedom, the self-confident capacity to take dangerous initiatives coupled with alertness, agitation and perseverance in adversity,[15] was one which the Jews had always been obliged to pay.

The observations of Tocqueville leave no doubt but that any contemporary historical assessment of the worth of the Anglo-Jewish community has, though with some caution of interpretation, to be set against the backcloth of appreciation or denigration of British, and even Anglo-Saxon, life and culture. This testified to the belief in individual autonomy, and Adam Smith himself had drawn a most pertinent contrast with the Continent when, heralding the advent of capitalism and the Industrial Revolution, he felt he could confidently compare England's commercial progress with that étatist 'policy of Europe' which, by limiting individual enterprise, diminished the wealth of nations. The Jews were readily identified with the free-market climate associated with Adam Smith and his Manchester School successors. The republican Michelet compared his own France, which he conceived of as the harbinger of peasant revolutionary progress, with England, supposedly the country of *statu quo* and of gold; the Jews, represented by Michelet as having in their hands the funds of every state and as guaranteeing the settlement of 1815, 'that armed peace, that motionless war', were therefore seen to be at home in the exchange of London.[16] Marx, who likewise argued that to the Jews the world signified little other than a stock exchange, was even more simplistic; he differed from Michelet only in seeing New England, where Mammon was idolized by the pious and politically free inhabitants, as the Jews' natural home.[17] This identification of Jews with Anglo-Saxons was felt as strongly by the criticized as by the criticizers. Byron's 'The Age of Bronze' and its ironical lament 'Was ever Christian land so rich in Jews?'[18] conveyed the scorn of the English liberal Romantics for all that the Rothschilds and the Metternich-Castlereagh system stood for.

Some present day readers of these nineteenth-century intellects may be tempted to pass over such implied denunciations as exceptionally reprehensible manifestations of antisemitism. But then, if consistent, they must attach similar criticism to Hazlitt, whose most moving appeal through the medium of the essay for the admission of Jews to Parliament yet turned on the argument that past treatment had made of the Jews unsocial beings and that emancipation from political restrictions, emancipation by others, was necessary precisely because this was the essential precondition of the Jews' own self-emancipation.[19] Even Emerson would have to fall victim to the charge of antisemitism. Touchstone of liberal opinion on every issue from Catholic Emancipation and penal reform to slave emancipation and the triumph of the American Union, Emerson advocated the remission of disabilities and yet was led, after twice visiting England in 1833 and 1847–48, to comment on that very same trait, the paying of an absolute homage to the acquisition of money and wealth, which had also impressed Tocqueville; Emerson decried that Englishmen, no longer transcendentalists or Christians in anything but name, now espoused exclusively the doctrine of the Old Testament and lived under the 'Jewish law' of a brutal utilitarian political economy.[20]

Hazlitt and Emerson disdain Jewishness but support Emancipation; in the mind of each writer there may be detected a duality of thought which a modern interpretation might construe, almost nonsensically, as revealing an uneasy Manichaean coexistence of both philosemitism and antisemitism.

In reality, Hazlitt's understanding of human nature led him to expose the connection between Jewish vices and gentile hypocrisy; Emerson's worship of the intellect and admiration for the German philosophers, 'those Greeks who think for all Europe', made him naturally unsympathetic when writing of the change which had come over the English character. The author of *English Traits* deplored the metamorphosis of the contemplative poetic and democratic Englishmen of Sir Francis Bacon's time into the mentally priapistic [*sic*], mechanistic, selfish manufacturers of his own day, men whose cant in favour of the practical as opposed to the ideal seemed to him to betray nothing other than effeteness of intellect and a Macaulayan concern for 'solid advantage' and sensual benefit.[21] A more understanding interpretation of this transformation of character may be found, not surprisingly, in the writings of J. R. Green and other of the Victorian historians. For they discerned in this evolution a biblical triumph.

Nineteenth-century Englishmen did not recognize themselves as worshippers of the Golden Calf; they drew rather upon the tradition of puritanism—conviction of the need for independent judgement based on conscience and Bible-reading—which had discarded the time-honoured European objective of dissociation from Jews in favour of a biblical ideal of association. The Jewish campaigners for Emancipation knew well that they were the beneficiaries of a kinship which drew inspiration from the Old Testament: how the stand for liberty inspired by Hampden's refusal to pay Ship Money was that very same stand against kingly despotism given divine blessing by Elijah in the matter of Naboth's vineyard. Revered as the descendants of the

patriarchs and prophets, marvelled at as the scattered remnant of the old
Zion and exalted as the builders of the old Jerusalem, the presence of some
Jews in England had long since been deemed by many as indispensable for
the building of the *New* Jerusalem. Radical Protestantism ran counter to the
tradition which stressed both the early Christian breach with Judaism and
the extent to which the cultural history of Europe had drawn strength from
native cultures; the Old Testament was regarded as the forerunner of the
Gospel and the puritan reverence for the moral precepts enshrined in the
Mosaic Law, Psalms, Proverbs and Prophets provided as strong a contrast
as imaginable with, for example, the Pauline Lutheran condemnation of
obeisance to the Law as tantamount to a sinful preoccupation with self-
righteousness akin to justification by works.

The religion of the New Zion was aniconic to the point of smashing the
graven images, extirpating Mariolatry and whitewashing church walls; her
people were frequently christened with names redolent of the Old Testament; the polity of many of her Churches looked to the congregational
example set by the Hebrews of old; the whole land willingly fell sway to the
practice of sabbatarianism, observation of which was so rarely to be encountered on the Continent. This affinity was felt no less strongly by the Jews.
The religious climate explains why, in unique contrast with the Jewries of
the Continent, the community in Britain, though containing a preponderance
of Ashhenazi Orthodox Jews, should have been content to use a Christian
Bible, the King James Version; incongruous would have seemed some Men-
delssohnian cry for a version of the vernacular answering particularly to the
needs of the Jews. When, at the inception of University College, London, in
1828, Hyman Hurwitz was appointed to be Professor of Hebrew he became
the first occupant of such a chair anywhere; in the German lands, despite the
achievements of distinguished scholars, not one university post in biblical
studies or post-biblical literature was to be conferred on a Jew during the
course of the nineteenth century.

For it was through the Bible that the Anglo-Saxon world discerned the
meaning of the designation 'chosen people', a religious concept of godly
election quite the opposite of those most obviously secular appeals to some
superior provenance which came invariably to preface the use of such self-
designations by Zionist Jews and nationalist-minded gentiles in the Europe
of the late nineteenth century. Addison and Steele, in their assessment of the
Jews' contribution to the economic life of the Old and New Worlds, were
greatly influenced by the writings of Jacques Basnage, pastor-divine and
diplomatic minister-pensionary in the United Provinces in the years after the
revocation of the Edict of Nantes; Basnage, whose Calvinism led him to
ponder the fate of God's elect, was so closely acquainted with the sufferings
of his own people as to be able to give in his *L'Histoire des Juifs* an accurate
and perceptive account of the hardships which had befallen those other
chosen people.[22] When, from the retrospect of the middle years of the

nineteenth century, the philosopher-historian Harriet Martineau had occasion to refer to the 'chosen people', or Jews, residing in Britain during her own times she did not cavil, for she knew that fears of a religious score were fears of proselytization and that the Jews were not a proselytizing people.[23]

The religious connotation of 'chosen people' explains too the attitude towards Jews of many of the eighteenth-century Anglican bishops. *The Divine Legation of Moses* written by Bishop Warburton and published between 1737 and 1741 was of interest partly for the very arguments which sought to prove that the survival of the Jews constituted evidence of their being the chosen people; of others among the episcopate Butler, Newton and Hurd were all led to marvel at the survival of the Jews as a unit in dispersion, believing this to be one of the miracles which provided evidence of the authenticity of Scripture and of the Christian revelation. In attempting to discern what was portended by this dispersion the problem seemed, at least to the evangelicals, to resolve itself into the question as to whether the Jews had not been preserved by God for some special providential purpose. One attempt to unravel the mystery was made in 1795 with the choice of millenarianism and the accuracy of prophecy as the subject for the Norrisian Prize essay at Cambridge. There followed in 1808 the establishment of the London Society for promoting Christianity among the Jews, related to the Evangelical London Missionary Society, and in 1826 the London Society itself gave birth to an offshoot, the Philo-Judean Society. The purpose of this particular evangelical group, as defined by the *Christian Register,* was initially twofold: as prelude to their conversion the Jews should be relieved from civil disabilities and persuaded through kindliness to regard the Church more favourably. Many of the earliest and foremost advocates of Emancipation subscribed to this second aim of the Philo-Judean Society.

The influence of Methodism and the Evangelical Revival had not however been able to erase the legacy of the rationalizing, naturalist school to which Warburton and Butler must more correctly be assigned; to eighteenth-century individuals of a secure and classicist Pelagian disposition, more inclined as semi-deists to thank Christ for his moral teaching than to look to him as future Saviour, the question of the Jewish or any other dispensation was simply not one deemed worthy of consideration. The temper of politics, with the refusal to incur the risk of reviving religious strife by making assent to any one set of credos a matter of concern, had reflected this indifference; indeed few men ever can have been more averse to attempting 'final solutions' than the latitudinarian Whigs of Walpole's and the immediately succeeding generation. The centrifugal dynamic of a bibliolatrous Protestantism, finding expression in a congeries of sects each in theory comprised of godly men who must be guaranteed freedom of religious conscience, had first been upheld by Selden and his fellow anticlerical Erastian lawyers of the Long Parliament in their appreciation of the truth of Milton's dictum 'New *Presbyter* is but old *Priest* writ large.' Only a few months before the readmission of the Jews to England in 1656 the Venetian ambassador had been led to comment with some exaggeration that Englishmen 'are divided into as many faiths as there are heads';[24] the multiplication of Presbyterians, Independents and Baptists under the Commonwealth, the failure to effect a comprehensive religious settlement after the Restoration and the timely transfers of power to monarchs dependent upon the Whigs, the first in 1688–89 and the second in 1714, had involved the irrevocable recognition of Dissent.

This recognition, identified with the Whigs, was grounded on the Lockeian assumption that political security, not religious conformity, should be the criterion adopted by Government in respect of religion. As Locke had emphasised, 'laws are not concerned with the truth of opinions, but with the security and safety of the commonwealth.' Thus the Jews, unlike atheists, whose godlessness seemed to invite anarchy, or Catholics, whose avowed intolerance of other men's opinions was the very negation of their own claims to tolerance, could reasonably expect almost an equality with the sects.

> Those whose doctrine is peaceable, and whose manners are pure and blameless, should be on equal terms with their fellow-citizens. And if others are allowed assemblies, solemn meetings, celebrations of feast days, sermons, and public worship, all these should with equal right be allowed to Remonstrants, Anti-remonstrants, Lutherans, Anabaptists or Socinians. Indeed, to speak the truth, and as becomes one man to another, neither Pagan nor Mohametan nor Jew should be excluded from the commonwealth because of his religion.[25]

If Walpole and the Whig politicians of the eighteenth century had to be mindful of the claims of the Church and popular opinion, the renewed Parliamentary approval after 1719 of the practice of Occasional Conformity, whereby Protestant Dissenters were enabled to qualify for public office by occasionally receiving Anglican communion, together with the introduction of Acts of Indemnity, almost invariably renewed at annual intervals, by which the Protestant Dissenters were protected for successively temporary periods after 1727–28 from the penal consequences of refusal to subscribe the necessary oaths upon entry to certain municipal and political offices and employments, signified the triumph of a lax and languid tolerance and set a precedent for the formal removal of political disabilities. In the hundred years after 1727–28 Jews became natural supporters of those Whiggish and other reforming groups within parliaments which, under the guidance of such politicians as Fox and Canning, moved to espouse the cause of civil and religious liberty.

Montesquieu and Voltaire perhaps saw most clearly the connection between a number of interlocking factors. Montesquieu, in commenting that the English 'had progressed the farthest of all peoples of the world in three important things: in piety, in commerce, and in freedom',[26] and Voltaire, noting the social intercourse of men of different religions in a commercial context and observing that 'if there were only one religion in England, one would have to fear despotism; if there were two, they would cut each others' throats; but they have thirty, and they live happy and in peace',[27] perceived the connection between liberty and trade, the benefits of diversity and the flourishing of commerce.

In Britain not only did the social respectability of successful business entrepreneurs, commented upon by Defoe, mitigate the stigma which formerly had attached to trade; the marriage of the Dissenters to an overlapping range of principally commercial occupations, enjoined upon them by virtue of their exclusion from the universities and a proscription in respect of innumerable civic and military offices, was impressively sanctified by an individual work ethic whereby conscientiousness and the particular *innerweltliche Askese* of the puritan were deemed to be the true marks of the elect. By the 1820s this work ethic could draw on a pedigree reaching back two centuries to the time when Archbishop Laud had animadverted to emulating the 'error of the Jews' or acting on the belief that 'Christ's kingdom should be temporal', an implied rebuke to such as the puritan divine Richard Sibbes who were to persist in preaching 'a holy violence in the performing of all duties' as counter to a Popery 'set up by the wit of man to maintain stately idleness'.[28] The individualist work ethic, assiduously fostered by classics of literature which included the allegory of *The Pilgrim's Progress* by Bunyan, the *Political Mischiefs of Popery* by the Huguenot exile De Souligné, and the economic myth of the enterprising *Robinson Crusoe* by Defoe, was encouraged by John Wesley and was to reach its apogee in the secular hagiographies of Samuel Smiles, whose wildly popular *Self-Help* was published during the very years at the end of the 1850s when the Jews were first enabled to sit in Parliament.

The currency of the adage 'One drop of Huguenot blood in the veins is worth a thousand a year' not only bore witness to the monopoly of Huguenot expertise in the carrying and manufacture of silks and fabrics but also pointed to the circumstance that in England Jews were not the most conspicuous of the religious groups seen to possess business acumen. The presence of the Jews has emphatically to be set in the Anglo-Saxon context of the overlap—frequently to be encountered—between possession of a fierce sense of individualism in matters of conscience and dissent from the norm in the shrewd conduct of one's material affairs. Insofar as the smallness of numbers held the key to the successful integration of non-indigenous minorities, the numbers of Jews, rising imperceptibly from the figure of no more than eight thousand a century after the resettlement to an estimated twenty-seven thousand in 1828 and forty thousand in 1860, never at any time before the last third of the nineteenth century constituted more than 0.2 per cent of the population of Britain. This percentage was tiny not only in comparison with that prevailing in many of the European territories from which the Jews of the mid-nineteenth century or their forbears had emigrated; the proportion of Jews was very small when set beside that of the Huguenots, still an identifiable community in both Britain and Ireland when Smiles wrote a study of them in the 1860s. The eighty to a hundred thousand Huguenots who had fled across the Channel in consequence of the revocation of the Edict of Nantes came to comprise between 1.5 and 2 per cent of England's population at that time; this particular influx was, moreover, only one in a succession of immigrant waves which had earlier brought to England more than thirty thousand Flemings and Walloons fleeing from the Spanish persecution. Of some thirty-five thousand Jews living in Britain at the beginning of the 1850s the largest concentration, reckoned both in absolute numbers and as a proportion relative to the gentile majority, was to be found in cosmopolitan London where a community of not many more than twenty thousand persons comprised less than one per cent of the capital's total population; of the three most substantial communities in the provinces Liverpool contained no more than approximately two and a half thousand Jews; Manchester, where the Unitarian cotton-spinners were arguably the most conspicuous enterprising group, approximately two thousand Jews, and Birmingham slightly fewer than a thousand Jews.

Of the entrepreneurs who dominated the commercial life of these cities the Jews appeared to share most in common with the Quakers. Within each community there existed the same clandestine suspicion of outsiders and refusal to contemplate marriage outside the faith, the same concern for partnerships and for the fecundity which could ensure the forging of business dynasties and the consolidation of family firms. The Anglo-Jewish cousinhood was not unique and in the deposit-bankers among the Quakers the Jewish merchant-bankers found their counterparts; the pre-eminence of financiers, bankers, brokers and underwriters in the Jewish community was matched by the preeminence of those many, often biblically named, bankers, ironmasters, mineowners and grain merchants among the Quakers. Instances of Quaker-Jewish rapport are legion: it was a Quaker, Joseph Avis, who on building the Bevis Marks Synagogue in 1700/1701 then generously returned the fees to the Sephardi congregation. That at the end of the eighteenth and beginning of the nineteenth centuries two Jewish institutions for the care of orphans, the elderly and the poor, should have been helped into existence by virtue of half the donors being gentile was not only remarkable in itself for revealing a Christian interest quite without parallel on the Continent; the subscription list for the establishment in 1807 of the second of these two institutions, the Mile End Hospital for the aged and indigent, was of note insofar as one Quaker contributed £500, the second largest donation, while two others contributed donations of £100 apiece. This rapport was particularly evident in the City: in 1824 the Quakers Samuel Gurney, Alexander Baring and Thomas Fowell Buxton cooperated with Nathan Mayer

Rothschild and Moses Montefiore to found the Alliance (British and Foreign Fire and Life) Assurance Company.

This collaboration augured well for the success of integration; the predominantly business-oriented Anglo-Jewish community could participate the more easily in the life of a society whose values so overlapped with their own. The campaign for the admission of the Jews to Parliament was coincident with the heyday of the capitalist economy and was one of the scenes in a drama which saw political power initially moving from an oligarchic base to one which could accommodate equally the interests of duke and mill-owner. This preparedness or acquiescence on the part of the traditional wielders of power to concede Protestant Dissenting and Roman Catholic claims for relief from religious disabilities and a limited measure of Parliamentary and municipal reform was all important. The bankers and manufacturers whose rise to power was confirmed between 1828 and 1835 owed their success not to any republican or democratically puritan transformation of institutions such as had been attempted and decisively checked in the seventeenth century, but to the industrial strength which they had acquired during the previous half-century. Politically interested Jews did not, as so often on the Continent, find themselves attracted to the ranks of those seeking to overturn the established order; the institutions of the country were adaptable, not brittle.

The Jews would have to learn from the example set by other non-Anglican groups how best to overcome the inertia which invariably attaches to well-entrenched institutions and they could do worse than observe how, in a Britain grown up on an eighteenth-century tradition of stability, a conservative resistance to change seemed to be finding justification in the formula that 'it is the excellence of the constitution' that no law can anticipate the public opinion. Ultimately—albeit ostensibly—the question of Jewish Emancipation was a political one; however important social and economic factors may have been, the case for the admission of Jews to Parliament would have to come to rest on constitutional precedent.

And here the criteria were no longer those of religious conformity but the Lockeian ones of political security. By the 1820s the Protestant Dissenters, though occasionally still suspected of harbouring republican sympathies, had successfully freed themselves from the taint of regicide. By contrast the inability of atheists to bind over their consciences to the Creator when asked to subscribe oaths was thought by a not inconsiderable number of religious believers to betray proof of an anarchic disrespect for the divine order. The Roman Catholics in Britain, whose memories of past treatment at the hands of the lay power could not but set them at least one remove apart from the Continental Catholic exponents of social and political conservatism, enjoyed more trust than atheists but rather less than most of the Protestant Dissenters: striving to appear as simply one more sect or denomination they yet laboured under the stigma of falling within the embrace of an authoritarian Church and of being associated, as so often in the past, with co-religionists who were suspected of being enemies of the Crown.

In 1828 the Protestant Dissenters, including the Unitarians with their heterodox disbelief in the doctrine of the Trinity, won formal relief from the operation of legislation which had disabled them from sitting in Parliament. The vital Anglican principle of the constitution had been breached; when in 1829 the Catholics too were conceded Parliamentary Emancipation some at least of the leading members of the Anglo-Jewish community seemed to interpret this further instalment of relief legislation as almost an incitement to begin their own campaign. Because the Roman Catholics, in common with the Jews, belonged to a universal religious membership which transcended national boundaries, once the problems of dual loyalty to spiritual and temporal authority had been resolved in the case of the one group the claims of the other would be correspondingly enhanced.

Here it is germane to retrace in some detail the strategy which had been deployed by the Catholics in the half-century prior to the concession of 1829.[29] During this period, as indeed during the greater part of the two and more previous centuries, the Catholics were accused of submitting to a divided obligation. Opponents of Catholic Emancipation held—as had Locke—that so long as certain subjects of the Crown continued to acknowledge the supremacy of the Pope the threat of a Catholic reimposition of power could not be banished; consequently, as a safeguard against emergency, there was a need to retain the post-1688 Revolution Settlement. The Catholics argued in reply that the Test Acts of the 1670s had been panic measures, while the Revolution Settlement had been essentially a transitory arrangement. In the eighteenth century the constitution had not been static and disabling legislation had been undergoing repeal. Catholic Emancipation would represent not some revolutionary change but rather the consummation of a liberalizing adjustment to the constitution; the benefits of such adjustment, though withheld from the Catholics, were presently being inconsistently granted through the annual Indemnity Acts to the Protestant Dissenters.

Accusations of foreign allegiance and dual loyalty were vigorously denied by the English Catholics. In 1788 they obtained from five Continental Catholic universities a statement declaring that the Papacy would find itself unable to absolve Catholics from the requirement, enjoined upon them as upon all other subjects of the Crown, of having to subscribe the oaths of allegiance. This denial became a recurring and persistent theme in all Catholic arguments, being emphasised even to the extent that the members of the second committee formed in 1787–88 for the purpose of negotiating Emancipation with the Government—the first had been in 1782—decided to call themselves the Protesting Catholic Dissenters. In 1788 this committee was so bold as to compose a statement which they described as a 'Protestation'.

This both denied temporal authority to the Pope and rejected any notion of Papal infallibility. These declarations were partly reproduced in an oath embodied in the Relief Act of 1791 and were adopted in principle by the Cisalpine Club, founded in 1792, which announced that it would resist any ecclesiastical interference which might seek to restrict the freedom of English Catholics. Persistent ridicule of the idea that the security of the realm might come to be threatened by Papal jurisdiction or encroachment seemed, after many years, to point to the futility of continued exclusion.

Yet, whereas in England Cisalpinism naturally commended itself to an impressive aristocratic and lay Catholic leadership which stood to gain most from the remission of disabilities, in Ireland not only was religious orthodoxy in the ascendant, as from 1800–1801 strengthening the feeling of separateness in a predominantly Protestant Union, so too was a peasant nationalism; this was embryonic in a movement for Emancipation which served as a vehicle for the remedying of social and economic grievances. Although Catholic Ireland had always been considered a standing threat to the unity and security of the British Isles, conjuring up fears and dangers of alien powers and enemy forces joined in league with the Crown's Catholic subjects, after the end of the Napoleonic Wars the imputation of divided allegiance was held in particular to imply obedience to the Irish Catholic hierarchy and was thus associated with the growth of an Irish identity.

The relevance of the Catholic success to any claims which might be advanced by the Jews lay in the circumstance that, although the concession of 1829 was to be explained by the Irish situation and was an actual response to the political pressure which the Irish had brought to bear on the Government, British politicians could scarcely be expected to share with the Irish a relish of the memories of the pressure which had extracted Catholic Emancipation. Those compelled to grant concessions under duress need subsequently to reassure both themselves and others that their former policies had constituted not some panic response to the threat of violence but had been conceived aforethought in altruistic spirit. Many of the English Catholics later became only too pleased to help save the face of their former opponents by generously subscribing to the view that Emancipation represented not a triumph of strength but rather a victory for abstract principles of liberality. The Jews were fortunate that, inasmuch as this almost perverse misrepresentation was compounded by misunderstanding of the relative importance of religion and of embryonic socio-economic nationalism as motivating forces which had lain behind the Catholic campaign, the concatenation of circumstances which retrospectively attended the concession of 1829 came after a decade and a half to appear as a good augury for the prospects of Jewish Emancipation.

But in more than one sense did appearance belie reality. The very achievements of the Protestant Dissenters and of the Roman Catholics in winning Emancipation bore not an unqualified augury of deliverance but rather their own omen. Are not group absorption and group preservation two contending manifestations of this selfsame *Emancipation?* The individual bearer of a distinctive religious culture, the ethos of which has been tempered by the circumstances of exclusion, must necessarily, in any new circumstances conducive to inclusion, reach his own *modus vivendi* with the demands and pressures of participation. Tocqueville was one of many who observed that sociologically there existed two religions in England, the one aristocratic, the other democratic;[30] would emancipated Jews emulate certain of the emancipated Protestant Dissenters in forsaking their own religion for that of the establishment? Or would Jews, perhaps exaggerating the extent of a future revival of Papal influence among the Catholics in Britain, misconstrue such Ultramontanism as a licence for treating with levity their own claims to be regarded, after the Protestant Dissenters and the Roman Catholics, as the third branch of non-Anglican religious dissent?

The forthcoming question of Jewish Emancipation would prove to be a threefold one. To that which at the beginning of the campaign was upper-most in the minds of politically interested persons, 'How might Jews be able to secure the concession of Parliamentary Emancipation?' we must add those two which impart to Emancipation its almost elusively chimerical quality, 'Where would Jews, first as individual disputants in discussion and ultimately as a community in agreement, come to draw the line between religious tradition and secular innovation?' and 'How would they satisfy both themselves and the gentile majority in reconciling expectations of due conformity with the retention of a dignified distinctiveness?'

Henceforward the initiative would lie with the Jews themselves and with any individual among their number who might come forward to act upon that most 'just and excellent' of maxims handed down by Lord Mansfield more than sixty years before in the case concerning the Protestant Dissenters and the Shrievalty of London and Middlesex:

'By their fruits ye shall know them.'

NOTES

1. Translation from J. Katz, *Exclusiveness and Tolerance. Studies in Jewish-Gentile Relations in Mediaeval and Modern Times* (1961), pp. 21–23.
2. Heinrich Heine, *Sämmtliche Werke* (Leipzig, 1828), IV, pp. 287–88.
3. Pejoratives taken from Jules Michelet, *Le Peuple,* first published, 1845, trans. C. Cocks (3d ed., 1846), pp. 72–73.
4. E. Hodder, *The Life and Work of the Seventh Earl of Shaftesbury, with Extracts from Lord Shaftesbury's Diaries and Journals* (1892), p. 270, quoting from *Lord Ashley's Private Holiday Journal of a Visit to Europe* (1843), Carlsbad (14 August 1843).
5. Richard Monckton Milnes, *Hansard's Parliamentary Debates,* Third Series, 82 (17 July 1845), 642.
6. Theodor Herzl, *The Jewish State. An Attempt at a Modern Solution of the Jewish Question,* first published 1896, trans. S. D'Avigdor, revised by I. Cohen (1946 edn.), pp. 15–25.
7. Johann Gottfried Herder, "Über die politische Bekehrung der Juden" in *Adrastea und das 18 Jahrhundert,* 1801–3.
8. For the following brief discussion, see most particularly the essay by Karl Marx 'On the

Jewish Question', 1843–44, in *Writings of the Young Marx on Philosophy and Society,* trans. and ed. L. D. Easton and K. H. Guddat (New York, 1967), pp. 216–48.

9. *The Complete Letters of Lady Mary Wortley Montagu,* ed. R. Halsband (3 vols., 1965–67), vol. I, years 1708–20 (1965), pp. 354–55, letter from Lady Mary Wortley Montagu to the Abbé Conti, written from Adrianople, 17 May 1717.

10. Jacques Basnage, *L'Histoire des Juifs,* first published at Rotterdam, 1706, English trans. T. Taylor (1708), pp. 718–19.

11. See, in this connection, F. Landsberger, *Rembrandt, the Jews and the Bible,* translated from the German by F. N. Gerson (Philadelphia, 1945–46).

12. *Cases argued and determined in the Court of Common Pleas. Reports of Chief Justice Willes,* 1737–60; ed. C. Durnford (1799), Hilary 18 Geo II [Omichund *v* Barker, 23 February in Chancery], pp. 538–54.

13. Joseph Addison in *The Spectator,* essay no. 495, 27 September 1712; *The Spectator,* ed. D. F. Bond (1965), IV, pp. 255–58. Bond here comments on the similar observations made by Richard Steele in *The Tatler,* no. 85.

14. Daniel Defoe, *The Complete English Tradesman,* 2 vols., first published 1725–27, 4th and revised edn. (1738), vol. I, pp. 322–23.

15. Alexis de Tocqueville, *Journeys to England and Ireland,* trans. G. Lawrence and K. P. Mayer, ed. J. P. Mayer (1958), pp. 114–17. Observations recorded by Tocqueville, 7 July 1835.

16. Michelet, *Le Peuple,* pp. 72–73.

17. Marx, 'On the Jewish Question', p. 244.

18. George Gordon, Lord Byron, 'The Age of Bronze', XV.

19. William Hazlitt, 'Emancipation of the Jews', first published in *The Tatler,* 28 March 1831, in *The Complete Works of William Hazlitt,* ed. P. P. Howe (1930–34), 19 (1933), pp. 320–24.

20. Tocqueville, *Journeys to England and Ireland,* pp. 114–17; Ralph Waldo Emerson, *English Traits,* first published 1856, in *The Complete Essays and Other Writings of Ralph Waldo Emerson,* edited, with a biographical introduction by Brooks Atkinson (New York, 1940), pp. 521–690, a persistently recurring theme.

21. Emerson, *English Traits.*

22. Basnage, *L'Histoire des Juifs.*

23. Harriet Martineau, *The History of England during the Thirty Years' Peace: 1816–1846* (3 vols., 1849–51), vol. I, p. 547.

24. W. K. Jordan, *The Development of Religious Toleration in England* (4 vols., 1932–40), III, p. 171.

25. John Locke, *Epistola de Tolerantia: A Letter on Toleration* (first edn. published at Gouda, 1689), trans. J. W. Gough, ed. R. Klibansky (1968), pp. 123, 143, 145.

26. Montesquieu, *De l'esprit des lois,* book XX, chapter 7.

27. Voltaire, Lettre VI, *Lettres philosophiques,* ed. G. Lanson (2 vols., 1909), vol. I, p. 74.

28. Archbishop William Laud and Richard Sibbes, quoted in C. Hill, *Society and Puritanism in Pre-Revolutionary England* (1964), pp. 131, 203; Richard Sibbes, quoted also in L. Stone, *The Causes of the English Revolution, 1529–1642* (1972), p. 99.

29. The perspectives to be found in G. I. T. Machin, *The Catholic Question in English Politics, 1820 to 1830* (1964), have been of particular help, here and in the succeeding paragraphs, in retracing the stages of the campaign for Catholic Emancipation.

30. Tocqueville, *Journeys to England and Ireland,* p. 79.

2
The Legal and Juridical Position of Mid-Nineteenth-Century Anglo-Jewry

Legally and juridically the Jews in Britain found themselves at a comparatively early date pronounced members of the host community—a *constitutional* evolution having appeared to pre-empt the need for that process of *democratic* integration which in many of the lands of post-1789 Europe was to see the break-up of a social order based upon 'estates' and the supersession of those communal laws to which the Jews had hitherto been subject. As the Lord Chancellor, Brougham, declared to the Upper House in 1833: 'His Majesty's subjects professing the Jewish religion were born to all the rights, immunities and privileges of His Majesty's other subjects, excepting so far as positive enactments of law deprived them of those rights, immunities and privileges.'[1]

And because the Jews were subject to the same law, they were also subject to the same 'defects' of that law: if their status was not clearly defined this was not a factor to occasion them, as Jews, undue anxiety. A natural corollary of Britain's long historic evolution was the lack of any ideal codification of the law or of a constitution held to be of immutable validity. Jews came but gradually to enjoy the benefits of an adaptable constitution and, in common with other groups, came to discover their rights and disabilities largely through test cases in the lawcourts. Brougham's somewhat bald statement therefore requires qualification. The rulings of judges in test cases, the practical undermining of penal legislation and the related phenomenon of disabling laws almost casually being allowed to fall into desuetude, the *ad hoc* alterations induced by expediency, as with the concession of Catholic Emancipation in 1829: these were typical of the factors which imparted to English law its distinctive character.

Brougham was, however, correct to emphasise the importance attaching to birth. British nationality law has traditionally been grounded on the feudal or territorial principle that all persons born within any of the dominions over which the monarch has at the time of their birth sovereign power owe allegiance to the monarch and are therefore deemed natural-born subjects of the monarch's realm.[2] To be born within the monarch's dominions almost equals allegiance, the state of being born under the rule and protection of a particular ruler, but dominions or territory and allegiance are not always interchangeable and a person must 'be born within the ligeance of the ruler' in order that his alien status can be modified.[3] Those Jews born in England as the children of alien Jews would have come within the ligeance and would thus have been considered as subjects or citizens.[4]

This definition of British nationality, with citizenship conferred on the native-born, brings the question of the naturalization of foreign-born Jews into perspective. Naturalization, conferring on the foreign-born the full rights and privileges of British subjects, could be granted either through private Acts of Parliament—the purchase of such constituting an option open only to the wealthy—or in the form of concessions to selective groups of foreigners engaged in the public service and in especially beneficial branches of trade.[5] But naturalization was important only for the first generation of immigrants and not for their descendants; in essence naturalization was never at any time concerned with the question as to whether Jews should or should not reside in Britain. Consequently the act of 1753 for naturalizing foreign-born Jews, repealed in the following year on account of popular agitation, cannot be regarded as a substantial act of policy.[6] The act 6 Geo IV, c. 67, of 1825, abolished in all cases the necessity for receiving before naturalization the Sacrament according to the rites of the Church of England and in repealing a law of 1609, 7 Jac I c. 2 and c. 6, thereby achieved incidentally, and without even either mentioning the Jews or attracting any public attention, the object of the legislation of 1753. And by 1828 another form of conferred privilege had long since fallen into desuetude: denization, which could be granted to single individuals but not necessarily to their heirs. Denizens were created *ex donatione regis* and enjoyed a status intermediate as between that attaching to aliens and that attaching to natural-born subjects. They could reside anywhere within the realm and could own land but, unlike those benefiting by naturalization, they were subject to various impositions, including payment of alien duties. During the reigns of Charles II and James II more than a hundred Jews had been favoured by grants of denization letters but with the decline of the royal prerogative it was natural that the practice should gradually cease to commend itself to the approval of Parliament.[7]

The laws governing the entry of Jews into Britain became, for a period extending over half a century, unusually important. After the Ukrainian massacres of 1768, which resulted in the emigration of many refugees from Eastern Europe, the Government declared that no Jews could be permitted to come to Britain on British packetboats unless they had previously paid passages in full and possessed passports granted to them by an ambassador or minister abroad. In 1774 the Postmaster-General reinforced his earlier order.[8] After the outbreak of the French Revolution Jews, along with some of the republican-minded Protestant Dissenters, were suspected of Jacobin sympathies and of having links with malcontents abroad, and the 1793 Aliens

Act, 33 Geo III, c. 4, placed foreigners in Britain under strict control. The Crown was empowered to direct, by Proclamation or Order in Council, that any alien or aliens should leave the realm, and the Government was enabled to draw up regulations for the landing and subsequent residence of foreigners, if necessary expelling or imprisoning disobedient aliens. The 1793 act was renewed periodically during the Napoleonic Wars and was enforced until 1826, when it was repealed by the act 7 Geo IV, c. 54. Thereafter, until the last third of the nineteenth century, the rate of Jewish immigration was so small as not to warrant restrictions.

The use of the royal dispensing power in 1664, in 1673–74 and again in 1685, on the two latter occasions exercised through special Orders in Council, had exempted the Jews from the harshness of the penal laws, had confirmed them in the free exercise of their religion—approved earlier during the Protectorate—and had recognized their rights as subjects in the law-courts. There was thus never any doubt as to the Jews' recognition in statute law and in 1818 Mr. Justice Abbott recognized the right of a synagogue to be represented in a Court of Law.[9] Nevertheless it took some time before one potentially harmful notion came to be discarded. This arose from a proposition expounded by Lord Coke that all infidels in law must be considered as perpetual enemies 'for between them, as with the devils, whose subjects they be, and the Christian there is a perpetual hostility, and can be no peace.'[10] Yet there never existed any doubt that Jews could be called as witnesses in a Court of Law. As early as 1667, in the case of Robeley v Langston, several Jewish witnesses were sworn on the Old Testament by the Chief Justice.[11] One eminent jurist, Sir Matthew Hale, in his *History of the Pleas of the Crown* published nine years later, forcefully disagreed with Coke's interpretation.[12] The capacity of a Jew to sue was admitted by Chief Justice Jeffreys in 1684 and was confirmed in the case of Wells v Williams of 1697.[13]

The rejection of Coke's notion in this case of 1697, and the reasons given for the Court's ruling, found more than an echo in the striking pronouncement in favour of a mercantile liberty issued by Lord Chief Justice Willes almost half a century later. In the case of Omichund v Barker of 1744, tried in the Court of Common Pleas, the question as to whether a witness, provided he acknowledged a Supreme Being, might be sworn in the form which he expressly or impliedly declared to be binding on his conscience was resolved in the affirmative. Of Coke's dictum Willes declared:

But this notion, though advanced by so great a man, is I think contrary not only to the scripture but to common sense and common humanity. And I think that even the devils themselves, whose subjects he says the *Heathens* are, cannot have worse principles; and besides the irreligion of it, it is a most impolitic notion and would at once destroy all that trade and commerce from which this nation reaps such great benefits. . . . We are commanded by our Saviour to do good unto all men, and not only unto those who are of the household of faith. . . . It is a little mean narrow notion to suppose that no one but a Christian can be an honest man.[14]

The third section of the statute 53 Geo III, c. 127, of 1813, declared invalid the once-accepted maxim that excommunication necessarily entailed a disability to bring a court action, and so finally reversed 12 Henry VIII, c. 4, upon which Coke had strengthened his conviction that infidels were perpetual enemies.

The most important questions affecting the status of Jews, after citizenship and recognition in a Court of Law, concerned marriage. Here Jews shared with Quakers, though not with other non-Anglicans, the privilege of having secured special Acts of Parliament legalising their respective forms of marriage, and Lord Hardwicke's Marriage Act, 26 Geo II, c. 33, of 1753, devised for the purpose of curbing clandestine marriages, had specifically excluded Jews and Quakers from its scope. Where both parties professed, respectively, Judaism or the Quaker form of Christianity they could marry according to their own rites: the only doubt concerning the operation of Jewish marriage law arose as the result of the legislation 5 & 6 Will IV, c. 54, of 1835, which could be construed as bringing Jewish marriages and divorces within the jurisdiction of civil law. If this construction of the 1835 act were accepted Jews would be barred from validly marrying within degrees permitted by Jewish law but prohibited by English law; for a short period in 1857 during the drafting of the Matrimonial Causes Bill it seemed that Jewish marriages might be expressly exempted from dissolution by the Civil Divorce Court first set up by the 1835 act.[15] As this legislation, 5 & 6 Will IV, c. 54, did not in practice infringe rabbinical powers as otherwise defined by English law, the importance both of its existence and of the amendment mooted in 1857 related rather to the debate among the leading members of Anglo-Jewry concerning the relative claims of civil and communal ties. Likewise, the importance of the Marriage Act, 6 & 7 Will IV, c. 85, and of the Marriage Registration Act, 6 & 7 Will IV, c. 86, both of 1836, lay not in their confirmation of the validity of Jewish marriages but in the framing (section 30 of the latter act) of a special provision for marriage registration which gave statutory recognition to the Jewish Board of Deputies—up to this time the *putative* representative body of British Jews—as the competent authority to certify places of worship. This legislation entrusted the Board, and particularly its President, with such discretionary powers as to explain why, once disagreement arose in connection with the request from the West London Reform Synagogue after 1841 that its minister be allowed to register marriages, dissension concerning the rights of Reform Jews as dissidents was to influence communal attitudes towards Emancipation. If the 1836 legislation came to dissatisfy the Reform Jews it met from the outset with the more important disapproval of the Protestant Dissenters, and in 1855 further measures were proposed.[16] Once again objections were raised by almost all the interested parties, including the Orthodox Jews and the Quakers, both of whom feared that the proposed legislation would infringe their respective privileged positions. The measures were laid aside until the following session, but when an amended bill was produced in February 1856 the various parties were still dissatisfied, including the Orthodox Jews who strongly objected to the proposed twenty-second section which would have enabled twenty householders to certify the appointment of a Marriage Secretary and would thus have allowed not only the West London Reform Synagogue but also the provincial Reform congregations to authorise marriages.[17] All the groups affected by the bill were finally conciliated, including the Orthodox and Reform Jews who agreed on their own compromise. An Act to Amend the Provisions of the Marriage and Registration Acts, 19 & 20 Vict, c. 119, of 1856, besides confirming the special status of Jewish marriage law, gave statutory recognition to the West London Reform Synagogue, though not to the provincial Reform congregations.

Another recurring issue of controversy, though far less important than the legislation concerning marriages, arose in connection with the ownership of land. In 1738 the antiquary D'Blossiers Tovey published his erudite *Anglia Judaica; or the History and Antiquities of the Jews in England*. The most surprising aspect of Tovey's research had been the unearthing in the Bodleian Library at Oxford of the 1271 ordinance (54 & 55 Henry III) forbidding Jews to own land.[18] This rediscovered ordinance undermined the validity of the act 10 Geo I, c. 4, of 1723, based on judgments given in 1718 by the Attorney-General, Sir Robert Raymond, and in 1723 by ten eminent counsel, that Jews could own and purchase lands.[19] The validity of the 1271 legislation was itself called into question, not merely because some subsequent legislation of 1275 (3 Edw I, *Statutum de Judeismo*) appeared to qualify it but on account of certain abstruse technicalities. The question became highly academic and lawyers interested in the status of the Jews split into two parties, the larger of which contended that the Jews could own land.[20] Yet even if Jews could not in theory own freehold land there was nothing to prevent their acquiring land on lease on a peppercorn rent for an indefinitely long period, and this amounted to the same thing.[21] Jews did indeed own land, and one Chief Justice, Lord Ellenborough, gave a practical proof of his concurrence in the belief that Jews might hold land by purchasing from Benjamin Goldsmid a freeholding at Roehampton. In answer to an enquiry by Peel, the Prime Minister, in 1845 I. L. Goldsmid imparted the information that neither his landholding in Hampshire nor his title to plots of building land which he had sold in Brighton had ever been questioned, although the title had passed through the hands of many solicitors.[22] The law on landholding was finally clarified in 1846 when the first section of an act, 9 & 10 Vict, c. 59, removed from the statute book and explicitly declared void and invalid all legislation derived from, or thought to be derived from, the pre-expulsion period, including the 1271 ordinance and the *Statutum de Judeismo* of 1275.

In certain spheres of opportunity the Jews had to contend with disabilities which were more often designed for non-Anglicans in general than for Jews in particular. In 1697 the Corporation of the City of London had permitted the total of 124 brokers on the Royal Exchange to include a maximum of twelve Jews[23]—yet this quota was disproportionately generous considering the number of Jews then in England. But as for retail trade within the City of London the laws of the City confined retail trade to freemen and Jews could not be admitted to the Freedom of the City: in a test case of 1739 the Chief Justice, Sir Robert Raymond, ruled that Jews were barred from trading within the City boundaries unless they subscribed, on the New Testament, the stipulated Oaths of Allegiance, Supremacy, Uniformity and Abjuration.[24] It was only after another ninety years, in 1829, that Apsley Pellatt, one of the keenest supporters of the Jewish cause among the Protestant Dissenting Deputies, was able to observe how the recent expansion of the City had mitigated the harshness of this restriction and that Jews were now selling retail from warehouses classified as wholesale. Then, in the following year, 1830, the Freedom of the City was opened to the Jews and the provisions of 1697 were finally rendered obsolete. Many times during the previous century and a half had Jews been charged excessively for the transference of their brokers' medals, although it had been the Protestant Dissenters who had suffered most from discriminatory practices in the City.[25]

Although no Jews were admitted to the Bar before F. H. Goldsmid in 1833 this was largely to be explained by the circumstance that prior to the establishment of London University in 1828, in which F. H. Goldsmid's father Isaac Lyon played a prominent role in cooperation with other non-Anglicans, Jews had been prevented by restrictions at Oxford and Cambridge from receiving the necessary preliminary training. One Joseph Abrahams had however been admitted to the legal profession as a solicitor in 1770, after having been allowed to omit the words 'upon the true faith of a Christian' in the Oath of Abjuration.[26]

It was indeed in the field of education that disabilities remained longest. Jews, together with Protestant Dissenters and Roman Catholics, were prevented from teaching in schools other than those catering for the education of children of their co-religionists, and for long Jews were excluded from attending many of the Public Schools on account of compulsory prayers or because of regulations in the school charters.[27] The 1846 act, 9 & 10 Vict, c. 59, did however provide comfort for the Jews insofar as it conferred on them equal status with Protestant Dissenters in respect of their schools, other educational establishments, places of worship and charitable foundations.

There were many deterrents at Oxford and Cambridge for those intending to read for bachelors' degrees. For the two universities insisted on the statutory oaths and on religious tests, including subscription to the Thirty-Nine Articles. At high Tory Oxford these tests had to be taken before matriculation or admission to membership, but at Cambridge, owing to a provision dating back to 1775, they could be deferred until candidature for a degree. Lower degrees were opened to all non-Anglicans, including Jews, at Oxford in 1854 (17 & 18 Vict, c. 81, s. 43, 44) and at Cambridge in 1856 (19 & 20 Vict, c. 88, s. 45, 46). But at both universities Jews were still prevented from assuming any office or taking any share in the work of the governing bodies: at Oxford by virtue of the fact that they could take only lower degrees, at Cambridge on account of their exclusion from membership of the Senate. At Cambridge however, although still ineligible for Fellowships, Jews were also able after 1856 to take higher degrees and until 1871, when the Universities Tests Act (34 & 35 Vict, c. 26), finally removed all disabilities, Cambridge was naturally the more favoured by Jews.[28]

Almost all the disabilities imposed on Jews arose as a consequence of the oaths which they were required to subscribe, yet whereas most civil disabilities were incurred on account of the New Testament form in which the oaths had to be taken, political disabilities were usually to be met with as a result of the actual wording of the parliamentary tests and oaths;[29] of these the most important was the Oath of Abjuration to which were appended the words 'upon the true faith of a Christian'.

It was ironic that these words—so objectionable to Jews—had not originally been devised with the intention of excluding them. They had first appeared in 3 Jac I, c. 4, s. 15, as part of the oath required by 'an Act for the better discovering and repressing of popish recusants'; when they reappeared almost a century later, in 13 Will III, c. 6, s. 11, they were included with the express purpose of disqualifying from public life any individual 'popish recusant convict' who refused to abjure Jacobite claims to the Crown. The explanation for the use of these words 'upon the true faith of a Christian', designed to ferret out recusants and to deter any who might otherwise dissemble, lay with the Jesuits. When the first of these two acts had been passed, after the Gunpowder Plot, the legislators had been concerned with the casuistry of a Jesuit book, *A Treatise on Equivocation,* discovered in the chambers of one of the conspirators. The words 'upon the true faith of a Christian' had then been so phrased as to prevent 'any equivocation, mental evasion, or secret reservation whatsoever'. As there were no Jews allowed in England during the reign of James I it would have been superfluous to have excluded them from office.[30] Furthermore, when the words were revived in 1701 there existed no body of 'Jewish Jacobites' who could have been suspect under the Abjuration Acts.

In respect of the exercise of the parliamentary franchise Jews often fared better than Catholics. For of the three Oaths of Allegiance, Supremacy and Abjuration which presiding officers might respectively be required to administer if so requested by one of the contestants Jews baulked only at the prospect of subscribing the Abjuration Oath. Although in 1707 it had been laid down in the legislation 6 Anne, c. 78, s. 13, that any person who wished to vote at a parliamentary election could be made, if this were so requested, to take the Abjuration Oath, prior to 1707 the legislation 7 & 8 Will III, c. 27, had enacted that no person should be permitted to vote in any parliamentary election if he refused to subscribe the oaths of Allegiance and Supremacy which the sheriff or other poll officer might likewise be required to administer; as there was nothing objectionable to Jews in either of these oaths they were never so drastically affected by disabling legislation in general. Nevertheless it was not until 1835 that such legislation, by this time virtually obsolete, was finally rendered ineffective: one section of an act of that year, 5 & 6 Will IV, c. 36, s. 6, concerned with eliminating some of the tedious and protracted procedures customary on election days, dispensed with the necessity of administering such oaths and thus, typically of English law, relieved the Jews from a particular disability in as incidental a manner as it had once been imposed on them. Only with the Statute Law Revision Act of 1867 (30 & 31 Vict, c. 59) was the 1707 act explicitly repealed.

For it was the Abjuration Oath which prevented any conscientious and professing Jew from sitting in Parliament. Every member of the legislature was compelled to subscribe the Oaths of Allegiance, Supremacy and Abjuration (with the exception of Quakers, who conscientiously objected to oath-swearing and were as from 1833 allowed instead to affirm): in the Commons the three oaths were administered by the Speaker at the beginning of a new parliament to all those returned at the previous general election, and the oaths were also administered to any who might subsequently be returned at by-elections arising during the life of that parliament. The Oaths of Allegiance and Supremacy would have presented no problems to an elected Jew: the difficulty arose as a result of the words 'upon the true faith of a Christian' to be found in the Abjuration Oath.

The campaigners for the admission of the Jews to Parliament thus looked forward to the day when an elected Jew might be enabled to subscribe the three oaths in common with all other Members, with the all-important proviso that he would be allowed to omit the controversial words in the Abjuration Oath. Most efforts to remove disabilities aimed at this amendment to the existing legislation but attempts, initiated by Lord John Russell in 1854 and 1857, were made to introduce into Parliament comprehensive oaths bills which would have repealed the existing statutory requirements and introduced, in their stead, a single modified oath to be taken by Jews and Catholics alike. For the Catholics, by virtue of the Emancipation Act of 1829, 10 Geo IV, c. 7, were allowed to subscribe to a single modified oath, instead of to the three oaths as hitherto, and this act seemed to provide a suitable precedent. But the Commons as from 1833 and the aftermath of the Reform, though unlike the Lords favourable to Emancipation, would not consider simplification of legislation until the Jews had been admitted to Parliament on the merits of their own case and in a straightforward fashion. Thus not until the less than satisfactory compromise between the willing Commons and the reluctant Lords, 21 & 22 Vict, c. 48 and c. 49, of 1858, had yielded to a permanent statutory and constitutional recognition of the Jews' rights to sit in Parliament, achieved by the act 23 & 24 Vict, c. 63, of 1860, could a new simplified oath be introduced as part of the Parliamentary Oaths Act, 29 & 30 Vict, c. 19, of 1866. This last act omitted all reference to the Abjuration Oath of the past and allowed any Jew, if ennobled, to be sworn in as a member of the Lords.

The one other important sphere of political and public service where Jews were affected by disabilities concerned municipal office. As municipal office was less important than membership of the legislature it was to be expected that the lesser problem would have to be overcome before the removal of parliamentary disabilities could be realized. Prior to 1828 the Corporation Act of 1661 (13 Car II, c. 2) and the Test Act of 1673 (25 Car II, c. 2), both of which required the holders of municipal office and of any civil or military office under the Crown to take the sacraments according to the Church of England, had together been supposed to guarantee the exclusion of non-Anglicans. Yet, so typically of English law, the legislators paid homage to an established principle whilst doing much to undermine it in practice. The Indemnity Acts, the first of which had been passed in 1727–28, were renewed annually until 1868, when the Promissory Oaths Act (31 & 32 Vict, c. 72), rendered unnecessary their continuance. The Indemnity Acts had shielded from prosecution anyone who had not taken the prescribed oaths at the appointed time, for a period lasting until some future day in the following year.[31] In 1828 the act 9 Geo IV, c. 17, repealed these disabilities as they affected Protestant Dissenters, but in so doing replaced the sacramental tests with a declaration containing the words 'upon the true faith of a Christian'; an attempt during passage of the measure to remove these words so that the Jews too might be included within the scope of the act proved unsuccessful. It was inconceivable that such disabilities affecting Jews could have been outlawed in 1828 at a time when Catholics were still subject to them: not until 1845, as a consequence of the legislation 8 & 9 Vict, c. 52, were the last of the barriers preventing Jews from serving in municipal office removed. Yet it was in 1828 that the Jews had first seen their opportunity and it is in connection with the parliamentary debates of April in that year, leading to the promulgation of 9 Geo IV, c. 17, that the campaign for Emancipation can be said to have begun.

NOTES

1. Brougham, Lord Chancellor, *Hansard,* Third Series, 20, 1 August 1833, 239.
2. H. S. Q. Henriques, *The Jews and the English Law,* p. 233.
3. H. S. Q. Henriques, *The Law of Aliens and Naturalization,* p. 62.
4. Ibid., p. 30.
5. H. S. Q. Henriques, *The Jews and the English Law,* pp. 237–40.
6. T. W. Perry, *Public Opinion, Propaganda, and Politics in Eighteenth-Century England. A Study of the Jew Bill of 1753,* Harvard Historical Monographs, no. 51, p. 178.
7. H. S. Q. Henriques, *The Jews and the English Law,* pp. 158, 234–38; H. S. Q. Henriques, *The Law of Aliens and Naturalization,* pp. 17–18.
8. C. Roth, *A History of the Jews in England,* pp. 235–36.
9. H. S. Q. Henriques, *The Jews and the English Law,* pp. 2–3, 32–33, 117–18, 147–50, 153–54, 173, 179, 183–85.
10. Ibid., pp. 185–87.
11. Ibid., p. 179.
12. Ibid., pp. 178–79.
13. Ibid., pp. 188–89.
14. *Cases argued and determined in the Court of Common Pleas. Reports of Chief Justice Willes, 1737–60* (ed. C. Durnford), Hilary 18 Geo II, [Omichund *v* Barker, 23 February in Chancery] pp. 538–54.
15. I. Finestein, *A Short History of Anglo-Jewry,* p. 95; I. Finestein, 'Anglo-Jewry and the Law of Divorce', *The Jewish Chronicle,* 19 April 1957, p. 11; I. Finestein, 'An Aspect of the Jews and English Marriage Law during the Emancipation: The Prohibited Degrees', *The Jewish Journal of Sociology,* vol. VII, no. 1, June 1965, pp. 3–21, discuss the following far more competently than I am able: 5 & 6 Will IV, c. 54, An Act to render certain Marriages valid, and to alter the Law with respect to certain voidable Marriages [31 August 1835]; *Parliamentary Papers, Public Bills,* 1857, 30 April–28 August 1857, I, A Bill intituled An Act to amend the Law relating to Divorce and Matrimonial Causes in England, 25 June 1857, pp. 541–56, bill no. 86; *Parliamentary Papers, Public Bills,* 1857, 30 April–28 August 1857, I, A Bill [as amended in Committee] intituled An Act to amend the Law relating to Divorce and Matrimonial Causes in England, 19 August 1857, pp. 557–74, bill no. 197.
16. *Parliamentary Papers, Public Bills,* 1854–55, 12 December 1854–14 August 1855, II, pp. 25–64 (drafts of bills to amend the Dissenters' Marriage Acts).
17. *Parliamentary Papers, Public Bills,* 1856, 31 January–29 July 1856, III, A Bill to Amend the Provisions of the Marriage Act relating to Dissenters, 7 February 1856, pp. 11–12.
18. D'Blossiers Tovey, *Anglia Judaica; or the History and Antiquities of the Jews in England,* pp. 187–91, re. Bodleian MSS, 1 Cod MS Bib Bod N.E.A. 19.
19. H. S. Q. Henriques, *The Jews and the English Law,* pp. 191–92.
20. For the case upholding the view that the Jews could own land, cf. F. H. Goldsmid, *Remarks on the Civil Disabilities of British Jews,* pp. 37–61. For the case upholding the view that Jews could not own land, cf. J. E. Blunt, *A History of the Establishment and Residence of the Jews in England with an Enquiry into their Civil Disabilities,* pp. iv–xvi, 77–128. Blunt was personally in favour of the removal of all disabilities affecting Jews.
21. C. Roth, *A History of the Jews in England,* p. 248.
22. F. H. Goldsmid, *Remarks on the Civil Disabilities of British Jews,* p. 4; Peel Papers, B. M. ADD. MSS. 40563, ff. 27–28, 17 March 1845, I. L. Goldsmid to Peel.
23. C. Roth, *A History of the Jews in England,* pp. 194–95.
24. H. S. Q. Henriques, *The Jews and the English Law,* pp. 198–200.
25. A. Pellatt, *Brief Memoir of the Jews, in relation to their civil and municipal disabilities,* pp. 23–27; H. S. Q. Henriques, *The Jews and the English Law,* pp. 200–202; B. L. Manning, *The Protestant Dissenting Deputies* (ed. O. Greenwood), pp. 119–29.
26. H. S. Q. Henriques, *The Jews and the English Law,* pp. 203–6.
27. Ibid., pp. 206–8; U. R. Q. Henriques, *Religious Toleration in England, 1787–1833,* p. 180.
28. H. S. Q. Henriques, *The Jews and the English Law,* pp. 208–11.
29. Ibid., p. 198.
30. F. Pollock, *Essays in Jurisprudence and Ethics,* pp. 186–88, noting the judgment of Baron Alderson in Miller *v* Salomons, 7 Ex, 536–37.
31. H. S. Q. Henriques, *The Jews and the English Law,* p. 203.

Part II
THE JEWISH INITIATIVE

3
Abortive Attempts at Emancipation

Propitious as circumstances may have appeared on the morrow of the Parliamentary concessions to both the Protestant Dissenters and the Roman Catholics three decades were to pass before any Jew was allowed to sit in the legislature. For these years were to see no less than fourteen attempts to remove parliamentary disabilities. One bill was presented in each of the years 1830, 1833, 1834, 1836, 1847–48, 1849, 1851, 1853, 1854 and 1856 and four further measures were considered in 1857 and 1858. The first bill was rejected by the unreformed House of Commons, the next twelve passed the Commons but were rejected by the House of Lords, while only the fourteenth, a compromise between leading members of the two Houses, proved acceptable.

One reason, if not the most important, for the initial failure to secure Emancipation lay in the conflict of aspirations to be found among the leaders and self-appointed leaders of the Jewish community.

In the years after 1828 the unquestioned lay leader of Anglo-Jewry was Moses Montefiore. He had been born into a merchant family in 1784, at a time when his parents were visiting Leghorn, the traditionally Medici-controlled refuge to which his ancestors had come from Ancona and the Papal States and from which his grandfather had emigrated to England in 1758. By 1828 Montefiore had been enabled virtually to retire from a successful career as merchant-banker and insurance-broker in order to devote more time to the affairs of both Anglo-Jewry and world Jewry. In 1818 he had been elected President of the Spanish and Portuguese congregation; in 1835 he was to be elected President of the Board of Deputies. Ranking next in importance among the lay leaders in the years after 1828 were the two Goldsmids, Isaac Lyon and his son Francis Henry, descendants of Aaron Goldsmid, a prosperous Dutch merchant who had emigrated from Amsterdam in the mid-eighteenth century. I. L. Goldsmid had followed the family tradition in becoming a broker and merchant-banker and had helped to finance first the London docks and then the railways; by 1828, at the age of fifty, he too had renounced most of his business interests in order to devote time to such affairs of Jewish concern as the establishment of the new London University and the remission of disabilities. F. H. Goldsmid, who was soon to establish a reputation as a prolific pamphleteer in the cause of Emancipation, became in 1833 the first Jew to be admitted to the Bar. Then, almost inevitably, there were the Rothschilds, heirs in England to such earlier financiers as Solomon de Medina, Samson Gideon and Joseph Salvador, though on a considerably larger and more international scale; between 1811 and 1816 almost half of the British subventions to the Continental powers passed through the hands of the Rothschilds and after the restoration of 1815 they became loan-mongers for the legitimist rulers of Europe. Nathan Mayer Rothschild was the Frankfurt-born head of the British branch of the family until his death at the age of fifty-eight in July 1836. Of his four sons the eldest, Lionel Nathan, was to take his seat in Parliament as the first professing Jew in 1858, while the three younger sons, Anthony, Nathaniel and Mayer Nathan were also involved in the campaign from its earliest stages. Scarcely known by 1828 in comparison with the Rothschilds was David Salomons, born in 1797 of an Ashkenazi family established for at least two generations as merchants and underwriters in the City and on the Royal Exchange. Salomons's own incursion into the Quaker sphere of deposit banking as underwriter and founder of the Westminster Bank constituted something of a break both with family and with Anglo-Jewish tradition.

The lay leadership was drawn together in the London Committee of Deputies of the British Jews, to be renamed in 1835 the Deputies of the British Jews, but usually known as the Board of Deputies. This committee can be traced back in embryo to 1746, when the Bevis Marks Synagogue had formed a Committee of Diligence to redress two rejections by the Irish legislature of a Jewish Naturalization Bill, and to the circumstances of 1754, when Parliament had suddenly repealed the previous year's legislation for the naturalization of foreign-born Jews. Both of these episodes had underlined the importance of constituting a Jewish body of elected lay representatives similar to the Protestant Dissenting Deputies, established in 1732 with between twenty-one and twenty-five laymen drawn from the London congregations of the 'Three Denominations', the Presbyterians, the Independents (the future Congregationalists) and the Baptists. The Board of Deputies, which emerged in 1760 from the moribund Committee of Diligence, was at its inception comprised solely of the Sephardim or *Deputados* of the Portuguese Nation, but before the year's end this group had admitted to its deliberations members of the Ashkenazim or German Secret Committee for Public Affairs. Thenceforth the Deputies nicely dovetailed into the British scene: emulation of the Protestant Dissenters apart, the Board's substitution of Portuguese by English for the recording of minutes as from the decade or so before 1789 attested to a trend akin to the prevailing Catholic Cisalpinism.

The newfound importance of the religious leadership of the Ashkenazim testified to their growing prominence in Anglo-Jewry relative to that of the Sephardim; by the middle years of the nineteenth century four out of every five Jews in Britain could be reckoned as Ashkenazim, a preponderance which had become ever more evident for a century past and which could be attributed to the arrival of Jews from Dutch, German and Central European territories rather than to any substantial flow of immigration from Russia and Eastern Europe. The tenure of the Chief Rabbinate by Solomon Hirschell lasted for forty years, from 1802 until 1842; Nathan Marcus Adler, who in 1845 succeeded to a similarly long pastorate, came like his predecessor from a rabbinical family, his father having been the Chief Rabbi of Hanover. And one of the most exotic of all the *dramatis personae,* lay or religious, in the forthcoming struggle was to be the Hungarian-born Joseph Crooll, who in a semi-official capacity taught Hebrew to interested members and particularly Fellows of Colleges at Cambridge University during the years when the Royal Professors of Hebrew were absentees.

From the earliest days of the campaign for Jewish Emancipation none had cause to doubt that the question at issue was essentially concerned with resolving yet a third set of claims, consequent upon those advanced by the Protestant Dissenters and the Roman Catholics, for admission to seats in the legislature. Municipal grievances would, however, have to be outlawed before parliamentary Emancipation could even be considered and in April 1828 the Board of Deputies drew up a petition to protect the interests of Jews in the forthcoming bill to relieve Protestant Dissenters from disabilities for public office.[1] During passage through Parliament of a measure for the relief of Protestant Dissenters from the sacramental tests imposed by the Corporation and Test Acts, Edward Copleston, Bishop of Llandaff, proposed that the words 'upon the true faith of a Christian' be appended to the new declaration which was to be taken upon admission to any corporate office. The original anti-recusant intention of these words appeared to explain Llandaff's speech drawing attention to the need to defend the Church of England against external danger, the more so as another amendment, proposed by the Earl of Winchelsea, to append to the declaration the words 'and in our Lord and Saviour Jesus Christ' was defeated by 113 votes to 15, a majority of 98. In spite of the disapproval of those such as Lord Holland, the nephew of Charles James Fox and as Whiggishly devoted as his late uncle to the cause of extending civil and religious liberty, Llandaff's amendment was carried without a division: a week later Llandaff disingenuously, if plausibly in view of the remission of Catholic disabilities, told Holland that he had not originally been aware of the anti-Jewish construction on the clause—though admitting that he would still have proposed it even had he realized the full implications.[2] It was in vain that I. L. Goldsmid pointed out to the Prime Minister the discriminatory effect of Llandaff's amendment, for Wellington replied that any modification of the bill in favour of the Jews would be impossible;[3] the protest entered on the Lords Journals by Holland and a small group of the Jews' supporters in the Lords was equally unsuccessful.[4] The Dissenters meanwhile were understandably so concerned for the success of their own measure that they were not prepared to jeopardize their chances for the sake of a group for whom they could anyway do little: when John Bowring, the confidant of Jeremy Bentham and one of the most influential among the Dissenting Deputies, wrote to Goldsmid at the beginning of May to inform him of the Dissenters' opposition to the Christian faith compelling clause he confessed to the failure of his own attempts to persuade the Deputies to communicate their displeasure with the Government to Lord John Russell, himself one of the keenest Whig advocates of the remission of disabilities.[5] And so the declaration containing the words 'upon the true faith of a Christian' passed into law as the act 9 Geo IV, c. 17, of May 1828. What little measure of encouragement the Jews received at this time came not from the Dissenters but indirectly from the Catholics; the role which an effective Board of Deputies might play was illustrated in June when Daniel O'Connell, the Irish champion of Catholic Emancipation, defeated Vesey Fitzgerald, the new Tory President of the Board of Trade and Treasurer of the Navy, in a by-election at Clare. For this result marked the culmination of five years' hard work undertaken by the Dublin-based Catholic Association, an organization dedicated to the achievement of Emancipation through peaceful agitation.

But an O'Connell strategy was yet to find a standard-bearer from within the Jewish community; I. L. Goldsmid, who at this time stood in the forefront of the campaign for Emancipation, was more attuned to the thinking of the Whig establishment. Holland, choosing to minimise rather than dwell upon the importance of developments at home, advised Goldsmid and the Rothschilds that at their next meeting with Wellington they should attempt to relate the benefits of Emancipation to possible desirable objectives of Britain's foreign policy as the Prime Minister would surely be susceptible to such an approach. His letter, with its sophisticated calculations of *Weltpolitik,* may be taken as a response to the occupation of the two Principalities of Moldavia and Wallachia in the aftermath of the Greek Revolt of 1827, a move on the part of Russia which seemed to justify fears that her oft-proclaimed policy in the half-century since the Kuchuk Kainardji Treaty of 1774, of seeking merely to protect the interests of subjugated Greek Orthodox Christians in the Balkans and Near East, was little other than a pretext for gaining control of areas vacated by the Turks, and ultimately of the Straits themselves. Holland observed that there was a need to counter the support which the Russians as natural protector and ally enjoyed amongst the Greek Orthodox peoples of the Balkans and among the Christian minority of Persia, a considerable moral influence which combined with geographical and military advantages had come greatly to incur the jealousy of British governments. Contending that the Jews might best be able to advance Britain's interests Holland remarked on the characteristics for which they were renowned throughout the East: active, intelligent, opulent, a compact and united people who were, as everywhere, remarkable for rapid and confidential communication between their communities. They possessed, moreover, many of the most lucrative trades and professions of Turkey and Persia. 'They must therefore have, and in fact they have, much moral though indirect influence on the councils of the state, and still more on the disposition of the people.' Jews everywhere, being sensitively alive to the treatment of their co-religionists by other governments, were intensely interested in the outcome of the Emancipation struggle in Britain: accordingly

> their inclination to favour or to baffle the views of the various Cabinets of Europe, would in a great measure be regulated by their sense of the greater indulgence or severity with which they are treated in the countries those Cabinets represent. If then the Jews of England were on an equal footing with all their other fellow-subjects, would not their brethren of Constantinople, Turkey and the Levant, feel that in promoting the political objects of Great Britain they were furthering the views of a friendly power, and the more so as it is notorious, and for very obvious reasons, that Jews everywhere are predisposed to regard Protestants with less suspicion and dislike than either Greeks or Roman Catholics, inasmuch as from both of those sects they have at no very distant periods and in various parts of the world experienced such cruel persecution?

Holland recalled the aid rendered to Napoleon by Jews in Poland, Egypt and Turkey, grateful not only because he had treated them with common justice but also because he had acknowledged their equality and their rights; 'if England had the *good sense* as well as the justice to court in the real spirit of amity and good-fellowship the goodwill of the Jews, as Napoleon did, I believe every Jew banker, Jew physician, Jew merchant throughout Turkey, would become an active and useful partisan of the English system of policy in the Levant, whatever that system may be.'[6]

Whatever the merits of Holland's arguments the Jews were bound to be preoccupied with domestic developments. At a meeting of the Deputies on 17 March 1829 I. L. Goldsmid emphasised that the insertion of the words 'upon the true faith of a Christian' in the act for the relief of the Protestant Dissenters meant that the position of the Jews compared unfavourably with that existing hitherto. He related to the Deputies the substance of his interviews with members of both Houses and read out various letters which had promised support for any Emancipation measure which might be submitted to Parliament. The Deputies, after resolving 'that the present era appears to this meeting propitious for the Advancement of the Civil Interests of the Jews of the United Kingdom', decided that as soon as the bill for the relief of the Catholics had passed into law the Board should be reconvened in order to determine what further steps should be taken.[7]

Although the Roman Catholic Relief Bill did not satisfy the grievances of the Deputies they were content to follow the lead of the Government. When, early in April 1829, Parliament found itself preoccupied with the Catholic Emancipation legislation the Lord Chancellor, Lyndhurst, advised a delegation led by Montefiore to remain quiet until the matter was settled and public opinion had become favourable.[8] Nathan Mayer Rothschild conveyed a similar message in reporting to the Board the content of his discussions with the leading members of the Government. He recommended that a prayer to the Lords seeking relief should be prepared for presentation at the opportune moment, that this petition should apply to natural-born subjects only and should ask for full protection in the matter of the holding and conveying of landed property.[9]

In consequence of Rothschild's recommendation the Board instructed its solicitor, H. P. Pearce, to prepare for the preliminary approval of the Deputies a draft of a petition to the Lords. This document, which was subsequently presented, pointed out that the Jews, in the aftermath of the relief for Protestant Dissenters and Catholics, were actually worse off. For the Board was only too well aware that the exclusion, which had before 1828 placed Jews alongside all those dissenting from the Church of England, now rendered Anglo-Jewry the only numerically significant group still suffering from disabilities: the petitions of the Board would henceforth invariably refer to the 'relief afforded to his Majesty's other subjects not being members of the Established Church' and express the hope that this would—in the exact words of one—'entitle them [the Jews] to look to the Legislature for an equal measure of liberality and indulgence—to that dispensed . . . in favour of both Protestant and Roman Catholic Dissenters.'[10] In the Upper House the petition was presented by the keen conversionist Lord Bexley, a former Chancellor of the Exchequer; a bill for the remission of Jewish disabilities was subsequently drafted and presented by a small deputation to Bexley and to Dr. Stephen Lushington, the Parliamentary reformer and anti-slavery campaigner. Perhaps the Jews should have been forewarned not to expect a Parliamentary response to their pressure, and warning did indeed now come from a friendly quarter with Holland's advice to I. L. Goldsmid on 4 May not to stir up the passions generated by the Catholic question. 'I think such application [for the outlawing of municipal disabilities] during the present session would be more likely to do harm than good. There are all who voted against, and some, I fear, who voted for, the Repeal of the Test Act who think we have gone too far on the perilous road.' This was sound advice for when Bexley informed the deputation from the Board that he had seen Wellington he was obliged to reveal that as a result of the Prime Minister's emphatic opposition he and Lushington had deemed it prudent to withdraw their measure. Holland could do little more than mollify Goldsmid by pointing out that sponsorship of any future measure would carry most weight if drawn from such a sample and cross-section of political and ecclesiastical opinion as a minister and a bishop, high and evangelical churchmen and former opponents of Catholic Emancipation as well as erstwhile supporters.[11]

The year 1830 began familiarly with the Board of Deputies placing in synagogues copies of a petition to the Lords to be signed by natural-born subjects; to arrange for presentation to the Commons of this petition and to ascertain the sentiments of the Government there now came forward another active conversionist, Robert Grant, the philanthropist and politician of Indian affairs. Although, on the recommendation of a Board of Deputies committee which included among its members Moses Montefiore, I. L. Goldsmid and Lionel Rothschild, the decision was taken that unlike earlier proposals 'the Right of sitting in Parliament should not form so conspicuous a feature in the new Bill, provided the Privilege can be obtained in any other manner', a delegation was subsequently disappointed when informed by Wellington on 12 February that he could not commit the Government to Jewish Emancipation. Advising a postponement of their application to Parliament, as he could promise nothing, Wellington warned the Deputies that if they refused to heed his advice they would have to push ahead at their own risk.[12]

This they did, with the encouragement of such public figures as the socialist Robert Owen, one of the co-founders with Goldsmid of London University, and William Huskisson, a former Colonial Secretary and Leader of the Commons. As heir in political philosophy to the dead Prime Minister Canning, Huskisson helped to keep in existence until his own tragic death in September 1830 a shadow band of nominal Tories most of whom supported the cause of religious liberty and which included such established figures as Melbourne, Palmerston and Robert Grant. Huskisson, with the assistance of the Marquis of Lansdowne, arranged for the presentation to Parliament of a petition from the Jews of his own constituency of Liverpool and in a letter to a leading member of the Liverpool community, M. L. Mozley, undertook to speak in favour of the removal of Parliamentary disabilities in the forthcoming Commons debate.[13]

Uncanny foresight characterised the speech delivered by Grant as he presented to the Commons on 5 April 1830 the first bill for the remission of Parliamentary disabilities. 'What!' remonstrated Grant, 'after the Catholic question had been so decided, were they to permit the present question to pass through a period of similar agitation? Were they to discuss it for thirty years, and at the expiration of that period were the survivors to be told that the occupiers of the Treasury Bench saw their error, and that they agreed to toleration for ever?' Grant, in a fourfold division of his address, cogently examined the state of the law, the grounds of complaint against it, the remedy for such complaints and the possible objections to that remedy. He considered that the role of the law was crucial in determining the standing of every social group and, in implying that the legal recognition of assumed deficiencies was tantamount to an admission of defeat in finding a natural solution, he observed that an excellent way to corrupt people was to enact legislation as though corruption already existed among them. Supported in debate by Sir James Mackintosh, the philosopher and legal reformer, and by the historian Thomas Babington Macaulay, choosing this as the occasion for the delivery of his maiden speech, Grant saw the bill given a first reading by 115 votes to 97, a majority of 18.[14]

But the smallness of the majority was a bad omen for the advocates of Emancipation: many men in public life were not prepared to commit themselves to support of the Jewish cause before being able to assess the effects of recent relief legislation and reservations in 1830 could not be construed as hostility. Even so sympathetic a figure as the poet and cleric H. H. Milman, author at this time of a *History of the Jews* which won renown for its realistic treatment of Old Testament figures, felt constrained to confess to I. L. Goldsmid his doubts concerning admission of Jews to the legislature.[15] Such reservations were, however, little heeded. Grant and his fellow sponsor, Lushington, were entreated by the Deputies to persist with the measure and on 14 April N. M. Rothschild and his son Lionel gave an account to Montefiore of their meeting with the President of the Board of Trade, J. C. Herries, who had informed them that the Government was to discuss the bill with its sponsors the following morning.[16] Admittedly some strong support for the Jewish cause was evident in the cities, with petitions to Parliament emanating from Bristol, Liverpool and London, but to this pressure the House of Commons, its composition of seats not yet reflecting the new power of the urban centres, might almost have been expected to remain impervious.[17]

And so events proved. On the second reading of Grant's bill on 17 May Russell observed that both Roman Catholics and Unitarians had been allowed to sit in Parliament, although the former regarded the Church of England as an apostasy and the latter believed it to be a corruption. Huskisson then developed this argument for Emancipation on grounds of consistency by stating that the exclusion of the Jews was the only exception remaining to the principle of toleration on which the law was now based. But the Commons was not yet receptive to the consistency argument, nor did it heed the wisdom of the shrewd and experienced O'Connell: 'Affect to scorn a man for his opinions, or to deprive him of civil power on their account, and he became wedded to them more firmly than ever.' Grant's bill was thrown out by 228 votes to 165, a majority of 63, though it was of some comfort to the advocates of Emancipation that of the twelve Members of Parliament who represented those London constituencies in which the vast majority of Britain's Jews lived every one recorded a vote for the removal of disabilities. For the present the Board could do little other than thank Grant for his exertions.[18]

Yet the Deputies, at the very moment when their enthusiasm for the struggle was waning, might have looked more closely at the circumstances attending this setback. Scarcely perceptible, but auguring well for the Jews, was the existence among the present parliamentary opponents of Emancipation of a group whose rejection of Grant's bill was to be explained more on grounds of pragmatism than of principle. Foremost among these was Peel, the Home Secretary, whose reasoned objections to the measure in winding up for the Government considerably irritated such influential Tory members as the essayist and reviewer J. W. Croker; Peel's contention that the removal of disabilities would be both untimely and inconsistent with the exclusion of other religious minorities, notably the Quakers and Separatists, was interpreted by the Tory diehards as recognition of the very worth of the consistency and timeliness arguments! Peel, once again the tergiversator? The day after the debate Croker wrote to Vesey Fitzgerald, the loser to O'Connell in the celebrated Clare by-election of two years before, to suggest that the Home Secretary was still smarting from the wounds inflicted upon him at Oxford by the evangelical and Eldonine ultra-Tory diehard Sir Robert Inglis in February 1829, the by-election in which Peel had suffered defeat for reversing his previous stand of opposition to Catholic Emancipation. 'We threw out the Jews' Bill last night', wrote Croker 'after a very *faint* speech from Peel. He did not at all grapple with the real question, and seemed as if he wished to be beaten. What can this mean? Does he resent against the Church the rejection of Oxford? He last night *in principle* gave up the whole connection of Church and State.' *John Bull* likewise complained of the 'long temporizing speeches' emanating from the ranks of those opposed to the bill, 'soft and soothing, in which those who made them, seemed, really, to palliate the disbelief of the infidels, and apologize for the expediency which forced them to shut the door against them'.[19]

The heterodox Unitarians, disbelieving in the divinity of Christ, were the Christians in closest religious affinity to the Jews and at the beginning of June Bowring of the Protestant Dissenting Deputies communicated to I. L. Goldsmid a resolution passed at a Finsbury Chapel general meeting of the British and Foreign Unitarian Association. The Association had then pledged itself to work for the 'complete triumph' of religious liberty and had instructed its committee 'to take such measures as may appear likely to remove from their Jewish brethren the stigma inflicted on them by exclusive statutes'.[20] This backing was undoubtedly welcome to Goldsmid although it might reasonably have been anticipated; what now came as an unexpected boon was the support lent by William Hazlitt. For the essayist, himself the son of a Unitarian minister, was scathing in his condemnation of the prejudices which had caused the vicious circle of degradation.

Hazlitt's sensitive appeal for Emancipation, published in *The Tatler* of March 1831 six months after his death, expressed more effectively, in his own inimitably terse and aphoristic style, a point made by Sir James Mackintosh in the Commons' debate of April 1830. 'We throw in the teeth of the Jews', remonstrated Hazlitt,

that they are prone to certain sordid vices. If they are vicious it is we who have made them so. Shut out any class of people from the path to fair

fame, and you reduce them to grovel in the pursuit of riches and the means
to live. A man has long been in dread of insult for no just cause, and you
complain that he grows reserved and suspicious. . . . The Jews barter and
sell commodities, instead of raising or manufacturing them. But this is the
necessary traditional consequence of their former persecution and pillage
by all nations. They could not set up a trade when they were hunted every
moment from place to place, and while they could count nothing their own
but what they could carry with them. They could not devote themselves to
the pursuit of agriculture, when they were not allowed to possess a foot of
land. You tear people up by the roots and trample on them like noxious
weeds, and then make an outcry that they do not take root in the soil like
wholesome plants.[21]

Any disinterested observer must be tempted to ask whether Hazlitt's
essay was not more helpful to the Emancipation cause than the facetiously
clever ridicule indulged in at this time by Macaulay, to the effect that Jews
enjoyed the substance of power whilst being deprived of the shadow. This
was a line scarcely likely to commend itself to a nation (*pace* Lytton Bulwer
and Emerson) somewhat hypocritically priding itself on 'salvation by taste',
attached to decency of forms and respectability of appearances. Jews,
pointed out Macaulay, had property, knowledge, the power of principal over
clerk, of master over servant, and of landlord over tenant. The influence of
the Jew was paramount in war and in the plans of princes, but still were they
deprived of the principle. In noting the political influence of Jews Macaulay
can scarcely have swayed, for example, Sir Robert Peel, who had been
reduced after his rejection by Oxford in 1829 to securing the nomination
borough of Westbury from its converted Jewish patron Sir Manasseh Lopes.
Jews could make money and money, contended Macaulay, could make
Members of Parliament. Jews could own pocket-boroughs without inhabitants and could bribe electors, they could behave as Dukes of Newcastle and
command the loyalty of Members of Parliament. Jews were prevented from
becoming Privy Councillors to a Christian king, yet they could govern the
money-market and ministers often found it necessary to seek the advice of
Jews on finance. 'The scrawl of the Jew on the back of a piece of paper',
jibed Macaulay, 'may be worth more than the royal word of three kings, or
the national faith of three new American republics. But that he should put
Right Honourable before his name, would be the most frightful of national
calamities.' More straightforward was Macaulay's resort to the Benthamite
maxim of striving to secure 'the greatest happiness of the greatest number':
the philosophy that every human being has a right to be allowed every
gratification, every right to political power, on the condition that such claim
does not inflict pain on others, and that a human being should be spared
every mortification productive of no benefit to others.[22] Considered as a
whole the value of Macaulay's essay to the Emancipation cause may have
lain more in boosting the morale of the Jews themselves than in rallying
gentile support. In Parliament there continued to be little enthusiasm for an

early reconsideration of the Jewish question and in June 1832 Wellington's successor as Prime Minister, Lord Grey, refused to commit the support of the Whig government to any legislation which might, in some unlikely event, be contemplated for the near future.[23]

Undaunted by the lack of parliamentary support but encouraged rather by the success of the organized agitation in favour of emancipating the slaves I. L. Goldsmid persevered in enlisting the backing of those most renowned for their humanitarian stance on this issue, the Dissenters. In March 1833 Elizabeth Fry gave a warm reply to a letter she had received from Goldsmid though reminding him that the better judge of political questions was considered to be Joseph Pease of the railway-pioneering family; Pease, only the month before, had been allowed to affirm as the first Quaker to take his seat in the Commons. 'I have so high a view of the *real* Christian principle', declared Elizabeth Fry,

> that I wish all who govern our country to be really influenced by it, though I lament to say I think far too many who take a part in this important work are only Christians in *name,* and I fully believe many of our Jewish brethren are examples to them in life and conversation, and even where they do not fully acknowledge it, they are much guided by the high moral standard inculcated in the Holy Scriptures. I therefore believe there are amongst you who would fill a place in the House of Commons to the satisfaction of their constituents.[24]

The day after Elizabeth Fry had written in praise of the Jews, William Cobbett, in answer to a petition to the Commons requesting the remission of disabilities, fiercely denigrated them. Cobbett was already known as 'the sauciest' opponent of the Jewish cause.[25] His stigmatizing of the Jews as blasphemers of Christ and as purveyors of the deist and atheist 'reason' which had damaged France and killed Poland had constituted the theme of *Good Friday; or the Murder of Jesus Christ by the Jews.* Although this interpretation offered in 1830 had merited a refutation from Hyman Hurwitz, the first Professor of Hebrew at University College, London,[26] it had been repeated in the Commons three weeks before in answer to the assertion of another Member that Jews were to be counted among the Crown's most industrious subjects. Cobbett had challenged his fellow Member as to 'whether he could produce a Jew who ever dug, who went to plough, or who ever made his own coat or his own shoes, or who did anything at all, except get all the money he could from the pockets of the people?'[27]

William Cobbett was the self-educated son of a labourer and by his own efforts he had risen to become a small farmer; to the supporters of Emancipation he seemed the English counterpart to those rural populists of the Continent who served up a brand of Jew-hatred as a substitute for curing the genuine ills of society. There could be no doubt as to Cobbett's dislikes. He was xenophobic, having once declared that as an Englishman he despised all other nations on earth; he was anti-negro, having portrayed slaves as 'fat and lazy niggers' laughing from morning until night, and he was antipathetic to Dissenting religion, having condemned the Methodists who fought on the slaves' behalf as 'the vilest crew God ever suffered to infest the earth'. Cobbett further gained a reputation as an opponent of every one of the half dozen successive changes which seemed to have characterised the transformation of English society over a period of three centuries. Traversing England on horseback Cobbett witnessed the passing away of long-established rural communities, of cherished village customs and of the stable continuity of family life and so became a convinced opponent of urbanization. As this trend towards urbanization could be attributed to the demands of industrialization Cobbett was further established as an opponent of this too: he saw industrialization as favouring the 'loanjobbers, contractors and nabobs, butchers, bakers, bottle-corkers and old-clothesmen'[28]—this last an unmistakable reference to the Jews formerly prominent in the peddling and selling of old clothes. These men had ruined the old system of domestic industry and by driving country folk to the towns had destroyed the happiest state of existence that could be imagined; meanwhile they bought up the countryside as prelude to keeping foxhounds and tracing their descent from the Normans.[29] As industrialization relied upon both a government funding system and a government taxation system which respectively entailed debt for the nation and penury for its inhabitants Cobbett was brought to oppose the capitalism of which these evils were the manifestation. Agglomerations of capital by means of taxation and government loans, contended Cobbett, were caused by the surplus printing of paper money, this inflation being the device by which hard-earned wages were conjured away into the pockets of Jews and stock-jobbers: Cobbett's definition of capital as 'money taken from the labouring classes . . . given to army tailors and suchlike'[30] was another clear reference to the many clothes-dealing Jews of London and the seaport towns during the Napoleonic Wars. Because the advent of capitalism was to be attributed to those who were tangibly its beneficiaries Cobbett was opposed to the display of individualism as represented by 'The Thing', a huge, intricate combination of knaves which included all the parvenus and plutocrats, Mammon-idolaters and money-changers, city-magnates and borough-mongers. The term Jew, declared Cobbett, was 'synonymous with *sharper, cheat* and *rogue*', as was 'the case with *no other* race of mankind'.[31] In this world of jobbery, placemen and corruption Cobbett thinks, among others, of the Jewish Ricardo family; he dubs as a 'blood-sucker' Abraham Goldsmid, the City financier who had committed suicide on the failure of the government loan in 1810,[32] and—this in the days before Peel's Westbury connection—he denounces Sir Manasseh Lopes, or 'Massa-Massa Lopez' as he calls him, who had in 1819 been convicted of bribery in connection with his pocket-boroughs and sentenced to a fine of a thousand pounds and three years' imprisonment. The Jews, according to Cobbett, were a people 'living in all the filthiness of *usury and increase*', who were singularly uncreative, 'extortioners by habit and almost by instinct'.[33] Cobbett's condemnation of 'The Thing' led him in turn to denounce the materialist flight from faith which he associated with the Jews' incorporation into society: the Jews had been a pernicious scourge to every country that had possessed 'the weakness and the wickedness to encourage anything approaching towards *fellowship*'.[34] Here Cobbett, in the Continental Catholic tradition, identified materialism with Protestantism and the re-admission of the Jews to England with the mid-seventeenth-century ascendancy of the puritans. Which led him, finally, to a denunciation of the Reformation. Debt was the one monster evil ravaging society, and taxes to support it a Protestant invention made necessary by the original act of monastic plunder; the poor law was deemed a mere partial atonement for the robbery and extortion by fear of what was the poor man's patrimony. Ultimately it was the treachery of the Reformation which was to be held responsible for all the evils which had since occurred, including the debt, the banks, the stock-jobbers and the American Revolution.[35]

Cobbett was protesting not only against the Jews but also against the age which they seemed to epitomise. He wrote nostalgically of a Catholic monastic world and his dislike of the Jews was derived from an outlook akin to the *völkisch* philosophy to be found in Justus Möser's *German History* of 1773 which had portrayed the Middle Ages as the 'golden time' of the tillers of the soil. But the replacement of wartime inflation by peacetime solvency and the accession to political power of a puritanical middle class soon came—at least in Britain—to render Cobbett's thinking as redundant and irrelevant as that of his fellow radical, Thomas Duncombe, who was to be observed in February 1828 attributing the break-up of the previous Tory Government to the financial power of the Rothschilds[36]—but who was to emerge two decades later as a keen advocate of Emancipation. All but a few of the radicals favoured the remission of disabilities and in the parliaments which followed the Reform Act of 1832 they were to be found in the vanguard of that new majority which represented rather the interests of trade than of land. The generation of Cobden and Bright looked enthusiastically to capitalism to remedy the poor man's ills; only after the heyday of capitalism had passed did a leading radical, in the person of Joseph Chamberlain, emerge to champion a modification of that urban, 'Mammonish' order against which Cobbett had forewarned.

When in April 1833 Grant was given leave to introduce the second bill for the remission of disabilities the radical Joseph Hume, declaring his support, related that John Quincy Adams, lately President of the United States, had informed him that in his country there were no better citizens than the Jews and had expressed the hope that before long the whole of Europe would see the justice and wisdom of freely conceding to them the fullest political privileges.[37] And now the first important conversion to the cause of Emancipation became known. *The Times,* recalling its earlier forebodings at the time of the 1830 bill that Jews might prove guilty of incivism on account of their supposedly alien nationality, admitted that these fears had been allayed by the lack of any instance in modern history to confirm them, and conceded that the objection had been reduced 'to a question of mere consistency on the part of the Legislature, as respects the previous liberal measures adopted towards other religious bodies, which hold no communion with the Church of England, and acknowledge not the ecclesiastical supremacy of our Lord the KING'.[38] Although the Commons gave Grant's bill a second reading in May by 159 votes to 52, a majority of 107, and a third reading two months later by 189 votes to 52, a majority of 137, these division figures were misleading. Peel, despite the private entreaties of Montefiore, was still to be found aligned with the opponents of Emancipation. The sets of division figures reflected I. L. Goldsmid's hectic canvassing of likely supporters and the July vote was further to be explained by the drifting away towards the end of the parliamentary session of those opponents who, in anticipation of the peers' opposition, considered that their presence in the Commons was scarcely required.[39]

When, on 1 August, the peers moved for the first time to a discussion of the Jewish question such anticipation of their sentiments did indeed prove justified, although not before Lord Melbourne had made known his support for the remission of disabilities. 'It was not the privileges and advantages of individuals which they had to consider', reflected Melbourne with seeming disinterestedness, '—the deprivation of these did not form the great ground of complaint; on the contrary, the complaint was, that the privileges of the State, the welfare of the country, and the advantage of the community, were seriously injured by those restrictions.' In maintaining that the exclusion of anyone from appointment to a Crown office necessarily involved a curtailment of the Crown's prerogative, because it could not then select the person who might perhaps be best fitted to perform the duties of that office, Melbourne anticipated the use of an argument which was to come prominently to the fore in the years after the election of Lionel Rothschild for the City of London in 1847, as to whether the House of Lords was not depriving constituents of the services of one of their Members of Parliament. Opponents of the measure preferred however to judge the issue of Emancipation with reference to the circumstances of the recent past. Wellington, conscious of the arguments which claimed that the admission of Jews to Parliament would be consistent with the innovatory changes of the 1820s, rejected the view that Catholic Emancipation had provided a precedent. Whereas Catholics, prior to the imposition of restrictions, had enjoyed all the privileges of which they had since been deprived, the Jews, having never enjoyed such privileges, were not entitled to claim their restoration. And Bishop Blomfield, on the threshold of establishing a reputation as prolific builder and endower of churches within his London diocese, put forward an objection considered by many Anglicans to be even more germane to the current problems surrounding church-state relations: he contended that the extension of relief to non-Christians, which he saw as almost tantamount to Parliament caring for the wellbeing of all faiths and thus, by implication, for the interests of none, would afford to the people further evidence of Parliament's growing indifference towards the true religion.

Grant's bill met its demise by 104 votes to 54, a majority of 50. The most important influence on the voting was probably not, as I. L. Goldsmid unreasonably surmised, the personal aversion of the Prime Minister—Grey, according to Holland, had sound reasons for remaining neutral—but episcopal opposition: whereas the Archbishops of Canterbury and York together with eighteen bishops voted against Emancipation, only three ecclesiastics voted in favour. One of these supporters was Archbishop Whately of Dublin, a former Professor of Political Economy at Oxford and an independent liberal, whose comparative youth at the age of forty-six and position as the most junior of the archbishops—'Little Benjamin' as Holland called him— seemed to indicate further advancement. The poignancy of Holland's observation to Goldsmid that 'one bishop is worth five laymen, so powerful is our tribe of Levi among us' should have alerted the Jews more to current considerations concerning church-state relations.[40]

For it was in this context that Wellington's reference to Catholic Emancipation assumed a particular importance. Although there was every chance that *in time* Catholic Emancipation would come to be seen as a precedent for Jewish Emancipation the *immediate* consequence of the 1829 concession was to affect somewhat adversely the Jews' claims. Although the Whig victory of 1830 was of note in drawing to a close half a century of almost uninterrupted Tory rule, the heady expectations of an early Emancipation which resulted therefrom, so evident in the false optimism of the Board of Deputies Minute Books during these years, were almost certain to be frustrated: the feeling prevailed that further concessions could scarcely be contemplated until such time as the original fears of 1828–29 had been dispelled and no evil consequences could be seen to have arisen as a result of transforming an Anglican Parliament first into a Protestant Parliament and then into a Christian Parliament.

Nor was this metamorphosis in the character of Parliament the only issue vexing those attached to the traditional established order in Church and State: the very method of bringing about these changes, as evidence of the Church's loss of jurisdiction to the State and the State's increasing hold over the Church, had of itself excited controversy. Only two to three weeks before the Lords debate on the Jewish question the divine and poet John Keble, provoked by the Government's proposal to suppress ten Irish bishoprics by act of the civil power alone, had fired the opening salvo of a campaign by delivering a sermon on *National Apostasy*. This was followed in September by the first *Tract for the Times*. The Oxford Movement, of which Keble, John Henry Newman and E. B. Pusey came in the ensuing years to be the acknowledged leaders, won over a number of adherents at Oxford University and a revulsion at some of the reforms for which the civil power was held responsible, in particular the establishment of the rival London university, united in common cause a number of anti-Erastian high churchmen and diehard evangelicals: to a proportion among both these groups the new institution appeared as the embodiment of Jacobin, utilitarian and atheistic teachings. Such politico-religious considerations lay behind the subsequent election of Wellington as Chancellor of Oxford University and this, in turn, considerably heartened the Tories. Thus, when in spite of the continued non-committal stance of Grey, Grant persisted in the spring of 1834 in introducing yet another measure for the remission of the Jews' Parliamentary disabilities, the Tory majority in the Lords displayed an especial keenness in reversing the decision of the Commons, where the bill had been granted an easy passage by 123 votes to 32, a majority of 91. On 23 June, after a debate during which Howley, the Archbishop of Canterbury, apart from dismissing the Jews as 'a money-getting people' whose prosperity seemed proof that no concession was required to increase it, alluded to the ultra-orthodox arguments against Emancipation of the type advanced by Rabbi Joseph Crooll as evidence that Jews were themselves divided on the wisdom of such a measure, the Lords refused their own second reading by 130 votes to 38, a majority against the bill of 92 votes which was almost twice as large as that of the year before.[41] The Upper House was in no mood to consider further reforms affecting non-Anglicans and in the remaining weeks of the parliamentary session there followed rejection of both an Irish Tithe Bill and a measure for the admission of Dissenters to the two universities of Oxford and Cambridge.

In November 1834 the Whig Government was replaced by a Tory one. Although the leaders of Anglo-Jewry might have been expected to let their campaign fall into abeyance until such time as the Whigs returned to office they were confident that the Tories could at least be persuaded to grant one rather limited request. In February 1835 a group which included I. L. Goldsmid, David Salomons and N. M. Rothschild wrote to Peel, the new Prime Minister, expressing the hope that Jewish enfranchisement might soon be enacted and enquiring whether such a measure would be supported by the Government. Peel replied that the Government was not proposing to introduce any measure with reference to the civil capacities of the Jews.[42] Only after the Whigs had returned to office in April 1835 were the Jews able to elicit a favourable response to such a proposal: at the beginning of May Melbourne gave I. L. Goldsmid a pledge of support for the granting of 'civil rights and franchises with the other subjects of His Majesty dissenting from the Established Church'[43] and in due course, in August 1835, there was enacted the legislation 5 & 6 Will IV, c. 36, which enfranchised all Jews who were otherwise qualified to vote in elections.[44]

In 1836 one further attempt was made to achieve Emancipation and a bill for the remission of disabilities was introduced into the Commons by the Chancellor of the Exchequer, Spring Rice. Sir Robert Inglis, who was fond of resorting to Crooll's arguments for evidence of the Jews' religious exclusiveness, questioned whether a community of Jews true to Judaism would admit Christians to their legislative assembly—he was sure they would not. Although the measure successfully passed through all its stages in the Commons, apathy in a thin House made the division figures look particularly unimpressive and the lateness of the parliamentary session explained why, soon after the bill's introduction into the Lords, all further discussion was curtailed.[45]

Unremarkable though this set of debates may have seemed they were not allowed to pass without one supporter, Archbishop Whately, being treated to an exceptionally articulate restatement of the principle underlying the opposition to the Jews' claims. In contrast to that argument which was fast becoming the most oft-deployed weapon in the armoury of the supporters of Emancipation, namely that Jews could fairly claim consistency of treatment with other non-Anglican groups, not least the Unitarians, a standard of an absolute exclusion of the Jews in the cause of the very extension of the Church was now raised by none other than Thomas Arnold, the innovating Headmaster of Rugby. Arnold, regarded by liberals as impeccably free-thinking and progressive on the main issues of social and political reform, was subsequently looked upon as the exemplar of a broad church movement by such as Milman, Whately, Tait, the future Archbishop of Canterbury, and Stanley, Arnold's biographer and a future Dean of Westminster. A patent need had arisen for an updated rationale of the particular objections to Jewish Emancipation because the kernel of the protest mounted by Eldon, the former Tory Lord Chancellor, and others at the time of the Corporation and Test Acts Repeal Bill in 1828, with its concern for the maintenance of a specifically Anglican Protestant qualification for office,[46] could no longer be employed to counter the arguments for consistency of treatment. Former adherents of religious exclusion were now presented with the opportunity of resorting to an argument which did not force them into a rearguard defence of a lost order but seemed, by reducing to *adiaphora* the particular differences dividing Christians and thus emphasising the Christian truths which still united them, to effectively exclude all non-Christians from political comprehension.

In his consideration of political questions this theory of Arnold's that the world was made up essentially of Christians and non-Christians was complemented by another: from classical antiquity was derived the ideal of the small self-contained entity of the city-state or republic, its citizens conscious of being bound together in one community. Arnold's biographer, by the employment of an analogy, was neatly to illustrate the conjunction of the two theories. Stanley wrote 'As, in answer to the question, "What is the

Tiers-État?'' Sieyès, the theorist of the French Revolution, was wont to reply, ''The nation, minus the clergy and the nobles''; so in answer to the question ''What is the Laity?'' Arnold would reply, ''The Church, *minus* the clergy''.'[47] Choosing to treat Emancipation as a national rather than as a religious question, but yet invoking religious criteria to define nationality, Arnold's resort to Roman laws of citizenship allowed him to view favourably the claims of the Irish Catholics whilst arguing that the Jews of Britain were no more than 'strangers'. The two letters despatched by Arnold to Whately in May 1836 expounded these views:

The Irish being a Catholic people, they have a right to perfect independence, or to a perfectly equal union: if our conscience objects to the latter, it is bound to concede the former. But for the Jews I see no plea of justice whatever; they are voluntary strangers here, and have no claim to become citizens, but by conforming to our moral law, which is the Gospel. . . . I would give the Jews the honorary citizenship which was so often given by the Romans, namely, the private rights of citizens, *jus commercii et jus connubii,* but not the public rights, *jus suffragii et jus honorum.* But then, according to our barbarian feudal notions, the *jus commercii* involves the *jus suffragii;* because land, forsooth, is to be represented in Parliament, just as it used to confer jurisdiction. . . . I cannot but think that you over-estimate the difference between Christian and Christian. Every member of Christ's Catholic Church is one with whom I may lawfully join in legislation, and whose ministry I may lawfully use, as a judge or a magistrate; but a Jew, or a heathen, I cannot apply to voluntarily, but only obey him passively if he has the rule over me. . . .

Undoubtedly I think that up to 1795 or 6—whenever the elective franchise was granted to the Catholics,—the Protestants were *de facto* the only citizens of Ireland;—and that the Catholic claims could not then be urged on the same ground that they are now.—Till that time, one must have appealed to a higher law, and asked by what right the Protestants had become the only citizens of Ireland:—it was then a question of the *jus gentium;*—now it is merely one of *jus civile.*—I never have justified the practice of one race in wresting another's country from it;—I only say that every people in that country which is rightfully theirs may establish their own institutions and their own ideas;—and that no stranger has any title whatever to become a member of that nation, unless he adopts their institutions and ideas.—It is not what a Government may impose upon its subjects;—but what a people may agree upon for themselves;—and though England does not belong to the King yet it belongs to the English;—and the English may most justly say that they will admit no stranger to be one of their society.—If they say that they will admit him, that is if Parliament pass the Jew Bill,—I do not at all dispute their right as Englishmen to do so;—and as an Englishman I owe obedience to their decision;—but I think they make England cease to be the πολις of a Christian, and we like the old Christians shall then become in our turn παροικοι. Politically, if we are the minority, I see no injustice in this:—but I think that we may wonder a little at those of the majority who are Christians;—seeing that we as Englishmen have a nearer claim to English citizenship than the Jews can have,—and Christians being the majority ought I think to establish their own ideas in their own land.[48]

Thus, in his careful selection of the Greek word for foreigners or aliens, παροικοι, Arnold likened the inability of Jews as strangers to sit in the British Parliament with the ineligibility of a lodger to share with his landlord the management of the house in which he finds himself temporarily domiciled.[49] In the Commons in December 1847, five years after Arnold's death, Gladstone, himself a former opponent of Emancipation, was to observe that in respect of the Jews' claims Arnold had examined them not on their own merits but had allowed himself to be misled by a 'bias' or 'notion' which seemed necessary to the integrity of his favourite theory;[50] the incontrovertibility of Gladstone's judgement may indeed be illustrated by Arnold's advocacy of compulsory qualifying examinations in divinity as a requirement for the Bachelor of Arts degree in the University of London, which proposal was rejected in 1838 as being contrary to the spirit of the original charter. And even such an ally on the Jewish question as the evangelical Lord Ashley, the future seventh Earl of Shaftesbury, was to concede on the same occasion that Arnold had 'certainly carried his opinions to the greatest possible extent'.[51] Peel was to point out to the Commons in February 1848 how untenable in law was Arnold's thinking, for British nationality was not in essence personal, an equivalent of that *jus civile* which had prevailed during the centuries between the Roman Republic's foundation and the subjugation of central and southern Italy, but territorial. Derived from the mediaeval English feudal concept of 'the ligeance' British nationality adhered without distinction to all who at the time of their birth fell within the royal jurisdiction: within the lands and dominions acknowledging 'the ligeance' of the Crown.[52] Arnold, as the first of the two letters despatched to Whately reveals, was of course aware of some of the flaws in his argument and these implied rebukes testify how limited was his immediate impact on informed opinion; inasmuch as Rugby's greatest headmaster may be accredited with exercising a lasting influence on British national life traces of that influence are scarcely to be detected in the mid-century House of Commons but rather in the Public Schools of a later generation which sought to transform Britain from a puritan 'Hebraizing backwater', as she was derisively dubbed by Arnold's son Matthew, into an imperial power led by Christian gentlemen.

The years after 1836 saw anyway a discontinuation of the struggle to achieve the removal of parliamentary disabilities. The advocates of Emancipation could not but acknowledge that, despite all efforts, their present approach continued to lack some ingredient of success. Yet, too consciously examining the problem, they had already resorted to debate, unaware that any agreement which might result therefrom would prove not the less elusive of a solution.

NOTES

1. Minute Books of the Board of Deputies, I, p. 36, 28 April 1828.
2. Copleston, Bishop of Llandaff, *Hansard,* New Series, 18, 21 April 1828, 1591–92; Winchelsea, *Hansard,* New Series, 18, 21 April 1828, 1609; Copleston, Bishop of Llandaff, *Hansard,* New Series, 19, 28 April 1828, 159, in reply to Holland.
3. Letter Books of I. L. Goldsmid, I, fol. no. 341, 24 April 1828, Wellington to I. L. Goldsmid.
4. Protest signed by Holland and others, *Journals of the House of Lords,* 60, 25 April 1828, 247.
5. Letter Books of I. L. Goldsmid, I, fol. no. 53, 1 May 1828, J. Bowring to I. L. Goldsmid.
6. Ibid., fol. no. 390, 10 February 1829, Holland to I. L. Goldsmid.
7. Minute Books of the Board of Deputies, II, pp. 1–5, 17 March 1829.
8. L. Loewe (ed.), *The Diaries of Sir Moses and Lady Montefiore,* I, p. 5.
9. Minute Books of the Board of Deputies, II, p. 8, 16 April 1829.
10. Ibid., p. 163, undated petition.
11. Ibid., pp. 12–27, 3 May–11 June 1829; Letter Books of I. L. Goldsmid, I, fol. no. 17, 4 May 1829, Holland to I. L. Goldsmid; fol. no. 29, Four Preliminary Questions for Consideration of Petitioning Jews, in Lord Holland's handwriting, 1829.
12. L. Loewe (ed.), *The Diaries of Sir Moses and Lady Montefiore,* I, pp. 78–79; Minute Books of the Board of Deputies, II, pp. 31–42, 22 December 1829–25 February 1830.
13. Letter Books of I. L. Goldsmid, I, fol. no. 93, 22 February 1830, R. Owen to I. L. Goldsmid; *Hansard,* New Series, 23, 10 March 1830, 72; Mocatta Miscellaneous Collection, Box 10, letter 2, March 1830, letter from W. Huskisson to M. L. Mozley in reply to Mozley's letter of 3 March 1830 which had accompanied the petition.
14. *Hansard,* New Series, 23, 5 April 1830, 1287–1336; Grant, cols. 1287–1303, 1334–36; Thomas Babington Macaulay, cols. 1308–14; Mackintosh, cols. 1314–23.
15. Letter Books of I. L. Goldsmid, I, fol. no. 103, 6 April 1830, H. H. Milman to I. L. Goldsmid.
16. L. Loewe (ed.), *The Diaries of Sir Moses and Lady Montefiore,* I, p. 79, 14 April 1830.
17. *Hansard,* New Series, 24, 4 May 1830, 375–77; *Hansard,* New Series, 24, 17 May 1830, 769–74.
18. *Hansard,* New Series, 24, 17 May 1830, 784–814; Russell, cols. 797–99; Huskisson, cols. 800–802; O'Connell, cols. 793–96. F. H. Goldsmid, *The Arguments advanced against the Enfranchisement of the Jews, considered in a series of letters,* 1831, letter 1, introduction, pp. 3–4; Minute Books of the Board of Deputies, II, pp. 52–53, 23 May 1830.
19. *Hansard,* New Series, 24, 17 May 1830, cols. 802–7 for Peel's speech; L. J. Jennings (ed.), *The Croker Papers, The Correspondence and Diaries of the late Rt. Hon. John Wilson Croker,* II, p. 62, 18 May 1830; *John Bull,* X, 1830, p. 164, 23 May 1830, editorial.
20. Letter Books of I. L. Goldsmid, I, fol. no. 189, 2 June 1830, I. Bowring to I. L. Goldsmid.
21. W. Hazlitt, 'Emancipation of the Jews', in *The Complete Works of William Hazlitt* (ed. P. P. Howe), 19, pp. 320–24.
22. Thomas Babington Macaulay, *Hansard,* New Series, 23, 5 April 1830, 1308–14, and 'Civil Disabilities of the Jews', *The Edinburgh Review,* 52, pp. 366–67.
23. Letter Books of I. L. Goldsmid, I, fol. no. 243, 11 June 1832, Grey to I. L. Goldsmid.
24. Ibid., fol. no. 246, 21 March 1833, Elizabeth Fry to I. L. Goldsmid.
25. Ibid., fol. no. 324, T. Perronet Thompson to F. H. Goldsmid, 12 February 1833.
26. H. Hurwitz, *A Letter to Isaac L. Goldsmid . . . on certain recent misstatements respecting the Jewish Religion.*
27. *Hansard,* Third Series, 16, 1 March 1833, 11–14; *Hansard,* Third Series, 16, 22 March 1833, 973–75.
28. J. M. and J. P. Cobbett (eds.), *Selections from Cobbett's Political Works: Being a complete abridgement of the 100 volumes which comprise the writings of "Porcupine" and the "Weekly Political Register",* I, pp. 443ff., from 'Paper Aristocracy', *Political Register,* September 1804.
29. Ibid., VI, 176, from 'Cobbett's Letters to Landlords on the Agricultural Report and Evidence', letter IV, *Political Register,* 1 October 1821, par. 133.
30. Ibid.
31. L. Melville, *The Life and Letters of William Cobbett in England and America,* I, p. 21.
32. W. Cobbett, *Paper against Gold or, the History and mystery of the Bank of England, of the Debt, of the Stocks, of the Sinking Fund, and of all the other tricks and contrivances, carried on by the means of Paper Money,* pp. 78–86.
33. W. Cobbett, *Good Friday; or the Murder of Jesus Christ by the Jews,* pp. 5–21.
34. Ibid.
35. W. Cobbett, *A History of the Protestant Reformation in England and Ireland.*

36. *Hansard,* New Series, 18, 18 February 1828, 540–43.

37. *Hansard,* Third Series, 17, 17 April 1833, 205–44; Hume, cols. 242–43.

38. *The Times,* 3 May, 1830, leading article; *The Times,* 19 April 1833, leading article.

39. *Hansard,* Third Series, 18, 22 May 1833, 47–62; L. Loewe (ed.), *The Diaries of Sir Moses and Lady Montefiore,* I, p. 92; *Hansard,* Third Series, 19, 22 July 1833, 1075–82; D. W. Marks and A. Löwy, (eds.), *Memoir of Sir F. H. Goldsmid, Bart. Q.C., M.P.,* pp. 44–45.

40. *Hansard,* Third Series, 20, 1 August 1833, 221–55; Melbourne, cols. 247–48; Wellington, cols. 245–47; Blomfield, Bishop of London, cols. 236–38. *Memoir of Sir F. H. Goldsmid,* p. 46; Letter Books of I. L. Goldsmid, I, fol. no. 253, July 1833, Holland to I. L. Goldsmid.

41. *Hansard,* Third Series, 22, 24 April 1834, 1372–73; *Hansard,* Third Series, 23, 21 May 1834, 1158–76; *Hansard,* Third Series, 24, 11 June 1834, 382–83; *Hansard,* Third Series, 24, 23 June 1834, 720–31; Howley, Archbishop of Canterbury, cols. 724–28.

42. Peel Papers, B. M. ADD. MSS. 40414, ff. 351–52, 17 February 1835, Salomons and others to Peel, and f. 353, 21 February 1835, Peel to Salomons.

43. Letter Books of I. L. Goldsmid, I, folio mark R. S., 2 May 1835, Melbourne to I. L. Goldsmid.

44. See above, chap. 2, 'The Legal and Juridical Position of Mid-Nineteenth-Century Anglo-Jewry'.

45. *Hansard,* Third Series, 33, 31 May 1836, 1227–38; Inglis, cols. 1228–31; *Hansard,* Third Series, 35, 3 August 1836, 865–75; *Hansard,* Third Series, 35, 12 August 1836, 1209–10; *Hansard,* Third Series, 35, 15 August 1836, 1236–39; *Hansard,* Third Series, 35, 19 August 1836, 1318.

46. Cf. protest signed by Eldon and others, *Journals of the House of Lords,* 60, 28 April 1828, 256.

47. A. P. Stanley, *Essays chiefly on Questions of Church and State from 1850 to 1870,* p. 275.

48. A. P. Stanley, *The Life and Correspondence of Thomas Arnold, D.D.,* II, p. 35, Arnold to Whately, Archbishop of Dublin, 4 May 1836, as quoted by Ashley, *Hansard,* Third Series, 95, 16 December 1847, 1278; and Peel, *Hansard,* Third Series, 96, 11 February 1848, 520–21; papers of Richard Whately, Archbishop of Dublin, Lambeth Palace Library, MSS. no. 2164, fol. nos. 30–31, Arnold to Whately, 16 May 1836.

49. παροικοι = foreigners, strangers, aliens, sojourners in alien lands, in another's house. A. P. Stanley, Dean of Westminster, *The Life and Correspondence of Thomas Arnold, D.D.,* II, p. 26.

50. Gladstone, *Hansard,* Third Series, 95, 16 December 1847, 1294–95.

51. Ashley, *Hansard,* Third Series, 95, 16 December 1847, 1278.

52. Peel, *Hansard,* Third Series, 96, 11 February 1848, 520–23.

4
The Intra-Jewish Debate

In their attempts to secure the remission of parliamentary disabilities during the years from 1828 to 1836 the Deputies had barely been able to preserve a united front and opponents of Emancipation had thus been enabled to argue that the differences among the Jews themselves constituted ground for opposition. These differences related firstly to the question as to whether Emancipation itself was considered to be a desirable objective and secondly to the problems concerning the pace at which such an Emancipation, assuming its desirability, should be achieved.

For Emancipation, by which was denoted not only the right of Jews to be allowed to sit in Parliament but, rather obviously, the preliminary measure of the enfranchisement of otherwise qualified voters, raised at the very outset of the campaign a fundamental divergence of view concerning its right or wrong as an abstract principle, and this was most evident in the polemical exchange between Rabbi Joseph Crooll and the young Francis Henry Goldsmid.

First to take a stance was Crooll, who between 1812 and 1829 wrote three small books devoted to stating the classic ultra-Orthodox case against Emancipation.[1] Crooll was an eccentric and incongruous figure in the Cambridge of his day and his teaching record, judged even by the lethargic standards of the eighteenth and early nineteenth centuries, was an odd one. Although in March 1828 he wrote a begging letter to a Cambridge don, complaining that the decision of the Vice-Chancellor two years earlier to allow converted Jews to teach Hebrew was rendering even more precarious than before the tenuous existence he had led for the previous twenty years,[2] at the time of his death it was reported that, instead of having adhered to the custom of the non-absentee Cambridge dons in giving twenty lectures a year, he had never delivered, and had never offered to deliver, a single lecture. Crooll could scarcely fail to attract note on account of the strangeness of his garb, which included an incredible parchment-girdle on which were inscribed passages from the Law and the Talmud, and his prejudices were no less bizarre, some later attributing to him the opinion that it was the Angel Gabriel who had appeared to the Fathers and the Prophets of the Jews.[3]

Crooll was so obviously a product of his native environment; as a Hungarian emigré, born about 1780, he may be regarded as the counterpart in

England of Moses Sofer, born in 1762 and one of the rabbis administering to the exceptionally influential Pressburg community from 1806 until his death thirty-three years later. Sofer, rigidly opposing all innovation and firmly adhering to the Talmudic dictum *Hadash asur min ha-Torah* (the Torah forbids everything new), was hostile to Emancipation not only because he feared the dangers which might befall Jews through the jettisoning of certain religious traditions but also because he considered that aspirations for Emancipation betokened both a dissatisfaction with the customary Jewish way of life and a yearning for partial assimilation with gentile culture. Sofer set an example to the ultra-Orthodox everywhere by his merciless be-labouring of the Reform and the embarrassment which he caused to fellow Jews through propagation of the idea that practitioners of Orthodox Judaism must necessarily be opposed to the granting of political rights was appreciated by Crooll in his own efforts to rally British parliamentary opponents of Emancipation.

In Central and Eastern Europe many centuries before, at the time when the Jewish communities had been organized and the famous schools established, the Ashkenazim had become acquainted with suffering and persecution. The writings of their learned men reveal a continuous consciousness of sin and guilt, a profound humility, a tendency to asceticism and a proneness to superstition, all these relating to remorse for the past, uncertainty of the present, and fear for the future.[4] All these traits are to be found in the works of Joseph Crooll.

The Jews constitute one people, one nation at present living among other nations, which will one day be restored to Zion; the Bible has foretold both the Exile and the Restoration. The sufferings of the Jewish people in the lands of the Dispersion (the *Diaspora*) during the Exile (the *Galuth*) are inevitable, for they have been incurred as a result of the sins committed against God by the Jews of the Bible.[5] Crooll, agreeing with this explanation often given by the writers of German Jewry, exhorts the Jews to bear their burden stoically.

> It is the order and is established as a law by God, that when the Jews are condemned to go into captivity among the nations and there to be punished during the term of their exile, if the nations slay them, pillage them, torture them, or whatsoever they do to them, the Jews, at the same time may cry aloud, weep, lament, fast, make much prayers, no redress can they obtain, God will not hear them, for suffer they must.[6]

Crooll entertains no doubts as to the election of the Jews. God, ruler of men, has declared 'And ye shall be holy unto me: for I, the Lord, am holy, and have severed you from the nations, that ye should be mine' (Leviticus xx, 26).[7] Crooll identifies himself with the separatist tendency of the Jewish religious consciousness finding classical expression in the story of the curse turned into a blessing: 'Behold, it is a people that dwelleth apart, and doth not reckon itself amongst the nations [Goyim]' (Numbers xxii–xxiii, 9).[8] God entered into a covenant with Moses and with all future generations to the effect that they must remember always to obey the Mosaic Law; this, His convenant with the Jews upon their exodus from Egypt, was renewed with the deliverance from Babylon. Even he who has been converted is still to be deemed a Jew. 'And it shall come to pass on that day the Lord shall beat off from the channel of the river unto the stream of Egypt, and ye shall be gathered one by one, O ye children of Israel (Isaiah xxvii, 12).[9] The converted Jew cannot isolate himself by saying he will not go. God takes no note of the views of the converted Jew, but as being born under the covenant of the Law. A Jew he was born, and a Jew he must be again.'[10] Choice of religion is open to no man, and Judaism, moreover, is no ordinary religion. The Reform idea of Jews constituting a religious community—however universal that may be—is completely alien to Crooll. To him the one religion of the covenant dictates the Jews' separatism.

The religion serves to bind the Jews together. Strict observance and asceticism must eventually restore the nation in the sight of God. To the unassimilated Jews of Central and Eastern Europe the preservation of Judaism in its ancient exclusiveness was made to seem a holy trust and all private transactions, public undertakings and national acts were to be measured by the rigid standard of religion; here Crooll, insistent that men's sins may be remedied only through a religion governed by wisdom, contends that sinners yearning for a true expiation must look to past tradition and observance. Men's wrongs betray their corruption and this is tantamount to sin. Sin invites God's wrath, although divine retribution may be withdrawn if man offers a true and sincere repentance. Repentance will lead to godliness, which itself is conducive to everlasting happiness.[11]

Strict observance and asceticism are however only the prerequisites of repentance: mysticism, dwelling upon the gloomy forebodings of the past, must also be invoked. Jewish customs are to be interpreted as symbols of *Galuth* and as signs of mourning for former glory.[12] Self-affliction or *Teshubah* combines the necessary approaches: the German Chasidim, for example, practised such Draconian forms of self-punishment as the exposure of their bodies to bee-stings.[13] Unlike the Sephardim, who had rejected most of the superstitious practices originating in the non-Jewish world, the Ashkenazim, because they lived in environments of low culture, had been more influenced by the Cabbalah and by the beliefs of their Christian neighbours, both adopting and adapting from them practices grounded in, for example, folk-medicine, magic, sorcery, incantations, conjurations and demon-belief.[14] In the combination of ultra-Orthodoxy, Chasidism and Cabbalistic mumbo-jumbo may be discerned as sufficient an explanation of the titles of Crooll's books as of his extraordinary personal appearance. Crooll's reckoning in respect of *The Fifth Empire* was that the first four

Empires, as revealed to Abraham, had been those of Babylon, Persia-Media, Alexander the Great, and Rome.[15]

Religiosity serves a high ideal. The Jews, as a separate nation, must ever be wary of sinking roots among their hosts in the lands of the *Galuth*. For the stronger the attachment of the Jews to the land of their civil devotion the correspondingly weaker must be their adherence to the Jewish religion. More than six centuries before, Rabbi Judah Hehasid had declared that a Jew should not build for himself a house of stone, for might not such a symbol of permanent domicile imply a surrender of any hope of the return to Israel? The appearance of stone buildings in lands which were not their own would furnish proof that the Jews had surrendered all hope of redemption.[16] Rabbi Solomon Kluger, a Continental contemporary of Crooll's, strongly criticized Jews who took advantage of Emancipation in order to acquire villages and estates, for in so doing they betrayed their lack of faith in the speedy redemption of the Jewish people.[17] The Orthodox Rabbis of Pressburg, whose influence was so marked in the thinking of Crooll, had earlier advised their congregations to issue a petition calling upon the Jews of Hungary to refuse Joseph II's grant of civil Emancipation, any such desire for political equality being considered by the Rabbis as sinful and inconsistent with Israel's hopes for the future.

Crooll not merely affirms that Israel's destiny will be fulfilled but claims to know exactly when such a restoration will occur. His earliest work, *The Restoration of Israel*, surveys the course of universal history and gives an interpretation of the biblical prophecies. There is no problem in dating biblical events—the time, for example, between the appearance of Adam in the Garden of Eden and the building of Noah's Ark is given as 1,656 years. Four empires have risen and fallen, as foretold in a vision which came to Abraham, and now the world, which Crooll compares to a ship without a rudder, drifts towards the time when the last generation of the peoples who have maltreated and persecuted the Jews are to be punished for all the sins of former generations. Then too shall Israel be restored. The gentiles cannot constitute God's ministry, for according to Ezekiel xx, 38, this privilege is reserved exclusively for the Jews. Except for the converts amongst them who cannot be admitted to restored Zion. Such renegades shall never find a home and are doomed to wander the earth for ever.[18] Crooll summons up biblical evidence in predicting the worst possible fate for converts. He especially resents all friendly approaches to the Jews by philosemitic Christian societies which seek to proselytize; those who attempt to convert the 'chosen people' will perish as assuredly as did the gourd which protected Jonah after his ordeal.[19]

Already in 1812 Crooll is to be found firmly predicting that the restoration of Israel will take place in 1840, the Jewish year 5600.[20] He arrives at this date after the customary Cabbalistic reckonings and in a later work it emerges that his calculations derive their credence largely from prophecies given in the Book of Ezekiel.[21] In this *annus mirabilis* the Messiah will assume possession of his Empire, the enemies of the Jews will be vanquished and the Temple will be rebuilt to mark the permanent restoration.[22] Crooll's interpretation of biblical prophecies is here similar to those of earlier ultra-Orthodox Ashkenazim who had, in contrast to Maimonides and his Sephardi successors, discerned in the Bible a series of unalterable decrees and predictions.[23] Election is certain—and yet Crooll condescendingly spares a thought for England and the English. It is, he declares, 'our duty to pray for the nations at the present time, in particular for this country, for here we are used well, and treated better than in any other country: here we enjoy ease and security'.[24]

Crooll's arguments were frequently to be held up by parliamentary opponents of Emancipation as proof that a very pious Jew could not possibly desire the removal of disabilities. In the Commons' debate of May 1833 Sir Robert Inglis read from a letter which he had received from Crooll. 'Remember this, you can be no freemen except in the land of Canaan. . . . Jews, whether they spend two days, or two months, or twenty years in a country, are equally strangers and sojourners. They must look to another home and another country.'[25]

Crooll may have stiffened the resistance to Emancipation always evident among a minority of Jews; he certainly appears to have scared considerably more by alleging that the introduction of Jewish to Christian Members of Parliament, as the natural outcome of Emancipation, would make conversion a temptation too difficult for these accepted Jews to resist.[26]

Crooll, contending that the Jews' sojourn in the lands of the Diaspora is about to yield to the imminent restoration to Israel, implied that Jews were incapable of sharing the feelings of Englishmen: this supposition, alone, to the gentile opponents of Emancipation seemed to render the Jews unworthy of British rights and privileges. With this interpretation, and the assumptions, reasoning and theory on which it is based, Francis Henry Goldsmid, the keenest challenger of Crooll's views, most fiercely disagrees.[27] Eschewing the theoretical approach, Goldsmid argues that the experience of Jews, whenever and wherever they have been treated as full citizens, far from disqualifying actually qualifies those living in Britain for the enjoyment of full rights and privileges.

Enquiring as to the causes of patriotism Goldsmid believes that these lie in the entrusting by the institutions of a country to the citizen of a large proportion of the liberties and franchises indispensable to good government and social order.[28] The Jew at present shares all other motives for patriotism and if granted political liberty he would come to feel as fully patriotic as his Christian fellow countrymen. Crooll has dwelt upon the imminence of the restoration to Zion but Christians wait upon the Second Coming and Jews therefore are not the only people whose awareness of God's immanence assumes the miraculous.[29] Could not the line of reasoning employed to demonstrate that Jews are failing in patriotism be here used against Christians, to prove that they too must be indifferent to temporal matters and cannot therefore be entrusted with responsibilities?[30]

Goldsmid brushes aside the Cabbalistic time-reckonings of Crooll. Men, lacking the necessary foreknowledge of any divine scheme, must needs be governed by considerations transient and worldly. In an obvious reference to the notion of a return to Zion in 1840 Goldsmid emphasizes that 'the devout Jew has no greater reason for supposing, that the re-establishment of his race in Palestine will take place during the next twenty, than that it will be delayed to the end of the next one thousand years'.[31]

Goldsmid further notes that Crooll, disregarding factors other than religious, has ascribed the Jews' preference for mobile possessions over landed property to a supposed refusal on their part to bind themselves to their respective countries of domicile pending the imminent restoration. To this Goldsmid replies that the true causes of Jews being unable to hold land have been those persecutions which formerly drove them from kingdom to kingdom, their hereditary habits, and in England the additional factor that possession of land even now does not confer upon Jews the same privileges as it confers upon others.[32] Goldsmid denies that Jews, any more than other men, think of ordering their worldly estate with a view to a miraculous future.[33] There is nothing either in the Jewish character or in the Jewish religion which militates against patriotism.[34]

Goldsmid realizes, however, that some opponents of Emancipation seek justification for their stand in the tradition of Jews constituting themselves 'a separate people' and so he sets about examining the meaning of the phrase. Applied to the past this separatism recalls the Jews' formation as a political entity, a singling out from the pagan tribes which surrounded them. Applied to the future the phrase signifies the belief in the Jews' reestablishment as a nation.[35] But with reference to the present, Goldsmid doubts if the phrase 'a separate people' has any relevance and whether indeed, as Jews are scattered so widely, with those in one country ignorant of the existence of those elsewhere, it can be said that they are conscious of forming a national entity. Goldsmid states that no religion, not even Judaism, can induce such a feeling of national unity and in so doing thus follows the Continental Reform Movement in exorcising the national idea from Judaism.[36]

Having dismissed the concept of Jews as a nation, Goldsmid finally turns to those passages of the Bible which foretell the Dispersion and finds in them nothing to forbid political identification with the people among whom Jews live. The example of the prophets during the First Captivity teaches the Jew that to serve the state and government which protect him is not a crime but a duty, 'for Jeremiah more than once enjoined cheerful submission to Babylon; and Nehemiah and Daniel were ministers and servants of Babylonian and Persian kings'.[37] Goldsmid is suspicious of those avowed opponents of

Emancipation who, resorting to Crooll's ultra-Orthodox arguments, instruct Jews to shun as irreligious the performance of those very civil functions and duties which were recommended and performed by the teachers of Judaism themselves.[38]

Taken to an extreme such a statement of the invalidity of Crooll's reasoning could be as productive of hostages to fortune as the very arguments they were meant to disprove. Where Crooll specifically insisted that the restoration of the Jewish nation to Israel would occur in 1840, the medical practitioner Barnard Van Oven, a close and active ally of the Goldsmids on Emancipation and related politico-religious issues, later issued a shrill disclaimer that there existed any bond at all linking Jews in Britain with their co-religionists in other countries. When *The Noble Friend* in his imaginary conversation with *The Jew* alludes to the probable election of one of the latter's 'nation' to Parliament he is met with the retort that there no longer exists any such Jewish nation. 'Born in England of English parents', proclaims *The Jew*, 'I acknowledge no other land as my country, no other nation as my nation.' *The Noble Friend*, still requiring reassurance, remonstrates that surely *The Jew* looks upon Jews of all lands as his brethren. *The Jew* then declares that 'politically speaking, in duties and in feelings, attachment to country or Sovereign, the British Jew is as distinct from the French Jew, as the English descendant of any one of the Barons who came over with the Conqueror is distinct from the French descendant of the brother of that same Baron, who may be now ploughing the fields of Normandy or in the *Chambre des Deputés* at Paris, declaiming *la perfide Albion!*' Here Van Oven is so emphatic as to offer a variant on the same theme. 'The British Jew is as distinct in political feeling and duty from the American Jew, as is the descendant of any other branch of the same family who may have remained in England: although both springing from the same progenitor, although of the same race and blood, their duties, feelings, attachments and opinions are different, they may have met in the field of battle, and may do so again, even although their religions may remain unaltered and alike.'[39]

Crooll's case was the first to be discredited, not on account of any superiority of scholarship evinced by the Goldsmid–Van Oven school but simply because the millennium failed to arrive in 1840. In consequence there ebbed away whatever support Crooll may hitherto have enjoyed among the more favourably-inclined rabbinical guardians of Orthodoxy who belonged to the zealously governing Beth Din of Hirschell's last years. The more profound reason, explaining why the redundancy of such millenarian predictions should this time have proved permanent in a predominantly Christian country, may be attributed to the defeat now inflicted on the interconnected theories of catastrophism, finalism and providentialism. Prior to the early 1830s, and the dissemination of the findings expounded in Sir Charles Lyell's *The Principles of Geology*, accepted orthodox theories of the earth, informed more by deductions from the Bible than by scientific observation, held that violent upheavals in the universe, coupled with sudden inundations and cataclysms, had imparted to the world its shape and structure; these theories accorded with the traditionally-accepted account of the Mosaic cosmogony and the relatively brief biblical chronology, tracing God's creation of the universe to the year 4004 B.C., propounded in the mid-seventeenth century by Archbishop Usher. Now, displacing this belief that the hand of the Creator was to be found in every work of nature, an interpretation developed in the 1680s by Thomas Burnet in his *The Sacred Theory of the Earth* and subsequently reiterated by Paley, the Anglican divine, as recently as 1802 in the standard textbook *Evidences of Christianity,* there emerged acceptance of Lyell's finding that geological change must have come about as a result of regular processes spanning an immeasurably long period of time.

Crooll was obsolete.

The debate between the ultra-Orthodox and the Goldsmid–Van Oven faction was concerned with the merits or demerits of Emancipation conceived as a principle. But there were, of course, those whose opinions lay situate at varying points on the spectrum between these two extremes. In 1845 the editor of *The Voice of Jacob,* moved to comment on the correspondence received by its rival *The Jewish Chronicle* during the first four years of its existence, offered a threefold classification of the divisions on Emancipation which appeared to bedevil the Jewish community:

1. Those who desire a complete fusion of the Jews with their fellow subjects of every other denomination; and who would pledge the body of the English Jews to repudiate any legislative concession, short of complete equality in every respect.—This class (in other countries) demand to be drawn into the army, and to be arrayed in arms against the Jews of any other country happening to be at issue with their own.
2. Those who are content to deal with each disqualification as the opportunity serves; that is, to take advantage of the progressing liberality of the Christian public, in order to get rid of each disability as it can be demonstrated to be inexpedient, unjust, or unpopular; to accept every such concession as it can be best secured, separately, and as the occasion for, or propriety of, each additional privilege can be reconciled to the objections of the following class.
3. Those who dread a diversion of the Jewish mind from the religious interests of the Jews, as a people, through the seductions offered by the opening of new avenues to personal ambition, the ardent pursuit of which, they maintain, is calculated to estrange the individual from certain higher duties, that devolve upon him in common with all Jews. These hold that there are public offices which a pious Jew cannot conscientiously discharge with efficiency.[40]

Preeminent as the leading lay representative of the second group was Sir Moses Montefiore; his long tenure of the Presidency of the Board of

Deputies was to appear in retrospect as the inevitable sequel to his earlier incumbency of the Presidency of the Spanish and Portuguese Congregation.

Oral and religious tradition has always been an ingredient of Jewish life: differences of outlook and mentality forged during the course of centuries could not disappear within a few generations. The Sephardim have ever harboured a nostalgia for the age of Maimonides and Averröes, when Spain had served as the scientific and cultural bridgehead linking the Arabic and Christian worlds, largely responsible for giving to Latin Europe a new version of Aristotelianism. Many Sephardim hankered after the past and were resistant towards change. After Passover in 1829 the *Yehidim*, or members of the Bevis Marks Synagogue, entered into a debate as to whether English should replace Portuguese as the language of the synagogue. A generation gap soon revealed itself. The older members pointed out that those Sephardim who had been dispersed to lands as far and as widely removed from their second homeland as those of Asia Minor, Northern Africa, Central and North-Western Europe, still maintained the usage of Spanish or Portuguese in respect of their prayer-books, Bibles and codes of communal laws; the younger, more energetic members displayed enthusiasm for the innovation. After five and a half hours of discussion, the opinions of the latter party prevailed and a resolution was adopted 'to have all religious discourses delivered in the synagogues in English, and also henceforth to have all proclamations made in the same tongue.'[41]

This debate afforded evidence of the residual strength of religious conservatism more than a century and a half after the resettlement. Montefiore was among those prepared to welcome the use of English at Bevis Marks and he was prepared to welcome Emancipation. But he was never a militant, declaring some years after the removal of parliamentary disabilities: 'I am an enemy of all sudden transitions. The Jew must, in his claims and wishes, not outstrip the age. Let him advance slowly but steadily; let him gradually accustom his Christian fellow-citizens to his gradual progress and success in public life, and what may not be obtainable even by an arduous struggle, will, after a certain time, fall into his lap like ripe fruit.'[42]

This choice of simile betrays Montefiore's passive conception of Emancipation; almost any attempt to hasten its passage could be construed as premature. Although believing in 1829 that the time was indeed ripe for a campaign, adducing here the circumstances of a still united community, the distinction achieved by Jews in society and the distinctly liberal tendency of national thought as illustrated in Parliament by the enactment of Catholic Emancipation, he considered—as he was always thereafter to consider— that he must defer to the rabbinical leadership for guidance. Dr. Loewe, a future influential fellow member of the Board of Deputies who became in later years the close personal friend entrusted with the task of editing Montefiore's diaries after death was to offer an invaluable assessment of this pro-rabbinical bias:

He [Montefiore] entertained the most liberal principles in matters of religion; although himself a staunch supporter of the time-honoured usages of his religion, he did not interfere with the opinions or acts of those who differed from him unless compelled to do so by actual duty. But when, as President of the Board of Deputies, or of any other institution, he had to give his opinion on religious matters, he invariably referred to the Spiritual Head of the community for guidance; he regarded a word from him as decisive, and obeyed its injunctions at whatever cost to himself. There was never any doubt in his mind as to the spirit which should prevail in their deliberations on the intended reform in the community; and he maintained that the religious tenets of Israel, as revealed in the Code of Sinai, would invariably stand the test of reason. 'They are', Montefiore would add in the words of Scripture, 'to show our wisdom and understanding in the sight of nations.' He did not consider that he would be acting in accordance with the dictates of truth and justice if he were to accept laymen, however learned they might be, as authorities on religious subjects for the guidance of the whole community. Some of his colleagues at the Board, however, did not acknowledge the authority of the Ecclesiastical Chief of the community, and relying entirely on their own judgement, would not accept the dictates of the ancient teachers by whose decisions and interpretations of the sacred text Hebrew communities had been guided for thousands of years.[43]

Ipso facto the Chief Rabbi's position was Montefiore's position. In reply to an enquiry by I. L. Goldsmid in 1836, Hirschell declared that it was not in his power and was not his desire to take a hostile attitude towards Emancipation or to hold back the good from Anglo-Jewry: the Jews should aim for the achievement of their Emancipation so long as they were not thereby caused to turn away from God and His written and oral Law or to surrender their religious duties.[44] This also was Montefiore's stand and thus, on every occasion that I. L. Goldsmid was to be found pressing for Emancipation Montefiore was as likely to be found holding back. When in the excitement of the circumstances surrounding the passage of the Roman Catholic Relief Bill through Parliament in April 1829 the delegation led by Montefiore had first conveyed to Lyndhurst their dismay with the legislative draft and then been deflected by the Lord Chancellor's advice to relax their pressure, Montefiore had given the assurance that the Jews would be entirely guided by his advice and would do nothing for the present; in so deferring to the Government's counsel he was supported by Nathan Mayer Rothschild who advised the Board of Deputies that nothing should be published in the daily papers on the subject of Emancipation, as any controversy might prove fatal to the object in view.[45]

I. L. Goldsmid would brook no such caution. Indeed, the initiative taken in February 1830 to place in synagogues a number of petitions to be signed by natural-born subjects was a response to Goldsmid's pressure.[46] And although the committee of the Board of Deputies which was constituted at this time subsequently agreed to relegate in importance the particular matter of remitting parliamentary disabilities the decision can scarcely have been reached in unanimous spirit. Grant, while piloting his bill through the Commons, enquired of Montefiore as to how insistent the Jews were on obtaining parliamentary Emancipation to the exclusion of otherwise piecemeal concessions. After Montefiore had informed Grant that the Jews would be best advised to 'take what they could get' and let it be known that he would acquiesce in Wellington's non-committal stand, I. L. Goldsmid let it equally be known that he disagreed with Montefiore and that he would refuse to surrender the ultimate claim of gaining entry to Parliament.[47] The disagreement spilled over into the consultations which Herries held in mid-April 1830, a few weeks before the second reading of Grant's bill. Montefiore at this time confided to the Rothschilds that as far as the views of I. L. Goldsmid were concerned 'I decidedly differ with him; we should accept all we can get'.[48]

With the defeat of Grant's bill the Deputies became far more worried than Goldsmid about the expenses of a campaign which seemed, at least in the foreseeable future, unlikely to attain its objective. When Goldsmid recommended presentation to the Lords of the petitions entrusted to the Board's care several Deputies reported that because of the heavy outstanding debts incurred by their congregations they could no longer pledge their financial support. Once again the assurance was given by Montefiore, this time to Dr. Lushington, that the Deputies would gladly accept anything the Government could offer, however far short such concession might fall of the repeal of all disabilities. I. L. Goldsmid, who on this occasion accompanied Montefiore, not only let known his disagreement with the majority of the Deputies but offered to his critics an insight into the close links which for him appeared to exist between political Emancipation and those religious forms conducive to achievement of that goal. Reiterating that he did not care for halfway measures Goldsmid hinted that he might establish a new synagogue with the assistance of young men in the community and would so alter the present form of prayer as to make it conform with that in use at the Reform Synagogue in Hamburg.[49]

The publicity involved in the next three years of campaigning rendered it impossible to conceal any longer the division which had arisen between the majority who were prepared to settle for a piecemeal approach and that party which, in demanding the outright repeal of all disabilities, campaigned for legislation which would encompass the ultimate goal of realizing parliamentary ambitions. The split, when overlaid by rumours emanating from Crooll and the ultra-Orthodox, could easily be misconstrued by those parliamentary opponents of Emancipation who wished to portray Montefiore and the majority of Jews as hostile to even the mildest concession, enfranchisement. So keenly did the Deputies apprehend the dangers of misrepresentation that in April 1833 almost all the members of the Board, together with more than forty other leading members of Anglo-Jewry, decided to despatch a letter to Grant. This began by denying the rumours that, while only two or three individuals among the Jews were enthusiastic for Emancipation, the greater portion of the community, including its most influential members, regarded the issue with indifference. The very recent petition signed by nearly a thousand Jews in London, and the similar petitions from almost every part of the country where Jews were resident, provided proof enough of the falseness of such rumours; the signatories, including among their number Montefiore, I. L. Goldsmid, F. H. Goldsmid and Salomons, affirmed their enthusiasm for enfranchisement and expressed gratitude to Grant for his exertions on their behalf.[50]

This letter, however, achieved little other than to serve as a disclaimer of Crooll's right to speak for Anglo-Jewry; when Grant saw his bill passing from the Commons to the Lords in the closing days of July 1833 but yet thought it prudent to warn I. L. Goldsmid that the peers might insert into the legislation a proviso which would exclude Jews from sitting in Parliament he was met with a characteristically uncompromising response. I. L. Goldsmid, at this time attracting praise from Frankfurt for his 'well-known and successful efforts' to procure Emancipation, refused to countenance any half-measure which 'instead of removing, would deliberately establish, that which now appears to be merely the effect of chance'.[51]

The Board of Deputies, finding itself unable to share in any sanguine appraisal of I. L. Goldsmid's ability to negotiate Emancipation, soon became more anxious than ever to bring the question under its control. The marriage legislation of 1836 presented the Board with its opportunity. The Deputies decided on 24 May to inform Spring Rice, as Chancellor of the Exchequer, that the Board constituted the only official channel of communication for the secular and political interests of the Jews[52]—and this claim to an unrivalled and undisputed exercise of authority came, indeed, to seem all but confirmed with the enactment of the marriage and registration legislation 6 & 7 Will IV, c. 85 and c. 86, which first gave the Board statutory recognition.

The Board's assertiveness exacerbated tensions and less than a fortnight after the Deputies had asked the Chancellor for a copy of his proposed bill for the removal of civil disabilities an unofficial 'meeting of British Jews' was held at the house of the young David Salomons. Here two resolutions were passed, one inviting the active assistance of all Jews in promoting the passage of the Jews' Relief Bill, the other calling upon the Deputies to cooperate. On 7 June a letter communicating these two resolutions was considered by the Deputies, whereupon the decision was taken to answer Salomons's cool persiflage in kind. The Deputies extended to Salomons and to any other of 'the few gentlemen' who had passed these resolutions a 'courteous invitation' to meet at a conference which would be held under the auspices of the Board; another invitation was despatched to I. L. Goldsmid and F. H. Goldsmid, asking also for their cooperation. When, in consequence of these developments, the Chancellor received a letter from Montefiore restating that the Board of Deputies was the *only* institutional organ which could satisfactorily represent the Jews he cannot but have suspected that in continued factiousness lay the reason for the Board abandoning an exclusive reference to the marriage legislation as a pretext for the assertion of its own supremacy: the Board was no longer embarrassed to proclaim its status openly.[53]

And yet, in deceptive contrast to its public stance, the Board was now tactfully attempting to heal the rift: its four leading critics, I. L. Goldsmid, F. H. Goldsmid, Barnard Van Oven and David Salomons, were among those who attended a meeting held on 13 June 1836 at Montefiore's house in Park Lane. Montefiore referred to the resolutions passed at Salomons's house, and after the Board had conferred with the four critics they then retired, leaving the Deputies to deliberate on their own. The outcome was a formula according to which a six-man sub-committee of the Board would cooperate with not more than six persons outside its membership, with the proviso added that the Deputies must not be held responsible for defraying the further financial expenses which support of the 1836 bill might entail. The proposal of such a compromise was a tacit recognition on the part of the Board that, with none of the four critics presently included as members, the Deputies could no longer monopolise discussion of the question by claiming to be the sole representatives of Anglo-Jewry. The Deputies accepted the compromise by nine votes to three, a majority of six, and when the outsiders rejoined the meeting they expressed themselves satisfied with the arrangement.[54]

Yet the Board still desired to assert its authority, and in December 1836, after passage of the Marriage Act which made the President of the Board of Deputies a vital intermediary between the Government and the Jews, the Deputies 'invited'—or rather notified—its constituent congregations to 'entrust their political Interests to us as recognised representatives of the British Jews'.[55] Such marriage legislation, for having conferred on the lay leadership powers of controlling and disciplining deviant groups within the community, was to assume a significance quite out of proportion to its intrinsic importance. This, however, lay in the future: when, in July 1837, Montefiore wrote in his diary 'I am most firmly resolved not to give up the smallest part of our religious forms and privileges to obtain civil rights',[56] he was referring rather to those controversial clauses of Lord Lyndhurst's Matrimonial Causes Act of 1835 which had, according to one construction, brought the law on Jewish marriages and divorces within the jurisdiction of English civil law. Montefiore, ever concerned for the observance of those religio-national laws and *mores* which he believed to have been sanctioned by antiquity and divine authority, was striving for an amendment to the Act or for an authoritative opinion in support of the contrary construction of the Act.[57]

Montefiore felt strongly that a too hasty concession of Emancipation would be sure to weaken the Jews' attachment to their religion, and his comment was a reflection of his anxieties concerning the growth in Britain of the Reform Movement. In 1836 several members of the Spanish and Portuguese community had presented a petition to the governing body of the Bevis Marks Synagogue in which they requested the introduction into the religious service of 'such alterations and modifications as were in the line of the changes introduced in the reform synagogue [at Hamburg] and other places', and for several years thereafter this same group of members pressed the authorities for changes which included fewer prayers, a more convenient hour of service on the Sabbath and on holidays, English sermons and a choir, and the abolition of the second day of the Festivals.[58]

This was the religious manifestation of a discontent which the June compromise between the Board of Deputies and its critics could not for long assuage. And indeed two years later the communal breach as far as it concerned Emancipation, if not Reform, was all but consummated with I. L. Goldsmid's repudiation of the Board's authority. In a letter to the Great Synagogue, of which he was a member, Goldsmid attacked the Board for its bureaucratic methods and unwieldiness, its inefficiency, passivity and inertia. Referring first to the constitutional changes of 1835, according to which twenty-two places on the Board were reserved for the Deputies from four London congregations, Goldsmid contended that

> the great number of Deputies is quite sufficient to make the body wholly unsuited to watch proceedings before Parliament. So much time is lost in issuing circulars and calling a meeting of a numerous body like this, that the proper season for acting has usually passed before the Deputies have begun to deliberate. And if by some rare chance a meeting is obtained, when the right moment for action has not gone by, the unanimity, and above all, the promptitude and decision are wanting, which can only be found in a small committee, and without which any attempt at originating or influencing legislative measures will either fail to be made or will be feeble and useless.

Goldsmid, by way of criticizing the new method for election of the Board and arguing that this did nothing to remedy the particular shortcomings inherent in its essential composition, unwieldy bulk and lack of authority to delegate powers to a sub-committee, then took issue with the new regulations. Most objectionable to him appeared to be the third and twenty-first which declared the Deputies to be the only official medium of communication with the Government for the purposes of their appointment, including all matters affecting the political interests of the British Jews. 'What experience', remonstrated Goldsmid, 'have we of the efforts of the Deputies for procuring a recognition of the civil rights of the Jews being so much superior to the efforts of individuals that we ought to transfer all power from the latter to the former?' Referring next to the three bills in favour of parliamentary Emancipation which had been passed by the House of Commons in 1833, 1834 and 1836 Goldsmid expressed the opinion that this partial success 'was owing to my devoting to the purpose my time and best energies from night to night, from week to week, and from session to session, whilst I found, it is true, in some a disposition to cooperate warmly with me, but experienced from others, and among them influential members of the Board of Deputies, a great unwillingness to contribute their personal exertions and a total refusal of pecuniary assistance.'

Goldsmid continued his letter by recalling certain developments of recent years which might prove to be the harbinger of parliamentary Emancipation— his son's admission to the Bar in 1833, the pamphleteering of Barnard Van Oven, the tenure by Salomons first and then by Montefiore of the office of Sheriff and by other individuals too in respect of the offices of magistrate and alderman, the right to trade retail which was a consequence of the admission of Jews to the Freedom of the City of London in 1830, and, not least, his own particular role in helping to establish the University of London. 'And now let me inquire', demanded Goldsmid indignantly, 'what during the progress of all these changes has been accomplished or attempted by the Deputies? . . . The answer is (as it has been said a battle should be) decisive. Nothing!' Goldsmid arrived at the reluctant conclusion: 'But when I find the first acknowledgement of my services in the adoption of a regulation which, if acquiesced in, would make it almost impracticable for me or others who are younger than I now am to render similar services for the future, I am reluctantly compelled to state what I have done and at the same time to say that I cannot possibly consent to entrust my political interests to the charge of the Deputies.'[59]

In November the Great Synagogue despatched this condemnation to the Deputies who then invited the Goldsmids to confer with them.[60] At the subsequent meeting on 4 December 1838 there was disagreement with I. L. Goldsmid's interpretation of the third, sixteenth and twenty-first regulations of the new constitution, if such be taken to mean that persons, through adherence to a synagogue congregation, were thus deemed to have collectively bound themselves to approval of a constitution which deprived them of the right of independent action. To remove misunderstanding, the Deputies resolved 'that it is the opinion of this Board that no individuals, by being members of a Synagogue or of the Board of Deputies, are precluded from exerting their influence with the Government of the Country for the promotion of their civil rights and privileges'. Then, 'to make assurance doubly sure', the Deputies agreed to amend the controversial clauses of the constitution.[61] But I. L. Goldsmid was no more mollified by this compromise than by the one reached in June 1836: when in 1839 he was elected to the

Board as a Deputy for the Great Synagogue he declined to take up his position.[62]

For discord was now as much engendered by religion as by politics. The Board encountered great difficulties during 1839 in persuading provincial congregations to accept that, by the terms of the 1836 Marriage Act, no Marriage Secretary of a synagogue could enter upon his duties unless he had first been certified to the Registrar-General by the President of the Board. Already in January the Maiden Lane Synagogue had decided to withdraw its representation from the Board;[63] thirteen months later, as if to proclaim more dramatically its independence of the Deputies, Maiden Lane seized the initiative in presenting a Loyal Address on the occasion of Queen Victoria's marriage to Prince Albert. It cannot have come as any surprise to the Deputies to discover that this address on behalf of Maiden Lane had been presented by none other than I. L. Goldsmid. The wrath of the Deputies was further increased when several other synagogues followed suit. The Board protested against such 'public unauthorized acts', castigated these synagogues for having manifested to the world 'a want of general cooperation and of unanimity', and in despatching its own Loyal Address once again reasserted the claim to be the only acknowledged representative body of British Jewry.[64]

The authorities may have dealt with the symptoms of discontent but they were soon confronted with the explosion of its undercurrent. At the Bevis Marks Synagogue there seemed to be too few common points of possible agreement between the traditionalists and the reformers, and so, in April 1840, acting upon the surmise that the rabbinical authorities would remain intransigent, eighteen members of the community together with six from other synagogues resolved to found a West London place of worship which would be neither Sephardi nor Ashkenazi, but British. The dissidents might have anticipated too the response of Montefiore; from the earliest times of the Inquisition in their former homeland the Sephardim had inherited a marked suspicion of any manifestations of 'heresy' among their own number. Thus when, in February 1842, Hirschell wrote to Montefiore as President of the Board trusting that the Deputies would refuse to certify the young David Woolf Marks as Rabbi of the West London Synagogue he was instantly obeyed. But the Reformers were not thereby deterred and the establishment of the synagogue proceeded as planned.[65]

The Reform Movement in England, as in Europe, denoted a shift of emphasis as to where the Jew should focus his loyalty: the pamphlets of the Goldsmid–Van Oven school, stressing how loyal the English Jews were to the country of their adoption, reflected the new criteria of assimilation. Yet the English movement was, characteristically, less ideological than the German; it was more concerned with those adjustments in religious practice which some thought necessary to match the new tempo of modern life, such as the omission of Law-readings on the second day of Festivals. Interestingly, in the 1870s Marks, then still Chief Minister of the West London congregation of British Jews in addition to occupying the Chair of Hebrew at University College, London, was publicly to declare in the presence of Dr. Hermann Adler, Delegate Chief Rabbi, that there would have been no secession in 1841 had the Orthodox synagogues then been the institutions which they had since become.[66] The Reformers of the 1840s did indeed indicate clearly that drastic action involving litigation against the Board of Deputies would be taken only in the event of practical difficulties being encountered by their minister in the matter of marriage registration.[67]

As for Emancipation, as distinct from its by-product of Reform, Montefiore was firmly of the opinion that civic duties must never be allowed to take precedence over divinely-prescribed religious duties or to interfere in spheres of life regulated by rabbinical authority. When his friends, noting the climate of change, remarked on how differently others might act in a similar position, Montefiore would reply 'Very well, I will not deviate from the injunctions of my religion; let them call me a bigot if they like; it is immaterial to me what others do or think in this respect. God has given man the free will to act as he may think proper. He has set before him life and death, blessing and curse [Deuteronomy xxx, 15]. I follow the advice given in Holy Writ, and choose that which is considered life, which is accounted a blessing.'[68] For was not the negative indignity of political disabilities blessing indeed compared to the hardships, misery and insecurity suffered by many Jews abroad?[69] Montefiore personally investigated the case of the Catholic Father Tommas, whose murder had allegedly been committed by Jews with the intention of mixing his blood into their Passover cakes. The pogroms at both Damascus and Rhodes aroused considerable sympathy for the Jews and at public meetings Peel and Russell lent their support.[70]

Not surprisingly therefore the reasons for the conferment of a baronetcy on Montefiore in 1846 were significantly different from those which had lain behind the award of a baronetcy to I. L. Goldsmid five years earlier. The citation to Montefiore expressed 'the hope that it [the baronetcy] may aid your truly benevolent efforts to improve the social condition of the Jews in other countries by temperate appeals to the justice and humanity of their rulers';[71] Goldsmid's baronetcy owed much to the recommendation of the fourth Lord Holland, whose father had worked so closely with the Goldsmids to achieve the removal of disabilities.[72] If, particularly during the early years of the campaign, I. L. Goldsmid appeared as the standard-bearer of Emancipation, no less should Montefiore, as an effective counterbalancing influence, be credited with helping to keep the issue within a broader Jewish perspective. Yet, though the motives of the two men may have been equally worthy, neither Montefiore nor I. L. Goldsmid can be acquitted of remaining in some degree prisoners of their respective preconceptions of Emancipation: to this extent their differences find a place at points in that spectrum of which the extremes had earlier been charted by Crooll and F. H. Goldsmid.

NOTES

1. *The Restoration of Israel;*
The Fifth Empire, delivered in a discourse by thirty-six men; every one made a speech, and when the one had finished another began; and it is decided among them that the Fifth Empire is to be the inheritance of the people of Israel;
The Last Generation.
2. Whittaker Papers, Jewish Central Library, Woburn House, MSS. No. 4 (1), formerly MSS./30, letter from Crooll to the Revd. J. W. Whittaker, 24 March 1828, in the Jewish year 5588.
3. *The Jewish Chronicle,* 30 June 1848, p. 590; an obituary notice, based on a letter from the Revd. F. R. Hall published in the *Cambridge Independent Press,* 11 June 1848.
4. H. J. Zimmels, *Ashkenazim and Sephardim,* p. 233.
5. Ibid., p. 234.
6. *The Last Generation,* p. 9.
7. *The Fifth Empire,* p. 4.
8. Ibid., p. 5.
9. Ibid., pp. 8–10.
10. Ibid.
11. *The Last Generation,* pp. 3–5.
12. H. J. Zimmels, *Ashkenazim and Sephardim,* pp. 236–37.
13. Ibid., pp. 240–42.
14. Ibid., pp. 246–49.
15. *The Restoration of Israel,* p. 51.
16. H. J. Zimmels, *Ashkenazim and Sephardim,* p. 238.
17. Ibid.
18. *The Fifth Empire,* pp. 8–10; *The Last Generation,* p. 8.
19. *The Fifth Empire,* pp. 5–8.
20. *The Restoration of Israel,* pp. 59–60.
21. *The Last Generation,* p. 26.
22. *The Restoration of Israel,* pp. 72ff.
23. H. J. Zimmels, *Ashkenazim and Sephardim,* pp. 249–50.
24. *The Restoration of Israel,* p. 4.
25. Inglis, *Hansard,* Third Series, 18, 22 May 1833, 50–51. For other references to Crooll, cf. Inglis, *Hansard,* Third Series, 35, 3 August 1836, 869–70; *Hansard,* Third Series, 57, 10 March 1841, 90; *Hansard,* Third Series, 95, 16 December 1847, 1263–64; Samuel Wilberforce, Bishop of Oxford, *Hansard,* Third Series, 98, 25 May 1848, 1373–75.
26. *The Jewish Chronicle,* 30 June 1848, p. 590.
27. F. H. Goldsmid, *Two Letters in Answer to the Objections urged against Mr. Grant's Bill for the Relief of the Jews,* and second and third letters of *The Arguments advanced against the Enfranchisement of the Jews considered in a series of letters,* particularly letter 2: 'Reply to the objection that the Jews are in constant expectation of their Return to Palestine', pp. 6–7, referring to the argument implicit in Crooll's contention. For an example of gentile opposition, albeit soon to be abandoned but at the time finely mirroring Crooll's arguments, see *The Times,* 3 May 1830, leading article: 'What can the Jew care about the cause for which *HAMPDEN bled in the field, and SIDNEY on the scaffold?* . . . The names of SOMERS, of LOCKE, of HOLT, and RUSSELL, at the sound of which every Englishman's heart leaps with sympathy, must to him be *a mere sounding brass and tinkling cymbal.*' A general rejection of Crooll's arguments may be found in the Deputies' letter to Robert Grant of 11 April 1833, Letter Books of I. L. Goldsmid, I, fol. no. 358, and in two pamphlets written by B. Montagu: *A Letter to Henry Warburton. Esq. M. P. upon the Emancipation of the Jews,* and *A Letter to the Rt. Revd. the Lord Bishop of Chichester, upon the Emancipation of the Jews.*
28. F. H. Goldsmid, *The Arguments advanced against the Enfranchisement of the Jews,* letter 2: 'Reply to the objection that the Jews are in constant expectation of their Return to Palestine', p. 8.
29. Ibid., p. 9.
30. Ibid., p. 10.
31. Ibid., p. 11.
32. Ibid.
33. Ibid., p. 12.
34. F. H. Goldsmid, *The Arguments advanced against the Enfranchisement of the Jews,* letter 3: 'Reply to the Objections, that the Jews consider themselves as a separate nation, and that their religion forbids their political identification with the state in which they live', p. 13.
35. Ibid., p. 14.
36. Ibid.

37. Ibid., p. 16.
38. Ibid., p. 17.
39. B. Van Oven, *Ought Baron de Rothschild to sit in Parliament? An Imaginary conversation between JUDAEUS and AMICUS NOBILIS*, pp. 6–10.
40. *The Voice of Jacob*, 31 January 1845, p. 89, for the Jewish year 5605.
41. L. Loewe (ed.), *The Diaries of Sir Moses and Lady Montefiore*, I, pp. 69–70.
42. L. Wolf, *Sir Moses Montefiore. A Centennial Biography. With extracts from letters and journals*, pp. 47–48.
43. L. Loewe (ed.), *The Diaries of Sir Moses and Lady Montefiore*, I, p. 301.
44. Letter from Solomon Hirschell, the Chief Rabbi, to I. L. Goldsmid, recently in the possession of the late Sir H. d'Avigdor Goldsmid, translated from the Hebrew and published in S. Stein, *The Beginnings of Hebrew Studies at University College*, 1952, p. 7, appendix B, p. 27, for the original Hebrew version.
45. L. Loewe (ed.), *The Diaries of Sir Moses and Lady Montefiore*, I, p. 66; Minute Books of the Board of Deputies, II, p. 8, 16 April 1829.
46. Minute Books of the Board of Deputies, II, pp. 31–42, 22 December 1829–25 February 1830.
47. L. Loewe (ed.), *The Diaries of Sir Moses and Lady Montefiore*, I, pp. 78–79.
48. Ibid., I, p. 79 14 April 1830.
49. Ibid., I, p. 82.
50. Letter Books of I. L. Goldsmid, I, fol. no. 358, 11 April 1833, the Deputies to R. Grant.
51. Letter Books of I. L. Goldsmid, I, fol. no. 333, 2 August 1833, P. Ellissen to I. L. Goldsmid; D. W. Marks and A. Löwy (eds.), *Memoir of Sir F. H. Goldsmid*, pp. 153–54, letter from I. L. Goldsmid to Lord Bexley, 30 July 1833.
52. Minute Books of the Board of Deputies, II, p. 105, 24 May 1836.
53. Ibid., pp. 106–9, June 1836.
54. Ibid., pp. 111–12, 13 June 1836.
55. Ibid., pp. 109–10, 12 December 1836. For some reason the Secretary of the Board entered the record of the December meeting on an earlier page of the Minute Book than that of the 13 June meeting.
56. L. Loewe (ed.), *The Diaries of Sir Moses and Lady Montefiore*, I, p. 111, 9 July 1837.
57. I. Finestein, 'An Aspect of the Jews and English Marriage Law during the Emancipation: The Prohibited Degrees', *The Jewish Journal of Sociology*, VII, no. 1, June 1965, pp. 3–21, for interpretation of Montefiore's stance.
58. D. Philipson, *The Reform Movement in Judaism*, pp. 128–31.
59. Minute Books of the Board of Deputies, III, pp. 30–45, 13 November 1838, at which I. L. Goldsmid's letter of 26 September was read out and discussed.
60. Ibid.
61. Ibid., pp. 46–48, 4 December 1838.
62. C. H. L. Emanuel, *A Century and a Half of Jewish History*, p. 32.
63. Minute Books of the Board of Deputies, III, pp. 49–56, 4 February 1839.
64. Ibid., pp. 84–90.
65. D. Philipson, *The Reform Movement in Judaism*, pp. 128–31; H. J. Zimmels, *Ashkenazim and Sephardim*, pp. 300ff.; Minute Books of the Board of Deputies, V, February–May 1842, and particularly p. 82, 7 February 1842, for the Board's response to the Chief Rabbi.
66. L. Wolf, *Sir Moses Montefiore*, pp. 124–25.
67. D. Philipson, *The Reform Movement in Judaism*, p. 142.
68. L. Loewe (ed.), *The Diaries of Sir Moses and Lady Montefiore*, I, p. 108.
69. L. Wolf, *Sir Moses Montefiore*, p. 164.
70. Minute Books of the Board of Deputies, III and IV. The last half of the third volume and the first half of the fourth volume contain little material other than that relating to these questions. File of Louis Cohen–Moses Montefiore Letters (1837–74), pp. 9–13, letter VI, Montefiore to Cohen, from Alexandria, 14 August 1840. On 7 November 1840 the Sultan bowed to Montefiore's pressure and issued a *firmân* condemning the accusations against the Jews; Cohen–Montefiore File, pp. 35–37.
Disraeli's novel *Tancred*, which supported Jewish claims to political rights, struck a familiar chord of public sympathy in referring to Damascus and parodying the prejudices which had there harmed the Jews. Fakredeen, the villain of the plot in *Tancred*, describes Passover cakes as the 'festival bread of the Hebrews, made in the new moon, with the milk of he-goats'. B. Disraeli, *Tancred or The New Crusade*, pp. 438–40.
71. L. Loewe (ed.), *The Diaries of Sir Moses and Lady Montefiore*, I, p. 388, letter from Peel to Montefiore 28 June 1846; Peel Papers, B.M.ADD.MSS. 40594, ff. 259–66, 25–29 June 1846, four letters of Peel-Montefiore correspondence. Cf. Extant Letter-Books of Sir Moses Montefiore, Mocatta Library, which illustrate clearly Montefiore's preoccupation with the fate of Jews abroad.
72. Cf. Letter Books of I. L. Goldsmid, I, f. 133, 24 August 1841, Lord John Russell to J. Allen.

5
Benjamin Disraeli, Marrano Englishman

In discussing almost any aspect of Disraeli's politics conventional interpretation has customarily come to regard expediency as the determining factor. Yet most authorities, concerned with tracing Disraeli's rise to the Tory leadership, are agreed that his writings cannot be appreciated without reference to Judaism in general and to his Sephardi descent in particular. And so a chain of thought becomes easily detectable. Such interpreters contend that Disraeli, finding necessary the espousal of religious principles as integral to his Toryism and yet unable to accept Anglican prejudices against Judaism, transmuted his monotheism into a Semitic-Tory creed. Religion and politics having become indivisible Disraeli could then arrive at support for that Church of England form of Christianity the profession of which, at a time when Jews were still excluded from Parliament, was indispensable to the fulfilment of his youthful ambition to become leader of the Tory party and Prime Minister. Indeed so convenient have these views been made to seem as to tempt some observers to place their own even less obvious constructions on his words and actions: while Cecil Roth, attaching undue importance to the immature Disraeli of the novel *Alroy* (1833), uncovers a forerunner of Zionism,[1] Lord Blake has seen his subject rather as an Italian in England, incompetence in the handling of his financial affairs, supposedly untypical of most Jews, being adduced as evidence for his lack of Jewishness.[2]

But what if one regards Disraeli as Marrano rather than *manqué?* He undoubtedly possessed what one might loosely describe as a Marrano mentality. The state of being a Marrano in itself presupposes assimilation for, whereas the Ashkenazim had been involuntarily shut off from Christians, many Sephardim had taken advantage of the choice which had often been offered them of mixing with gentiles. Not uninterestingly some of the more adventurous and ambitious even of the English Sephardim had been tempted to leave the Jewish community: these included the economist David Ricardo who, as a Member of Parliament in the period before his death in 1823, nonetheless won identification with the Jewish community through his keen advocacy of religious liberty and free discussion,[3] and Ralph Bernal, chairman of Commons committees after 1830, whose father had left the Synagogue out of pique.

This last was the experience which befell Isaac D'Israeli. In 1817 he resigned from the Synagogue after a protracted dispute arising from his refusal to accept the presiding warden's office of *Parnas* or to pay the consequent fine of forty pounds. This incident was, however, essentially the culmination of a deepening disillusionment with Judaism. In the first volume of *The Curiosities of Literature* (1791), the Talmud was described as 'a compleat system of the barbarous learning of the Jews'.[4] Isaac seems to have evinced no pride in his Jewish origins and insensitively overlooking hundreds of years of involuntary reclusiveness from European civilization he once observed in a letter that 'the Jews have no men of Genius or talents to lose. I can count all their men of Genius on my fingers. Ten centuries have not produced Ten great men.'[5] Isaac D'Israeli's mature views on Judaism were revealed in *The Genius of Judaism* (1833) which, significantly, was published anonymously—by this time he seems to have become almost ashamed of orthodox Judaism. Though Isaac never formally became a Christian he wrote as if he were a zealous convert: 'let those who are born in the happy faith of Christianity compassionate the Jew, for we cannot relieve him.'[6] He strongly disagreed with the rabbinical interpretation of the Mosaic Laws which he condemned for having contributed to the separation of the Jews from other people. Indeed the Jews' belief in the divine origin of the Mosaic Laws had been the 'first great cause of their separation', while secondary causes had included observation of the Sabbath, the many peculiar rites such as circumcision, and difficulties about eating with gentiles.[7] Disraeli's mother, moreover, appears to have nurtured an even greater antipathy than his father towards her ancestral religion for she 'regarded Judaism not as a religion but as a misfortune'.[8]

With this family background Benjamin might almost have been expected to grow up scarred with the complexes of the convert, not merely a Jew devoid of Judaism but rabidly hostile to Judaism and all things Jewish. He might well have become a neophyte anxious to prove his zealous fidelity to the newly espoused creed or philosophy, virulently denouncing his former co-religionists—the successor to the *converso* of former times, sapping the morale of Judaism and hated by those who have been deserted.[9]

Benjamin Disraeli was one of those *déraciné* Jews who does not attempt to conceal his past but rather to recreate it. He was 'the heir to that legacy of the puritanical visionary, the Hebraic tradition, embodied by the Jew who does not feel comfortable unless the prophet's cloak is warming his shoulders, the living communicant of Judaism's greatest contribution to Western civilization'. One writer has even stated that Disraeli's views taken together, of the Sphinx, the Asian Mystery, the patriarchal principle, the Religion of Sinai and Calvary, make him the last of the Jewish prophets with a religious-political mission,[10] while another has seen in Disraeli yet a more recent 'dreamer of the ghetto', his philosophy an example of the Jews' unifying sweep of idea.[11]

As Disraeli believed that his argument in favour of Emancipation would be

best served by first convincing others of the Jews' superiority, he began by
stressing the superiority of his own Sephardi ancestry. Here he was only one
of many. For the Sephardim the norm had always been a society in which
they, as individuals of the Jewish faith, could contribute to its social and
cultural development; in the golden age of Judeo-Spanish symbiosis they had
been integral to European life. Contact with Arabs and Christians had
imparted to the Sephardim distinctive traits: appreciation of culture, a love
of general knowledge and scholarship, a faculty for statesmanship coupled
with pride and self-assertiveness.[12] These Disraeli certainly possessed in
abundance. He was aware of how the Sephardim in the centuries since the
Expulsion had come to provide the statesmen, the professional men and the
many merchants who kept themselves free from usury; though the Sephardim formed self-supporting communities, their abilities had ensured that
these never became, as with the Ashkenazi communities, alienated and
isolated groups.[13] In a passage in *Tancred* Disraeli compares the Sephardim
of the Mediterranean with the Ashkenazim of the Houndsditch and Minories
settlements or of the Hamburg and Frankfurt *Judenstrasse,* and he remarks
on the contrast between life in the bleak northern cities and the celebration
of *Succoth,* the Feast of Tabernacles, in the sunny climes of the south. Of
the beauty of the booth of Besso at Damascus, Disraeli enthuses: 'A race
that persist in celebrating their vintage, although they have no fruits to
gather, will regain their vineyards. What sublime inexorability in the law!
But what indomitable spirit in the people!'[14]

The assumed superiority of the Sephardim manifested itself in a snobbery
based upon nobility of birth, this being in some measure the answer to
Ashkenazi claims of descent from great scholars and martyrs. At Leghorn,
the town from which Disraeli's grandfather had emigrated to England in the
mid-eighteenth century, the Jews would proudly point out at their burial
ground those of their monuments upon which were engraved coronets, in the
belief that these were the tombstones of brethren who had been able to claim
membership of the Spanish nobility.[15] The strongest argument on which the
Sephardim based their claim to regard themselves as of nobler birth than the
Ashkenazim was that while all Jews formerly of the Iberian Peninsula were
descendants of the tribe of Judah, the very nobility of Jerusalem, the
Ashkenazim were descendants of the inferior remaining tribes.[16] Disraeli
was thus sustaining a very long tradition in asserting this superiority;
although intermarriage between Sephardim and Ashkenazim had become
almost acceptable by the 1840s there were still to be found some overtones
of that fawning attitude evident in the letter which one Sephardi Jew had
despatched to Voltaire, explaining that if a Sephardi Jew in England or
Holland were to marry an Ashkenazi Jewess he would be disowned by his
relatives and denied burial in their cemetery.[17] The reasons for this Sephardi
snobbery had emerged very clearly in 1802 when a bill for a communal poor
law, supported if necessary by compulsory communal taxation, had been

introduced in Parliament. The Bevis Marks congregation had subsequently sought the assistance of Members of Parliament so that they might secure the exclusion of the Sephardim from the bill's provisions and they had even prepared a document to make clear to the Parliamentarians the difference between themselves and the Ashkenazim. This emphasised that the Spanish and Portuguese Jews had been the first to settle in England and that to provide for their own poor the Sephardim had formed various charitable institutions in addition to a hospital and schools. These charitable institutions were directed solely to assisting those of their Sephardi brethren who had either fled from abroad or been reduced by other misfortunes. They had thus been formed, declared the document disparagingly, 'not for the purpose of encouraging German, Dutch, or Polish adventurers'. The document further noted how the German Jews, differing from the Portuguese, periodically erected various synagogues 'in order to follow their own peculiar method'; as the Ashkenazi pronunciation of Hebrew was anyway 'so different from that of the Portuguese' it was impossible for the two groups to read prayers together. More honestly revealing of the Sephardi outlook was the further observation that 'not having increased in number, their [Sephardi] establishments for looking after the poor, sick, aged, orphans, etc. remain competent to their wants, where within the last fifty years the German Jews have increased prodigiously in number, coming from all parts of Germany, and mostly of the poorer class'.[18]

This Sephardi snobbery enables us to imagine Disraeli's delight when, in 1872, he received a letter from Dr. Moses Margoliouth, the historian of the Jews in Britain, informing him that 'the name to which you have added immortal renown is of considerably earlier date than you supposed.' Margoliouth's researches had uncovered a certain Isaac D'Israeli, who had been one of the twelve Hebrew savants attached to the Astronomical Academy at Toledo established and patronised by Alfonso XI. This distinguished 'master in Israel' had in 1310 written a very learned work on mathematics and astronomy entitled *The Foundation of the Wold* [sic], which had remained in manuscript until the mid-eighteenth century and had since been published in three editions.[19] But Disraeli had long since been confident of his ancestry: there is no error in the claim of Sidonia concerning his line of the family, as compared to the pedigree of a cousin's, that 'we are pure Sephardim'.[20]

Disraeli goes further and transfers the snobbery of the Sephardim to the 'race' as a whole. The qualities which have rendered the Sephardim such an asset to Europe in the past are in refined form those of the Jewish 'nation'; where others simply argue that Jews are no worse than other men, Disraeli argues that they are indeed better.

Disraeli sees the survival and prosperity of the Jews in so many countries as proof that it is useless to attempt to defeat that inexorable law of nature which has decreed that a superior race shall never be destroyed or absorbed by an inferior.[21] 'Sidonia and his brethren could claim a distinction which the

Saxon and the Greek, and the rest of the Caucasian nations, have forfeited. The Hebrew is an unmixed race.'[22] This virtue is partly to be explained by the original home and subsequent migration of the Jews. While 'the decay of a race is an inevitable necessity, unless it lives in deserts and never mixes its blood',[23] and though pure blood groups other than Jews may be found in the desert, 'the Mosaic Arabs are the most ancient, if not the only, unmixed blood that dwells in cities. An unmixed race of a first-rate organization are the aristocracy of nature. . . . When he [Sidonia] reflected on what they had endured, it was only marvellous that the race had not disappeared. . . . To the unpolluted current of their Caucasian structure and to the segregating genius of their great lawgiver, Sidonia ascribed the fact that they had not been long ago absorbed among those mixed races, who presume to persecute them, but who periodically wear away and disappear, while their victims still flourish, in all the primeval vigour of the pure Asian breed.'[24] This theme is not merely reiterated: 'The fact is you cannot destroy a pure race of the Caucasian organization. No penal laws, no physical tortures work—where mixed persecuting races disappear, the pure persecuted race remains';[25] Eva in *Tancred* goes further in reiterating Sidonia's proud boast that the Jews have never blended with their conquerors.[26]

The Jews have such a debt owed to them by the English and European peoples that they are entitled to Emancipation. For it was none other than the Jewish race which was responsible for having given Christianity to the world.[27] Moses, Christ, the prophets and the apostles were all Hebrews. The Churches of Asia and of Rome were founded by Hebrews.[28] Christ is the eternal glory of the Jewish race,[29] the descendant of King David, the last and greatest of the Hebrew princes.[30] And so Tancred the Englishman comes 'from a distant and northern isle to bow before the tomb of a descendant of the kings of Israel, because he, in common with all the people of that isle, recognizes in that sublime Hebrew incarnation the presence of a Divine Redeemer'.[31] Eva asks Tancred: 'Pray, are you of those Franks who worship a Jewess; or of those other who revile her, break her images, and blaspheme her pictures?' only to remind him that Christ and Mary had been Jews. Tancred's admonition to Eva to read the history of the life of Christ is met with the retort that she already has—'a very good one, written, I observe, entirely by Jews'.[32]

Disraeli's continual assertions as to the superiority and purity of his race bear some resemblance to those of Joseph Crooll. But, whereas to Crooll the covenanted separatism of the Jews as they await the return to Zion demands their resistance to all emancipatory blandishments, to Disraeli the Jews' election as the Messianic nation must needs command their immediate Emancipation. In a passage in *Tancred* which describes Jerusalem by moonlight Disraeli enthuses:

There might be counted heroes and sages, who need shrink from no rivalry with the brightest and wisest of other lands; but the lawgiver of the time of the Pharaohs, whose laws are still obeyed; the monarch, whose reign has ceased for three thousand years, but whose wisdom is a proverb in all nations of the earth; the teacher whose doctrines have modelled civilized Europe; the greatest of legislators, the greatest of administrators, and the greatest of reformers; what race, extinct or living, can produce three men such as these!

While Disraeli asks of Israel: 'Is it not the land upon whose mountains the Creator of the Universe parleyed with man, and the flesh of whose anointed race He mystically assumed, when He struck the last blow at the powers of evil?'[33]

Jehovah's people constitute the chosen race and this explains their superior faculties.[34] In comparison the English and European peoples suffer grave defects. Disraeli remarks on how Europeans are harassed by complicated conventionalisms which have increased in exact proportion as their possessors have seceded 'from those Arabian and Syrian creeds that redeemed them from their primitive barbarism'. He then describes in glowing terms the 'land of Canaan' where live the Arabs who so value tradition and truth. On seeing the landscape Tancred becomes nostalgic for the past age of Solomon, but he soon realizes that all such ancient glories have vanished and that in the absence of wise kings and bright-witted queens there now reigns only desolation.

And yet some flat-nosed Frank, full of bustle and puffed up with self-conceit (a race spawned perhaps in the morasses of some Northern forest hardly yet cleared), talks of Progress! Progress to what, and from whence? Amid empires shrivelled into deserts, amid the wrecks of great cities, a single column or obelisk of which nations import for the prime ornament of their mud-built capitals, amid arts forgotten, commerce annihilated, fragmentary literatures and populations destroyed, the European talks of progress, because, by an ingenious application of some scientific acquirements, he has established a society which has mistaken comfort for civilization.[35]

Tancred, spellbound by the personality of Sidonia, feels compelled to acknowledge the debt that Europe owes to the Jews and humbly he admits to being sprung from a horde of Baltic pirates who were never heard of during the greater annals of the world, 'a descent which I have been educated to believe was the greatest of honours'. Tancred further confesses to the errors of his earlier thinking. 'What we should have become, had not the Syro-Arabian creeds formed our minds, I dare not contemplate. Probably we should have perished in mutual destruction. However, though rude and modern Gentiles, unknown to the Apostles, we also were in time touched with the sacred symbol.'[36]

Europeans therefore can scarcely refuse to accept Jews in their midst. In spite of centuries of degradation the Jewish mind, so Sidonia informs

Coningsby, has been able to wield a vast influence on the affairs of Europe. 'I speak not of their laws, which you still obey; of their literature, with which your minds are saturated, but of the living Hebrew intellect. You never observe a great intellectual movement in Europe in which the Jews do not greatly participate.' Disraeli then makes Sidonia recall the influential positions held by Jews past and present—though here the fantasising of Disraeli makes it difficult to distinguish fact from fiction. According to Sidonia the Jews had provided the first Jesuits, and more recently most leading Russian diplomats and German university professors have been Jews. Their importance in business, in the transaction of loans for example, has been considerable. In politics the positions of Russian Finance Minister, Spanish Prime Minister, President of the French Council, and Prime Minister of Prussia are all currently held by Jews or New Christians. Sidonia, then asked why the Jews have produced no great poets, orators, or writers, directs Coningsby's attention to David, Isaiah and Ezekiel. The Jews remain as a people 'after acts of heroic courage that Rome has never equalled; deeds of divine patriotism that Athens and Sparta and Carthage have never excelled'. They have endured 1,500 years of slavery. 'The Hebrew child has entered adolescence only to learn that he was the pariah of that ungrateful Europe that owes to him the best part of its laws, a fine portion of its literature, all its religion.' The Jews have produced the poetry of the Bible, the orators of the temples, and as for great writers 'what are all the schoolmen, Aquinas himself to Maimonides; and as for modern philosophy, all springs from Spinoza'. Sidonia claims for the Jews 'the passionate and creative genius that is the nearest link to divinity': music. Referring here to the Jews' past contribution he boasts to Coningsby that 'at this moment even, musical Europe is ours. There is not a company of singers, not an orchestra in a single capital, that are not crowded with our children under the feigned names which they adopt to conciliate the dark aversion which your posterity will some day disclaim with shame and disgust.' Almost all the great composers, skilled musicians and singers 'spring from our tribes. . . . The catalogue is too vast to enumerate; too illustrious to dwell for a moment on secondary names, however eminent'.[37] Of the great civilizations of the past only Israel lives on, whereas Greece and Rome have perished. Alexander and Caesar 'were both deified: who burns incense to them now? Their descendants, both Greek and Roman, bow before the altars of the house of David. The house of David is worshipped at Rome itself, at every seat of great and growing empire in the world, at London, at St. Petersburg, at New York.'[38] So all-pervasive is Israel's influence made to appear that Disraeli seems at times engaged in an attempt to convince his readers that Europe owes an almost exclusive debt to the Jews. Disraeli contends that whereas the nations which welcome Jews flourish, those others which reject them decay. Spain provides a perfect example of the latter. In *Coningsby* Sidonia, recalling the establishment of the 'Saracen kingdoms' of Spain and the value of the Judeo-Spanish symbiosis, presents an exaggerated, albeit essentially true, picture of mediaeval Spanish Jewry. 'That fair and unrivalled civilization arose, which preserved for Europe arts and letters when Christendom was plunged in darkness.'[39] Sidonia presents Tancred with a letter of introduction to Alonzo Lara, Spanish Prior at the Convent of Terra Santa at Jerusalem and explains that Lara is a fourteenth-century Nuevo. 'You see, he is master of the old as well as the new learning; this is very important; they often explain each other. Your bishops here know nothing about these things. How can they? A few centuries back they were tattooed savages. . . . Theology requires an apprenticeship of some thousand years at least; to say nothing of clime and race. You cannot get on with theology as you do with chemistry and mechanics.'[40] Lara has benefited from the unique symbiosis of many centuries before. Now, asks Sidonia, 'Where is Spain? Its fall, its unparalleled and its irremediable fall, is mainly to be attributed to the expulsion of that large portion of its subjects, the most industrious and intelligent, who traced their origin to the Mosaic and Mohammedan Arabs'[41] . . . 'the fall of Spain was occasioned by the expulsion of her Semitic population: a million families of Jews and Saracens: the most distinguished of her citizens for their industry and their intelligence, their learning and their wealth'.[42]

It is however not merely European civilization in general which is indebted to Judaism, but more particularly the religion of Christianity. Whereas opponents of the Jews have alleged that the dispersion of the Jewish race was the penalty incurred for the Crucifixion, Disraeli points out that at the time of the advent of Christ the Jewish race was as widely dispersed throughout the world as at the present time, and had indeed been so for many centuries before. There were at the time of Christ more Jews living in Alexandria than at Jerusalem itself. Nor is the contention historically true that the small section of the Jewish race then dwelling in Palestine rejected Christ: the first preachers and historians of the Gospel were Jews. 'No one has ever been permitted to write under the inspiration of the Holy Spirit, except a Jew.' For many years none but Jews could bring themselves to believe in Christ. The very man who diffused the faith was a Jew of Tarsus, founder of the seven churches of Asia. And the Church itself was founded by another Jew, a Jew of Galilee. The penal assumption which relates the dispersion to the Crucifixion remains, moreover, dogmatically unsound; the mob at the Crucifixion cannot be said to have implicated with guilt all the members of their nation, let alone to have transmitted such guilt to their posterity.[43] Too rarely have Christians been conscious of their debt to the Jews; the people of Europe, when only recently converted, considered that atonement for their past idolatry was to be had in avenging themselves 'on a race to whom, and to whom alone, they were indebted for the Gospel they adored'.[44] Moreover, 'if the Jews had not prevailed upon the Romans to crucify our Lord, what would have become of the Atonement? But the human mind cannot contemplate the idea that the most important deed of time could depend upon human will. The immolators were pre-ordained like the victim, and the holy race supplied both.'[45]

Disraeli argues that the responsibility for persecution of the Jews is to be attributed not to the Holy Books but to the Churches. 'We have saved the human race and you persecute us for doing it.'[46] This is a quite different explanation of the sufferings of the dispersed Jews from that advanced by the ultra-Orthodox Jews. Where Crooll follows the orthodox Ashkenazi tradition in arguing that the Jews have brought their sufferings on themselves and that these had been foretold in the Bible, Disraeli, in contending that the traditional plight of the Jews bears witness to the ingratitude of Christian Europe, tends rather to agree with the alternative theory that the Jews have been made to shoulder the sufferings of mankind. This had always been the Sephardi view: Judah Halevi, the twelfth-century philosopher, in noting that the heart is more sensitive to pain than any other organ of the body and that Israel, by analogy, stands in the same relationship to mankind as does the human heart to the body, logically concluded that Israel must be more quickly affected by any calamity which befalls mankind than any other nation.[47]

Christianity, indebted to Judaism for its doctrines and writings, is built on the foundations of the Old Testament and is Judaism completed. As the Revd. Mr. St. Lys admonishes Lord Egremont: 'In all these church discussions, we are apt to forget that the second Testament is avowedly only a supplement. Jehovah-Jesus came to complete the *law and the prophets*. Christianity is completed Judaism, or it is nothing. Christianity is incomprehensible without Judaism, as Judaism is incomplete without Christianity.'[48] To Disraeli it is deplorable that several millions of the Jewish race, and not least Baron Lionel Nathan de Rothschild, should unfortunately persist in believing 'only in the first part of the Jewish religion',[49] and he trusts that time will remove the anomaly. His optimism rests on three premises. Firstly, that the existing Jews are descendants of those who would have been found in colonies and emigrations long before the advent; secondly, that Christ had been able to gain acceptance amidst the carnage of the Roman Wars; and thirdly, that since the Christian religion had been sustained solely by the Jews of Palestine during the greater part of the first century it was therefore improbable that there might still remain any descendants of these Jewish Christians, or 'true Jews', avowing to a disbelief in Christ.

Disraeli gives some fanciful reasons for the existence of Judaism at the present time. When, after many centuries, Christianity was first heard of by the Jewish colonies it seemed to embrace idolatrous practices and to hold up the Jewish race to public scorn and hatred. No wonder that the Church of those times had failed to win converts. All the Spanish Jews knew of Christianity was that 'one of its first duties was to avenge some mysterious and inexplicable crime which had been committed ages ago by some unheard of ancestors of theirs in an unknown land'. After enduring so much suffering and persecution it is scarcely surprising that many Jews should not believe in 'the most important portion of the Jewish religion'. But there can be nothing 'very repugnant to the feelings of a Jew when he learns that the redemption of the human race has been effected by the mediatorial agency of a child of Israel'. Disraeli is confident that when the Jews come to realize that the doctrines of Christianity originated with a member of their own race they will readily accept them. 'It can hardly be maintained that there is anything revolting to a Jew to learn that a Jewess is the queen of heaven, or that the flower of the Jewish race are even now sitting on the right hand of the Lord God of Sabaoth.'[50] The one undeniable fact, even if Christians continue to persecute Jews and Jews persist in rejecting Christianity, is that Jesus, Incarnate Son of the Most High God, is the eternal glory of the Jewish race.[51]

Christianity, claims Disraeli, has been created by the Jewish race for the peoples of the world. Tancred, as a Christian, and his adversary Fakredeen, as a Jew, argue their respective cases before the court of the mysterious and beautiful Queen Astarte. Asked at what epoch men ceased to worship gods and goddesses, and whether this was 'before the prophet', Tancred gives the reply that it was when truth descended from Heaven in the person of Christ. With this Fakredeen disagrees. He observes that truth had descended from Heaven before Jesus, 'since God spoke to Moses on Mount Sinai, and since then to many of the prophets and princes of Israel'. 'Of whom Jesus was one', adds Tancred, 'the descendant of King David as well as the Son of God. But through this last and greatest of their princes it was ordained that the inspired Hebrew mind should mould and govern the world. Through Jesus God spoke to the Gentiles, and not to the tribes of Israel only. That is the great worldly difference between Jesus and his inspired predecessors. Christianity is Judaism for the multitude, but still it is Judaism, and its development was the death-blow of the Pagan idolatry.'[52] Christendom is so exclusively the creation of Jews that they will even condescend to carry the responsibility for its faults. 'Sons of Israel, when you recollect that you created Christendom, you may pardon the Christians even their Autos da Fè!'[53]

Disraeli, with consummate skill and at great length, has justified his own *Marrano* status. Blending Sephardi tradition with his own idiosyncracies he has established the superiority of those to whom the civilized Christian world is so heavily indebted: the Jews in general and the Sephardim in particular. Now, in Disraeli's own lifetime, Christian Europe seeks to discover in Israel her own true purpose, her destiny and her mission.

Who can point the way? In Disraeli's novels it is Sidonia, the shaman who greatly intrigues Coningsby at their first chance encounter. When the young man tells Sidonia 'your actions should be heroic', he receives the reply,

'Action is not for me. I am of that faith that the apostles professed before they followed their Master.'[54] Most writers have seen in Sidonia the banker and philosopher, the combination of a Rothschild and a Disraeli. Perhaps he is also Sir Moses Montefiore, who 'in his comprehensive travels had visited and examined the Hebrew communities of the world . . . had found in general the lower orders debased; the superior immersed in sordid pursuits'.[55]

But is not Sidonia—or Disraeli—something more? Sidonia continues with his observations on the Jews of the world.

> He perceived the intellectual development [of the Jews] was not impaired. This gave him hope. He was persuaded that organization would outlive persecution. When he reflected on what they had endured, it was only marvellous that the race had not disappeared. They had defied exile, massacre, spoliation, the degrading influence of the constant pursuit of gain; they had defied time. For nearly three thousand years, according to Archbishop Usher, they have been dispersed over the globe.[56]

'They had defied time.' *The Turkish Spy* Wandering Jew of the age of Louis XIV, the aptly-named Sieur Paule Marrana, whom tradition has ever compared favourably with the degraded hovel-ridden German Jew, is the same sphinxlike witness of time as Sidonia, witness to the endurance of Israel as the one fixed point in an ever-changing landscape.[57]

> You might call him the youngest brother of Time. This Wandering Jew understood all languages, knew all Christian and Moslem dynasties, their rise and fall, their follies, and their aimless actions. He had seen from a lofty hill the flames of Rome when Nero set it alight. He had been at the Court of Vespasian, and spoke of the catastrophe that brought about the destruction of the Temple of Jerusalem. This Wandering Jew had passed through the tortures and horrors of the Inquisition in Spain, Portugal and Rome, and at this his auditor is astounded as at a miracle.[58]

We are back to the inn where the young Coningsby is listening spellbound to the stranger,[59] to Sidonia whom Disraeli considers by temperament so suited to English life with its 'masculine vigour' and 'active intelligence'.[60]

For Sidonia, self-consciously reflecting upon his acquired status, now proclaims that mission which, since time immemorial, has been entrusted to his people. Moses was 'summoned to be the organ of an eternal revelation of the Divine will, and his tribe were appointed to be the hereditary ministers of that mighty and mysterious dispensation'.[61] Here Disraeli is conspicuously a Sephard of the Marrano type who, in the cause of conceiving the universal mission of the Jewish people, seeks to merge his religious identity with loyalties to his adopted nation. The idea of a mission to the nations does not however necessarily entail the abandonment of Judaism. Maimonides had seen the period of the Pentateuch in a 'stained-glass light', of Abraham,

Isaac and Jacob having been entrusted with a didactic mission. The Jews of the Diaspora must continue the work of the patriarchs, for the Jews are a people who have been taught to know God and whose task it is to make God known.[62] Was not the wandering of thousands of years almost pre-ordained to fit Israel for her task? Emigration of Jews began long before the rise of Christianity and was at first voluntary; when, at a later time, the Wandering Jew came to be directed by the hand of Providence the expulsion served the ideals of Judaism.[63]

Up to this point Disraeli would agree with Crooll: the Jews' mission is to teach nothing other than the original faith implanted by God among men, the faith of Abraham.[64]

But then he goes his own way: whereas the Orthodox would contend that the Jews' mission is dependent upon both the triumph of the Old Testament and the Jews' ingathering from exile,[65] Disraeli would obviously disagree. He visualises the ideal of mission set in an English context: it is precisely because the English are so preeminently the heirs of the Hebrew race that they have been entrusted with the legacy of Zion. The Jews have defied the axiom that life demonstrates the survival of the fittest: the spirit of a nation overcomes military might. The Greek material ideals of beauty and knowledge and the Roman ideals of expansion, conquest and practical political organization are evanescent in comparison with the timeless ideals of the Jews.[66]

Tancred, as he sets out on his Crusade to the Promised Land, requires those qualities of self-sacrifice, martyrdom and witness to the truth which had sustained the prophets, the poets and the exemplar of Sinai.[67] Sidonia gives Tancred a Delphic note and confers upon him a blessing: 'a pilgrim who aspires to penetrate the great Asian mystery . . . may the God of Sinai in whom we all believe, guard over you, and prosper your enterprise!'[68]

Tancred is won over. As a prisoner in the desert he broods over his misfortune. He remembers his determination to come to the East and reflects on the influence of the wilderness thirty centuries ago. He asks where the English people look when they stop working and demand 'that exponent of the mysteries of the heart, that soother of the troubled spirit, which poetry can alone afford'. Not in their Wordsworths or Byrons, in any of the Augustans, or even in Shakespeare. 'No; the most popular poet in England is the sweet singer of Israel!' And since biblical times 'there never was a race who sang so often the odes of David as the people of Great Britain. . . . Vast as the obligations of the whole human family are to the Hebrew race, there is no portion of the modern populations so much indebted to them as the British people.' It was 'the sword of the Lord and of Gideon that won the boasted liberties of England; chanting the same canticles that cheered the heart of Judah amid their glens, the Scotch, upon their hill-sides, achieved their religious freedom'.[69] Disraeli broadens his appeal to the puritan conscience of Britain. The people of the rural town of

Marney where the 'Holy Church had forgotten her sacred mission . . . took refuge in conventicles, which abounded; little plain buildings of pale brick, with the names painted on them of Sion, Bethel, Bethesda; names of a distant land, and the language of a persecuted and ancient race; yet such is the mysterious power of their divine quality, breathing consolation in the nineteenth century to the harassed forms and the harrowed souls of a Saxon peasantry'.[70] 'Independently of their admirable laws which have elevated our condition, and of their exquisite poetry which has charmed it; independently of their heroic history which has animated us to the pursuit of public liberty, we are indebted to the Hebrew people for our knowledge of the true God and for the redemption from our sins.' Tancred is finally convinced of his good sense in embarking upon such a crusade. 'Then I have a right to be here. . . . I come to the land whose laws I obey, whose religion I profess, and I seek, upon its sacred soil, those sanctions which for ages were abundantly accorded.'[71]

Christ, having conquered Europe and changed its name into Christendom, far exceeded the wildest dreams of the Rabbis. The Jews are therefore entitled to reflect on his achievements: of having made their history the most famous in the world, of having spread and disseminated their laws, vindicated their wrongs and vanquished the Caesars. The 'northern and western races' are indebted for their civilization to the 'oriental intellect' and although there have been occasions, as in Revolutionary France, when this has been denied, Disraeli sees the Semitic principle as now dominant in Europe, America and Australia.[72]

What is 'the Semitic principle'? It represents all that is spiritual in man's nature, for the Jews are the trustees of religion and the conservators of the religious element; it is based upon the Jews' greatness of energy and enterprise, strength of will and fertility of brain.[73] In time the Semitic principle will come to inform Britain's imperial role but first Disraeli must convince the Tory Party of its worth. In *Tancred* the Semitic principle becomes the way and the life; the elixir of tradition, natural aristocracy and religion which the clear-headed Eva gives Tancred to rescue him from Liberalism and Materialism, Scepticism and Atheism, Anarchy and 'moonshine idealism',[74] might equally well be labelled Toryism. For the Semitic principle, translated into political language, *is* Toryism: The Jews 'are a living and the most striking evidence of the falsity of that pernicious doctrine of modern times—the natural equality of man . . . the native tendency of the Jewish race, who are justly proud of their blood, is against the doctrine of the equality of man.'[75] As Sidonia tells Coningsby, 'Toryism indeed is but copied from the mighty prototype which has fashioned Europe.' The Jews, independently of the capital qualities for citizenship which they possess in their industry, temperance and vivacity of mind, are essentially monarchical, deeply religious, and 'shrinking from converts as from a calamity are ever anxious to see the religious systems of the countries in which they live, flourish'.[76] One Jewish characteristic is the faculty of acquisition and although the laws of Europe have sought to prevent Jews from obtaining property they have become remarkable for their accumulated wealth.[77]

The consequences for the Tories, as for the nation, of continued refusal to grasp the constructiveness of the Semitic principle are grave indeed. 'The life and property of England are protected by the laws of Sinai.' And yet, recriminates Disraeli, these Saxon and Celtic societies persecute the Jews and hold up to odium an Arabian race to whom they are indebted both for their sublime legislation, which alleviates the lot of the labouring multitude, and for their literature in the pages of which they have found perpetual delight, instruction and consolation.[78] It is at their own expense that the Tories make opponents of potential natural allies. Disraeli recalls both the general election result for the City of London of June 1841, when Lord John Russell had won his seat by the majority of a mere nine votes, and the further Whig-Liberal victory achieved in the same constituency in a by-election of October 1843 when James Pattison, the Liberal candidate, had beaten his Tory opponent by a majority of only 165 votes. This result with Pattison polling 6,532 votes as against the 6,367 of the financier Thomas Baring, had provided encouragement for the Anti-Corn Law League of Richard Cobden and John Bright at a crucial stage of its campaign, and the victory had owed something to Rothschild personally for having exerted his influence in persuading Jews to cast their votes, most unusually, in a Saturday poll. 'The Tories lose an important election at a critical moment; 'tis the Jews come forward to vote against them.' Disraeli then makes allusion to I. L. Goldsmid's role in the foundation of London University. 'The Church is alarmed at the scheme of a latitudinarian university, and learns with relief that funds are not forthcoming for its establishment; a Jew immediately advances and endows it.'[79] Such Jews as even the Rothschilds whilst finding that they possess the substance of power are yet deprived of its shadow: here Disraeli also makes a timely appeal for the removal of the renowned anomaly concerning the ownership and holding of land—in 1845, one year after the publication of *Coningsby*, the issue was clearly resolved in the Jews' favour. Sidonia reasons with Coningsby:

> Can anything be more absurd than that a nation should apply to an individual to maintain its credit, and with its credit, its existence as an empire and its comfort as a people; and that individual one to whom its laws deny the proudest rights of citizenship, the privilege of sitting in its senate and of holding land; for though I have been rash enough to buy several estates, my own opinion is that by the existing law of England an Englishman of Hebrew faith cannot possess the soil.[80]

Disraeli is a convinced proponent of the axiom that the power and danger of the Jews must increase in proportion to the iniquities borne by them.[81]

Institutions have been threatened and events afford evidence that the Jew would prefer to cooperate with levellers and latitudinarians 'prepared to support the policy which may even endanger his life and property, rather than tamely continue under a system which seeks to degrade him'.[82] Jews are found cooperating with atheists and communists in the leadership of revolutionary movements and their influence may be discerned in the last outbreak of the 'destructive principle' in Europe: here he cites the example of Manini [Daniel Manin] in Venice as evidence of the Jewish mind behind the upheavals of 1848. Disraeli considers as tragic this recent identification with the destructive principle, for the Jews are not natural revolutionaries; in this matter Metternich receives praise for having appreciated Jewish potential in his wise appointment of Frederick Gentz as Secretary to the Congress of Vienna.[83]

To Disraeli the choice could not be clearer. The English already possess the key that will open up the Great Asian Mystery: as an osmotic force the Semitic principle has done its preliminary work of casting the English as the People of the Book, the Chosen People.[84] Now, however, regeneration must resume afresh; here Disraeli no more than romanticises the feelings nurtured by a whole generation. 'By the law of contraries,' writes Emerson in 1856, 'I look for an irresistible taste for Orientalism in Britain. For a self-conceited modish life, made up of trifles, clinging to a corporeal civilization, hating ideas, there is no remedy like the Oriental largeness.'[85] But what of Asia? That continent too is in need of regeneration. 'The world, that, since its creation, has owned the spiritual supremacy of Asia, which is but natural, since Asia is the only portion of the world which the Creator of that world has deigned to visit, and in which he has ever conferred with man, is unhappily losing its faith in those ideas and convictions that hitherto have governed the human race. . . .'[86]

The puritan visionary and the Wandering Jew see in one another the palladium of their cause. If 'the time has arrived when Asia should make one of its periodical and appointed efforts to reassert that [spiritual] supremacy' she need not seek for an agent. Is not the Church already 'a sacred corporation for the promulgation and maintenance in Europe of certain Asian principles'?[87] Asia stirs. Beckons. And is heeded. Disraeli perceives with Heine that as puritan Britain is already the heir of ancient Palestine, and its State Church only the guardian of the Semitic principle popularised, so is it by its moral and physical energy the destined executant of the ideals of Zion; that it is planting the Law like a great shady tree in the tropic deserts and arid wastes of barbarism.[88]

In the intra-Jewish debate on Emancipation Disraeli speaks only for himself. His influence, however, was to be anything other than extraneous. Entrusted with reminding puritan Britain of that past Jewish mission which was responsible for bringing Christianity and civilization to its peoples, Disraeli champions the Anglo-Saxon cause of liberty—but it is assuredly the Old Testament polity of the Hebrews that he aspires to emulate. As to the problem of resolving the Great Asian Mystery, Disraeli anticipates the union of the four component parts of the Christian home empire with those territories which three thousand miles away comprise the Great Mogul Empire; this endeavour, though, he conceives to be the mission not of England but of Asia. Self-appointed to the task of forging a political instrument which will achieve these goals Disraeli turns, as if naturally for a philosophy, to the Semitic principle. In short Disraeli is *the* Marrano Englishman.

NOTES

1. C. Roth, *Benjamin Disraeli, Earl of Beaconsfield*, pp. 74–75.
2. R. Blake, *Disraeli*, pp. 49–50.
3. David Ricardo, *Hansard*, New Series, 8, 26 March 1823, 722–24; *Hansard*, New Series, 9, 1 July 1823, 1386–91.
4. J. Ogden, *Isaac D'Israeli*, p. 194.
5. Isaac D'Israeli to Francis Douce, 1794, in Bodleian Manuscripts, Douce, d. 33 ff. 7–8, quoted in J. Ogden, *Isaac D'Israeli*, pp. 194–95.
6. *The Genius of Judaism*, p. 212, quoted in J. Ogden, *Isaac D'Israeli*, p. 202.
7. J. Ogden, *Isaac D'Israeli*, p. 202.
8. C. Roth, *Benjamin Disraeli*, p. 21.
9. Such *conversos* would include Torquemada, the first Spanish Inquisitor, Deza, his successor, Lainez, the designated successor of Loyola as head of the Jesuit order, and St. Teresa of Ávila.
10. Oscar Levy, postscript to *Tancred*, Munich and Berlin, 1914 edn., p. 505.
11. I. Zangwill, *Dreamers of the Ghetto*, p. 386. Disraeli's two speeches in the House of Commons on the Jewish question, *Hansard*, Third Series, 95, 16 December 1847, 1321–30, and *Hansard*, Third Series, 113, 5 August 1850, 788–95, contain his views in rather compressed form: their value lies in confirming the authenticity of those views which may be reliably attributed to Disraeli in his writings.
12. H. J. Zimmels, *Ashkenazim and Sephardim*, p. 233.
13. I. M. Jost, *Geschichte des Judenthums und seiner Sekten*, part 3, 1859, book 7, pp. 199–200.
14. B. Disraeli, *Tancred or The New Crusade*, 1880 edn., pp. 388–92.
15. M. Margoliouth, *The History of the Jews in Great Britain*, vol. III, p. 176, referring to Narrative of a *Mission of Enquiry to the Jews from the Church of Scotland*, 1839. This practice of distinguishing rank on tombstones may have been imitated from the Moors, who organized their families in any one community in a hierarchy according to the number of famous ancestors.
Cf. also H. J. Zimmels, *Ashkenazim and Sephardim*, pp. 280–81. Great importance had been attached to nobility of birth even before the Expulsion. Often a Sephard on being called up to the Torah (Law) refused to read the portion if the man who was next to him was not of the same rank as himself. In 1567 Rabbi Abraham Saba of Venice had complained bitterly about the problems concerning reading of the Torah which turned the synagogue into a place of quarrels on Sabbaths and Festivals.
16. R. D. Barnett, 'Anglo-Jewry in the Eighteenth Century', in *Three Centuries of Anglo-Jewish History*, ed. V. D. Lipman, p. 62; and H. J. Zimmels, *Ashkenazim and Sephardim*, p. 282.
17. R. D. Barnett, 'Anglo-Jewry in the Eighteenth Century', p. 62; H. J. Zimmels, *Ashkenazim and Sephardim*, p. 282, citing Isaac de Pinto, *Letter addressed to Monsieur Voltaire*, 1777.
18. Minute Books of the Board of Deputies, I, p. 27, 14 February 1802.
19. Hughenden Papers, Box 136; B/xxi/M/199, 21 May 1872, Dr. M. Margoliouth to B. Disraeli, 'The antiquity of the patronymic D'Israeli'.

20. *Tancred*, p. 125; see C. Roth, *Benjamin Disraeli, Earl of Beaconsfield*, chap. 1, for an examination of Disraeli's claims.
21. B. Disraeli, *Lord George Bentinck: A Political Biography*, 1872 edn., p. 355.
22. B. Disraeli, *Coningsby or The New Generation*, 1959 edn., p. 182.
23. *Tancred*, p. 150.
24. *Coningsby*, pp. 182–83.
25. Ibid., pp. 207–8.
26. *Tancred*, p. 191.
27. *Coningsby*, p. 403, noting preface to 1849 edition of *Coningsby*. 'In vindicating the sovereign right of the Church of Christ to be the perpetual regenerator of man, the writer thought the time had arrived when some attempt should be made to do justice to the race which had founded Christianity.'
28. *Tancred*, p. 122.
29. *Lord George Bentinck*, p. 364.
30. *Tancred*, pp. 167, 190, 426–27.
31. Ibid., p. 169.
32. Ibid., p. 188.
33. Ibid., pp. 168–70.
34. Ibid., p. 192.
35. Ibid., pp. 223–27.
36. Ibid., p. 427.
37. *Coningsby*, pp. 208–11.
38. *Tancred*, p. 428.
39. *Coningsby*, p. 174.
40. *Tancred*, p. 125.
41. *Coningsby*, p. 176.
42. *Lord George Bentinck*, p. 366.
43. *Lord George Bentinck*, pp. 346–50; *Coningsby*, pp. 402–3, noting preface to 1849 edn. of *Coningsby*.
44. *Coningsby*, pp. 402–3. In note C of the 1849 preface Disraeli amplifies his views.
45. *Lord George Bentinck*, p. 350.
46. *Tancred*, pp. 194–96.
47. H. J. Zimmels, *Ashkenazim and Sephardim*, p. 233.
48. B. Disraeli, *Sybil or The Two Nations*, 1880 edn., pp. 129–30.
49. W. F. Monypenny and G. E. Buckle, *The Life of Benjamin Disraeli, Earl of Beaconsfield*, I, p. 847. Disraeli was so consummate a master of presentation that one argument, central to his thesis, was not stressed—either in his public utterances or in his writings. This was his impatience with the Jews for not accepting Christianity. A scrappy and undated note, possibly of 1863, among the Hughenden Papers, reads as follows: 'I look upon the Church as the only Jewish institution remaining—I know no other. A vulgar error to consider circumcision one. . . . If it were not for the Church, I don't see why the Jews should be known. The Church was founded by Jews, and has been faithful to its origin. It secures their history and their literature being known to all? . . . publicly reads its history, and keeps alive the memory of its public characters, and has diffused its poetry throughout the world. The Jews owe everything to the Church, and are fools to oppose it. . . . The History of the Jews is developement or it is nothing. If ever a history were a history of developement, it is that of the Jews.' Hughenden Papers, Box 26: A/x/A/6.
50. *Lord George Bentinck*, pp. 358–63.
51. Ibid., p. 364.
52. *Tancred*, pp. 426–27; *Coningsby*, pp. 402–3, noting preface to 1849 edn. of *Coningsby*.
53. *Tancred*, p. 431.
54. *Coningsby*, pp. 94–100.
55. Ibid., p. 182.
56. Ibid., pp. 182–83.
57. H. Graetz, *Historic Parallels in Jewish History*, pp. 4–6.
58. Ibid., pp. 4–5.
59. *Coningsby*, pp. 94–100.
60. Ibid., p. 183.
61. *Tancred*, pp. 226–27.
62. L. Roth, *Judaism, a Portrait*, pp. 93–94.
63. H. Graetz, *Historic Parallels*, pp. 13–14.
64. The common points of agreement as between Disraeli and Crooll may be illustrated from H. Graetz, *Historic Parallels in Jewish History*, pp. 11–12, and are summarised below:
   i) Jews, as predestined, could establish and spread both the ideal of a purer knowledge of God and a higher morality;

ii) as a Messianic nation the Jews must 'carry light to the people';

iii) to do this it was necessary for the Jews to wander;

iv) the Talmud has expressed the deep symbolism of the fateful dispersion in the interpretation of the biblical verse: 'God has been good unto Israel in ordaining that he should be scattered through all the earth';

v) dispersion was a blessing, inasmuch as it was now impossible to destroy all Israel at one and the same time, but only separate members;

vi) because the wanderings of the Jews enabled them to fulfill their mission of enlightening the nations this constituted a further blessing in the development of their own world history.

Here is it important to observe that the term 'universal mission' as understood by Reform Jews denotes something very different from that discussed above in connection with either Disraeli or the Orthodox Jews.

65. L. Roth, *Judaism, A Portrait*, p. 94.
66. H. Graetz, *Historic Parallels*, pp. 7–12.
67. Ibid.
68. *Tancred*, p. 166.
69. Ibid., pp. 265–66.
70. *Sybil*, p. 63.
71. *Tancred*, p. 266.
72. *Lord George Bentinck*, pp. 363–64; *Tancred*, pp. 170–71.
73. *Lord George Bentinck*, pp. 355–56.
74. O. Levy: postscript to *Tancred*, Munich and Berlin, 1914 edn., pp. 506–10.
75. *Lord George Bentinck*, pp. 356–58.
76. *Coningsby*, p. 207.
77. *Lord George Bentinck*, p. 356.
78. *Tancred*, pp. 265–66.
79. *Coningsby*, pp. 207–8.
80. Ibid., pp. 206–7.
81. Ibid., pp. 207–8.
82. *Coningsby*, pp. 206–7.
83. *Lord George Bentinck*, pp. 356–58.
84. Ibid., pp. 355–56; *Coningsby*, p. 402, noting preface to 1849 edn. of *Coningsby*.
85. Ralph Waldo Emerson, *English Traits*, in *The Complete Essays and Other Writings of Ralph Waldo Emerson*, ed. Brooks Atkinson, p. 660.
86. *Tancred*, p. 421.
87. Ibid.; *Coningsby*, p. 402, noting preface to 1849 edn. of *Coningsby*.
88. I. Zangwill, *Dreamers of the Ghetto*, p. 386.

6
David Salomons's Emancipated Jewishness

With David Salomons we come to the most enterprising figure to be found among the mid-nineteenth-century Anglo-Jewish leadership. Surveying the emancipation of the Jews in those parts of Europe where there existed an active Reform Movement, enthusiasm for the acquisition of civil and political rights invariably appears to accompany a corresponding enthusiasm for Reform. In Britain no such correlation is evident. Emancipation was primarily the achievement not of a Goldsmid or a Montefiore but of one who personified the community as a whole and more particularly its younger half; the political demands of Protestant Dissenters and Roman Catholics having been conceded when David Salomons was little over thirty he belonged to a generation which viewed Emancipation as a right and not merely as a privilege.

Salomons was held in high esteem by all sections of Anglo-Jewry: his membership of the Orthodox community, his inexhaustible patience even in the face of setbacks and his willingness to compromise were all vital factors which explain why he continuously enjoyed the confidence of both the Montefiore 'establishment' and the Reform Movement—if on occasion serious disagreements did occur they were always settled within a relatively short period.

Although Salomons was as militant as the Goldsmids he did not join them in 1828 at the outset of the campaign in demanding the immediate remission of all disabilities. Nor was he at that time established as a fighter for Emancipation; his reputation was forged in the mid-1830s with the first of the campaigns to remove municipal disabilities in the City of London. Salomons's individual position within the community did not therefore become apparent until November 1838 when, after only a few weeks' tenure of the Presidency of the Board of Deputies (an incumbency brought about by one of Montefiore's temporary absences abroad), he resigned from that office. Very probably he was embarrassed by the effusive praise heaped on him by I. L. Goldsmid's letter of September 1838, which had subsequently been passed on to the Board, and was further deterred from remaining as President in view of the invitation now extended to the Goldsmids to confer with the Deputies—a meeting which would have cast Salomons in the unnaturally pontifical role of having to critically examine the case of those

115

who shared his militant position on Emancipation.[1] In December 1839 Salomons went further and actually resigned from the Board itself; although the incident which brought about this resignation belongs to another chapter in the story of Emancipation, relating as it does to a disagreement over the tactics adopted by Salomons in pursuit of his campaign strategy, his return to the fold at the time of the Damascus crisis symbolized the closing of ranks.

Then came the Reform split and a clear demonstration of how Salomons, absolutely committed to the achievement of political Emancipation and therefore to the maintenance of the unity of the community without which he believed that goal would not be attained, refused to align himself with one or other of the warring factions; rather, in combining zealous enthusiasm for Emancipation with religious orthodoxy and even more particularly, in having earlier attempted to placate the reformers at the Orthodox New Synagogue to which he belonged by advocating some alterations and improvements in the conduct of the services, Salomons considered himself ideally suited to heal the rift between the conservatives and the reformers. In the early months of 1841 the Board issued a number of warnings against the establishment of a new synagogue and at the second full meeting of the 1841 session the members were asked to ponder an urgent letter from the Chief Rabbi and from Dr. Meldola, Rabbi of Bevis Marks. This deprecated the threatened establishment of a dissenting congregation which intended 'to depart from the Laws, Statutes and Observances which our fathers bequeathed to us' and strongly urged the Board to take measures of defence and resistance lest ensuing disunity encourage the development of subdivisions with their weakening influence. Two of the Deputies, Louis Lucas and H. H. Cohen, consequently proposed a motion which declared

> that it is with feelings of profound regret that this Board learns that any persons professing the Jewish Religion should be capable of endeavouring to undermine the sacred principles of our Faith by attempting to introduce innovations inconsistent with the Laws and Customs which have been in practice for so many centuries and that this Board does solemnly protest against any authority assumed for such purpose.

The eirenic Salomons, realizing that this censure was so blunt and uncompromising as to be scarcely capable of healing the breach it condemned, now recorded his opposition to such an organization as the Deputies presuming themselves justified in championing the Montefiore concept of a corporate Jewish community comprehended or defined by one rabbinic authority. He devised an amendment which, while as firm in its upholding of Orthodoxy and as reproving in its criticism of Reform, managed to adopt a conciliatory and understanding approach towards those who had felt compelled to set up a new congregation. The motion proposed by Salomons, and seconded by Hyam Hyams, read that this Board has received with the utmost reverence and respect the communication addressed to it by the Reverend Solomon Hirschell and the Reverend David Meldola, the Spiritual heads of the Jewish community, from which it learns with feelings of the deepest regret that individuals should be found associating together to form a distinct congregation not under the sanction of the Ecclesiastical authorities, and in contravention of the Laws and customs of the Jews, observed for so many centuries, and that the Board deprecates and deplores a course of conduct so vitally injurious to the welfare of the Jewish People, and earnestly prays that the persons so associated will abandon such course which must be destructive of that unity so essential to the happiness and security of the Jews in this kingdom: and this Board is prepared to lend its best assistance to any attempt that may be made to conciliate every individual of the community.

Salomons's amendment was, however, defeated by thirteen votes to six and, with one more member of the Board voting, the original motion of Lucas was adopted by thirteen votes to seven.[2]

It was not long before the crisis engendered by the Reform split assumed an added dimension; with the establishment of the West London Reform congregation there naturally followed a request from members for certification of their minister, David Woolf Marks, as a fit person to perform the celebration of marriages. According to the legislation of 1836 celebration of marriages without such prior certification by the Board of Deputies would have been deemed legally invalid; the Deputies, taking advantage of this exceptional measure of autonomous power conferred upon them by the marriage legislation, argued that the place of worship in question could not be considered a synagogue. Here the Board seemed to be spurning one of the most important of the responsibilities which had lain behind its foundation as a Jewish lay organization corresponding to the Protestant Dissenting Deputies, and the acceptance of which responsibility was implicit in its statutory recognition: that of presenting to the Government for consideration the grievances of any aggrieved individuals or groups within the community. The Board chose instead to act characteristically at the instance of the rabbinical authorities in refusing certification and this refusal was, of course, considered justified by counsel's opinion.

Salomons was one of the small minority opposing this action. Furious with the Deputies for abusing their authority as impartial representatives and for operating a double standard, on the one hand asking their fellow countrymen to emancipate them politically while simultaneously betraying in matters involving their own internal affairs an establishmentarian intolerance of nonconformists, he gave notice of a resolution in which he particularly berated the leaders of the community for attempting to repress their own deviants with the selfsame legislative instrument fashioned originally to protect as non-Anglican dissenters all groups of Jews. Salomons pointed out

that the privileges granted to the Jews by Parliament of appointing the

Secretary of a Synagogue as a Registrar of Marriages of persons professing the Jewish Religion was an act of grace and favour conferred upon
them, to enable them to register their marriages in a manner most in
accordance with their own peculiar customs and usages. That to withhold
this privilege from a congregation of persons professing the Jewish religion
in consequence of their alleged nonconformity is an endeavour to maintain
ecclesiastical discipline by the aid, and through the operation of the
Marriage and Registration Acts, the object of those Acts being to extend
and not to restrict religious liberty.[3]

As a consequence of proscription any adherent of the Reform congregation wishing to become a Member of the Board of Deputies would have
found it necessary to persuade an Orthodox congregation that he was a fit
person to represent their interests. November and December 1853 found the
Deputies preoccupied in discussing the question of such representation;
when a decision was called for as to whether members of the Reform
synagogue who represented Orthodox congregations should be eligible for
election to the Board the votes of the Deputies were found to be evenly
divided, twenty-three votes being cast for and against the motion. Salomons
was emphatically in favour of cooperation with the new community, arguing
that no religious test was justified so long as the candidates were Jews by
religion, no matter of what complexion. Sir Moses Montefiore, as President
of the Board and chairman of the meeting, then deployed his casting vote to
defeat the proposal, whereupon Salomons resigned as representative of the
New Synagogue.[4] According to family tradition the particular reasons for
the resignation lay not only in what Salomons considered to be the irregular
voting action of Montefiore but also his overbearing attitude:[5] this charge of
autocratic self-importance serves as a reminder of the extent to which
personal factors exacerbated the divisions in the community. In his letter of
resignation Salomons advocated complete reconciliation with the Reform
community, going further than simply advocating that Reformers be allowed
to represent other congregations but boldly claiming that the Reform community was entitled in its own right to representation on the Board. The New
Synagogue implored Salomons not to resign, informing him that should he
persist in his decision he would be unanimously reelected: when Salomons
felt unable to heed the appeal the New Synagogue carried out its declared
intention. It was, of course, indicative of Salomons's stature in the community that his continued presence on the Board should have been required for
providing a counterweight to the autocratic figure of Montefiore, but the
whole episode, culminating with this reelection, represented something
more. Salomons's views on communal affairs were now widely shared: the
New Synagogue made known to the Board its sympathy with him, declaring
in a resolution that although the congregation promised always to submit to
ecclesiastical authority in religious affairs the refusal of lay Deputies to allow
Reformers to sit on the Board was to be deplored.[6]

Victory in this respect was soon assured. Ever since the Marriage Act of 1836 the Board had claimed to be the sole official representative body of Anglo-Jewry; now, twenty years later, the Government was intending to introduce a Dissenters' Marriage Bill which contained a clause whereby any twenty householders might be enabled to certify the appointment of a Marriage Secretary. As the effect of such a clause would have been to blunt the Board's statutory powers, by eliminating its effective supervision of marriage registration, it is not surprising that a later chronicler of the Board should have pointed an accusing finger at the West London Synagogue.[7] Whether or not such suspicion was justified remains uncertain, since the measure applied to other non-Anglicans. Anyway, the Chief Rabbi and the Board felt impelled to protest to the Government, whereupon it was agreed that the new clause should apply only to the West London Reform Synagogue and not to the provincial Reform congregations. How should the compromise be interpreted? Any concession, however slight, was in reality gall and wormwood to those such as Montefiore; by the same token the measure represented a limited victory for the Reformers. But this is to view the issue purely as an aspect of the struggle between Orthodox and Reform; the very achievement of a compromise represented a great victory for Salomons. It afforded evidence of the degree to which Anglo-Jewry was now committed to maintaining that communal unity which was widely acknowledged—in Parliament and out—to be a precondition of Emancipation; it was a sign that the Board was now reverting to its originally conceived role as an impartial, independent lay body entrusted with the task of acting as intermediary between all sections of the community and the Government; it vindicated Salomons's long-held conviction that the Reformers within the Jewish community bore the same relationship to the traditional body of Jewry as Protestant Dissenters enjoyed in relation to the Anglican establishment; finally, it seemed to hint that emancipation for Reform Jews was so manifestly a microcosm of the struggle for political Emancipation as to be almost a harbinger of it.

Salomons probably perceived more acutely than Montefiore the attitudes expected of the Jewish community by its friends in English public life—here another aspect of marriage law provides an instance. In 1857 the Government, wishing to overhaul all such legislation as the Marriage Act of 1835, the Lyndhurst measure which had arguably brought the Jews within the scope of English law, carefully considered inserting a clause in the Matrimonial Causes Bill which would have exempted Jewish marriages from dissolution by the civil Divorce Court first set up by the 1835 act. One authority has seen the inclusion and subsequent abandonment of the clause in successive drafts of the bill as representing a victory for Salomons and Lionel Rothschild over the Chief Rabbi and the Board of Deputies.[8] Adler and the Deputies, though appreciative of the advantages of Continental forms of autonomy in matters of religious law, were indeed reluctant to embarrass the leading protagonists of Emancipation by promoting at such a delicate stage of the campaign any measures which might enhance or confirm the special status of the Jews; Salomons, convinced that Jewish marriage law should resemble English marriage law as nearly as Jewish religious requirements might permit, believed that conditions were ripe for the entire abrogation of the rabbinic power of divorce in England.

In this Salomons was conspicuously a man of his time. While Jewish Emancipation in its strictly political context was all too obviously the protracted sequel of the earlier struggles between the competing claims of Anglicanism and Dissent, such questions germane to that Emancipation as, for example, the aforementioned reform of marriage law or the preferred type of school for the education of Jewish children seem rather to belong to a phase characterized by a struggle as between doctrinal and undenominational concepts of national life.

On the Reform issue Salomons had repeatedly demonstrated his annoyance with the rabbis for assuming Draconian powers of coercion in matters which he considered to fall largely within the jurisdiction of laymen. Then, in the early 1850s, some members of the Board of Deputies chose to defy the rabbinical 'diktat' on an issue not related to Reform. In the belief that Jewish schools dependent upon the receipt of grants from the Government should not be subject to rabbinical control this group sought to remove from a Model Deed, drafted by the Board in 1852, a provision whereby the Chief Rabbi and his Sephardi counterpart would exercise in such schools an exclusive jurisdiction over religious instruction.[9] Although the result of subsequent deliberations was a compromise the episode was important for revealing that in Aaron Asher Goldsmid and his small group of collaborators on the Board there existed the Jewish counterparts of such Erastians as Peel and Russell: the animosity the rabbinic authorities may have harboured toward the Jewish advocates of an undenominational system was a reflection of the resentment borne by some of the Protestant Dissenters, adherents of the Voluntary principle of privately-financed sectarian schooling, towards Russell for having attempted to advance the cause of a universal state-financed system of education based upon denominational equality under the aegis of a preponderantly Church establishment—a resentment which, in the 1847 general election in the City of London, had at one stage threatened to unseat Russell as Prime Minister.[10]

But Erastian as these critics of the Board may have been, their radicalism could not compare with that of Salomons. He had long since evinced a preference for a type of education for Jews which precluded the least measure of rabbinical influence and had, for many years past, favoured the City of London School with generous financial gifts. In the autumn of 1845, to celebrate the legislation of that year outlawing municipal disabilities, he had donated a scholarship, to the value of fifty pounds a year, to be awarded annually for the purpose of maintaining a former pupil of the school who had entered one of the English universities. The endowment of the scholarship was a remarkably unsectarian gesture and the 'Resolution of Thanks' from the Court of Common Council, whilst expressing gratitude for the actual sum of the annual scholarships, went further in recording appreciation 'more especially on account of the truly liberal and philanthropic spirit in which Mr. Salomons has expressed his desire, that the advantages to be derived from his generosity shall be available to members of every religious persuasion.'[11] The inclusion, moreover, of Oxford and Cambridge within the provisions of the bequest was a selfless gesture in itself, as Jews were still unable to take degrees at either of the two universities.

Given Salomons's preference for the City of London School and similar establishments it was not surprising that he should have dissociated himself from the Chief Rabbi's scheme for a Jews' College which would be devoted both to the educational training of ministers and to providing an education for the lay majority. Adler envisaged that while Jews' College would emulate the standards of the best gentile schools in respect of secular content it would resist the incursion of those studies into that part of the timetable formerly reserved for Hebrew and biblical education. In February 1852 Salomons informed the Chief Rabbi that he wholly disapproved of the proposed day school as 'unadvisable' and 'unnecessary'; in reluctantly proferring a financial donation to Adler he stipulated that this should remain distinct from the funds of the *Beth Hamedrash*, the institution for Hebraic and Talmudic studies, and should be used solely for the educational training of ministers.[12]

The ability of Salomons to free himself from that exclusiveness to which any minority is prone was coming to be demonstrated so clearly as to disarm those opponents of Emancipation who struggled to maintain that the Jews' allegedly excessive resolution 'not to give up the smallest part of . . . religious forms and privileges to obtain civil rights'[13] negated the validity of their political claims.

As for his fellow Jews Salomons had long since come to command great respect. On the Board of Deputies this was attested as early as October 1838 when, on the occasion of one of Montefiore's missions abroad, he had been unanimously elected to fill the temporary Presidential vacancy.[14] And his resignations from the Board of 1839 and 1853 were both very short-lived: on the former occasion he voluntarily returned to the Board, while on the latter he was unanimously reelected. To the Jewish community as a whole Salomons was coming to represent progressive orthodoxy, for he combined respect for Orthodox Judaic teaching with a sensitivity to the demands of the age and the country to which he belonged. And his altruism was self-evident because the particular conception of tolerance which he embodied and which he believed should serve to unite Anglo-Jewry seemed ever to be promoting his personal strategy for the achievement of political Emancipation.

NOTES

1. Minute Books of the Board of Deputies, III, pp. 30–45, 13 November 1838.
2. Ibid., V, pp. 16–23, 20 May 1841.
3. Ibid., February–May 1842 for controversy on the marriage question.
4. Ibid., VII, pp. 232–35, 7 December 1853, pp. 238–39, 5 January 1854; cf. in connection with the controversies of 1853, I. Finestein, 'The Anglo-Jewish Revolt of 1853', *The Jewish Quarterly*, XXVI, 3–4 (97/98), autumn–winter 1978–79, pp. 103–13.
5. A. M. Hyamson, *David Salomons*, pp. 43–44.
6. Minute Books of the Board of Deputies, VII, pp. 239–49, 18 January 1854.
7. C. H. L. Emanuel, *A Century and a Half of Jewish History*, p. 69.
8. I. Finestein, 'Anglo-Jewry and the Law of Divorce', *The Jewish Chronicle*, 19 April 1957, p. 11; I. Finestein, 'An Aspect of the Jews and English Marriage Law during the Emancipation: The Prohibited Degrees', *The Jewish Journal of Sociology*, vol. VII, no. 1, June 1965, pp. 3–21. See also the statutory and legislative references given above, in chap. 2, 'The Legal and Juridical Position of Mid-Nineteenth-Century Anglo-Jewry'.
9. Minute Books of the Board of Deputies, VII, pp. 48–56, 79–99, 105–7, 111–16, 127–30.
10. For the complexities of the triangular debate between Erastians, Voluntarists and Churchmen during these years, the context in which developments within Anglo-Jewry should be placed, cf. for an introduction, G. F. A. Best, 'The Religious Difficulties of National Education in England, 1800–1870', *The Cambridge Historical Journal*, vol. XII, 1956, no. 2, pp. 155–73; O. J. Brose, *Church and Parliament. The Reshaping of the Church of England, 1828–1860*, particularly pp. 94, 181–83; G. I. T. Machin, *Politics and the Churches in Great Britain, 1832 to 1868*, passim.
11. David Salomons House, Broomhill, wall certificate no. 13, 5 November 1845.
12. A. M. Hyamson, *Jews' College, London, 1855–1955* pp. 21–22.
13. L. Loewe (ed.), *The Diaries of Sir Moses and Lady Montefiore*, I, p. 111. Cit. supra, this being of course the statement made earlier by Montefiore.
14. Minute Books of the Board of Deputies, III, pp. 23–30, 30 October, 1838.

7
David Salomons's Emancipation Strategy

If—to adapt a simile of Montefiore's—the *Salomons* frame of mind was one which might seem conducive to Emancipation falling into the Jews' laps *like ripe fruit,* (readers, please excuse my teasing of Montefiore), the answer to the pivotal question of Emancipation took longer to discern: what choice of strategy could be seen to lie behind the Jews' pursuit of their aims?

Would the Jews emulate, for example, Daniel O'Connell? For O'Connell, on the morrow of that Emancipatory legislation making valid his election to Parliament, had despatched a letter to I. L. Goldsmid outspoken in its advocacy of militancy. 'I am much obliged to you for your kind congratulations on the event of the Clare election,' wrote O'Connell.

Ireland has claims on your ancient race, as it is the only Christian country that I know of unsullied by any one act of persecution of the Jews—I entirely agree with you on the principle of freedom of conscience, and no man can admit that sacred principle without extending it equally to the Jew as to the Christian. . . . I have not ability to offer you, but I have zeal and activity. Allow me at once to commence my office of your advocate, and to begin by giving you advice. It is: Not to postpone your claim of right beyond the second day of the ensuing session. Do not listen to those over-cautious persons who may recommend postponement. Believe an agitator of some experience that nothing was ever obtained by delay—at least in politics. You must to a certain extent force your claims on the Parliament. You cannot be worse, recollect, even by a failure, and you ought to be better by the experiment. As far as you and your friends may entrust the measure to me, I will bring it forward in twenty different shapes if necessary to advance its success. . . . Confided or not confided in, my course will be the same, that is, I will, on every *practical* occasion, struggle to extend the full effect and operation of the principle of freedom of conscience to all your people. . . . You must, I repeat, *force* your question on the Parliament. You ought not to confide in English liberality. It is a plant not genial to the British soil. It must be *forced.* It requires a *hot-bed.* The English were always persecutors. Before the so-styled Reformation the English tortured the Jews and strung up in scores the Lollards. After that Reformation they still roasted the Jews and hung the Papists. In Mary's days the English with their usual cruelty retaliated the tortures on the Protestants. After her short reign there were near two centuries of the most barbarous and unrelenting cruelty exercised towards the Catholics, a cruelty the more emaciating because it was sought to be justified by imputing to them tenets and opinions which they always rejected and abhorred. The Jews too suffered in the same way. I once more repeat, Do not confide in any liberality but that which you will yourself rouse into action and *compel* into operation—After all you are the best judges of your own affairs, and if you deem my advice unwise, you will not the less receive every assistance from me in my poor power.[1]

On reflection the Jews might deem O'Connell's advice unwise. His campaign for Emancipation and Repeal had been conducted on behalf of several million people, the threat of whose force would have been ignored by a British Government at its own peril. The number of Jews in Britain, rising imperceptibly from a mere 27,000 in 1828 to a total of 40,000 in 1860, were never in a position to threaten a recalcitrant legislature. In his capacity as President of the Jewish Association for Obtaining Civil Rights and Privileges, the campaigning organization based on the City of London with the Rothschilds among its patrons, I. L. Goldsmid was rather more certain to appreciate the prudence of Lord Holland who counselled the members of the organization that they 'should so conduct themselves as to show that their exclusion was a really practical grievance. . . . Make yourselves . . . beloved by, and useful to, your fellow countrymen in your counties and in cities, and when they shall elect you to be their representatives or magistrates, and the law will not allow you to take office, it will be a practical grievance on them as well as on you, and must be amended.'[2]

One of the incidental merits of Holland's strategy was to turn the question of numbers from a disadvantage to an advantage. Fewness of numbers could come to be a precondition of that integration without which Emancipation was inconceivable. While many Jews or their forebears had come from lands where their co-religionists comprised 10 per cent or upwards of the population, in Britain throughout the period from 1828 to 1860 the proportion of Jews to non-Jews remained constant at 0.2 per cent, rendering correspondingly more soluble the problems of absorption. Estimates even for London, which contained the largest absolute and relative concentration of Jews, suggest that never at any time during this same period did the Jewish percentage of the population rise above approximately 1 per cent: while in the years between 1821 and 1861 the capital's total population increased from 1,600,000 to 3,227,000, during the almost overlapping period of the Emancipation campaign from 1828 to 1860 the number of Jews in London increased from between perhaps 15,000 and 18,000 to between 25,000 and 30,000.

The wisdom of Holland's advocacy, of eschewing an ideological approach in favour of an empirical one based upon a shrewd appraisal of the factors most likely to enhance the appeal of the case for Jewish Emancipation, was almost certain to commend itself more favourably to David Salomons than to the Goldsmids. A pragmatic approach was compatible with the argument that the Jews were fighting for nothing more than admission to a legislature each one of whose members could subscribe to a generalised religious outlook; an ideological approach would *ipso facto* polarise into doctrinal blocs those whose initial feelings upon the matter had predisposed them to view the matter with anything other than concern.

But lest the aforegoing chapter might seem to suggest that Salomons was a placid figure, conciliatory and eirenic to the last, it is important to recall that the issues which required such an approach were precisely those which had arisen in connection with the intra-Jewish debate on Emancipation; there was nothing to suggest that Salomons could not be pugnacious when confronted with genuine opposition or uncompromising in meeting what he deemed to be implacable hostility. Indeed, already by February 1835 he was to be found concluding a pamphlet with the promise of a militant campaign: 'Conscious of the Justice of their Cause, the Jews of England can never cease pressing it on the Legislature, until they are placed on a parity with those of their Fellow-citizens, whose tenets also differ from the doctrines of the Established Church.'[3]

Such a choice of parallel at this particular time was of significance: Salomons himself was about to draw upon the precedents set in the previous year by John Illidge, a Protestant Dissenter, and Alexander Raphael, a Roman Catholic, in having themselves elected as the two Sheriffs for London and Middlesex for the year 1834–35. Insofar as their joint election had drawn attention to the triumphs of 1828 and 1829, so too would Salomons's own candidature to succeed them as one of the two Sheriffs now draw attention to the Jewish cause. Yet here the importance of his campaign lay less in the fact that it attracted the backing of such City radicals as William Thornborrow, Charles Pearson, Sir George Carroll, David Wire and the Quaker banker Samuel Gurney, and was to result in the success of procuring the unanimous electoral support of the City Livery; of greater consequence was the removal of an obstacle which the very fact of such success entailed, an obstacle of precisely the type referred to by Lord Holland in his letter of counsel to I. L. Goldsmid. The act 5 & 6 Will IV, c. 28 of August 1835, in abolishing the requirement that an elected Sheriff subscribe a declaration containing the words 'upon the true faith of a Christian', as prescribed by the act 9 Geo IV, c. 17, rectified the exceptional anomaly whereby Jews had been barred from the City Shrievalty whilst finding themselves eligible, on account of the workings of the Indemnity Acts, to assume the County Shrievalties (and thus in theory, Middlesex, had it not been linked to the City).

Salomons's creditable performance in office reflected well on the Jewish community. On 29 September 1836 the Common Hall, a General Meeting of the citizens, passed a resolution thanking John Lainson and David Salomons for their performance during their year of office. The testimonial followed the conventional pattern in praising the two Sheriffs but departed from it when recording particular appreciation of the action taken by Salomons to improve the accommodation and conditions of the City prisons. 'This Common Hall think it right to advert to the fact that one of them [the Sheriffs] David Salomons is the first gentleman of the Jewish persuasion who has served any office of trust and honour in this City . . . and this Common Hall congratulate their fellow-citizens upon having selected a gentleman whose highly meritorious conduct both in and out of office, has obtained for him golden opinions from men of every creed and party, and this Common Hall earnestly hope that the advancement of this worthy individual will be but the precursor to the entire removal of the Jewish disabilities. . . .'[4]

The measure of Salomons's breakthrough was in the first instance felt most keenly by the Anglo-Jewish leadership. Had Salomons not set a precedent on almost every conceivable occasion it is possible that Montefiore would never have held any important civic office. Early in 1837 Montefiore was presented with the opportunity of becoming one of the two Sheriffs for London and Middlesex; instead, however, of taking heart from the assurances of support which came from some of the most influential members of the City of London he began to prevaricate and to cavil at the prospect. If actually elected he wished to retain his freedom as to whether or not he would feel able to accept the office; although having no objection to sending his money Montefiore stressed the impossibility of attending church and how at all City feasts he must be allowed to have his own meat and dishes in conformity with the Orthodox dietary requirements. On being told that to all these reservations there could be no possible objection Montefiore took a resigned line; apparently he believed that ultimately he would not be conscripted to stand. And when this supposition about his candidacy was proved wrong he even thought of declining the Shrievalty on grounds of health. He brooded on the difficulties appertaining to the fulfilment of official duties, noting for example that the very first day of his term coincided with the date of the New Year: not only, therefore, must he walk to Westminster instead of travelling in the Sheriff's carriage, he must also endeavour to persuade his colleagues to advance by a few days the timing of the inauguration dinner which 'from time immemorial' had been given on the last day of September.[5]

Montefiore did serve a term as Sheriff for the year 1837–38. Nonetheless even though in the case of the London Shrievalty an obstacle had been most demonstrably overcome, Salomons had not forgotten that the winning of office was almost as important as performance in office. Here O'Connell's example of making as great a nuisance of himself as possible cannot have failed to have impressed, even if it was not realistic to attempt to force the claims of the Jews in like manner as O'Connell had forced the claims of the Catholics. Salomons knew that he had to mask his militancy and seek a nice balance, keeping the grievances of the Jews in the forefront of public attention without at the same time alienating the ever-more tolerant sympathies of those very people whom he wished to conciliate. For municipal office was now open to Jews in most places, mainly owing to the circumstance that the restrictive declaration containing the words 'upon the true faith of a Christian' as enacted by 9 Geo IV, c. 17, was not usually enforced by returning officers. This climate of languid tolerance, of which the Jews were now as favoured a group of beneficiaries as the Protestant Dissenters had once been during the century of Indemnity Acts, was appreciated by Salomons. In 1835 he observed that from their 'benignant' fellow countrymen Jews received kindness and forbearance 'and are by them permitted to exercise many privileges which the strict application of disqualifying Statutes would not allow.'[6] And in the debate on the Municipal Officers' Declaration Bill of December 1837 O'Connell commented on the flexibility of English law which had made possible such an apparently extraordinary situation according to which Jews could hold certain municipal offices by 'a sort of trick and dexterity of law.'[7]

Indeed, before an almost *de facto* recognition of the Jews' right to hold municipal office gave way to a *de jure* recognition in 1845, most of the remaining pockets of discrimination were seen to exist only in some of the City Aldermanries. Here Salomons's general strategy was one of attrition in wearing down the resistance of opponents; his usual tactics were to present himself as a candidate for an office for which he was clearly ineligible, to comb the relevant legislation which excluded him from that office for vague and faulty drafting, and then either to fight his case before the body to which he hoped to be admitted or alternatively to proceed to litigation. Many years later, after his by-election victory at Greenwich in 1851, Salomons attempted to use at the parliamentary level the methods he had earlier tried out at the municipal level.

In the last two months of 1835 Salomons as a Cooper—and now moreover as one of the Sheriffs—was elected an alderman for the ward of Aldgate, polling 75 votes as against 68 votes and 67 votes respectively for his two opponents. The election was then declared void because of Salomons's refusal to subscribe to 9 Geo IV, c. 17. Two protests were lodged, one by certain electors of the Aldgate ward and one by Salomons himself, both of which were communicated to the Court of Aldermen at a meeting on 17 December. In his own letter Salomons stated that he would not admit the legality of any new election; he was still the Alderman and any election of another person would be void. He gave notice that he would take further his protest against the decision of the Court of Aldermen and would contest their ruling. The other letter, from fifty-nine petitioners of the ward, remonstrated that the ruling on the election constituted an 'illegal assumption of authority by the Court of Aldermen tending to make your Petitioners' right of electing an Alderman a mere farce'. The petitioners further protested against the seating of one who had actually come third in the wardmote election with 67 votes, alleging that the candidate in question, John Humphery, was on account of his trade unworthy of the office. Yet another complaint by the petitioners, a claim that insufficient notice had been given of the intention to elect Humphery in Salomons's place, was also rejected; the Court of Aldermen declared Humphery duly elected.[8]

Litigation was then undertaken by Salomons. That the case should drag on for almost the next four years was partly to be explained by the fate which, towards the end of 1837, befell an amendment to the Municipal Officers' Bill, introduced into the Commons by Edward Baines, one of the two Members for Leeds. This bill, though altering that declaration of 9 Geo IV, c. 17, containing the words 'upon the true faith of a Christian' which was supposed always to be taken by persons entering upon admission to civil offices, had been expressly devised for the singular purpose of relieving Quakers and Moravians of the scruples which these sects entertained in respect of oath-swearing.

The Jews considered that they too ought to benefit from such legislation. On 29 November Salomons was co-opted to serve on a sub-committee of the Board of Deputies which had been delegated the task of scrutinizing the bill; at the end of a long day, consisting of two wearying sessions, the Deputies resolved to persuade Baines to include the Jews.[9] Then, on 30 November, as the Municipal Officers' Bill was about to be given a second reading, George Grote, the historian of Greece and at this time a radical Member for the City of London, quite suddenly gave notice of his intention to move an amendment which, by extending relief from the obligation of taking an oath to persons of all religious persuasions, would have achieved precisely the same effect as the amendment proposed by the Deputies; on the same day Salomons was to be found petitioning the Common Council of the City of London in what proved to be a successful effort to persuade its Court to adopt unanimously a motion in line with Grote's amendment.[10]

The Commons' debate of 4 December, with the bill at the committee stage, was to leave no doubt as to the impropriety of the Salomons-Grote tactic; Disraeli articulated the opinion of the majority when he dubbed the debate 'the Jew question by a sidewind'. Baines feared that the device of tacking on the Jews would jeopardize the measure; Lord Melbourne as Prime Minister, the Marquis of Lansdowne as Lord President of the Council and Lord John Russell as Home Secretary and Leader of the House had already intimated to the Jews the inadvisability of such amendment to the bill as would have to surmount the hurdle of the Lords; now Russell was seen openly to concur in Baines's opinion. Grote's amendment was rejected by 172 votes to 156, a majority of 16; the postscript to the episode, in the form of a last minute amendment to the measure (1 & 2 Vict, c. 5 and c. 15) which included Separatists within its scope, was however of interest for leaving the Jews as the only religious group still liable to disabilities.[11]

So no legislation intervened to render unnecessary the litigation arising from Salomons's refusal to subscribe 9 Geo IV, c. 17. First to pronounce Judgment, in May 1838, was the Court of Queen's Bench. The judges here, holding the opinion that Salomons should have been admitted to office prior to the tendering of the oath and that the Court of Aldermen had consequently acted prematurely in declaring his election void, gave a decision against Humphery. The aggrieved party then applied for a writ of error, which in June 1839 came on before the judges of the Court of Exchequer Chamber; there, by seven votes to four, the Judgment of the Court of Queen's Bench was itself overruled and Humphery was declared duly seated. Salomons believed that in the event of his appealing to the House of Lords such eminent figures as Brougham, the former Whig Lord Chancellor and Cottenham, the present Whig occupant of the Woolsack, might prove disposed to view his claims with sympathy; insofar as there existed a snag this concerned defrayal of the additional expenses which such appeal would incur. And so began that wrangle with the Deputies which was to culminate in the first of Salomons's two open breaches with his colleagues. He addressed the Board as the body professing to take charge of public questions of importance; the Deputies' reply, to the effect that it would be more expedient to obtain the required relief by direct legislation rather than by appeal to the Lords against the Court of Exchequer Chamber decision, led to Salomons's resignation later that year.[12]

During 1840 little pressure was exerted on the Government to introduce legislation in respect of municipal offices, the members of the Board of Deputies being more concerned with the fate of the Jews in Damascus and the East than with domestic problems. Salomons, however, remained restless and it was at his instigation that in February 1841 Edward Divett, one of the two Members of Parliament for Exeter, introduced a bill into the Commons which would have unreservedly exempted those Jews elected to municipal office from any requirement to take the prescribed oaths. If it might almost have been expected that the Jewish Board of Deputies would present a petition to both Houses, confirmation of the extent to which those represented by the Protestant Dissenting Deputies considered their religiosity to be derived no less from Old Testament precepts of morality was afforded by the wording of a petition which contended that 'to exclude from civil offices believers in the Laws of Moses is to condemn those Laws as making men bad Citizens'. The House of Commons was now prepared to accept, by majorities of 113 and 77, the measure introduced 'by a sidewind' four years earlier, but there were still important figures such as Gladstone among the small band of almost three dozen opponents. The division at the end of the second reading debate in the Lords, with 48 votes in favour of Divett's bill and 47 votes against, raised hopes among some Jews that they might now achieve the immediate objective of seeing municipal disabilities outlawed. On the contrary, this one vote margin caused opponents to rally. They knew of those disagreements racking the Jewish community as to the tactics, the strategy and even the principle of Emancipation, and could exploit them by arguing that as the Jews were not in agreement themselves about what they were demanding and until such time as they were, it would be impossible to contemplate further action by Parliament. On the third reading in the Lords Divett's measure was decisively defeated by 98 votes to 64, a majority of 34.[13]

The passions roused by the campaigns of Salomons were now to impinge upon the electoral fate of one most closely identified with his cause. For the Whigs the session of 1840–41 was one marked by a series of by-election defeats and voting setbacks in the House of Commons; as these culminated on 4 June 1841 in a one-vote defeat for the Ministry in a no-confidence debate Melbourne was led to seek a dissolution. Whereupon Lord John Russell pledged the Whigs to support 'the great cause of civil and religious freedom' as inspired by 'the principles of Mr. Fox'.[14] Russell's known support for the Jewish cause made his candidature in the City of London constituency especially controversial, and some of his opponents believed that in the Jewish question they had found the issue whereby they could terminate his political career. A campaigning ditty, entitled *A New Song to an Old Tune*, reminded the electorate of Russell's supposedly carpet-bagging parliamentary career, involving past campaigns for Tavistock, Huntingdon, Bandon-bridge, Devon and Stroud. The twelfth and last verse combined an attack on Russell's support for the Jews with a sneer at his diminutive figure:

> From Parliament,
> They have you sent,
> As sorely you'll remember;
> We won't have you,
> You little Jew,
> You *homoeopathic member*.[15]

To counter such propaganda I. L. Goldsmid despatched an address to the Jewish electors of the constituency. He argued that the election of Russell would evince gratitude for his past services, for his support for the removal of all municipal disabilities and for the even earlier encouragement which, as a minister, he had offered to the scheme for the establishment of the University of London. And he concluded on a characteristic note. Emancipation would 'enable us [the Jews] to devote our energies, free and unfettered, to the advancement of the welfare of our native land.'[16] In the event Russell had every reason to be grateful to Goldsmid and his supporters: when the poll was declared on the afternoon of 30 June Russell emerged as the last in the list of the successful two Tories and two Whigs who had been elected for the City, having polled 6,221 votes as against 6,212 for the third Tory candidate in fifth place. Russell had gambled somewhat in staking his career on being elected for the City, for a defeat could have proven disastrous. It certainly cannot be conclusively argued that the Jewish question was responsible for having reduced Russell's potential majority to only nine votes; the two Whig candidates who had been defeated were not particularly associated with support for the Jewish cause, and thus for Russell personally the election result may have been the best obtainable in the general political circumstances of 1841.

In a sense the election result of 1841, with the return of a Tory Government, drew to a close the first phase in the campaign to remove Jewish political disabilities. Success, now more than ever, was to depend almost exclusively on what the Jews could achieve by themselves, rather than on what could be achieved for them by a reforming majority in Parliament. For two years there was a respite in the campaigning; then, from November 1843 until his grievances were remedied in July 1845, Salomons was responsible for conducting almost single-handed the campaign for the remission of all municipal disabilities.

Two important letters despatched to Peel in November 1843 drew the Prime Minister's attention to the recent tenure of municipal office by Jews. The first letter took the form of an impressive list, 'the facts of his case' as Salomons called them, which he deemed evidence of favourable public opinion. Salomons pointed out that Jews had been admitted as freemen of the City of London, not only as brokers but also as members of the City Livery. (In 1831 Salomons had become a Liveryman of the Coopers' Company, in 1835 a member of its court of assistants, and in 1841 master of the same company.) Two Jews had been Sheriffs of London. Four Jews were currently serving as Commissioners of the Peace. Two Jews had become High Sheriffs of Counties. (In 1839 Salomons had been Sheriff of Kent and E. Lousada was completing a term as Sheriff of Devon for the year 1842–43.) Salomons referred to the work of J. M. Montefiore as a Commissioner of the Peace for Sussex and to his own responsibilities in the same capacity for Kent and Sussex. (Each of these three appointments had been made in 1838.) He also noted that for the current year Sir Moses Montefiore had been appointed a Commissioner of the Peace for Kent and for the Cinque Ports. Finally Salomons's list recalled that Jews had been serving as councillors at Southampton, Birmingham and Portsmouth (A. Abrahams at Southampton since 1838; D. Barnett at Birmingham since 1839; E. Emanuel at Portsmouth since 1841). Salomons also drew Peel's attention to certain anomalies other than those existing in the City: whilst during his term as High Sheriff of Kent he had been considered a fit person, as holder of the highest county office, to entertain the Maidstone Corporation, in a less exalted capacity he would have been prevented from holding even the meanest of offices in the government of this county town. In his second letter of 20 November Salomons referred to the pending court proceedings in respect of a Mr. Cohen, elected assessor at Exeter but unable to take the declaration prescribed in 9 Geo IV, c. 17. Subsequent to this correspondence Peel granted Salomons an interview but found himself unable to give any undertaking that the Government might accede to his wishes.[17] Nor was the Prime Minister in any better position to oblige in May of the following year when Salomons once again sought a private interview to discuss the problems raised by 9 Geo IV, c. 17.[18] The question had in fact now reverted to the hypothetical one of what line the Government might adopt in the event of a Jew being elected to a City Aldermanry; as Lord Holland had surmised, pressure on the Government to succumb would become irresistible only after a Jew had been elected, so posing once again the practical dilemma of how to reconcile the will of the electors with the inexorable demands of the law.

Another test of the issue was called for and in the autumn of 1844 Salomons as Cooper sought election for another Aldermanry in the City. In a contested ballot for the ward of Portsoken he was elected by a majority of 32 votes, polling 168 votes as against the 136 of his opponent, Sheriff F. G. Moon. The oath prescribed by 9 Geo IV, c. 17 was duly administered to Salomons; in consequence of his refusal to take the declaration the Court of Aldermen deliberated and voted on the question of his admission. Nineteen of the Court's total of twenty-five votes were recorded: six were cast in Salomons's favour, thirteen were cast against him. In consequence of this adverse majority of seven the aldermanic office was declared void. The respective letters of protest against the seating of Moon which Salomons and some members of the Portsoken Ward despatched to the Lord Mayor, David Wire, proved to be of no avail.[19]

Salomons was most aggrieved: he confided to Peel the deep sense of degradation and humiliation caused to him by such an anomalous and galling disability and asked the Prime Minister to grant him another interview.[20] Salomons expected immediate Government action; when this was not forthcoming he became even more impatient than usual, mobilising his supporters in the City so that he might badger Peel the more effectively. He also managed to arouse from its lethargy the Board of Deputies which had, in the three and a half years since the failure of Divett's bill, scarcely concerned itself with Emancipation. At a meeting of the Board on 23 January 1845 the Deputies resolved that in view of the advancement of liberal feelings, particularly in respect of religious questions, the time was now ripe for a recommencement of the agitation for Emancipation. A committee of five Deputies, which included Salomons, Montefiore and Lionel Rothschild, was appointed to act on this decision and a public subscription was opened to defray the necessary expenses.[21] On 9 February Salomons wrote to the Prime Minister, conveying to him not only the sense of great expectations entertained by himself and his supporters, but explaining how, politic to the point of exasperation, they had deliberately concealed any such open manifestation of feeling. Now, however, they had become open to a charge of supineness. Salomons argued—indeed almost insisted—that the decision of the Court of Aldermen rendered imperative the introduction of legislation, for this action had so blatantly revealed the limitation on the rights of the electors and demonstrated the disadvantageous status of Jews relative to that enjoyed by other dissenters. And in concluding his letter Salomons somewhat presumptuously laid claim to be the voice of City opinion, informing Peel that there had grown up a conviction that the time was ripe for the Government to interfere to apply a remedy for a practical grievance.[22]

On 18 February the Deputies again conferred and on the following day the five-man deputation from the Board had an audience with Peel. At this meeting there were to be heard echoes of the intra-Jewish disagreements of the 1830s; the Prime Minister surprised Montefiore by informing him of a letter he had received from the Goldsmids stating that the Jews would not be satisfied with any incomplete measure. Peel confided that he had been considering some measure of relief in respect of municipal offices but that in view of this difference of opinion he might not now proceed with a bill. The need for Peel to tread warily, to be able to assure his party that the Jews would not take immediate advantage of a small concession, was obvious; he would first have to obtain such an assurance from the Deputies. However, at the delegation's request, the Prime Minister did consent to see Goldsmid and he informed the Deputies that they would be asked to come and see him again within a fortnight. Peel naturally preferred to discuss Emancipation with Montefiore as a fellow espouser of the belief that 'half a loaf was better than none'. The Prime Minister was sure the Jews would feel as well satisfied with partial Emancipation for they would not thereby be precluded from procuring further Emancipation at a later stage; as proof of his goodwill he consented to present a petition from the Deputies to the House of Commons.[23]

For at last the Government felt free to act. On 22 February Peel wrote to the Lord Chancellor, Lyndhurst, requesting him to direct the immediate preparation of a bill for the outlawing of all remaining municipal disabilities as they affected Jews;[24] on the same day a Royal Commission was appointed under Lyndhurst's chairmanship, entrusted with the broader task of reporting on penalties and disabilities in regard to religious opinions as they affected all non-Anglicans. With, of course, the important proviso that the question of those disabilities disqualifying Jews from the legislature be excluded from consideration. While the Commission was sitting the scope of the bill was specifically widened so as to leave no doubt as to the Jews' eligibility to serve in all corporate offices, including those of Recorder and Town Clerk, although it was not eventually considered necessary to emphasise the Jews' admissability to office in trading corporations and all lay corporations connected with commerce, as Peel had originally suggested.[25]

From the Commission's 160-page report, as it appeared on 30 May, the inference to be drawn was that Jews were a group set apart from the religious norm only by differences of degree, as denominational in character as the differences dividing Catholics or Protestant Dissenters from Anglicans; it was significant that the report should have surveyed the history of Anglo-Jewry within the context of that whole body of legislation deriving from the

Edwardine and Elizabethan Acts of Uniformity, the purpose of which had been to suppress those who refused to conform at a time when there simply did not exist in England any errant Jews who might have rendered themselves liable to such a suppression.[26] The summary of the report, apart from recommending the repeal of obsolete laws, for example those governing landownership, advised that Jews should 'be admissable to various offices and situations of trust and emolument. . . . A test of submission and attachment to the Government would be substituted for such tests as have reference to religious opinions in nearly all the cases in which any tests would be required.'[27]

Despite the recommendations of Lyndhurst's Royal Commission there remained some staunch opponents of even so limited a concession as the outlawing of municipal disabilities. Lyndhurst himself favoured the further removal of parliamentary disabilities but had of course to weigh in the balance the opinion of Church and party.[28] As the member of the Cabinet responsible for initiating in the Lords the relief legislation such caution was well justified. Bishop Blomfield of London articulated the views of the majority in the Lords when he warned that his acquiescence in the measure—given so as to avoid needless dissension—should not be misinterpreted as betokening the abandonment of opposition to the Jews' parliamentary claims. Although the bill met with little opposition from his fellow peers, Lyndhurst did deem it vital to give a reassurance that the proposed legislation would represent nothing more than a *de jure* recognition of the *de facto* situation whereby Jews such as Salomons and Montefiore had been able to fill a variety of civic and municipal offices, the City Aldermanries alone excepted.[29] The Protestant Dissenting Deputies was one group, however, which refused to recognize the necessity of limitation and during passage of the bill from the Lords to the Commons their committee petitioned that Jews should be eligible not only to all municipal offices but also to seats in the legislature.[30] In moving the second and third reading debates in the Commons Peel had therefore to reiterate Lyndhurst's proviso, though he did concede the necessity for removing all existing anomalies and uncertainties. It was because of the assurances given by Lyndhurst and Peel that in each of the two divisions only eleven members, with whom Gladstone was not this time associated, were to be found voting against the bill.[31] On 31 July 1845 'An Act for the Relief of Persons of the Jewish Religion elected to Municipal Offices', 8 & 9 Vict, c. 52, received the Royal Assent. Anyone of Jewish faith admitted to municipal office, with the inclusion now of the City Aldermanries, was permitted to substitute for the declaration enacted under 9 Geo IV, c. 17 one in a form more acceptable to his conscience. The act also rectified the old anomaly prevailing in the City, whereby a Jew refusing to serve as a Sheriff had been liable to the payment of a fine.

The act 9 & 10 Vict, c. 59, of August 1846, gave effect to the other recommendations contained in the report of the Lyndhurst Royal Commission; these concerned such problems raised by past legislation as the status of educational establishments and undisputed entitlement to land ownership. The act clarified existing law by decreeing that 'Her Majesty's Subjects professing the Jewish Religion in respect to their Schools, Places for Religious Worship, Education, and charitable Purposes, and the Property held therewith, shall be subject to the same laws as Her Majesty's Protestant Subjects dissenting from the Church of England . . . are subject to, and not further or otherwise.'

Although Montefiore had warmly welcomed the measure for the outlawing of municipal disabilities,[32] the demands of Judaism and of public office in a Christian country appeared to him to be almost incompatible. Salomons, by contrast, was an optimist in his belief that these loyalties could be successfully reconciled. But again, unlike Goldsmid, he had accepted that the piecemeal removal of the remaining municipal disabilities would have to be accomplished before the issue of the admission of Jews to Parliament could be seriously contemplated by the legislature. And now Lyndhurst's adaptation of the law seemed almost to mark the end of a rehearsal. What if a Parliamentary constituency, after Aldgate and Portsoken, were similarly to elect a Jew and that Member of Parliament were then to find himself ineligible to take his seat? The Jewish press at least was belatedly coming to appreciate the wisdom of the advice tendered to I. L. Goldsmid by Lord Holland at the outset of the campaign, that in the pursuit of a practical, and not ideological, approach lay the prospects of eventual success. For the abstract modified religious-cum-Whiggish case which could be made out in support of Emancipation, more than ever imparting to the concessionary measures of 1828 and 1829 in respect to other non-Anglicans a retrospective importance as precedents, constituted little more than simple justification of an evaluation of the Jews reached on empirical grounds, an evaluation relevant to that small and politically eligible class of City financier Jews which had, by 1845, come to the fore: the Rothschilds and the Goldsmids, Montefiore and Salomons. And here, in observing how theory does not weigh with English minds, it is worth recalling the non-ideological obverse in respect of intra-Jewish affairs: one of the most fortunate by-products of the Salomons strategy, absolutely at one with that Salomons perception of problems over education, marriage, etc., as currently moving towards a compromise resolution of the conflict as between doctrinal and undenominational concepts, was to reinforce the position of those leading figures in the Jewish community who subconsciously recoiled from so pushing principles to their extreme logical conclusion as to have to choose between the two mutually exclusive ideologies of ultra-Orthodoxy and Reform assimilation.

These nuances, these discernments as between the *a priori* and the *a posteriori*, the Germanic and the English, were not lost on either of the two leading Jewish newspapers. A leading article in *The Voice of Jacob* of August 1845 observed that 'English legislation, at this day, is an essentially practical one and the policy of the minister must necessarily exhibit that characteristic in an eminent degree. . . . Her Majesty's ministers preferred rather to present Mr. Salomons' exclusion as a practical grievance, and to expose its inconsistency'; the newspaper then paid tribute to Salomons as 'a gentleman to whose exertions the present progress of the question is so eminently indebted'.[33] A leading article in *The Jewish Chronicle* two months later was distinguished by a connexion of particularly shrewd insights. It declared that 'the removal, in part, of our civil disabilities . . . is a concession made to public opinion, rather than a recognition by the legislature of the abstract justice of our claims. But that very circumstance enhances the value of a boon . . .'; here the newspaper was fully appreciative of that more than compensating difference between the Emancipation which had come about as a result of a 'popular excitement' coloured by atheism and irreligion, so characteristic of those parts of Europe influenced by the Revolutionary tradition, and the Emancipation which, as in England, was 'the work of a Conservative government' responsible for facilitating the passage of legislation through 'a House of hereditary and ecclesiastical legislators.'[34] Time would confirm *The Jewish Chronicle* in attaching significance to the involvement of the Tories.

The middle decades of the century saw a large increase in the number of non-Anglicans, most notably Unitarians, who came forward to serve in public office and the preparedness of Jews to do so was thus characteristic of a trend: in 1846 B. S. Phillips became a Common Councilman for the ward of Farringdon-Within in the City of London; in 1847 Sir Moses Montefiore became Sheriff of Kent; in 1852 Philip Salomons became Sheriff of Sussex; in 1857 I. L. Levy became Mayor of Rochester. But it was for David Salomons himself that the greatest triumphs were reserved. In December 1847, only days before the House of Commons was asked for the first time in eleven and a half years to vote upon the issue of parliamentary disabilities, David Salomons as a Cooper was elected an Alderman for the Cordwainer Ward in the City of London. *The Jewish Chronicle* chose the occasion to reflect philosophically on the importance of Salomons's earlier campaigns, reminding its readers that Salomons

> was the cause, the proximate cause, that the disabilities affecting the municipal rights of the British Jews were abolished. . . . It frequently happens that those principles which men do not understand in a general sense, they are taught by the uprightness, and by the integrity of one man, and by the respect which, notwithstanding opposing tendencies, they are compelled to tender him. Without in any way attributing the entire change of public feeling towards the British Jews to the unaided efforts of Mr. Salomons, we yet with justice may assert that to him must be ascribed the merit of having broken down the barrier intolerance has raised against us, and thus permitted others to follow.[35]

The Cordwainer Aldermanry was an office Salomons was to hold until his death a quarter of a century later; its tenure meanwhile involved progression to a higher office: the Mayoralty of the City of London. The year 1855 was to find Salomons as long-serving Alderman and Cooper standing next in rotation to the mayoral incumbent, his former opponent in the Portsoken Ward, Sir F. G. Moon. Salomons's own election as Lord Mayor of the City of London on 29 September 1855, and the confirmation of this decision by the Court of Aldermen, were thus almost formalities.[36] Salomons's services during the year were warmly appreciated and an address from the merchants, citizens and almost all the bankers of the City at the conclusion of his term of office took the form of an endorsement of the tribute offered by one of the more prominent of their number, W. G. Prescott: 'On no occasion I may truly say, has the hospitality of the Mansion House been more conspicuous than during your Year of Office.' Of the Mayoralty the tribute added: 'It is the highest reward without the aid of the Crown or Parliament, that your fellow-citizens can give to a chief magistrate.'[37]

This commendation was recorded on 8 November 1856; a little more than a year and a half later Emancipation was achieved. Salomons became one of the first Jewish Members of Parliament and after a further decade a baronet. There seems nothing too panegyrical about the congratulatory address which was received by Salomons from the Board of Deputies in 1869, an address signed most appropriately by Sir Moses Montefiore acting on behalf of the Board:

That the honoured name of *David Salomons* will ever be gratefully cherished and remembered in connection with the great struggle for Jewish Emancipation of which he was one of the most able, indefatigable and devoted Champions; that to his indomitable efforts, the Jews of this Country are largely indebted for the complete removal of their Civil disabilities.[38]

NOTES

1. Letter Books of I. L. Goldsmid, I, fol. no. 55, 11 September 1829, O'Connell to I. L. Goldsmid.

2. Quoted in B. Van Oven, *Ought Baron de Rothschild to sit in Parliament? An imaginary conversation between JUDAEUS and AMICUS NOBILIS*, p. 3.

3. David Salomons, *A Short Statement on behalf of His Majesty's Subjects professing the Jewish Religion*, 9 February 1835, p. 26.

4. David Salomons House, Broomhill, wall certificate no. 9.

5. L. Loewe (ed.), *The Diaries of Sir Moses and Lady Montefiore*, I, pp. 107–8.

6. David Salomons, *A Short Statement on behalf of His Majesty's Subjects professing the Jewish Religion*, pp. 21–22.

7. O'Connell, *Hansard*, Third Series, 39, 4 December 1837, 515–16.

8. Corporation of the City of London, Guildhall Records. Repertories of the Court of Aldermen, vol. 240, 1835–36, pp. 61–71, minutes of meeting for 17 December 1835. Reference to Attorney's report of 8 December 1835.

9. Minute Books of the Board of Deputies, II, pp. 129–132, 29 November 1837; L. Loewe (ed.), *The Diaries of Sir Moses and Lady Montefiore*, I, p. 126.

10. *Hansard*, Third Series, 39, 30 November 1837, 423–25; L. Loewe (ed.), *The Diaries of Sir Moses and Lady Montefiore*, I, p. 127, 30 November 1837.

11. L. Loewe (ed.), *The Diaries of Sir Moses and Lady Montefiore*, I, p. 128, 17–18 December 1837; Minute Books of the Board of Deputies, II, pp. 133–34, 7 January 1838; *Hansard*, Third Series, 39, 4 December 1837, 508–21; W. F. Monypenny and G. E. Buckle, *The Life of Benjamin Disraeli, Earl of Beaconsfield*, I, p. 405, 5 December 1837; *Hansard*, Third Series, 39, 21 December 1837, 1372–74.

12. A. B. Beaven, *The Aldermen of the City of London*, I, pp. 15, 226; A. M. Hyamson, *David Salomons*, pp. 36–37; H. S. Q. Henriques, *The Jews and the English Law*, pp. 254–55.

13. *Hansard*, Third Series, 56, 9 February 1841, 504–7; Minute Books of the Board of Deputies, IV, pp. 231–33; B. L. Manning, *The Protestant Dissenting Deputies*, p. 212, Petition of 26 March 1841; *Hansard*, Third Series, 57, 10 March 1841, 84–99; *Hansard*, Third Series, 57, 31 March 1841, 754–68; *Hansard*, Third Series, 58, 3 June 1841, 1048–9; *Hansard*, Third Series, 58, 11 June 1841, 1449–58.

14. Russell, *Hansard*, Third Series, 58, 4 June 1841, 1210.

15. *A New Song to an Old Tune, etc.: On Lord John Russell's election as Member for the City of London*.

16. *Address from I. L. Goldsmid to the Jewish Electors of the City of London*, 18 June 1841.

17. Peel Papers, B. M. ADD. MSS. 40535, ff. 245–48, 8 November 1843, and f. 249, 20 November 1843, D. Salomons to Peel; ff. 250–51, 22 November 1843, Peel to Salomons; f. 252, 24 November 1843, Salomons to Peel.

18. Ibid., B. M. ADD. MSS. 40544, f. 217, 13 May 1844, D. Salomons to Peel.

19. Corporation of the City of London, Guildhall Records. Repertories of the Court of Aldermen, vol. 248, 1843–44, pp. 405–7, 9 October 1844; pp. 411–13, 15 October 1844; pp. 436–37, Minutes for 29 October 1844. Reference to Salomons's and petitioners' protests, 21 October 1844; Beaven, *The Aldermen of the City of London*, I, pp. 186, 188.

20. Peel Papers, B. M. ADD. MSS. 40553, ff. 298–301, 6 November 1844, Salomons to Peel.

21. Minute Books of the Board of Deputies, V, pp. 298–99, 23 January 1845.

22. Peel Papers, B. M. ADD. MSS. 40559, ff. 233–34, 9 February 1845, Salomons to Peel.

23. Minute Books of the Board of Deputies, V, pp. 308–9, 20 February 1845.

24. Peel Papers, B. M. ADD. MSS. 40442, ff. 263–64, 22 February 1845, Peel to Lyndhurst.

25. Ibid., ff. 265–73, 4 March 1845, and ff. 274–75, 9 March 1845, Peel to Lyndhurst.

26. First Report of Her Majesty's Commissioners for Revising and Consolidating the Criminal Law, appointed 22 February 1845, dated 30 May 1845; in *Parliamentary Papers*, 1845, 4 February–9 August 1845, XIV [631], pp. 1–160.

27. *Parliamentary Papers*, 1845, XIV [631], p. 45.

28. John, Lord Campbell, *Lives of the Lord Chancellors and Keepers of the Great Seal of England, from the earliest times to the reign of Queen Victoria*, VIII, pp. 155–56.

29. *Hansard*, Third Series, 78, 10 March 1845, 515–27; *Hansard*, Third Series, 78, 14 March 1845, 885–86.

30. B. L. Manning, *The Protestant Dissenting Deputies*, p. 212, Petition of 28 April 1845.

31. *Hansard*, Third Series, 82, 17 July 1845, 622–43; *Hansard*, Third Series, 82, 21 July 1845, 869–70.

32. Collection of Sir Moses Montefiore's autograph letters addressed to Dr Louis Loewe: album folio I, letter 2 (10 March A.D. 1845 or 5605), Montefiore to Loewe.

33. *The Voice of Jacob*, 1 August 1845, pp. 205–6, for the Jewish year 5605.

34. *The Jewish Chronicle*, 6 October 1845, pp. 249–50, leading article, 'Retrospect of Anno Mundi 5605'.

35. *The Jewish Chronicle*, 10 December 1847, pp. 341–42, leading article, 'Election of Mr. David Salomons as Alderman of the City of London'.

36. *The Illustrated Times*, 1855, p. 372.

37. David Salomons House, Broomhill, fol. no. 324 for the signatures of the bankers, merchants and citizens, and wall certificate no. 35 for Prescott's tribute on their behalf, 8 November 1856.

38. David Salomons House, Broomhill, wall certificate no. 48. Illuminated address to Salomons, to mark the occasion of Salomons receiving his baronetcy, from the London Committee of Deputies of British Jews, 12 October 1869, signed by Montefiore on behalf of the Board.

Part III
THE GENTILE RESPONSE

8
Climax of the Campaign

The life of Sir Robert Peel's Government was abruptly terminated in June 1846 by the major split in the Tory party caused by the Prime Minister's conversion to the cause of Corn Law Repeal, the abolition of those duties upon imports of cheaper grain which had been imposed after the end of the Napoleonic Wars so as to give support to domestic agriculture in a period of depression. The majority of the party repudiated Peel and his Free Trade supporters and formed themselves into a party of Protectionists, so named on account of their adherence to the abandoned policies. The Tory Administration was succeeded by a Whig-Liberal one, led by Lord John Russell, committed to the implementation of Repeal and Free Trade; in the House of Commons Russell's Government was supported by those who instinctively looked to Peel for a lead and who normally voted with him against the Protectionist Opposition on those questions which the latter made an issue. These Free Trade Conservatives, conveniently known by the designation of Peelite, included among their number such former Cabinet ministers as Sir James Graham, Home Secretary for the whole duration of Peel's recent Government, Henry Goulburn, an even longer-serving Chancellor of the Exchequer, Gladstone and Sidney Herbert.

An election appeared almost imminent; Russell's Government would wish to secure a mandate in its own right. And the Jews, in recalling Salomons's achievements, could reflect that no better preparation for a parliamentary career could have been obtained than through service in the Corporation of the City of London. In 1854 a Commission of Enquiry into the Corporation was to infer that as an administrative entity London was a miniature England, while its Corporation as a model legislature enjoyed powers which almost set it in rivalry to Parliament itself. The Commissioners commented upon the Corporation's exclusive possession of powers of municipal government in the metropolis, on how the customs of the City having been solemnly confirmed by Act of Parliament had themselves the force of an Act of Parliament so that even the highest legal authorities were divided as to the effect of general Acts of Parliament within the City when they conflicted with the City customs and did not repeal them by express enactment.[1]

When, however, a general election was called in the summer of 1847 it seemed probable that the Jew who would first emulate the precedent set by O'Connell at Clare almost twenty years before would be not the vanquisher of the City Corporation's disabilities, David Salomons, but the well-born

Lionel Rothschild. On 29 June 1847 a meeting of the Liberal London Registration Association was held at the London Tavern in order to consider the report of its committee.[2] Two of the incumbent Members of Parliament for the City of London, Lord John Russell and J. Pattison, were readopted as Liberal candidates; when the further nominations of Sir G. Larpent and Lionel Rothschild were considered these too were approved by the Association. Two particular considerations appear to have lain behind the choice of Rothschild. Firstly, the Liberals considered that such close identification with the Jewish cause would redound to the honour of the citizens of London who had ever been the 'uncompromising leaders' of civil and religious liberty; secondly, such a nomination would permanently attach to the Liberals 'a most influential class to whom on all occasions they have been much indebted', doubtless a reference to those two crucial City elections of 1841 and 1843, the respective results of which had seen the present Prime Minister elected by a majority of nine votes and one of his fellow Members, Pattison, similarly victorious by a margin of 165 votes.

The City of London constituency was a sizeable one, extending in the east to the Tower Hamlets area, and the four candidates were required to conduct a strenuous campaign with more than a dozen large meetings to address during the course of a month. As Prime Minister Russell's other duties prevented him from attending many of the meetings and of the other candidates Rothschild was most often present. Pattison and Rothschild were articulate speakers while Pattison shared with the Peelite Masterman the further advantage of being well-known to an electorate which they had both represented for the past few years. These were to prove crucial factors in determining a contest for which not only four Liberals but the additional Peelite entertained high hopes of being elected as one of the representatives for the four-member constituency; Larpent, as infrequent attender at meetings, as a relatively poor speaker and as one of the new candidates, may well have suffered in consequence.

The platform on which Rothschild campaigned was similar to that of the other Liberal candidates: freedom of religion, freedom of trade, extension of knowledge and consequently extension of the franchise. Rothschild's addresses, after extolling the merits of free trade and praising the Corn Law Repeal of the previous year, stressed the importance of the Jewish cause. In his exposition of policy Rothschild was fairly specific, expressing a preference for direct taxation as opposed to the prevailing indirect taxes on those commodities in general use; he favoured in the short term a reduction of the high duties on tobacco and on many articles of consumption and also the total abolition of the tea duties which pressed so heavily on the poorer classes. He further urged the introduction of a property tax. As for the question of religious endowments, still of concern following the decision in 1845 to increase and make permanent the parliamentary grant to the Roman Catholic seminary at Maynooth in Ireland, Rothschild considered wrong a policy which made an individual liable for the upkeep of a sectarian or religious establishment of which he was not a member. This stand, together with a declared dislike of capital punishment, won for Rothschild the personal support of some Dissenters. The Irish Poor Law was upheld on the grounds that it was only correct that Ireland should maintain its own poor. Rothschild supported reform of the City of London Corporation and hoped to see the establishment of a Hall or Chamber of Commerce in London, which was now almost the only city still without one. And although favouring extension of the franchise he was opposed to the introduction of secret ballots which would abrogate the tradition of keeping poll records.

Rothschild's reception on the hustings was warm, with vociferous cheering and a general waving of hats whenever he appeared. When, at the conclusion of the campaign, *The Spectator* was led to comment on the singularly mild tone of many of the electoral contests, it noted the good example set in this respect by the City. There were admittedly allegations that Rothschild had bought votes with his money and that he was purchasing large quantities of corn so as to keep up the price to the detriment of the poor; one of the Tory candidates, moreover, referred to him as a 'foreign baron' and a prominent Tory supporter jibed that rather than attempt to enter the legislature Rothschild 'ought to be one of the princes of Judah, in the land of Judah'. But these were isolated instances. It was rather Russell who had alienated the feelings, if not the votes, of a section of his supporters. His Erastian educational policies were disliked by those many Protestant Dissenters holding to Voluntary principles and at meetings some of the more militant of these unsuccessfully proposed that support be confined to the three other Liberals. The Jews were naturally very grateful to Russell for his past endeavours on their behalf and one of Rothschild's most successful evenings was at a meeting of the Aldgate and Portsoken Wards where David Salomons, most appropriately, proposed the motion in support of the four Liberal candidates. Salomons and other Jews were very active in the City, forming themselves into a Hebrew committee which issued pungent polemical appeals. *An Address of the Jewish Association for the Removal of Civil and Religious Disabilities, to the Electors and Inhabitants of the City of London,* copies of which were posted all over the constituency, declared that

religion is a matter solely between man and his Maker, that faith, like love, is free, that it never can be the result of constraint, that it must be the offspring of a conviction which it is not in man's power to call forth at pleasure: . . . to punish men for not doing that which they cannot do; all these are truths so immutably established, so universally recognized, that the voice which attempts to question or gainsay them, can only proceed from the graves of Philip II of Spain, of Mary, his Queen, and their mouldering inquisitors, and is not worthy of serious refutation in this nineteenth century.

The *Address* also refuted some of the standard arguments against Emancipation: that even native-born Jews should not be admitted to the full rights of Britons on account of a supposed dual allegiance and divided love of country, and that in the political privileges of a Christian land none but Christians ought to participate.[3]

Not all Whigs were as keen as Russell to fight the battle for civil and religious liberty. A fortnight before the poll Lady Russell, in the course of a conversation with Lady Grey, the wife of Lord Grey, the Secretary for War and Colonies and the active leader of the Whigs in the Lords, referred to the possibility of Russell's withdrawing from the City contest. Grey, son of the former Whig Prime Minister whose commitment to Emancipation had been marked by caution, entreated Russell to tread equally warily.

> The City is at any rate an inconvenient seat for a minister, and the contest by which it is to be obtained is one which in the peculiar circumstances in which it is to take place must involve you in endless difficulties not to mention the risk of being responsible for what Rothschild's friends may do—I am told he makes no secret of his determination to carry his election by money and with a joint contest this might very easily compromise you—The manner in which the Party in the City has used you by forcing upon you a needless contest ought to relieve you from any scruple in refusing to be the instrument for fighting their battle and supporting their very unreasonable pretensions. . . . I am anxious you should know how very strong an opinion I have in favour of your getting some quieter seat.[4]

Russell was not to be deterred and he campaigned with especial keenness towards the close of the campaign. The result, declared on 30 July, saw him returned at the head of the poll with 7,137 votes. Pattison polled 7,030 votes. Then came Rothschild, with 6,792 votes. Masterman, the Peelite, took the fourth seat, with 6,722 votes, so beating Larpent, the remaining Liberal, who with 6,719 votes just failed to secure election. The other candidates, three Tories and an Independent, polled respectively 5,268, 5,069, 4,704 and 513 votes; given Masterman's personal vote the result was thus further interesting for revealing the crucial margin of electoral advantage which might seem for the moment in the City to be enjoyed by a Peelite over three Protectionists.

Rothschild's election at once transformed what had always hitherto been a somewhat hypothetical question into an actual constitutional problem. Indeed, given Rothschild's re-election in 1849, in 1852 and twice in 1857—his shadow presence in the Commons thus covering the whole duration of the eleven-year period which preceded a solution—the issue could be seen to be resolving itself almost exclusively into a constitutional one, inviting not merely examination but settlement of an elected Member of Parliament's status of ineligibility to sit in the Commons as it related to the claims and rights of his constituents and to the jurisdiction of each of the two Houses of Parliament. One of the first to realize the significance of Rothschild's election was F. D. Maurice, the recently appointed Professor of Theology at King's College, London, who in future years was to act as philosophical guide to the Christian Socialist Movement. It is difficult to discern whether Maurice's 'Thoughts on Jewish Disabilities', published in *Fraser's Magazine* for November 1847, reveal him as supporter or opponent of Emancipation.[5] Although Maurice, in common with such other Christian Socialists as Charles Kingsley, the novelist, and Henry Mayhew, the chronicler of London life of the mid-century, did deprecate the Jews as the purest representatives of and embodying 'in its worst and most evil form, the money-getting principle', such a measure of their worth seemed to him irrelevant to the issue in question. Maurice's assertion that 'in the last election . . . the citizens [of London] did not well know whether they were asserting a majestic principle, or following their most Mammonish instincts' allowed him rather to develop a theme as to self-deception and confusion of belief and so to take issue with Arnold's contention that the profession of Christianity should be the title to citizenship. For in what form, enquired Maurice, would such a profession be made? One of Maurice's oft-expressed convictions concerned the worthlessness of mere dogmas or opinions as a philosophical foundation for a cohesive society, and here he emphatically stated: 'I do *not* admit that *Christianity* is identical with *belief* in Christianity.' Although in agreement with Arnold in deploring the present secularising trend of society Maurice therefore differed from him in asserting the distinction between Church and State; persuasion directed towards the hearts of the people would induce a return to faith, not Acts of Parliament or proscription of the votes of Jews. The electoral verdict of the City of London must meanwhile be accepted. As an exercise in thought Maurice's article was refreshingly above the usual low level of contemporary printed polemic; if the price of his philosophising was subjection to misunderstanding and misrepresentation he was at least to see certain of his points concerning Church and State taken up by Gladstone in the following month's debate in the House of Commons.

For on 16 December 1847 Russell introduced a bill to remove parliamentary disabilities, the first such measure in eleven years. In a two-day debate of particularly impressive quality Gladstone, Disraeli, and the leader of the Protectionists, Lord George Bentinck, were to be found amongst those joining with Russell in speaking in support of the measure, while some of the most interesting speeches opposing it came from the Tory diehard Inglis, the Peelite Goulburn, and the evangelical Lord Ashley, the future Earl of Shaftesbury.[6] A number of most influential newspapers also deemed the occasion suitable for declaring a stand. Apart from *The Times,* with a daily circulation of approximately forty thousand copies, those newspapers averring their support for Emancipation included *The Morning Advertiser, The Morning Chronicle* and the liberal journal of the Lancashire cotton merchants, the *Manchester Guardian,* which with its bi-weekly circulation of approximately nine to ten thousand copies was almost twice as popular as its nearest northern rival. *The Standard, The Morning Post* and the ultra-Tory *Morning Herald* all declared themselves opposed to the remission of disabilities.[7]

At the start of the debate Russell took up the point developed by F. D. Maurice as to the inadequacy of a formal profession of Christianity. He argued that conformity to the postscript of an oath ensured the worst of both eventualities: while it could not be certain of ensuring religious legislators it could be quite certain of excluding sincere, honest and conscientiously motivated men. Those who, subscribing to the declaration, threw off both their duties and the obligations of their religion were meanwhile not excluded. The Jews were accused of being revilers of Christianity, yet the irreverent *philosophe* Hume had represented George III at the French court and both the Tory Bolingbroke and the historian Gibbon, renowned by their respective contemporaries for their sneering and ironical criticism of the Scriptures, had taken Christian oaths and been admitted to the Commons.[8] Already *The Times* had resorted to the English historical experience since the Revolution Settlement to allay the anxieties of opponents of Emancipation for the security of Christianity. In November 1847 the newspaper had represented opponents of the Jewish cause as espousing the logic that 'religion should have flourished nobly while tests abounded and should decline when they were removed'. *The Times* compared the religiosity of the present day with the religious indifference prevailing at the time of the 1753 'Jew Bill', declaring of this earlier period 'nor did anything but a most exemplary Court under George III save us from worse morality than that of France'. The result of the concessions to religious freedom had not been religious indifference. 'Between the landing of William III and the accession of George IV there was no period in any degree comparable to the present for the sincerity, extension and activity of religious spirit, for the exertions, influence and authority of the church, for the general decency of morals, and the unmistakable manifestations of faith.' The remission of tests was 'compatible with sincere convictions and awakened energies; with undiminished faith and laborious works'. As far as the real and imagined strengths of Christianity were concerned there appeared to *The Times* to exist a clear link between penal restrictions and a disrespectful indifference towards religion, while conversely there could be detected a correlation between enlightened toleration and religious improvement; on 17 December, in preparation for the second day of the Commons debate, *The Times* furnished a more vivid illustration of the same argument. During the time that faith had been protected by restrictions on all non-Anglicans the Church of England had been 'at its lowest ebb of laxity and incompetence'. It had risen 'to its highest flood' under a series of concessions and the present age was one of religious faith and deep convictions. If yielding on disabilities indicated national indifference to religious truth—a favourite Puseyite contention—

then England ought by now to have become avowedly latitudinarian. Yet the very opposite had come to pass: the present time might be compared with the day when 'Sir Robert Walpole might have made his bishops out of any material he pleased with as much security as any one of his secretaries might have nominated an exciseman.'[9]

Opponents saw differently the experience of British history and in answer to the demands that Parliament should pursue at home the 'precedents' of having relaxed the disabling laws in such colonies as Canada, Jamaica and Barbados, Sir Robert Inglis raised a Burkeian protest at major changes being unnaturally grafted on to the constitution. There was, contended Inglis, a most vital difference between changing the British constitution and establishing one for another country 'even if a man should not be so sensible of the value of our own constitution as to be willing to establish it everywhere else.'[10] Others, out of Parliament as well as in, did not confine themselves to such highly principled objections. Carlyle was fast acquiring a reputation for illiberalism whether in respect of Jews or Negroes; emancipation from slavery he equated with 'emancipation for horses'. Particular objections were harboured by Carlyle towards certain Jewish writers and intellectuals: Heine he described as a 'slimy and greasy Jew', while Disraeli, the only man of whom he claimed to have 'never spoken except with contempt' was dismissed as 'a cursed old Jew not worth his weight in bacon'.[11] In a letter to Monckton Milnes, the former Peelite of liberal views who was now more identified with the Whigs, Carlyle sought to exploit for the purposes of the Commons vote the personal antagonism which had sprung up between Monckton Milnes and Disraeli—in the event he could not dissuade Monckton Milnes from voting in favour of Emancipation. 'A Jew is bad', wrote Carlyle, 'but what is a Sham-Jew, a Quack-Jew? And how can a real Jew, by possibility, try to be a Senator, or even Citizen, of any country, except his own wretched Palestine, whither all his thoughts and steps and efforts tend?'[12]

This last point of Carlyle's was related to the contention of a quite dissimilar opponent of Emancipation. Lord Ashley, the future seventh Earl of Shaftesbury, was a curiously antique figure, a most untypical evangelical in an admittedly evangelical age. That age, with its optimistic faith in progress and improvement, feared that the moral and spiritual challenge of Christianity would be lost sight of unless religion succeeded in harnessing to itself the knowledge of Man and his Maker which stood revealed in historical, philosophical and scientific development; Ashley, by contrast, in rejecting the secularization implicit in modern biblical criticism and adhering to a fundamentalist God-centred view of the world, remained a millenarian who believed that the biblical prophecies indicated an early return to the Holy Land and that the return of the Jews would be associated with the Second Coming.

Jews for the Holy Land; they could look upon no other country as a permanent home and their conversion was necessarily a prerequisite of admission to any definably Christian legislature.[13] Ashley, by his own interpretation of the Scriptures, found himself cast as an opponent of Emancipation, though he was sincerely full of benevolent, patronising compassion for those 'erring, lost souls' whose departure from true religion had been the cause of the destruction of their own civil polity and of their subsequent dispersion. To contemporaries Ashley must have invited comparison with the leading millenarian Jewish counterpart; the ring engraved with the words 'Oh, pray for the peace of Jerusalem!' which he always wore on his right hand,[14] was scarcely less strange than Crooll's garb of a parchment girdle on which were inscribed passages from the Law and the Talmud. It was with some trepidation that Ashley had approached the December debate;[15] in the event he summoned up sufficient reserves of courage to deliver a long and interesting speech.[16] He maintained that the truths of religion should be closely identified with civil politics and asked his fellow Parliamentarians to join with him in reflecting on the likely consequences of any eventual concession to the Jews. The day would then approach, feared Ashley, when the legislators would 'have to stand out for a white Parliament; and perhaps they would have a final struggle for a male Parliament'.

Ashley was gloomily disappointed by the support for the measure and must have been dismayed in particular by certain reasoning which distinguished the contribution from Gladstone which followed his own.[17] In March 1841 Ashley had abstained from voting on the merits of Divett's bill for the outlawing of municipal disabilities in the politically naïve belief that such a vote was unimportant; he had then taken issue with Inglis for opposing the measure as though it involved the admissibility of Jews to · Parliament.[18] Now, six and a half years later, Ashley was still to be found asserting the 'wide and palpable' distinction between administrative and legislative functions. Executive office was delegated to a Jew by a Christian head and was executed for Christian purposes, such a Jew was bound by law and on him was imposed a public responsibility from which the legislator was free. Gladstone, on the contrary, ever as mindful as Ashley of the consequential relationship of parliamentary to municipal Emancipation, held as consistently to that opposing viewpoint for which he too had become known in March 1841, namely that no such breadth of distinction was to be discerned. Gladstone had then felt so strongly that the natural consequence of the outlawing of municipal disabilities would prove to be the remission of parliamentary disabilities, involving collapse of that interwoven Church-State superstructure according to which Parliament bore responsibility for the 'frame and form' of the established State religion, the regulation of the public worship of the whole nation and the performance of duties connected with religion, that he had acted as one of the tellers opposing the third reading of Divett's bill.[19] But by 1847, after the outlawing of municipal restrictions, the occupancy of a number of magistracies by Jews, the extension of the franchise and the remission of parliamentary disabilities in respect of the Unitarians 'who refuse the whole of the most vital doctrines of the Gospel', Gladstone, no less than Ashley the victim of his logic, felt compelled to support parliamentary Emancipation.[20]

Thus, as in such other matters of religious controversy as characterised these years—the Maynooth endowment, the preferment of the evangelical Dr. Hampden, and the appointment to a living of the allegedly heterodox Revd. G. C. Gorham—Gladstone was to be found abandoning, or at least *ostensibly* abandoning, his earlier politico-religious opinions. Freshly reacquainted with many of the arguments in favour of Emancipation by a reading of Barnard Van Oven's *Ought Baron de Rothschild to sit in Parliament?* and wisely taking the advice of a friend not to be tempted, as was his wont, into emulating the notoriously recondite Professor Maurice,[21] namely by arguing furiously in earnest on both sides of the question, Gladstone veered almost to the other extreme and offered to the Commons a deceptively straightforward explanation for his change of opinion; he maintained, in direct confutation of Ashley's arguments, that in present times and with the substance of power granted it would be foolish any longer to withhold the shadow.

Gladstone was insistent that the question of the maintenance of a Christian Parliament could not be adjudged without reference to the mutability of the British constitution. Contemporaries could not say of any one point of time in the past that 'this is the British constitution'; all legislation from, for example, Magna Carta through the early Anglican Acts of Uniformity to the Bill of Rights might be seen as 'data', fixed points only in discussion, to be applied and developed in a spirit of fairness and justice. Gladstone taunted Ashley for claiming, in regard to considerations of religion, that he was fighting for the maintenance of a long-established and ancient system while yet at the same time conceding that such a defence came only after generations of perpetual conflict, constant change and progressive movement, all in one and the same direction. Impartial application of the prevailing rules was imperative; contending that Ashley should have reached further back in time, Gladstone recalled that

the first contest of all was a contest for a Church Parliament; and the battle for a Church Parliament, fought between the period of the Restoration, when in point of fact formal dissent began, and the period of the Hanoverian succession, or perhaps I should say of the Occasional Conformity Act, was as fierce a conflict as any of the others. Even after Nonconformity had received the sanction of the law by the Toleration Act, it was still attempted to dislodge or to exclude the Nonconformist from the possession of political power. It appears, then, that you first contended for a Church Parliament—you then contended for a Protestant Parliament; in both cases you were defeated. You were not defeated unawares; you were not defeated owing to accident. You were defeated, owing to profound and powerful and uniform tendencies, associated with the movement of the human mind—with the general course of events, perhaps I ought to say with the providential government of the world. . . . It appears, then, we have now arrived at a stage in which, after two or three generations had contended for a Church Parliament, and two or three generations more contended for a Protestant Parliament, each being in succession beaten, we are called upon to decide the question whether we shall contend for a Christian Parliament.

Gladstone's retort to those opponents of Emancipation who so confidently claimed the ability to discern God's will was that Providence should be preferred as arbiter of the Jews' fate. If it were true that the concession of rights to non-Anglicans had been guaranteed to incur the wrath of the Almighty then the damage had already been committed: in 1828 and 1829 and through the admission of Jews to municipal office. Gladstone admonished his fellow Members that they would be more likely to incur the wrath of the Almighty by acting out of prejudice or through apprehension of clamour and the displeasure of others than through doing what they believed to be correct.

The degree to which the influence of Christianity in forming the character of the legislature would be adversely affected by Emancipation was naturally the question which troubled Gladstone the most deeply. It was, he implied, carrying logic too far to state that every legislator must be a Christian: more important was the composition and temper of society. Gladstone defended Russell and other supporters of Emancipation from the allegation levelled against them by Ashley that they were in favour of a severance between politics and religion. So long as the vast and overwhelming majority of those in Parliament should continue to be Christians there was no necessity for absolutely excluding the Jew from a legislature whose first duties were anyway secular and civil.

The discussion, therefore, in which we are engaged does not turn upon the question whether the Christian religion is needless for the work of government and of legislation. It must first of all be shown that the admission of an extremely small fraction of Jews into Parliament would paralyse and nullify the Christianity of all those who sit there. We may consistently affirm that Christianity is in the highest degree needful for our legislation, and yet decline to follow out that proposition to a conclusion so rigid as this, that every individual who is not a Christian should be excluded from the possibility of becoming a legislator.

Parliament would continue to derive its character mainly from the personal attributes of those who elected and those who composed it and thus the qualities of a man were more important than any letter of regulations as embodied in oaths and declarations. The formal profession of Christianity should not be unduly emphasised, for it was often little more than the most vague, naked, and generalized acknowledgement.

Gladstone directly refuted the arguments that Jewish Emancipation would be tantamount to unchristianization of the legislature and would afford evidence of indifference towards Christianity, that it could be regarded as a concession which would provide a precedent for the admission to Parliament of yet additional non-Christian groups who in turn would facilitate such unchristianization of the legislature and contribute to the growth of religious indifference. In the instance of the Jews Parliament would be dispensing with reference to a Christian profession which had no relation to any defined standard external to the individual mind. The profession of Christianity, in the sense of titular adherence, did not indicate concurrence in a fixed body of revealed truths. Whilst true that one might unchristianize the Parliament in name it was not true in substance and although it was painful to part 'with even the title of an exclusive Christianity. . . . Yet to qualify this title as we are now asked to qualify it, to surrender it as an universal and exclusive title, is not to deprive ourselves of such substantial Christianity as we may really now possess.'

Admonition to his fellow Members that with the substance of power granted it would be foolish any longer to withhold the shadow seemed almost peculiarly impossible of rejection in view of earlier predictions. In 1841 Gladstone had disagreed with Ashley's estimate of the importance of outlawing municipal disabilities, at that time pointing out to the Commons that because municipal office was concerned with the work of the magistracy and with the execution of civil offices and because any Jews entering upon such office would be involved in the administration of Christian laws and of Christian oaths to Christian men, it would be only realistic to expect advocates of the Jewish cause to follow up a municipal success with a campaign for parliamentary Emancipation.[22] Now, not only had the outlawing of municipal disabilities been achieved, but the franchise too had come to be enjoyed by many Jews, so that it could be said that they held real power in yet another sense for being able to count themselves among those who made the makers of laws.

For a general comment on the Gladstonian approach, transcending the single issue of Jewish disabilities, the essay written by Bagehot some years later was to provide as judicious assessment as any by a political scientist. 'These successive changes', wrote Bagehot with reference to the Maynooth, Jewish, Hampden and Gorham questions, 'do credit to Mr. Gladstone's good sense; they show that he has a susceptible nature, that he will not live out of sympathy with his age.' Gladstone, having come gradually to abandon the theory of the exclusive union of a visible Church with a visible State, here seemed to epitomise appreciation of one of the requirements of the new age of construction which Bagehot thought must necessarily succeed the abolitions consummated in Peel's day, namely 'how the natural union of Church and State is to be adapted to an age of divided religious opinion, and to the necessary conditions of a parliamentary government.'[23]

But if Gladstone did reveal a capacity for adaptation he was no political weathercock, as a simple reading of Bagehot's essay might suggest. Nor was he guilty, except upon a most superficial interpretation, of tergiversation. There lay behind Gladstone's rethinking and switch of vote on the Jewish question a fundamental consistency of attitude which, far from indicating some breach with that conception of a self-governing *Ecclesia Anglicana* held by many of his erstwhile Tory colleagues, seemed rather to divide him from the Erastian considerations of policy which guided Russell and many of the old Whigs. There was indeed no popularity to be gained by a switch of vote: still sitting with Peel on the Opposition benches of the House and still a member of the Carlton Club—a symbolic declaration of ideological allegiance which was not to be renounced until 1860—Gladstone courted considerable annoyance with those at Oxford who had previously been foremost in acknowledging both his political leadership and his high churchmanship.

For Gladstone was as Tractarian in 1847 as he had been in 1836 and 1841. This emerged most clearly in correspondence with Pusey. Referring to his support of Gladstone's candidacy prior to the recent July election Pusey, three days before the Commons' debate, remonstrated with his friend: 'Had I known that you would have joined in what I account an anti-Christian measure, I should not have helped to put you in a position which would have led to such a result. I would rather for your own soul's sake that you had been out of Parliament. . . . Your election seemed the one thing which could still interest me in politics. . . .'[24] In reply Gladstone explained that he could no longer act upon the assumption, however much he might privately be tempted to agree with it, that gains for non-Anglican dissent must necessarily entail a corresponding loss of influence for the Church. 'For what I thought the true principle of national religion I stood, until no man stood by me. Nor would it then have been time to retire had a standard been ordained for national religion without relation to the elements of which the nation is composed. The State recedes from its ancient and high position: in England more slowly than elsewhere, yet still truly and sensibly.'[25]

Gladstone indeed, whose religiosity compared with that of his captious followers at Oxford could the more easily transcend doctrinal differences, now believed that denominational barriers—and he extended the principle to the Jews—must be lowered in order that the whole country could unite behind a general religious and Christian standard. Prudential concessions to Dissenters, exchanging denominational equality in return for the assurance that the Anglican Church must remain among all Churches *primus inter pares,* would, maintained Gladstone, enable Anglicans the better to resist the encroachments of the State. Here, at the point in his career when Gladstone realizes that the Church must acclimatize itself to a more Liberal society, he proclaims his belief in a *quid pro quo* system according to which Anglicans would be prepared to bargain concessions with the Dissenters in return for 'the claim of the Church to have what is essential to her development done for her'.[26] The Church, and thus by implication judicious agreement to concessions which would remove some of the grounds of hostility to the Church, is all—and this explains Gladstone's diary entry in respect of his vote for the removal of the Jews' disabilities. 'It is a painful decision to come to. But the only substantive doubt it raises is about remaining in Parliamt. And it is truly & only the Church that holds me in there though she may seem to some to draw me from it.'[27]

A justificatory preface to the booklet edition of Gladstone's speech was of particular interest in providing yet more influential acknowledgement of how the political complexion of the Jewish question had been altered by Rothschild's election: Gladstone recalled how during the passage in 1845 of Lyndhurst's bill he had taken no part in the proceedings, then wanting time to reconsider his position rather than to decide prematurely on a question which had not practically arisen.[28] Some, however, of Gladstone's Peelite colleagues were not prepared to concede that the question had in the slightest degree been altered by Rothschild's election and Goulburn was foremost among those opponents of Emancipation who viewed the decision of the City electors as constituting a menacing challenge to the authority of the law. More akin to contemporary Continental conservatives than to his Peelite fellow Members, Goulburn was already renowned for his refusal to concede that legitimate pressures upon government could ever be exerted from below. Electors, he reasoned in a speech almost immediately following upon Gladstone's, could no more exceed their defined role and usurp the functions of the law than could jurors. If members of a jury in a particular case refused to convict prisoners charged with capital offences for the simple reason that they entertained an absolute objection to the infliction of the death penalty under any circumstance then those jurors could be accused of seeking by violation of their oaths to compel the legislature to abolish the death penalty; the repeal of oaths sought by the citizens of London in attempting to force upon the Commons as their Member a person subject to legal disqualification was, by the same token, tantamount to an abrogation of oaths in the courts of justice. The Commons should be jealous of any infringement of its rights; the admission of Gibbon was no precedent for defying the law but was, rather, an illustration of the inefficacy of human legislation as opposed to human depravity. It was interesting that whereas to Gladstone the criterion of 'consistency' invited the examination of parallels, to Goulburn use of the very same term suggested a search for analogies; stressing the evangelicalism of Christianity it was thus possible for Goulburn to argue that the 'inconsistency' or insincerity of admitting unconverted Jews to the legislature would effectively undermine the work of evangelists both at home and abroad.[29]

The speeches of Disraeli and of Lord George Bentinck in support of Emancipation are more germane to examination of the controversy which

they occasioned within the Protectionist ranks; if Disraeli was more cir-
cumspect in presenting his familiar thesis that Jews were entitled to Emancipation on grounds of Christian indebtedness—he smartly suggested that the
proof of conversionists' sincerity was an act of parliamentary Emancipation
precisely because the resulting mutual acquaintance would ensure
conversions[30]—the speech delivered by Bentinck was insouciant of his
supporters almost beyond expectation. Bentinck noted Goulburn's opinion
that it would be wrong to concede claims from the City of London of a
dangerous tendency, but then irritated the sensibilities of his party by
recalling how Catholic Emancipation had been effectively spurred on by the
forty shilling freeholders of Clare who had returned Daniel O'Connell. As for
the Jews' preparedness for parliamentary duty Bentinck remarked upon
their creditable performance in public office; a number of Jews had become
magistrates, recorders and jurors entrusted with the liberties of Christians,
and one of the Rothschilds had been chosen as High Sheriff to represent the
Queen in Buckinghamshire. Moreover, by their recent admission to offices
in the Corporation of the City of London, Jews in the capital would
eventually be enabled to become magistrates; Salomons, predicted Bentinck, would in due course become the Lord Mayor and thus an *ex officio*
member of the Privy Council.[31]

The Commons, prior to first reading, initially approved Russell's bill by
253 votes to 186, a majority of 67.[32] Analysis of the division—which was to
have momentous consequences for the future of the Tory or Protectionist
Party—reveals interesting features. Of the twenty-five Members (this
number does not include Rothschild) who represented the constituencies of
London and the major provincial cities which contained approximately
four-fifths of Anglo-Jewry (the City of London, Finsbury, Greenwich,
Lambeth, Marylebone, Southwark, Tower Hamlets, Westminster and
Middlesex; Birmingham, Liverpool and Manchester), no less than twenty-
three voted in favour of the measure, one either abstained, was paired or was
for some reason absent (T. Duncombe, the radical from Finsbury, who was a
maverick on questions relating to Jews), and only one voted against (J.
Masterman, the Peelite from the City of London). The two Members of
Parliament for Portsmouth and the two for Southampton, representing
municipalities where Jews had been elected to office, all voted for Emancipation and considerable support was received from the other urban centres
where Jews lived. The more rural a constituency the greater the likelihood
that a vote was cast against the measure: more than two-thirds of the bill's
opponents sat for country towns or districts predominantly agricultural in
character. But even in these rural constituencies, many of which were
represented in Parliament by two or more Members, the ratio of voting was
no more than approximately seven to five against the bill. As the Protectionists championed agricultural interests it was not surprising that the
character of a constituency should in so many instances have proved a guide

to the voting decision of a Member. Whilst only four Protectionists (Bentinck, Disraeli, Milnes Gaskell and T. Baring, the formerly unsuccessful candidate for the City in the 1843 by-election who was now Member for a rural constituency) supported the bill, Beresford, the Protectionist whip, noted that 138 opposed it and that 41 Peelites voted with them compared to the eleven, including Peel himself, who voted for Emancipation.[33]

Taking into account such factors as by-election vacancies, constituency disenfranchisement and the ineligibility of Rothschild, the working membership of the Commons was about 650 Members; the strength of the Peelites approached, almost exactly, half that of the Protectionists but as a Conservative combination the two groups could outnumber, by a dozen votes more or less, the ministerialist bloc of Whigs or Liberals and franchise, free trade radicals to which were appended as customary voting allies those Irish Members pledged to repeal the Union with Britain. If the two Protectionist and Peelite groupings, according to Beresford's tally, supplied 179 of the opposition votes and 15 supporters for the Emancipation lobby it would seem reasonable to deduce that, after pairing, the final factor leading to explanation of the ascendancy of 67 lies in the comparatively high level of abstentions among the Protectionists and the Peelites relative to those of the ministerialists. Leaving aside, therefore, those abstentions which cancel out each other, importance attaches to a like, surplus body of approximately 60 Protectionists and Peelites which constitutes the differential of abstention; Peelites, not surprisingly, are found to constitute the bulk of this group.

Russell, in reflecting that Peelite behaviour had assured that his majority would be a comfortable one, could look forward to the debates on further stages of the bill. On 7 February, during the second reading debate, Sheil, the Irish orator and playwright, advanced in the course of a passionately eloquent speech a variant on a theme long since expounded by such prolific pamphleteers of Emancipation as F. H. Goldsmid, J. E. Blunt, the advocate of Jews being able to own land as an incentive to patriotism, and Apsley Pellatt, the City manufacturer and politician and prominent Dissenting Deputy. 'In the same measure in which we have relaxed the laws against the Jews, that patriot instinct by which we are taught to love the land of our birth, has been revived.' Thus for perfect development in future, concluded Sheil, it was only necessary to concede to the Jews perfect justice.[34]

Four days later Sir Robert Peel addressed the Commons.[35] To a whole generation, to politicians as dissimilar as Palmerston and Cobden, Peel represented as did no other statesman 'the spirit of the times', 'the idea of the age', and it was therefore with the deepest respect, and not a faked interest in sitting through the speech of a lost leader, that the House listened to his arguments. Peel, in common with Gladstone, made much of the need for consistency. The precedents of 1828 and 1829 meant that no vital Eldonine principle remained to be breached; having conceded so much it was only consistent to concede the whole. Here Peel could claim that some of the same criteria which he had employed eighteen years before to justify continued exclusion now equally justified Emancipation.[36] For in the interval since the Jewish question had last been broached by him in 1830 the Quakers, the Moravians and the Separatists had been admitted to Parliament. And so too had the Unitarians, to whom there were no objections; they rejected one of the fundamental doctrines of the Christian faith and yet it was precisely this Christian character of the legislature which was often emphasised as a barrier to the Jews' admission. Jews also bore comparison with the Quakers, differing from them in not denying the right to tithes and entertaining no scruples as to the lawfulness of war.

Even in respect of oaths vital precedents had been set. The Quakers, the Moravians and the Separatists were all allowed to affirm and thus to waive upon entry to the Commons those words which they found personally offensive. Peel referred in particular to the case of Pease, the Quaker, adducing this as evidence that a set form of oath could no longer be deemed an essential prerequisite of admission to the legislature. The connection between the inquisitorial power of punishing men for religious error and the maintenance of a civil disability which was tantamount to infliction of such penalty led Peel to discussion of the secular, Lockeian distinction as to the necessity of oaths. Peel, in recalling the different motives of the legislature at various times, reminded Members that the words 'upon the true faith of a Christian' had not been a continuous qualification for the legislature since the reign of James I: allowed to lapse in the circumstances of 1688–89 they had only been revived more than a decade later for the purely political purpose of excluding Jacobites from office. The intent and effect of the 1701 oath had been quite different from the anti-Catholicism of that framed at the time of the Gunpowder Plot. Although the test of political attitude might happen to be religious opinions, as from the beginning of the eighteenth century until the repeal of disabilities it was for essentially political reasons that the Catholics had been excluded from power. They were excluded not on account of Mariolatry or transubstantiation but because it was feared they would abuse political power; exclusion was practised on account of the view that Catholics were considered to be dangerous and seditious subjects, in consequence of their acknowledgement of the supremacy of a foreign Power and their allegiance to another Sovereign. In such circumstances a religious test had been the only available guard. In the aftermath of 1829 the particular case to be weighed by Members was bound to be inclined the more heavily in favour of Emancipation because, unlike the Catholics, Jews could own to no rival religious establishment.

Consistency meant that regard should be paid not only to the admission of the other non-Anglican classes of religionists; for Peel, as for Gladstone, this criterion invited consideration of the point that Parliament, whilst yet withholding the shadow, had already conceded the substance. Peel observed that Jews possessed the elective franchise and that in respect of civil, political and municipal office their position had changed very considerably over the previous eighteen years. Baronetcies had been conferred upon such Jews as Montefiore and Rothschild; since 1845 all municipal offices had been open to Jews and all civil and military appointments were, with very few exceptions, also tenable by them. Peel, to meet the new circumstances presented by Rothschild's election, adapted a point made by Melbourne fifteen years earlier, remarking upon the anomaly which allowed Christian electors to suffer a curtailment of their choice whilst yet enabling the Crown to appoint Jews to important executive and civil offices.

Peel, noting that the Church of England was stronger than at any period in her history, advanced the view, wholly in character with his political philosophy, that one great cause of that strength lay in the disposition of the Church to admit timely and salutary reforms. And yet an even greater cause of the Church's strength was the deep religious feeling in the country; here Peel sought with *The Times* to distinguish between the real and imagined strengths of Christianity. The Church was rooted in the affections of the people and it was disparaging to the Church to contend that her safety depended upon the exclusion of a handful of Jews. Emancipation, tantamount to reparation for centuries of wrong, would carry abroad the moral authority of a just and benevolent example and make it impossible to look to England as justification for prejudice. The attraction of Christianity, thereby enhanced, would prove groundless the fears of Goulburn: the good work of Christian missions, far from being undermined by Emancipation, would be greatly encouraged. As for Sir Moses Montefiore's missions abroad, on behalf of distressed Jews, these would have proved more effective had disabilities been removed. Peel shared Hazlitt's understanding of where the responsibility lay for the origins of degradation, believing equally that it was erroneous to reproach Jews for separateness and for a deficiency of attachment to those institutions under which persecutory wrongs had been inflicted. Peel's contention that Emancipation would console such suffering, downtrodden Jews abroad whilst yet at the same time serving to weaken their opponents was more remarkable than would at first sight appear. On the very eve of European revolution here was the most respected contemporary British Conservative advocating Emancipation for a group which was to loom so menacingly in the van of opposition to the established order.

The Commons accorded Russell's bill a second reading by 277 votes to 204, a majority of 73. In a turnout generally larger than that of 17 December 1847 the respective ranks of ministerialists and Protectionists could be seen to be voting as one-sidedly along the predictable party lines; of the Peelites, however, while the total number opposing Emancipation varied little, the minority prepared to support Russell's bill increased to at least 20.[37] Some of the erstwhile abstainers had been convinced that the Peelite group to which they belonged had secured reelection to Parliament only by drawing upon a pool of anti-Whig votes, a conviction strengthened in the knowledge that more of these would have been theirs but for the support which the former Tory Government had given to Maynooth.[38] Peel's impressive commitment on this occasion influenced a number of the former abstainers to dispel their doubts about supporting Emancipation. The bill was now enabled to pass through its remaining stages in the Commons and, after being granted a third reading by a majority of 61,[39] it passed to the Lords.

But there progress was abruptly halted.[40] Strength of opposition to Jewish Emancipation invariably bore a correlation to the influence exercised by the episcopal leadership of the Church of England; while in the House of Commons some of the most vehement opponents of Emancipation were, to those outside of their party, tarnished by an equally vehement denunciation of such measures as the Repeal of the Corn Laws, in the House of the Lords the bishops proved a more influential focus of opposition. Since December there had been several important manifestations of feeling. While the Commons had been preparing for the first major division on Russell's bill, a petition conveyed through Lord Dartmouth to the Home Secretary, Sir George Grey, had expressed the objection to Emancipation recorded by the Birmingham Church of England Lay Association.[41] Then, a month later, the Bishop of Durham had been able to restrain some of his clergy from holding a meeting on the Jewish question only by emphasising how invidious it would be for the clergy to act collectively as a body on questions which involved the royal prerogative and the civil privileges of fellow citizens.[42] Religious objections to Emancipation were also bound to be rife in the two Church-dominated ancient universities. One pamphleteer, openly proclaiming his Cambridge connection, argued that the eighteen hundred years of wandering visited upon the Jews was a measure of the Divine displeasure which necessarily befell those who had sinfully rejected Christ; to admit the Jews to Parliament would thus represent a regression from Christianity to Judaism.[43] It was indeed symbolic of the controversy that one of the most acerbic speeches in the Lords opposing the second reading on 25 May should have come from the Bishop of Oxford, Sam Wilberforce; his words were closely heeded as reflecting the views not only of influential churchmen at Oxford, Puseyites included, but also as expressing the personal beliefs of one who, in his own right, deserved credit for having infused new life into the Church by some remarkable diocesan innovation. Insisting that the Jews hated Christianity and accusing them of having slain Christ as a malefactor, Wilberforce argued that in the event of admission to Parliament it would be impossible to assume any principle inconsistent with their avowed opinions.[44] Notable in standing out for the contrary view was Thirlwall, Bishop of St. David's. Robustly Whig in politics, Thirlwall had in 1834 been forced to relinquish his Cambridge Assistant Tutorship on account of his support for a House of Commons bill for the admission of Dissenters to university degrees and for his condemnation of the theological emphasis at the Cambridge colleges. On this occasion he was to be found reiterating the by now familiar argument in respect of the Unitarians; pointing out that in the crucial respect of not believing in the Divinity of Christ Jews and Unitarians stood on the same ground, Thirlwall noted that although the privilege of parliamentary Emancipation had been granted to the Unitarians it was still being withheld from the Jews.[45]

Lord Malmesbury, the future Cabinet minister in Derby's Tory Governments, was to recall towards the end of his life how he had never seen the Upper House so full as on this occasion. Both Lionel Rothschild, as elected Member of Parliament for the City, and his brother 'stood like elder sons of Peers on the steps of the throne, and would not even retire when the division took place'.[46] To their disappointment Russell's measure was rejected by 163 votes to 128, a majority of 35. Voting against the bill were the Archbishops of Canterbury and Armagh together with 16 bishops; voting in its favour were the Archbishop of York and 4 bishops. Two further supporters of relief legislation were absent: one bishop, who had ensured that he was paired off against an opponent, and Archbishop Whately, who was preoccupied with the crisis in Dublin.[47] The commitment of nearly the full complement of Lords Spiritual was now known and the extent of episcopal hostility invited some predictably waspish comment on the part of the Protestant Dissenting Deputies; their petitioning of Parliament in favour of the Jewish cause, after both the second and third readings of the bill in the Commons, had already thrown into contrast the conflicting attitudes of Church and Dissent.[48]

The Lords' decision marked too a personal rebuff for Russell, as sponsor of the bill and as Rothschild's party colleague in the City. Doubts about the constitutional propriety of a Prime Minister so closely involving himself in settlement of such an issue as the Jewish disabilities, aired almost a year before at the time of the election, now resurfaced. The Duke of Argyll, who had both spoken in favour of and voted for Emancipation in the Lords' debate of 25 May, heard a rumour soon afterwards to the effect that Russell was considering sending up to the Lords that very summer yet another relief bill in changed form. Doubtless with the current Continental and Chartist agitations in mind, Argyll emphasised the inconvenience and danger of such a proceeding. This was a moment when everything depended upon the preservation of good feeling between the various branches of the constitution and so distinct an expression of disrespect for the deliberate opinion of the House of Lords, given after what he considered to have been a good debate unmarred by any mixture of party spirit, would be most unjustifiable. Another bill in the present session could have one of only two consequences: the result would either discredit the peers for appearing so hastily to go back on their very recent careful deliberations, or it would court the danger of raising bad feeling between the two Houses. Another bill in the next session of Parliament would be quite acceptable. Argyll trusted that any further relief measure this session would be frustrated in the Commons; if, by chance, it were not he for one would have no hesitation in voting against it and he was sure that many others who had formerly voted for Emancipation would act likewise.[49]

In the event Russell did not attempt to push another measure through Parliament during the summer, but this prudence did not spare him from criticism during the 'business of the session' debate of 30 August 1848. On this occasion Disraeli delivered a speech which amounted to a constitutional *exposé* of Russell's handling of the Jewish Disabilities Bill and of the manner in which the Prime Minister had attempted to pilot it through Parliament. Disraeli pointed out that approximately fifty measures, some of them very important, had either failed to win approval or had been jettisoned as victims of the parliamentary timetable: for these ill-fated measures the Prime Minister was responsible, because he had neither decided beforehand which pieces of legislation should receive priority nor had he taken soundings to ensure that a sufficient number of votes could be relied upon in both Houses for the passage of such legislation. Whereas one of the Government's proposed measures, the repeal of the Navigation Laws, had been mentioned in the Queen's Speech, its introduction as late as 15 May had left insufficient time to procure enactment. And for the cause of that particular failure, opined Disraeli, one need look no further than to the introduction of a bill which had itself been omitted from the Queen's Speech—and that was the Jewish Disabilities Bill 'to which he [Russell] devoted all the strength and energies of the Government'. Russell, contended Disraeli, had generally demeaned the office of Prime Minister. 'Though I agree with [Russell] as to the principle which animated his legislation, I do not at all approve of his conduct as manager of the House of Commons.' Drawing on the Catholic Emancipation legislation for a precedent, Disraeli argued that a minister should not bring forward such a species of measure unless first confident of being able to carry it through Parliament. For failure imparted a party bitterness and a party spirit to subjects where there should be little party spirit and absolutely no party bitterness; the very incurring of a risk of failure was, moreover, both imprudent and impolitic because the defeat of a minister meant that the cause with which he was associated itself received a setback. All these points made by Disraeli elicited only a weak reply from the Prime Minister and events in succeeding years were to confirm that Russell did not accept such criticisms as valid.[50]

That the Emancipation struggle was to continue for another ten years was to be explained by the recalcitrance of the House of Lords—though the peers themselves could argue that it was not the unreconstituted Lords which was acting contrary to form, but rather the Commons which, having changed in social composition both since and as a result of the Reform, was failing to uphold its first negative vote given in 1830. No matter. The Lords did, in the final analysis, represent a world which could not easily acclimatize itself to freedom in questions of thought and religion, let alone be expected voluntarily to see its own territorial aristocracy give way to the interests of an industrial democracy—with which the Jews were so bound up. Rather, the peers sought by cleverly assimilating new men to their own world to postpone such a process of transformation. Here it is worth noting that post-1688 England, oligarchic if mercantile, gentlemanly if not closed to opportunity, was in a process of half-institutionalization; Emancipation of the Jews, whether it took ten or twenty years more to achieve, might prove to be one of the last victories of Whiggism.

Moreover the Lords were generally opposed to concessionary claims in the decade after 1848, that revolutionary year which could not but engender a reaction in defence of Throne and Altar: a speech of the Archbishop of Canterbury in June 1849 was to cite Continental experience as good reason for not yielding to the Jews' claims. Electoral considerations did not weigh with the peers and they resisted concessions if at all possible. For three decades the Lords thwarted attempts to relieve the Dissenters from payment of church rates for the upkeep of Anglican churches—relief was first discussed in the 1830s but did not fully come about until 1868. Likewise, the question of entrance for Dissenters at Oxford and Cambridge, which was first discussed in the 1830s: Jews were hardly the most affected by the disabilities which withheld the Bachelor of Arts degree at Oxford and Cambridge until the mid-1850s and all other non-divinity degrees at the two universities until 1871. Another question too remained unresolved for more than thirty years: although the substance of an Irish Church Temporalities Act was first discussed in 1833, the Irish Church was not actually disestablished until 1869. Indeed, with Ireland in mind, the Jews had even less to complain of when the circumstances of the Catholic Emancipation struggle are recalled. The Catholics had, after all, proved the theoretical case for relief by the late 1780s, only to see the French Revolutionary and Napoleonic Wars supervene, thus effectively postponing Emancipation for thirty to forty years. And although by the second half of the 1840s the fact of Catholic Emancipation was undeniably beginning to work in favour of the Jews, the revival of anti-Romanist feeling during the first half of the subsequent decade, as denoted by popular use of the term 'Papal Aggression', seemed, albeit for a fleeting moment, to jeopardize the value of even this concession.

Opposition to the Jews' claims, though in some instances justification for the most virulent of prejudices, was not only explicable: it was quite unexceptionable. Change here, as in all things English, would come but slowly.

NOTES

1. *Parliamentary Papers,* Reports from Commissioners: Twenty Volumes. Volume 8—Corporation of London. Session, 31 January–12 August 1854. Volume XXVI [1772]. Report of the Commissioners appointed to inquire into the existing state of the Corporation of the City of London, and to collect information respecting its constitution, order and government, etc. together with the Minutes of Evidence, and appendix (1854), pp. xiv–xv.

2. The following account of the 1847 election in the City of London is based on *The Spectator,* no. 991, 26 June 1847, p. 604; no. 992, 3 July 1847, p. 630; no. 996 31 July 1847, p. 721; *The Times* (all issues for 1847), 9 July, p. 8; 12 July, p. 3; 14 July, p. 7; 16 July, p. 7; 17 July, p. 8; 19 July, p. 8; 20 July, p. 8; 21 July, p. 7; 23 July, p. 8; 24 July, p. 8; 27 July, p. 8; 29 July, p. 2; 31 July, pp. 2, 6.

3. Address in M. Margoliouth, *The History of the Jews in Great Britain,* II, pp. 257–69.

4. Russell Papers, P.R.O. 30/22, 6d, 160–61, 15 July 1847, Grey to Russell.

5. F. D. Maurice, 'Thoughts on Jewish Disabilities', *Fraser's Magazine for Town and Country,* vol. XXXVI, July–December 1847, no. CCXV, November 1847, pp. 623–30.

6. *Hansard,* Third Series, 95, 16 December 1847, 1234–1332; *Hansard,* Third Series, 95, 17 December 1847, 1356–1401.

7. Leading articles in *The Times,* 22 November and 17 December 1847; *The Morning Advertiser,* 16, 17 and 20 December 1847; *The Morning Chronicle,* 15 and 20 December 1847; *Manchester Guardian,* 22 December 1847; *The Standard,* December 1847; *The Morning Post,* 15 and 18 December 1847; *Morning Herald,* 20 December 1847, p. 4, and 22 December 1847, p. 4.

8. Russell, *Hansard,* Third Series, 95, 16 December 1847, 1239–40; *Hansard,* Third Series, 125, 15 April 1853, 1284–85.

9. *The Times,* 22 November 1847, leading article; *The Times,* 17 December 1847, leading article.

10. Inglis, *Hansard,* Third Series, 95, 16 December 1847, 1257–58.

11. E. Williams, *Capitalism and Slavery,* pp. 195–96; J. S. Schapiro, 'Thomas Carlyle, Prophet of Fascism', *The Journal of Modern History,* vol. XVII, June 1945, no. 2, pp. 97–115.

12. J. Pope Hennessy, *Monckton Milnes,* I, *The Years of Promise, 1809–51,* p. 268, letter from Carlyle to Monckton Milnes, December 1847.

13. Cf., in this connection, E. Hodder, *The Life and Work of the Seventh Earl of Shaftesbury, with Extracts from Lord Shaftesbury's Diaries and Journals,* pp. 328–29, address to the Society for the Conversion of the Jews, 1845.

14. Ibid., p. 493.

15. Ibid., p. 388, diary for 15 December 1847.

16. Ibid., diary for 17 December 1847, recording feelings of the previous day. Ashley, *Hansard,* Third Series, 95, 16 December 1847, 1272–82, for the ensuing references to Ashley's speech.

17. For this and all succeeding references to Gladstone's speech see Gladstone, *Hansard,* Third Series, 95, 16 December 1847, 1282–1304.

18. E. Hodder, *The Life and Works of the Seventh Earl of Shaftesbury,* pp. 177–78, diary for 12 March 1841.

19. Gladstone, *Hansard,* Third Series, 57, 31 March 1841, 754–60.

20. J. Morley, *The Life of William Ewart Gladstone,* I, pp. 375–77 for Gladstone's correspondence with his father and others on the Jewish question, 1847–48.

21. Ibid.; M. R. D. Foot and H. C. G. Matthew (eds.), *The Gladstone Diaries,* III, 1840–47, p. 676, entry for Thursday, 16 December 1847, for the Van Oven reference.

22. Gladstone, *Hansard,* Third Series, 57, 31 March 1841, 754–60.

23. Walter Bagehot, 'Mr. Gladstone', *National Review,* XI, July 1860, pp. 219–43, in *The Collected Works of Walter Bagehot,* ed. N. St. John-Stevas, III, pp. 415–40.

24. Letter from Pusey to Gladstone, 13 December 1847, from the Pusey Papers, printed in appendix to article by L. Abrahams, 'Sir I. L. Goldsmid and the Admission of the Jews of England to Parliament', *Transactions of the Jewish Historical Society of England,* IV, 1903, pp. 123–24.

25. Letter from Gladstone to Pusey, 14 December 1847, marked 'private', from the Pusey Papers, printed in G. I. T. Machin, *Politics and the Churches in Great Britain, 1832 to 1868,* p. 194.

26. *Correspondence on Church and Religion of William Ewart Gladstone,* selected and arranged by D. C. Lathbury, I, pp. 79–80, letter from Gladstone to his brother-in-law, Lord Lyttelton, 10 September 1847, for this statement in relation to the *quid pro quo* bargaining notion. For the later development of Gladstone's thought along these lines, cf. G. I. T. Machin, 'Gladstone and Nonconformity in the 1860's: the formation of an alliance', *The Historical Journal,* XVII, 2 (1974), pp. 347–364.

27. M. R. D. Foot and H. C. G. Matthew (eds.), *The Gladstone Diaries*, III, 1840–47, p. 676.

28. W. E. Gladstone, *Substance of a Speech on the Motion of Lord John Russell for a Committee of the whole House, with a view to the removal of the remaining Jewish Disabilities; delivered in the House of Commons, on Thursday, December 16, 1847. together with a Preface*, 1848, Preface, pp. 20–21.

29. Goulburn, *Hansard*, Third Series, 95, 16 December 1847, 1314–21.

30. Disraeli, *Hansard*, Third Series, 95, 16 December 1847, 1321–30.

31. Bentinck, *Hansard*, Third Series, 95, 17 December 1847, 1381–90.

32. *Hansard*, Third Series, 95, 16 December 1847, 1234–1332; *Hansard*, Third Series, 95, 17 December 1847, 1356–1401.

33. R. Stewart, *The Politics of Protection: Lord Derby and the Protectionist Party, 1841–1852*, p. 122, noting letter from Beresford to Stanley, undated, Derby MSS, 149/1.

34. *Hansard*, Third Series, 96, 7 February 1848, 220–83 for first part of the second reading debate. Sheil, col. 278.

35. Peel, *Hansard*, Third Series, 96, 11 February 1848, 518–36.

36. Cf. Peel, *Hansard*, New Series, 24, 17 May 1830, 802–7.

37. *Hansard*, Third Series, 96, 11 February 1848, 460–540, for continuation of the second reading debate; cf. J. B. Conacher, *The Peelites and the Party System, 1846–52*, pp. 49, 220–25, for an analysis of Peelite voting behaviour based on a rather broad definition of what constituted a 'Free Trade Conservative'. Conacher's analysis, and definition, p. 65 and passim, may be compared with the even more fussy and fastidious definitions and analyses to be found in W. D. Jones and A. B. Erickson, *The Peelites, 1846–1857*.

38. G. I. T. Machin, 'The Maynooth Grant, the Dissenters and Disestablishment, 1845–1847', *The English Historical Review*, 82, p. 83.

39. *Hansard*, Third Series, 97, 3 April 1848, 1215–50; *Hansard*, Third Series, 98, 4 May 1848, 606–70.

40. *Hansard*, Third Series, 98, 25 May 1848, 1330–1409, for the following account of the Lords' debate.

41. Jewish Museum Papers, Jewish Central Library, Woburn House, MSS 66, 17 December 1847, Lord Dartmouth to Sir G. Grey.

42. Russell Papers, P.R.O. 30/22, 7a, 81–82, 11 January 1848, Bishop of Durham to Russell, 83–84, 13 January 1848, Bishop of Durham to one of his archdeacons.

43. A Graduate of the University of Cambridge, *A Few Words on the Proposed Admission of Jews into Parliament*, pp. 4, 7.

44. Wilberforce, Bishop of Oxford, *Hansard*, Third Series, 98, 25 May 1848, 1377.

45. Thirlwall, Bishop of St. David's, *Hansard*, Third Series, 98, 25 May 1848, 1361.

46. J. H. Harris, third Earl of Malmesbury, *Memoirs of an Ex-Minister. An Autobiography*, I, p. 230.

47. *Hansard*, Third Series, 98, 25 May 1848, 1330–1409 for proceedings of the Lords' debate, including speeches of Wilberforce and Thirlwall; cols. 1406–9 for the division.

48. B. L. Manning, *The Protestant Dissenting Deputies*, p. 212, noting petitions of 20 December 1847 and 14 February 1848 and the *Report of the Committee of the Protestant Dissenting Deputies for 1848*.

49. Jewish Museum Papers, Jewish Central Library, Woburn House, MSS 82, 5 June 1848, Duke of Argyll to an unknown correspondent.

50. *Hansard*, Third Series, 101, 30 August 1848, cols. 669–707 for Disraeli's speech and cols. 707–18 for Russell's reply.

9
The Tory Leadership Crisis

Impressive as may have been the quality of parliamentary debate on the Jewish question during the session of 1847–48 this factor cannot in itself explain why Emancipation should so suddenly have become an issue in British politics. The newfound importance of Emancipation derives, rather, from developments in the Tory Party arising from the two-day debate of December 1847 when Lord George Bentinck fell foul of his supporters by not only voting for Emancipation but also by speaking in its favour. The ensuing crisis involved the second deposition of a Tory leader within virtually eighteen months and the opening up of a vacuum which was eventually to be filled only by the emergence of Disraeli.

If 'liberty'—liberty mercantile and commercial, civil and religious—was the watchword uniting for the purposes of Government an assortment of Whigs or Liberals, radicals and Irish, 'protection', in matters of religion as well as of trade, epitomised to an equal degree the philosophy of the party committed to the defence of Throne and Altar. Jewish Emancipation, no less than Catholic Emancipation, constituted a talismanic divide marking out old Whig from old Tory; it was significant that those who, on other issues, had dissociated themselves at some time in the past from one or other of the two traditional alignments, now recalled those earlier disagreements by their respective stands on the Jewish question. There were the Peelites, who had broken with their fellow Conservatives over Free Trade, and the Canningites, who had seceded from the Tories in consequence of Wellington's initial refusal to concede Emancipation to the Catholics. Over the years the Jewish cause had come to attract, in particular, a number of eminent ex-Canningites: although by 1847–48 Lord Melbourne, the former William Lamb, and two of his contemporaries, William Huskisson and Robert Grant, had departed the political scene, Lord Palmerston, Lord Stanley, heir to the thirteenth Earl of Derby, and Lord George Bentinck, son of the fourth Duke of Portland and a former secretary to Canning, were now all three to the forefront of their respective parties.

But where Palmerston, through having transferred his allegiance, was to find himself in accord with the religious policy of his colleagues, Bentinck, in having remained with the Tories, was foredoomed to emerge on the Jewish question as an almost isolated dissentient. A popular figure, Bentinck had been elected to the Tory leadership of the Commons in the summer of 1846 primarily on account of his attack on Peel for having abandoned the Corn Laws: his religious views, apart from being known only to those with uncommonly good memories, then seemed scarcely relevant. Stanley's succession to the leadership of the Tory party as a whole was likewise to be attributed to a defence of agricultural protection; in view of their shared Canningite past, Bentinck cannot but have hoped that their working partnership, with Stanley leading in the Lords, might have extended to religious questions. In this he was to be cruelly disappointed. Although Stanley had begun life as a Canningite Tory and had in consequence transferred to the Whigs and served in Grey's Cabinet he had retraced his steps and recrossed the Commons to support Peel. The final renunciation of his Canningite-Whig past had been consummated in 1846; as fourteenth Earl of Derby he was to concede the substance of the Jews' claims only in 1858.

Had Bentinck's views on religious questions been more widely known future difficulties in connection with Jewish Emancipation might have been anticipated. He had voted in favour of the Maynooth grant[1] and in the election of the summer of 1847 had further offended some of his followers by recording in his address to prospective constituents at King's Lynn the opinion that some provision out of the land should be made to the Catholic priesthood of Ireland. Apart from offending certain religious sentiments the proposal had annoyed the many more Tories who considered that after Maynooth it would be inappropriate to encourage additional religious endowments. Nonetheless, at the time Bentinck's personal opinion was grudgingly respected; it was only when he manifested new deviance over Emancipation that former suspicions were revived.[2]

At the end of September 1847 Bentinck despatched a letter to Croker, outlining his own position in regard to the Jewish question. Bentinck wrote:

I have always, I believe, voted in favour of the Jews. I say I believe, because I never could work myself up into caring two straws about the question one way or the other, and scarcely know how I may have voted, viewing it quite differently from the Roman Catholic question, which I have ever considered a great national concernment. . . . The Jew question I look upon as a personal matter, as I would a great private estate or Divorce Bill . . . like the questions affecting the Roman Catholics, with the Protectionist Party it should remain an open question. I shall probably give a silent vote, maintaining my own consistency in favour of the Jews, but not offending the larger portion of the party, who, I presume, will be the other way. . . . The City of London having elected Lionel Rothschild one of her representatives, it is such a pronunciation of public opinion that I do not think the party, as a party, would do themselves any good by taking up the question against the Jews. It is like Clare electing O'Connell, Yorkshire Wilberforce. Clare settled the Catholic question, Yorkshire the slave trade, and now the City of London has settled the Jew question.[3]

Bentinck would the more easily have been able to explain his position to his followers had he enjoyed closer contacts with them. Stanley observed how Bentinck was alienating many members of the party by the distance he kept from them; Stanley was having to hold meetings of Protectionists in both Houses and in October 1847 he asked Bentinck to take a more decided lead in issuing notices and in calling meetings in his own name.[4] Such a firm lead was, however, precisely what Bentinck felt he could not give; it would achieve nothing except to exacerbate differences with his followers. At the beginning of November he complained of his predicament to Disraeli, as one of the few fellow dissentients on the Jewish question: 'Ld Stanley and all the Party are pressing me very hard to surrender my opinions about the Jews.—Has not Lord Stanley himself voted in favour of the Jews?—I confess I don't know how I have voted myself but I can not help thinking that Lord Stanley and I have both voted together in favour of the Jews.'[5]

Lord John Manners, former associate of Disraeli in the Romantic 'Young England' movement and better placed than most of the Protectionists to appreciate the value to the party of the few dissentients on the Jewish question, saw clearly the dangers which faced the Opposition in the weeks leading up to the parliamentary debates on Emancipation. Disraeli, one of the most promising leaders of the party, was known to favour the Jews, while Bentinck, likewise, was refusing to yield to Stanley's persuasion. Having earlier observed that the issue of the Corn Laws, that 'bond of union', was 'dead and buried',[6] Manners was vexed that at the very time when the Protectionists enjoyed a clear superiority 'in the three great spheres of debate', Ireland, Free Imports and the Currency, revival of the Jewish question should so jeopardize this party advantage. 'I see no daylight through that Cimmerian Darkness', wrote Manners to Disraeli.[7] Bentinck himself was equally gloomy: as a temperate supporter of Emancipation he could not understand the intemperate reaction of those in the party unable to keep the issue in perspective. 'I am lowspirited', he wrote to Disraeli, 'at seeing the Party occupying itself about the admission or exclusion of an individual from Parliament at a moment when the greatest Commercial Empire of the World is engaged in a life and death struggle for existence. It is tea table twaddling more becoming a pack of Old Maids than a great Party aspiring to govern an Empire on which the Sun never sets.'[8] Bentinck felt that in view of his own past support for Emancipation he could not now renege without incurring some dishonour for abandoning Disraeli. As he explained in a letter to Manners, 'I don't like letting Disraeli vote by himself apart from the party: otherwise I might give in to the prejudices of the multitude.'[9]

Disraeli was to recall how, as the days set aside for debate drew closer, Bentinck steadfastly refused to succumb to the least wishes of his party. First he was requested to vote against the Jews; then he was urged to absent himself so as to avoid having to vote at all; finally he was pleaded with merely to refrain from actually speaking in the Jews' favour.[10] Bentinck felt that any compromise with his party would itself actually compromise that very integrity which, in the split on Repeal in 1846, had seemed to the Protectionists to contrast so favourably with Peel's supposed lack of integrity. Declining last minute entreaties to use his poor health as an excuse for absenteeism, abstention and silence, Bentinck, with the characteristic courage of his convictions, chose the second day of the December debate to deliver his long speech.

Bentinck began uncomfortably: 'I never rose to address the House under such a sense of difficulty as on this occasion.' There followed the admission on his part that a silent vote would have been preferred, 'but I feel that I might be supposed to be slinking if I were to do no more than to register my vote upon this Motion'. Aggrieved by having to speak against his own colleagues, Bentinck made acknowledgement of the rumours that his actions might damage the Party, indeed might actually 'destroy the Party'. Yet to act against his own altruism might be to inflict an equally severe amount of damage on the Party. The absence of any misconduct by the Jewish community and the inapplicability to Emancipation of 'the more rigid and exclusive principles of Parliament' left nothing which he could cite as justification for reversing in 1847 the votes in favour given in 1830 and 1833.[11]

According to Sir James Graham, Peel's former Home Secretary, Bentinck faced such repeated interruptions from his own side that he even had difficulty in speaking; while Peel himself observed that Disraeli's assertion of the superiority of Judaism served only to aggravate this party discontent with the leadership. Peel wrote to Graham:

> The universal talk after the Jew Bill debate was that Mr. Disraeli's speech had given the greatest offence, and that Lord George Bentinck was formally deposed.—I never trust universal talk. The strongest proof of the virtual deposition of Lord George was the disinclination of all sides of the House to listen to him.—I hope to see Inglis in his proper place as the leader of a real old Tory, Church of England, Protectionist, Protestant party; and Lord Stanley acting in concert with him.[12]

Peel's sources were reliable: immediately after the vote, in which Bentinck and Disraeli were supported in the division lobbies by only two other members of the party (Milnes Gaskell and the erstwhile City candidate Thomas Baring, now sitting for a rural constituency), Beresford, one of the whips, informed Bentinck that he no longer commanded the allegiance of the party.[13] Here, in a confused situation, the role of the whips as channels of communication almost certainly assumed a particular importance. Manners wrote that Beresford was regarded by many of the party stalwarts as someone always to be found acting in opposition to the leaders;[14] his Protestantism was inflamed by fears of a Whig-Papal 'plot' of which the establishment of Catholic sees in England would supposedly afford evidence.[15] Beresford's fellow whip, C. N. Newdegate, likewise looked upon

Emancipation as a Papal plot masquerading in the guise of a pseudo-Whiggism. But though there could be no questioning of Newdegate's sincerity as manifested in the two-day debate and on subsequent occasions,[16] doubts on this score were entertained in respect of Beresford. In a letter to Disraeli of 29 December Manners pronounced Beresford

> an enigma—to me at least: but evidently possessed of considerable abilities and full of ambition. Beyond a certain traditionary hatred of Irish Priests, much softened down by living in England, I doubt his caring much for that Protestantism which he has so successfully evoked against his leaders. . . . I can't help entertaining a suspicion that he used the influence his position as Whip necessarily gave him to increase, not diminish, the intolerant agitation that has at last ended in this smash.[17]

Disraeli shared the opinion that Beresford had somewhat exceeded his authority. In the biography of his former leader, Disraeli was to recall how Bentinck's speech and vote in favour of the Jews led to dissatisfaction with his leadership being conveyed to him, but 'unfortunately he [Bentinck] received this when the House had adjourned for the holidays, and when Mr. Bankes [the unofficial chairman of the party], who had been the organ of communication with him in '46, was in the country, and when the party was of course generally dispersed'. Disraeli states that Bentinck, in ailing health, failed to ascertain whether the representation which was made to him was that of the general feeling of a large party, or that only of a sincere, highly estimable, but limited section, 'the opportunity of release coming to him at a moment when he was physically prostrate was rather eagerly seized'.[18] Disraeli was here echoing Bentinck's own feeling of disgust, conveyed in a letter to a supporter, as to the suspect timing of his opponents' moves; it was only on the very last day of the parliamentary session, Monday, 20 December, that he had received the intimation that the party would no longer consent to be led by him.[19]

Disraeli, bound by his loyalty to Bentinck, probably failed to appreciate the almost greater measure of resentment which was generated by his own intervention in the debate; many members of the party had been deeply offended by the speeches and votes of the two leaders. W. Monsell, an Irish member, let it be known that but for Disraeli's speech he would have voted for Emancipation, while Lord Henry Lennox had earlier warned that if Bentinck 'voted for the Jews without publicly dissenting from the gross blasphemies uttered by Disraeli' he would actually resign from the party.[20]

It was in retrospect significant that the move by a section of the party to depose Bentinck should have been staged only hours after a vehement denunciation of the Protectionist leadership had appeared in the influential Tory organ, the *Morning Herald*. The first leader of the *Morning Herald's* Monday edition was blunt: 'It would henceforth be traitorous to attempt, absurd to allow, the advocacy of a leadership which conducts us from our most sacred duties, and leads us to our ruin. . . . We abandoned the minister who insisted upon measures which we deemed inimical to the state. Can we stand by the leader who takes his place, and who calls for legislation which, as Christian men, we conceive, hateful to GOD?' Some begrudging respect must be had for Bentinck's candour and for the decision he had taken to act consistently with his earlier votes; these considerations, however, paled beside the demands of a greater principle. 'Let all who [favour Jewish Emancipation] depart with Lord G. Bentinck and Mr. Disraeli. Let the others remain to form a party if they will, and to call it—CHRISTIAN!' Disraeli was dismissed by the *Morning Herald* as simply ridiculous. 'Theology, Mr. Disraeli, is not your vocation. The "oh, oh's," and "loud laughter," of Thursday, in the House of Commons, conveyed the exact impression which your sermon has produced upon the minds of every Christian reader in the land.'[21]

As if the editorial of Monday, 20 December were not sufficient a clarion call to the Protectionists to change their Commons' leadership, another, even more strident, attack on Bentinck was launched by the *Morning Herald* two days later; the leading article this time raked up for the benefit of critics those other religious issues which had in the past proved a source of friction. Although party obligations to Bentinck 'cannot easily be overlooked, even now, when it becomes a question whether we are to desert his lordship or the religion in virtue of which we live or die', high principle regrettably demanded that they be set aside.

The leader of the Conservative party in the House of Commons, announces himself ready to unchristianise the state, and to endow that Popery which is inimical to the state, and he must be convinced that not a solitary voice behind him, or but a solitary voice, can re-echo the announcement. What, then, remains to be done? Are we to leave Christianity, Protestantism, and the Conservative party for his lordship, or his lordship for all three? . . . We need the heart and hand of every individual member of our party during our present trial, and Lord George Bentinck deliberately deserts us. We cannot spare the humblest follower of the camp in the great struggle for our religious rights, and the general himself walks over to the enemy. . . . Fidelity to his lordship would be disloyalty to GOD. . . . We rally to meet the foe, and, before the first blow is struck, we find ourselves forsaken by our chief and guide. . . . Nor is this, unfortunately, the first occasion upon which we have been so forsaken. It was our unthankful office, during the general election, to remonstrate with Lord George Bentinck for proclaiming to his constituents at Lynn, as leader of the Conservative party, his determination to vote for the endowment of Popish priests, and to show the impossibility of his lordship's retaining that leadership, whilst all his followers were resolved to refuse the endowment which he was prepared so liberally to concede. Are we to be perpetually at issue with his lordship on questions so vitally important to a Protestant state and Christian nation? Are we to be for ever playing into the hands of Papists, infidels, and others, indifferent to all religion, by such a mockery as is exhibited in the spectacle of a party feeling one way, and a leader voting another?[22]

Many of the Tory Members of Parliament felt no less strongly about the leadership. 'Must I vote with George Bentinck when he aids Atheism in legislation, or cheer Disraeli when he declares that there is no difference between those who crucified Christ and those who kneel before Christ crucified?' remonstrated Augustus Stafford, one of the more talented younger members of the party; his was a typically indignant reply to the professed indifference of Lord John Manners not to 'bury myself under the ruins of my country in order to keep Lionel Rothschild from entering that House [The Commons]'.[23]

Bentinck had been given no choice but to surrender the leadership; on 26 December he despatched to Croker his own version of the events which had forced him into resignation. 'I have ceased to be the leader of the House of Commons Opposition!' exclaimed Bentinck.

My vote and speech on the Jew Bill gave dire offence to the party, and on the Monday morning I got a long letter from Beresford, who, as you know, is the whipper-in of the party, the long and short of which was an intimation that for daring to make that speech I must be prepared to receive my dismissal. I need not tell you that a hint that any considerable portion of the party were dissatisfied with and wearied of me, was quite enough for me to proffer a resignation with a good grace, without waiting to be *cashiered*. . . .

Appointed on account of my uncompromising spirit, I am dismissed for the same reason; that which was my principal virtue in 1846 is my damning vice in 1847. In April 1846, they would have me, *nolens volens,* for their leader. I in vain warned them that my religious differences from them, as well as my want of capacity to lead a party, alike disqualified me for the office. I foretold all that has since come to pass—all in vain; they would not listen to me; and now, when standing as true as the needle to the North Pole, I get my *congé* from the whipper-in, and read in their *Morning Herald* that Lord George Bentinck has thrown over his party!—However, the great Protectionist Party having degenerated into a *No Popery, No Jew* Party, I am still more unfit now than I was in 1846 to lead it. A party that can muster 140 on a Jew Bill, and cannot muster much above half those numbers on any question essentially connected with the great interests of the empire, can only be led by their antipathies, their hatreds, and their prejudices; and I am the unfittest man in the world to lead them. Beresford, Newdegate, and Mr. Phillips, of the *Morning Herald* have raised all this artificial zeal in the cause of religion, and fanned the flickering embers of bigotry, till they have raised a flame, of which, as a matter of course, I am necessarily the first victim.

Bentinck continued by emphasising that the party could only be kept together by the choice of a *No Popery* leader and of this he had informed

Stanley long ago. 'I have put my resignation into the hands of Bankes, from whom, and through whose enthusiastic feelings and good offices, I originally received my appointment.' The tragedy of his own tenure of office, concluded Bentinck, was that he was 'a man who endeavoured to lead them [the Protectionists] by their understandings, but knew not how to sympathise in, or to pander to, their religious prejudices'.[24]

His own unsuitability for the leadership was something that Bentinck could accept; what rankled with him was the feeling of having been the victim of a *coup*. On 28 December he again wrote to Croker. 'I find all the leading men of the party are indignant; it is the bigoted rump that has created the dissension. The true-hearted of the party feel that without dishonour I could not have voted with them, or in my position contented myself with a silent sneaking vote. . . . I could not have looked the House of Commons, and certainly not Peel, in the face if I had turned my back upon all my former votes, and had joined in 1847 in the cry of *Unchristianizing the Parliament.*'[25] In another letter of the same date Bentinck was even less inhibited about those whom he saw as responsible for the leadership crisis. 'The National Club have done it all'; the party was threatened by 'the flickering embers of Bigotry now being fanned into a flame by the National Club'. However, continued Bentinck resignedly, 'it is best as it is—when with all my efforts I cannot bring 120 together on any one great question affecting the vital and substantial interests of the United Kingdom or her Colonial Empire, whilst 180 can be collected to keep Jews out of Parliament or Roman Catholicks from burying their dead in their own Churchyards according to the rites of their own Church, it is high time I resigned an office which practically gives none of the influence which its name imports'.[26] Loss of perspective was a loss for the Tory party: Bentinck, writing to a leading member of the Portsmouth Jewish community, supplied further affirmation that he regarded the Jewish question 'more as a *personal* than a national concernment from the smallness of the numbers of those affected by it'.[27]

The Tories, for the second time in two years, had now to set about the task of finding a new leader. There existed one obvious candidate for the succession. J. C. Herries, who had represented the Government in some of the earliest of the Emancipation discussions with the Jews, was yet another former Canningite who as long ago as 1827 had been Chancellor of the Exchequer. However, to many in the party Herries seemed to disqualify himself by a Laodiceanism for which indeed his earlier contacts with the Jews may have been partly responsible; an abstention at the close of the mid-December debate had been somewhat tactlessly explained away to the whips. As Beresford wrote to Stanley: 'He [Herries] says they [the Jews] are better than Roman Catholics!! Now bigoted Protestant as I am, I prefer a Christian to a Jew or infidel.'[28] Thereupon Stanley turned from one of the most experienced of politicians to one with least experience: it was with reluctance that the Marquess of Granby agreed to Stanley's request to serve as the nominal Protectionist leader in the Commons.

But Granby, as soon became evident, was not of the calibre to lead the party; as Herries was anyway considered—and indeed considered himself—too old to become a permanent leader in the Commons, the party necessarily had recourse to the distrusted *parvenu* whose speech in the December debate had been considered by many of the Protectionists to have been in bad taste. From the moment of Bentinck's deposition Disraeli was more and more relied upon by the Protectionists for the conduct of Commons business: a future annotator of Disraeli's biography of Bentinck was to recount how at the reassembly of Parliament on 3 February 1848 the deposed leader walked up to the head of the second bench below the gangway on the Opposition side and in this manner announced to the whole House that he was no longer the responsible leader of the Protectionist party. Disraeli, who as a front-bencher customarily sat by the side of Bentinck, wished honoura-bly to stand or fall by him; unwittingly and fortuitously already finding himself in the deposed Opposition Leader's seat he prepared to vacate it and was prevented from doing so only by Bentinck's magnanimous and earnest entreaty not to do anything so indicative of schism.[29]

Disraeli was emerging as leader; it was interesting that the four members of the party who had voted for Emancipation on 17 December almost monopolised the speaking talent on their side of the House, and with the party in Opposition this speaking talent was naturally equated with ability. A letter of Lord John Manners to Disraeli of 7 February noted, no doubt to the gratification of the recipient, that Disraeli and Thomas Baring had won distinction as the foremost opponents of the Government's finance bill. 'I hope too, the fact you note, of all the speaking on our side, coming from supporters of religious liberty, will not be lost on the squires. A month ago I asked a furious friend of mine if he thought the party was likely to be strengthened by the exclusion of you, G. B., T. Baring and Milnes Gaskell? It would be almost worth while to absent yourselves from the Navigation Laws debate in order to let these highfliers see what their real capacity is.'[30] Disraeli, with characteristic immodesty, soon confirmed Manners' assess-ment. Writing to his sister after another debate on financial affairs Disraeli boasted: 'I made a very successful speech last night; one of my best, . . . I never knew a better sustained debate. Lord George very vigorous and masterly . . . and Tom Baring a masterpiece. On the whole, this is by far the most sustained debate which has occurred since the formation of our party, and, singular enough, the three speakers who did it all are . . . members of the party who voted for the Jews! I don't know what they will do without us!'[31]

Disraeli underestimated the Protectionists' refusal to recognize the inevi-table; whilst the party remained in a cataleptic trance Stanley was able to keep up the illusion that Granby, Herries and Disraeli shared the command.

Of course, after such repeated demonstration of Disraeli's talent as was afforded, for example, by the performance in the end-of-session debate of 30 August 1848, the triumvirate arrangement or supposedly attractive combination of noble birth, Treasury experience and gifted oratory could henceforth serve only as piebald cover to conceal the individual shortcomings of each of the leaders—or, more particularly, of Granby and Herries. George Buckle, Disraeli's future biographer, was to see this impediment to advancement as carrying an implied tribute to his subject's sincerity: the Jewish question seemed to exonerate Disraeli from the customary charge that he lacked principle. 'He [Disraeli] had everything to gain by leaving the question alone, speaking not at all, and absenting himself on one pretext or another from the vote. . . . He knew well that there was no subject on which the men whom he aspired to lead felt more strongly than the proposal to admit to a share in the Government of a Christian State anyone who denied the Divinity of Christ.' The concurrence of leading Peelites on the Jewish question did Disraeli more harm than good: lined up against him were almost all those Tories he so needed to conciliate. These included Sir Frederic Thesiger, the leading lawyer of the party, Attorney-General in 1845–46, in the future first Derby Government of 1852, and as Lord Chelmsford-to-be, occupant of the Woolsack at the time of Emancipation in 1858; Bankes, the unofficial chairman of the party; Spencer Walpole, who was to be Home Secretary in 1852 and again in 1858; and—most important—Stanley himself. For ten years Disraeli was to be dependent on these men to secure and consolidate his leadership in the Commons, yet he was courageous enough to remind them year by year, regularly by his vote and sometimes by his speech, that he was himself of Jewish extraction, and that his religious convictions were very different from theirs, but quite as strongly held. Lord Morley, the future biographer of Gladstone, told Buckle that on one occasion when Disraeli was elaborating his thesis Russell could not resist turning to a colleague—this was Gladstone—and expressing his admiration for a parliamentary leader who could so intrepidly stand forward and enunciate views which he knew the men behind him abhorred.[32]

It was ironical indeed that whereas the issue of Emancipation had originally been impelled to the forefront of politics as a result of the defiant action of one leader, that leader's successor should subsequently have been enabled to consolidate his position and to see the controversy recede in importance despite an even greater defiance.

NOTES

1. R. Stewart, *The Politics of Protection: Lord Derby and the Protectionist Party, 1841–1852*, p. 63.

2. B. Disraeli, *Lord George Bentinck: A Political Biography*, p. 366.

3. L. J. Jennings (ed.), *The Croker Papers. The Correspondence and Diaries of the late Rt. Hon. John Wilson Croker*, III, p. 140, letter from Bentinck to Croker, 29 September 1847.

4. R. Stewart, *The Politics of Protection*, pp. 122–24, letters from Stanley to Charles Arbuthnot, 17 October 1847, to Wellington, 17 October 1847, and to Bentinck, 27 October 1847; copies in Derby MSS.177/2.

5. Hughenden Papers, Box 89: B/XX/Be40, letter from Bentinck to Disraeli, 3 November 1847.

6. C. Whibley, *Lord John Manners and His Friends*, I, pp. 272–73.

7. Ibid., pp. 279–81, letter from Manners to Disraeli, 8 November 1847.

8. Hughenden Papers, Box 89: B/XX/Be42, letter from Bentinck to Disraeli, 14 November 1847.

9. C. Whibley, *Lord John Manners and His Friends*, I, p. 283, letter from Bentinck to Manners.

10. B. Disraeli, *Lord George Bentinck*, pp. 367–68.

11. Bentinck, *Hansard*, Third Series, 95, 17 December 1847, 1381–90, particularly cols. 1381–82.

12. C. S. Parker (ed.), *Life and Letters of Sir James Graham, 1792–1861*, II, pp. 61–62, Graham's diary, and letter from Peel to Graham, 2 January 1848.

13. R. Stewart, *The Politics of Protection*, p. 123, letter from Beresford to Bentinck, 19 December 1847, copy in Derby MSS.149/1, and letter from Bentinck to Stanley, 24 December 1847, in Derby MSS.132/13.

14. C. Whibley, *Lord John Manners and His Friends*, I, p. 284.

15. R. Stewart, *The Politics of Protection*, p. 123.

16. Cf. Newdegate, *Hansard*, Third Series, 95, 17 December 1847, 1365–71, and the following speeches of Newdegate [all volume references to *Hansard*, Third Series]: 96, 7 February 1848, 278–83; 98, 4 May 1848, 660–61; 104, 7 May 1849, 1413–19; 105, 11 June 1849, 1388–95; 116, 1 May 1851, 367–82; 125, 11 March 1853, 114–17; 145, 15 June 1857, 1851–54; 148, 10 December 1857, 483–86, 497; 148, 10 February 1858, 1098–1105; 149, 22 March 1858, 490–506; 151, 21 July 1858, 1895–1900.

17. C. Whibley, *Lord John Manners and His Friends*, I, p. 284, letter from Manners to Disraeli, 29 December 1847.

18. B. Disraeli, *Lord George Bentinck*, pp. 368–69.

19. C. Whibley, *Lord John Manners and His Friends*, I, pp. 291–93, letter from Bentinck to a supporter, 28 December 1847.

20. Ibid., I, p. 284.

21. *Morning Herald*, Monday, 20 December 1847, p. 4, first leader.

22. *Morning Herald*, Wednesday, 22 December 1847, p. 4, first leader.

23. C. Whibley, *Lord John Manners and His Friends*, I, pp. 281–82, letter from Manners to Lord Lyttelton, 23 December 1847 and letter from Augustus Stafford to Manners, 24 December 1847.

24. L. J. Jennings (ed.), *The Croker Papers*, III, pp. 158–60, letter from Bentinck to Croker, 26 December 1847.

25. Ibid., pp. 163–65, letter from Bentinck to Croker, 28 December 1847.

26. C. Whibley, *Lord John Manners and His Friends*, I, pp. 291–93, letter from Bentinck to a supporter, 28 December 1847.

27. C. Roth, *Anglo-Jewish Letters*, 1158–1917, pp. 294–96, letter from Bentinck to J. Franklin, 9 January 1848.

28. R. Stewart, *The Politics of Protection*, p. 127, undated letter from Beresford to Stanley, in Derby MSS.149/1.

29. B. Disraeli, *Lord George Bentinck* 1905 edn., pp. 340–41.

30. Hughenden Papers, Box 106: B/XX/M/24, letter from Manners to Disraeli, 7 February 1848.

31. R. Disraeli (ed.), *Lord Beaconsfield's Letters, 1830–1852*, p. 210, letter from Disraeli to his sister, 18 February 1848.

32. W. F. Monypenny and G. E. Buckle, *The Life of Benjamin Disraeli, Earl of Beaconsfield*, I, pp. 893–95.

10
Hopes of Emancipation Thwarted

In May and June of 1849 an Emancipation bill was again brought forward in Parliament; it was interesting that Disraeli's brief reaffirmation of support at this time[1] should have won—or provoked—a backhanded compliment from Charles Dickens, who customarily regarded Disraeli as an impostor and humbug beside the worthy Peel: 'It delights me that D'Israeli has done such justice to his conscience-less self in regard of the Jews.'[2] The House of Commons approved the remission of disabilities by majorities of 93 and 66[3] but when the bill moved to the Lords it met with the predictable opposition. Sumner, the new evangelical Archbishop of Canterbury, pointing to past victories in India as typical of events which showed that the mark of Divine favour lay on Britain, then argued that it would be a poor return to Christ if the British appeared to behold in a similar light those from whom that Divine favour had been withdrawn. God did not regard with the same favour those who had accepted and those who had rejected his merciful offer of reconciliation; here Sumner was led by his Protestant certainty of election to compare the condition of the Continent in the wake of revolution with the condition of England, which still stood on firm foundations as a monument and example of freedom and social order. The nations adversely affected in 1848 had attributed the difference in Britain's circumstances to her national and scriptural religion, 'that religion which, cementing together the various orders of society, and hallowing our civil and social institutions, imparted a sanction to our laws which nothing else could give, and enabled us to stand secure against the storms of anarchy'; this was therefore emphatically no time for declaring it a matter of indifference whether such a religion be professed or denied by those who sat in Parliament. Sumner's argument was vigorously controverted by Archbishop Whately of Dublin, the former professor of political economy at Oxford, who entertained an intense aversion to the swearing of oaths on secular occasions. Christ, Saint Paul and the earliest Christians, having declared their kingdom to be not of this world, had thereby acknowledged the need for a healthy and clear delineation between the spheres of religion and politics; they had accordingly attempted to bring individuals to Christianity by conversion only, had renounced interference in political and secular affairs and so eschewed the use of any instruments of conformity. Christ and his followers had not called upon

Dionysius the Areopagite or Cornelius the centurion to resign their offices; similarly, when Paul had been brought to trial for speaking against Caesar and for setting up in his place another ruler by the name of Jesus he had disavowed all secular attempts to set up the Christian system. Whately's argument notwithstanding, the Lords rejected the Emancipation measure by 95 votes to 70, a majority of 25.[4]

This vote may have been expected but its effect was dramatic: Rothschild immediately resigned his seat in the City so that he might fight a by-election on the Emancipation issue.[5] Supporters of the Jewish cause considered that their case had already been sufficiently argued; they wished rather to develop the constitutional theme that the rights of a parliamentary constituency must be respected no less than those of the House of Lords. On 28 June *The Times* published a notice from Rothschild to the electors of the City constituency. 'The contest is now between the House of Lords and yourselves. . . . You alone can decide whether you will continue this honourable struggle, or give up your own declared wishes and the cause of freedom together.' As it was generally expected that Rothschild would win any City contest some difficulty was encountered by the Protectionists in finding a candidate to oppose him and momentarily the Liberals were to be found despondent as to the moral effect of a re-election carried without a struggle.

Then, on the very day of Rothschild's nomination, a Protectionist candidate appeared in the person of Lord John Manners. Little known in the City as one who had dissented from the harsh treatment accorded Bentinck after his support for the Jews in December 1847, Manners appeared rather as the dreamy aristocratic romantic and author of the couplet:

> Let wealth and commerce, laws and learning die,
> But leave us still our old Nobility.

Many of the commercially-minded supporters of Rothschild naturally resorted to this verse as ammunition with which to deride the Lords and in an election which was at all times good-humoured Rothschild had often to quieten his excited supporters on the hustings in order that Manners might obtain a hearing. That a warm welcome should have been accorded Manners even in those areas of the City where most Jews resided was to be explained not only by his personal qualities, good nature and evident respect for his rival but also because he acquiesced in fighting Rothschild not on an anti-Emancipation platform but on the theme already chosen, of the will of the Lords as opposed to that of the people. Manners campaigned as vindicator of the law and as upholder of the indefeasible privileges of the Upper House of Parliament.

The result of this July by-election constituted a triumph for Rothschild, who polled 6,017 votes as opposed to the 2,814 votes cast for Manners. Although Rothschild estimated that with the additional turnout of his more complacent supporters he could have polled between eight and ten thousand votes, the two-to-one majority of 3,203 votes was considered by him to furnish conclusive evidence of the state of public opinion and proof that the electors had not acted precipitately in returning him to Parliament two years earlier.

There arose now the problem of how best to follow up the advantage conferred by this convincing victory and from some of his leading supporters in Parliament Rothschild received some characteristically varied advice. On 4 March 1850 the radical J. A. Roebuck, whose intervention as champion of the 'modest middle class' in the Commons debate of June 1849 had been marked by a corresponding derogation of the peers' ability and of their claim to be the upholders of the religious character of the country, encouraged Rothschild to appear at the Commons on the following day in order that he might claim his seat.[6] Rothschild refrained however from making such a move and a week later his native caution was to seem the more justified when Peel, in the course of debate on a motion asking for a committee of enquiry to examine the question of oaths as they related to Rothschild, advised the Jews and their supporters in the Commons against the adoption of either of two radical tactics: attempting to undermine the authority of the Lords or adducing the case of the Quaker Joseph Pease as proof that the swearing of oaths was not compulsory.[7]

Rothschild again hesitated, in April conferring with Pease himself as to whether his own seating in 1833 had set a precedent;[8] it was only on 25 July, a full year after the by-election victory, that a meeting of City supporters at the London Tavern was able to persuade Rothschild to go to the Commons to claim his seat.[9] Even then he was to refrain from challenging the authority of Parliament and the law. When, on 26 July, Rothschild came to the table of the Commons to be sworn the Clerk of the House asked him whether he wished to subscribe the Protestant or the Catholic oath. Rothschild replied: 'I desire to be sworn upon the Old Testament.' The Speaker, Shaw-Lefèvre, wishing for time to consider Rothschild's case, then directed him to withdraw and there followed a debate concerned with technicalities.[10]

Three days later the Speaker brought to bear on the question his customary forensic skills and in summing up the points at issue he directed Members to make a vital distinction. Firstly there was the form and mode of swearing: whether the House should decide that a Jewish Member could be sworn on the Old Testament and be allowed, whilst taking the oath, to cover his head according to Jewish religious practice. This point as to the form and mode of swearing was one little emphasised hitherto for it obviously had not applied to the claims of non-Anglican Christians. The second point referred to by the Speaker concerned the more familiar and contentious issue of the wording of the oaths. Proceeding with the points one at a time so as to eliminate that which many thought presented no problem, the Commons decided that the Speaker should first enquire why Rothschild desired to be

sworn on the Old Testament. After Rothschild had given his reply—
'Because that is the form of swearing that I declare to be most binding on my
conscience'—the Speaker directed him to withdraw. Rothschild obeyed this
ruling and the House then went into a protracted debate on technical points,
during which the Government did not always appear to have a firm grasp of
the situation; eventually, by 113 votes to 59, a majority of 54, the House took
the very important—but not unexpected—decision that Rothschild might be
allowed to take the oaths in accordance with Jewish religious custom.[11]

It now remained for the Commons to resolve the second of the Speaker's
two points, as to the wording of the oaths. When, in consequence of the vote
of 29 July, Rothschild reappeared on the following day at the table of the
Commons there were first administered to him the Oaths of Allegiance and
Supremacy. These he swore in the prescribed form; then, when the Oath of
Abjuration was administered he repeated all the words until the Clerk came
to the controversial declaration 'upon the true faith of a Christian'.
Rothschild said: 'I omit those words as not binding on my conscience',
added 'So help me God!' then kissed the copy of the Old Testament which he
was holding. Thereupon the Speaker directed Rothschild to withdraw and
this instruction was immediately obeyed.[12] When the House resumed discussion of the question on 5 August—with Disraeli once again reaffirming his
support for Emancipation—a resolution was carried that Rothschild could
neither vote nor take his seat unless he took the Abjuration Oath as presently
worded; the only consolation afforded the Jews was the decision taken to
revive discussion of the question as early as possible in the next session.[13]

In presenting their own case for Emancipation the Protestant Dissenters
had recalled their loyalty to the Hanoverian sovereigns during the Jacobite
rebellions of 1715 and 1745;[14] now the Reverend Thomas Pyne, whose
knowledge of Jewish history was particularly extensive, eloquently remarked on the Jewish military contribution to Britain's fighting strength
during the Napoleonic Wars, noting indeed that such enthusiastic identification with the cause of their fellow countrymen had been responsible for the
heavy loss of Jewish army officers sustained by Britain on the battlefield of
Waterloo.[15] The effectiveness of such pamphleteering arguments notwithstanding, the cause of Emancipation received an unexpected setback
when the question was again debated in the spring of 1851. For on 1 May an
Oath of Abjuration (Jews) Bill, sponsored by the Prime Minister, received a
second reading in the Commons by a margin of only 25 votes, 202 votes
being cast in its favour and 177 votes being cast against.[16] The freakishness
of this result was probably to be attributed to the opening of the Great
Exhibition on the same day, this being an occasion which required the
attendance of a disproportionately large number of politicians from the
ministerial side of the House,[17] but to the Jews the reduced majority was
nonetheless a disappointment.

Then, with equal suddenness, fortune reversed itself. David Salomons secured election to Parliament, filling a by-election vacancy for the two-Member constituency of Greenwich.[18] Although Salomons's victory, with no Tory to oppose him, did not carry quite the same significance as Rothschild's two elections in 1847 and 1849, the fact that the Greenwich constituency, comprising the three large and important towns of Greenwich, Woolwich and Deptford, was a more typical one than the City, meant that the election of Rothschild could no longer be regarded as unrepresentative of public feeling. For it was obviously the Jewish question with which Salomons was most clearly identified; indeed, he even criticised Rothschild for not having boldly attempted to occupy a place on the Commons' benches. In fact Salomons's electoral platform was twofold: he presented himself as the champion not only of civil and religious liberty but also of the poor man. He stood for cheap food and for the reduction of taxes on essential commodities; defending the abolition of the Corn Laws he argued that food should be obtained at the price it was worth in the markets of the world. He advocated an extension of education and of the suffrage and declared himself in favour of the ballot. To many mid-century politicians the substitution of the prevailing method of recording each individual's vote in a poll-book by that of secret ballot in a polling booth seemed an essential corollary of suffrage extension, as it would prevent the dictatorial intimidation of workmen by employers; to this view Salomons added a rider in expressing the belief that a large extension of the suffrage would render the ballot unnecessary. The exorbitant cost of obtaining justice was another popular theme stressed at one particularly crowded meeting at the Greenwich Literary Institution; Salomons denounced a system whereby a poor man, fined one shilling or half-a-crown for a petty offence, could then be saddled with costs of some twenty-five shillings. The democratic hue of Salomons's electoral appeal reveals his Gladstonian susceptibility to the tendencies of the age; in this respect there was an interesting contrast, corresponding to those which featured in matters of intra-Jewish debate, between him and the more eighteenth-century patrician figure of Montefiore, who had at the time of the great Chartist agitation of April 1848 been rather more fulsome in his condemnation of the Chartists than might have been warranted by certain disagreements with either their methods or their democratic objectives.[19]

Salomons faced as his electoral opponent none other than D. W. Wire, the City of London alderman who many years before had assisted him in his campaigns for municipal offices and particularly for the City Shrievalty: as justification for his candidature Wire could reasonably state that as the alternative choice would entail the electors' own disenfranchisement they should accordingly vote for him as only he could hope to advocate Salomons's cause in the Commons. So the principle of Emancipation was even less in question in this campaign than in the City by-election of two years earlier, and *The Times* was correct in reporting on a good-humoured campaign, with an absence of rancour—and of drunkenness. But where Salomons proved to be a popular figure at the hustings, Wire was somewhat resented for the reason that he happened to be the vestry-clerk for the neighbouring village of Lewisham: this was considered, particularly by one of the regional newspapers, the *Kentish Mercury,* to constitute an affront to the dignity of the Greenwich electors. Another aspect of Wire's career held against him was the fact, emphasised by Salomons's supporters, that he had been thrice rejected in parliamentary contests for the constituency of Boston.

Salomons's claim that his personal success would best demonstrate the strength of feeling in favour of Emancipation was accepted by all the prominent Liberals in the constituency. If advocacy of a national education system unsectarian in character—consistent with the belief that the greater question of political Emancipation concerned admission to a legislature similarly defined—was to give Salomons a somewhat distinctive position within the Jewish community, this Erastianism did on balance gain him electoral adherents—even though the Catholics as a body declined to declare their support for him, consistent with their refusal to declare for Wire either. In the event the result of the poll was a very satisfactory one for Salomons: he won 2,165 votes as against 1,278 for Wire; this majority of 887 votes was to be explained by a two-to-one lead in the towns of Greenwich and Woolwich and a small lead in Deptford.

The fact of the Greenwich by-election victory could not perhaps quite redress the effect of the recent close vote in the Commons. The debate on the subsequent reading was scarcely of note for the Prime Minister's reiteration of the late Sir Robert Peel's argument that the intent of the Abjuration Oath had been quite simply the abjuration of the Stuarts; the interest of Members was turning away from examination of the relative strengths of pro-Emancipation and anti-Emancipation polemics to examination of the relative position of the two divergent Houses of Parliament. When Russell urged the peers to reconsider their attitude on the grounds that for the third time one or more Jewish candidates had been elected to the Commons, that two constituencies had elected Jews to represent them and that the Commons had several times passed bills in support of admission to Parliament, he was met by opponents with a display of cool bravado. First they bluffly alleged that Russell was having to cautiously time the Emancipation debates so as to avert defeat, then they nonchalantly waived their right to divide the House on the present third reading.[20]

Many opponents of Emancipation in the Upper House chose also to indulge in selective interpretation of the second reading division figures in the Commons, Lord Malmesbury recording in his diary that this result would encourage the peers.[21] It was through fear of such a stiffening of resistance in the Lords that Russell wrote to Sumner, the Archbishop of Canterbury, in the hope that he would reverse his previous stand of opposition and so influence other former critics of Emancipation to do likewise. The Primate had, however, already decided how he would vote and in reply to the Prime Minister stated his unwillingness to withdraw his proxy vote against the bill.[22] During the Lords' debate encouragement was afforded to the opponents of Emancipation by the contribution of Lord Shaftesbury, whose previous parliamentary speech on the question had been as Lord Ashley in the Commons' debate of December 1847. Restating that Christians could not yield up that authority entrusted to them by Christ, signified by those words of the Abjuration Oath which asserted the truth and maintained the supremacy of the Gospel, Shaftesbury once again recorded the belief that the ambition to sit in the British Parliament or take part in the councils of any empire could not be the predominant desire of the Hebrew nation, 'for a nation they are, and a nation they will continue to be to the end of time'. The Jews would not, as some of their number thought, be forever in the Diaspora, because such a future must necessarily be discounted by the biblical declaration that 'the people shall dwell alone, and shall not be reckoned among the nations'. The Diaspora assertion was degrading, said Shaftesbury, for it denied to the Jews the glories of their future career, 'a career the most brilliant, the most extensive, the most durable, and the most blessed in the entire history of the human race'. The bill was refused a second reading by 144 votes to 108, a majority against of 36; it was interesting that seven members of the episcopate were now to be found amongst the minority voting in favour of Emancipation.[23]

But any thought that the issue might have been settled, at least for the current session, was to reckon without the intentions of Salomons, who intended now to press his claim on the Commons. On 18 July, the day after the Lords' defeat of Russell's bill, Salomons arrived at Westminster with the purpose of taking his seat. There took place initially a repeat performance of Rothschild's abortive swearing-in ceremony of the previous 30 July. Then, however, Salomons went further than had his fellow Jewish Member of Parliament on that occasion, and in so doing rendered himself liable to prosecution. First he read out his own interpretation of the law relating to oaths and was consequently requested by the Speaker to withdraw; then he sat down on one of the lower benches so that the Speaker, in recalling both the form of the Abjuration Oath as prescribed by Act of Parliament and the verdict of the House as given on a former occasion, had once again to order him to withdraw. Salomons vacated the place which he had occupied on the benches but inadvertently failed to hold to the retreat behind the invisible line of demarcation which separated the space below the bar from the body of the House. When Sir Frederic Thesiger pointed out this unintentional intrusion the Speaker reinstructed Salomons to withdraw and this he finally did.[24]

The following day the Speaker, in answer to Russell's enquiries, clarified the legal position in which the Commons found itself as a consequence of Salomons's actions. He advised Russell that the penalties which a Member of Parliament incurred by sitting in a debate and voting, without having previously taken the oaths as required by law, could be sued for only if the Prime Minister himself initiated proceedings. The Government was not, however, actually obliged to direct the Attorney-General to prosecute. Conversely, if Salomons himself wished to try the question—and thus incur the risk of personal penalties—he should seek a plaintiff. The Speaker seems to have anticipated that Salomons would pursue such a course—his suspicions being confirmed within a matter of hours when Salomons despatched a cheeky letter to Russell complete with his own interpretation of the law and contention that the matter be referred to the judiciary. The Speaker, in his letter to Russell, further anticipated that Salomons would again attempt to take his seat on the following Monday, 21 July; if an order from the Chair to withdraw were then disobeyed there would have to be tabled a motion for withdrawal and if Salomons subsequently persisted in remaining seated the Serjeant-at-Arms would have to be directed by the Chair to remove him. Russell was advised that in this event he should move a Resolution similar to that agreed the previous year in Rothschild's case, while leaving it to others to move a new writ for the by-election in Salomons's former seat at Greenwich. For it was the Speaker's opinion that Salomons's occupancy during debate of a place on the Commons' benches, pursuant to the failure to subscribe the oaths, involved forfeiture of the Greenwich seat; here he added that there was an important difference between the Salomons and Rothschild cases insofar as the latter had never voted or sat during a debate.[25]

When the Commons resumed discussion of the question on Monday 21 July the Speaker conveyed to Members the contents of the correspondence recently received from Salomons, but then declared that it would be irrelevant to consider the points contained therein. Subsequently, Russell was asked if the Attorney-General was intending to prosecute Salomons: predictably the Prime Minister replied in the negative, though being careful to add that the Government reserved the right to change its mind at a later date. Sir B. Hall, one of the Members for Marylebone, argued that as Salomons had not descended to any subterfuge there was now no alternative but to letting him come within the House so that he might take his seat. Given his cue Salomons, who had hitherto occupied a seat below the bar, entered the chamber and took a seat within the bar, on the Treasury bench. There followed a scene of confusion. Silence was restored when the Speaker rose to declare that he had seen a Member taking his seat without having taken the oaths required by law, and that the said Member, Salomons, must in consequence withdraw. This pronouncement was followed by even greater confusion than before; the Prime Minister, twice denied a hearing, had to resume his seat. As Salomons remained seated within the bar the Speaker felt compelled to explain that his continued disobedience would require Members to uphold the Chair's authority as any order for withdrawal could be enforced only by vote of the House. Russell, belying suspicions that his impartiality on this particular question could not be relied upon, thereupon proposed 'that Mr. Alderman Salomons do now withdraw' and this motion was seconded by Sir Robert Inglis. But two Members, one of whom was Bernal Osborne, the radical Member for Middlesex, proposed a contrary amendment which would have enabled Salomons to take his seat. The result was bedlam. An adjournment motion, lost by a majority of 192 votes, was important for being the occasion which witnessed Salomons's first vote in the Commons. When a question personal to himself was next voted upon Salomons withdrew from the chamber, though he afterwards reentered to resume his seat. Once again the motion was proposed that Salomons withdraw. Hobhouse, the Member for Harwich, thought that the Member in question would weaken his own case if he did not speak for himself and thus it was that Salomons, rising amidst a scene of considerable confusion and excitement, with cries of 'withdraw' coming from one side of the House and much cheering from the other, addressed the House for the first time.

Salomons besought through the Chair a fair hearing from Members before the decision on his case was finally taken; explaining his appearance in the Commons Salomons said: 'I thought I was bound to take this course in defence of my own rights and privileges, and of the rights and privileges of the constituents who have sent me here. In saying this, Sir, I shall state to you that whatever the decision of this House may be, I shall willingly abide by it, provided that just such sufficient force be used to make me feel that I am acting under coercion.' Then another adjournment motion was lost, by a similar margin of 162 votes, this being the second occasion on which Salomons recorded a vote. The dramatic moment all Members had been waiting for had at last arrived. Russell's original motion, 'that Mr. Alderman Salomons do now withdraw', was put to the vote and accepted by 231 votes to 81, a majority of 150, with Salomons himself entering the division lobbies for the third time. The Speaker trusted that Salomons would now voluntarily withdraw; when it became obvious that no such compliance could be expected the Speaker had to direct the Serjeant-at-Arms to conduct Salomons from the seat he at present occupied to that place below the bar where Members customarily sat before they took the oaths.

In extremis it was significant that the Prime Minister should then have resorted to the experience of Catholic Emancipation for the precedent which might resolve the situation: he declared that Salomons could be heard at the bar of the House according to the example of O'Connell. Russell also refused to commit the Government to a prosecution of Salomons for having infringed the rules of the House.[26] Nonetheless, when the debate was resumed on the following day, 22 July, Russell did move the motion, 'That David Salomons Esq., is not entitled to vote in this House, or to sit in this House during any Debate, until he shall take the Oath of Abjuration in the form appointed by Law'. Then, after various amendments had been negatived which would have allowed Salomons to take his seat, either immediately or in consequence of an alteration to the Abjuration Oath, Russell consented to an adjournment.[27]

When the House resumed discussion of the question, on Monday 28 July, the Speaker informed Members that he had received a letter, dated 25 July, in which Salomons had explained that he had been advised that it was his duty to inform the House that two legal actions had been commenced against him for the penalties of sitting and voting in the Commons the previous Monday. At a trial of those actions any resolution or proceeding of the House might be given in evidence of them. There now ensued in the Commons a constitutional wrangle when Hall chose to recall the case of Wilkes, that libellous pamphleteering scourge of the executive in the early years of George III's reign, who had been unlawfully arrested by order of Government on a general warrant and expelled from the Commons, and been subsequently with tedious repetition re-elected for the Middlesex constituency and re-expelled until such time as his erstwhile electoral opponent had found himself declared seated by Resolution. The 1769 Resolution expelling Wilkes had been expunged from the Journals of the Commons twelve years later, on the grounds that it had been subversive of the rights of the whole body of the electors of the United Kingdom. The Commons refused to accept that such a precedent could be validly applied to the cases of Salomons and Rothschild, and petitions from their supporters in Greenwich and the City of London were defeated by, respectively, 135 votes to 75, a majority of 60, and 77 votes to 41, a majority of 36. The Prime Minister maintained that whereas in the case of Wilkes there had been an absence of law to guide the Commons, in the current instance Members could not avoid interpreting the legislation which was set before them; clearly Salomons would be breaking the law by not taking the whole of the prescribed declaration. Thereupon Russell's motion, that Salomons could neither sit in the House nor vote until he had taken the Abjuration Oath in the form appointed by law, was approved by 123 votes to 68, a majority of 55.[28]

In 1882 Sir Frederick Pollock was to observe that the Salomons case had come to interest only those lawyers with a taste for ingenious argument as to the construction and effect of statutes.[29] Two actions for penalties were issued against Salomons after proceedings had been instigated by a common informer, but one of these was subsequently withdrawn. The other, suing Salomons for his assumption of a seat in the Commons without having previously taken the Abjuration Oath, came on for trial in the Court of Exchequer on 9 December 1851, before Mr. Baron Martin and a Special Jury. A suggestion advanced by the presiding judge—that as the case involved important questions of law it should therefore be turned into a Special Verdict for the opinion of the full Court—was accepted by Counsel on both sides. On 26 and 28 January 1852 hearings began in the presence of

Baron Pollock, the Lord Chief Justice, Mr. Baron Parke, Mr. Baron Alderson and Mr. Baron Martin. Sir Fitzroy Kelly Q.C. acted as Leading Counsel for the Defendant, Salomons. The four points on which Salomons's case rested, as advanced by Kelly, were:

(1) The act of 6 Geo III, c. 53 was no longer in force, because it had not authorized the insertion from time to time of the reigning sovereigns' names and had therefore expired either at the end of George III's reign or at all events when there had ceased to be a king named George. The form of the oath could not here be altered. Where the change of name of sovereign had been considered necessary, the legislature had interposed by express enactment, expressly authorizing the substitution of one sovereign for the other. This had been the precedent followed from the time of William III to that of George III.[30]

(2) Even if an oath were still in force the law required that a man should assent to its contents in such manner and form as was binding on his conscience. Salomons saw in the Pease case of 1833 a precedent, for in allowing the Quaker to affirm, without swearing on the Gospel, Parliament had departed from its previous practice.[31] The only exemption from this rule was in cases where legislation concerned a religious or political test and 'that could only be the case where the language and intention of the Act clearly and positively required such a construction'.

(3) Assuming his first propositions to be doubtful, the defendant was bound and authorized to take the oath which he did take in the House of Commons by necessary implication under the Act 1 & 2 Vict, c. 105.

(4) The Act 10 Geo I, c. 4 was kept alive and in force by a succession of acts, continuing or enlarging the time given for taking the oaths, and with respect to Jews, without the words 'upon the true faith of a Christian' until 24 November 1766 and consequently beyond the time when the Act 6 Geo III, c. 53, was passed, and by its existence at that time qualified the meaning of the provisions of that Act.[32]

On 19 April 1852 judgment was delivered for the plaintiff by three judges out of four, the dissenting voice being that of Baron Martin; the words 'upon the true faith of a Christian' were deemed to constitute a material part of the oath and could therefore not be dispensed with otherwise than by legislation[33]—although Baron Alderson did here agree with Baron Martin that, as the oath was now being used for a purpose never originally intended, any exclusion deemed necessary should be enacted directly, 'and not merely by the casual operation of a clause, intended apparently in its object and origin to apply to a very different class of the subjects of England'.[34] Subsequently Salomons corresponded with Lord Derby, the new Tory Prime Minister, in the hope that the Government would introduce indemnifying legislation to overrule this verdict. Derby, after some Cabinet consultation, emphasised in reply that it was for Salomons himself to take any initiative he might consider appropriate; Parliament could not be expected to interfere with the case pending the appeal which Salomons was intending to make, in the first instance, to the Court of Exchequer Chamber and, ultimately, if need be, to the House of Lords; the Government would however, in the last resort, protect Salomons from the most serious consequences pronounced by the Court of Exchequer.[35]

It was with a view to meeting precisely these exigencies of the Salomons case that on 4 May Lord Lyndhurst, the former Tory Lord Chancellor, presented the Upper House with a limited indemnifying measure. Salomons was liable not only to a pecuniary penalty but to the pains of *praemunire*, according to which he might anciently have been put to death by any one who met him, as having *caput lupinum*. Lyndhurst's 'Disabilities Repeal Bill' to meet this and all similar contingencies left the law untouched as to the necessity for taking the Oath in the prescribed form, and preserved the pecuniary penalty, but swept away all the other punishments and disabilities. Unanimous confirmation, meanwhile, of the Court of Exchequer verdict by the Court of Exchequer Chamber made it even more unlikely that Salomons could escape incurring the obsolete penalties; consequently when Lyndhurst's bill was sent down to the Commons it was found to have the support of many of the opponents of Emancipation. To Spencer Walpole, the Home Secretary, the question was whether Parliament should leave on the statute book, in addition to the penalties incurred for the offence of voting in the Commons without taking the requisite oaths, the other very serious consequences which at present attached to such action. Walpole considered that as no person could have a seat in that House without taking the Oath which contained the words 'upon the true faith of a Christian' it would be mistaken to insist upon the retention of these other penalties. Lyndhurst's bill was then given a third reading by 50 votes to 4, a majority of 46.[36] So it was that, after an interval of six to seven years, the combination of Salomons and Lyndhurst could once again be seen to have achieved a removal of obsolete disabilities: the Act 15 & 16 Vict, c. 43, of June 1852, relieved of heavy penalties any persons who unlawfully participated in parliamentary divisions. Later in the year the Jewish Board of Deputies passed a noteworthy resolution thanking Salomons for the zeal and effort he had displayed after his by-election victory at Greenwich and praising him for the self-sacrifice in fines which he had incurred through the decision actually to take his seat in the Commons.[37]

Russell, however, was impatient for more than indemnifying legislation; towards the close of the parliamentary session in 1851 he had reconsidered the idea of devising a simple oath founded on the Oaths of Allegiance, Supremacy and Abjuration, which could be substituted for the series of oaths, taken at the table.[38] Prince Albert, on behalf of the Queen, had then demurred, replying to Russell that although such a simplified formulation of oath would be a great improvement it would also 'bring the question of the admission of the Jews on again'.[39] Nonetheless Russell persisted and at the outset of the next general election campaign in May 1852 he returned to the idea in his *Address to the Electors of the City of London*. Russell reaffirmed his personal commitment to the remission of disabilities and added: 'The oath taken by members of Parliament ought to be the same for all, simple, and not complex—a bond of union, and not a badge of distrust or a source of religious discord.'[40]

The electoral chances of Rothschild, Russell's fellow candidate in the City, retaining his seat were to be rated more highly than those of Salomons at Greenwich.[41] *The Kentish Independent* was a Liberal newspaper which commended Salomons as an imaginative Member of Parliament, in contrast to the Tory candidate, Rolt, whom it dismissed as a man of antiquated notions pertaining to the reign of Queen Anne; nevertheless at the same time the newspaper felt constrained to argue that it would be 'worse than nonsense' for the two-Member Greenwich constituency once again to half-disenfranchise itself by returning a silent or ineligible Member. When Salomons decided to stand the newspaper strongly criticised him for splitting the vote of the other two Liberal candidates, for his litigious actions in the courts and for the claim by some of his supporters that he was now eligible to sit in the Commons. Salomons did undoubtedly mislead some of the electors when choosing to emphasise that disabilities had been outlawed in the last Parliament, for he did not then specify which disabilities these were. But the mischief did not lie all on the one side. During the campaign some of those canvassing on behalf of the other Liberals spread a rumour that Salomons had withdrawn from the election and, by thus damaging his chances, afforded further opportunity for the Tory candidate to benefit from a split Liberal vote. The result was P. Rolt (Tory), 2,415 votes; M. Chambers (L), 2,360 votes; Admiral Stewart (L), 2,026 votes; and D. Salomons (L), 1,102 votes.

After the count Salomons was good-humouredly praised by Stewart, the man whose victory he had almost certainly denied; *The Kentish Independent* was less forbearing, furiously reproaching Salomons for his 'blind vanity' and 'concern for self' and for having helped to return a man [Rolt] 'pledged to oppose the manumission of his own sect'. Salomons's failure to secure re-election cannot be attributed to some supposed perceptible increase in anti-Jewish feeling during the short period which had elapsed since his by-election victory; the stand of *The Kentish Independent* provides answer to the rather different question as to whether electors were deterred from voting for Jewish candidates because the courts had so recently confirmed their disqualification to sit in Parliament. Many of the Greenwich electors refused to expend their votes on a candidate almost certainly ineligible to take his seat; some of them knew that Appeal to the Lords, to reverse the judgments of the Courts of Exchequer and Exchequer Chamber, was then in course of preparation and were aware that Salomons's loss of his seat would render pointless such further litigation. It is in these two senses that Salomons and those who campaigned for him might be accused of having displayed uncharacteristic lack of judgement in letting his candidature go forward. It caused them to divide attentions between two contests at a time when they could as well have chosen to repose their sole confidence in the electors of the City of London. Electors in other constituencies, lacking the four-Member representation possessed by the City, had no wish unnecessarily to half-disenfranchise themselves; in the event Rothschild did secure return to Parliament, taking last place amongst those successful in the City poll. The full result was J. Masterman, 6,195 votes; Lord J. Russell, 5,537 votes; Sir J. Duke, 5,270 votes; L. N. Rothschild, 4,748 votes; and R. W. Crawford (Ind. L), 3,765 votes.

Debate concerning the introduction of yet another Emancipation measure was revived in the House of Commons on 24 February 1853. Russell, referring to the argument sometimes deployed by opponents of Emancipation to the effect that the British Jews were descended from foreigners, denigrated such allusion as a betrayal of national prejudice and recalled instead those many other groups, for example the Huguenots, who had been granted the rights of British subjects. The diehard Tories remained impervious to such persuasion. Inglis resorted to a familiar theme in contending that everything held sacred by Christians was now under stronger attack from the Jews than it had ever been from individuals such as Wilkes and Gibbon. The present objections of the Jews were founded on principle whereas the resistance of these men had derived from their perverted natures, as they had not descended to open and avowed blasphemy it might be said of them that 'hypocrisy was the homage which vice paid to virtue'. Inglis's speech of opposition was as predictable as that of Russell in support; it was therefore a good augury for the Jews when Lord Drumlanrig, a Peelite who had both spoken and voted against Emancipation in the debates of the late 1840s, now reversed his stand by speaking and voting in favour of the measure. The division figures on this occasion were here somewhat misleading: Members' switches of opinion were invariably in one direction and the limiting of the majority favouring Emancipation to one of 29 votes might anyway have been partly anticipated in a House which contained a slightly larger minority of Tories than the previous parliament.[42]

Religious questions carried perhaps the greatest danger of jeopardizing that working arrangement between Whigs and Peelite Tories consummated before Christmas in the formation of a coalition under the leadership of Lord Aberdeen, and an eruption of disagreement was now to be sparked off by nothing more than the vote which had been cast against Emancipation on 24 February by an unknown junior Peelite member of the Government, Lord Alfred Hervey, one of the Members for Brighton and a Lord of the Treasury. Russell, who led for the Government in the Commons, wrote to the Prime Minister the day after the division to remind him of Hervey's vote; in the belief that this had constituted a denial of the doctrine of collective Government responsibility he added presumptuously: 'I conclude he [Hervey] has tendered his resignation.'[43] In reply Aberdeen recalled that the Peelites had only subconsciously moved towards adoption of a common Whig-Peelite line on Emancipation and he alluded to his own recent conversion on the subject.

> With respect to Lord Alfred Hervey's vote last night, he mentioned to me three or four days ago how he was situated, and perhaps might have offered to resign; but it really did not occur to me as necessary to exact it. I was so late a convert myself, that I felt it would be unreasonable to do so. Indeed, to say the truth, I had not the least notion of the Government being so united on the subject; for I think it was half-formed, before you were aware of the change which had taken place in my own case.'[44]

Aberdeen's tolerance towards Hervey was understandable: the Prime Minister could not in honesty exonerate himself from a charge of expediency in having very recently reversed his previous stand of opposition. Not a year had elapsed since so close an associate as Gladstone had learned for the first time of Aberdeen's conversion to the Jewish cause. The Court had then been extremely anxious to have a ministry in prospect to replace, whenever necessary, the minority Tory Government, and Baron Stockmar, the Queen's adviser, had intimated that the Peelites should in that contingency move beyond their former practice of 1846–51, of sustaining the Whigs in office simply by upholding the Government in critical divisions, to actually cooperating with Russell in a coalition. Yet Gladstone had known Aberdeen as a man who, for some years, had been anxious to reconstruct the Conservative party; baffled now by Aberdeen's 'liberal leanings', friendliness to a 'liberal policy' and readiness 'to join the liberal party', Gladstone naturally broached one of those questions on which Aberdeen had formerly seemed to share common ground with the Tories. Here, again, Gladstone detected the Court's influence: 'when I referred to his vote about the Jews [Aberdeen] told me in confidence he was prepared to change it.'[45]

Considerations of Government unity conspired to preclude the disciplining of Hervey. Aberdeen's primary concern was to hold together the disparate strands of opinion which comprised his Government; inasmuch as Russell sought identification as a paladin of religious liberty so equally did Gladstone, now Chancellor of the Exchequer, conceive himself to be a keeper of the Government's Christian conscience. Aberdeen was assailed on both sides, the first letter he received coming from Russell who refused to accept that attitudes towards Emancipation had not been fully determined two to three months before at the time of the Government's formation. 'I certainly never understood that it [Emancipation] was to be an open question', expostulated Russell with Aberdeen, 'and had I found that you meant to vote against it, I should at once have declined forming any part of your Government. I think the Jew question fully as important as the question of Maynooth.' With a mortified air Russell complained: 'My influence in the House of Commons is considerably weakened by Lord A. Hervey's vote;

still more by the concealment of his purpose from me'; he concluded with an implied rebuke to the Prime Minister for failing to maintain the tradition of close and candid consultation between those who led for the Government in each of the two Houses. 'Lord Grey and Lord Althorp, Lord Melbourne and I could only get on by constant communication of the most unreserved nature.'[46]

Next it was Gladstone's turn to display displeasure. Referring to the pressure to dismiss Hervey, exerted on Aberdeen by Russell, Gladstone reminded the Prime Minister of the anguish he himself had experienced several years before when he had broken with a number of fellow Tractarians over this very issue of Emancipation. 'Lord Alfred Hervey has spoken to me from time to time about the position of the Government in reference to the Jewish question: and I have heard with much surprise of the claim made upon you with respect to him—I believe I stand alone among the members of the Government in having *suffered* on account of that question: and it is so important to me that I write to beg that if anything is meditated which may be of a nature to invidify the original position of the Government in regard to it, I may have an opportunity of speaking to you before such a measure is determined on—If not, I need not trouble you.'[47] In the event Hervey remained in the Government, prudently varying his position to one of abstention in subsequent divisions on the question; the episode which had originated with his vote had been of interest in demonstrating that for the Government coalition at least, if not for Russell's own party, commitment to Jewish Emancipation was not an article of political faith.

Opponents of Emancipation were wont to contend that the political demands of the Jews constituted not a right but a privilege and on the occasion of the second reading debate of 11 March 1853 Sir Frederic Thesiger drew a distinction between the equality of civil rights to which all subjects in the country could lay claim, these being defined by him as the threefold entitlement to personal security, personal liberty and private property, and the qualification to political power of legislating and governing which only the state could confer. In rebuttal of this distinction Sidney Herbert advanced not merely the familiar negative objection that Jews, denied the shadow of power, already had possession of its substance; he chose, more positively, to extol the virtue of representation as an agent of integration in a country where it was wrong to confuse the principles of religion and sectarianism. 'If Parliament is to be a representation of the whole mass of the community, then I say that in a free country like this, with great licence in matters of religious debate, in a country in which religious bodies are divided into innumerable sects, this House must reflect their different opinions, or it is not an accurate representation of the country.' With a participation of Members greater than on 24 February the bill was granted a second reading by the more substantial margin of 51 votes.[48]

The third reading a month later on 15 April was notable for a characteristic intervention by Bright, the Quaker and radical champion of free trade; that Bright had already spoken in debates on Emancipation may have owed something to the very slight strain of Jewish blood which he seems to have inherited.[49] His speeches consistently bore witness to the Quaker testimonies of toleration, deprecation of oaths and protest against the Church establishment, and on the present occasion he mounted a sharp attack on the bishops who had so greatly contributed to the thwarting of past Emancipation bills. After declaring that 'high titles, vast revenues and great power, conferred upon Christian ministers, are as without warrant to my mind, in Scripture as in reason', Bright affirmed his expectation that such bishops could never be expected to give an unbiased, impartial judgement on the claims of the Jews. In the ensuing division Emancipation was approved by 288 votes to 230, a majority of 58: with the turnout of Members somewhat larger than the 439 and 475 of the February and March divisions respectively this vote provides the most reliable reflection of the true balance of opinion on the issue in the first year of the new parliament.[50] And the vote was of further interest for revealing additional Peelite support for Emancipation. Despite the assumption of the Peelites that approval of the Maynooth endowment had cost them votes in the 1847 election they had not taken an anti-Papal line on the Ecclesiastical Titles Bill of 1851 brought forward by Russell as reaction to the Papal reestablishment of a Catholic diocesan hierarchy in England; in 1852 evidence of the new Peelite alignment with the Whigs had been attested in the formation of the Aberdeen coalition and this recent development, coupled with the temperate response to developments within the Catholic community, makes it perhaps not so surprising that, according to one reckoning, no less than thirty-two of the remnant of the dissolving Peelite group should have voted in favour of Emancipation and that only four Peelites should have voted against, with another six absent.[51]

Passage of the bill to the Upper House provided Lord Aberdeen with the opportunity of openly admitting that conversion to support of the Jewish cause which he had undergone since the Lords' previous debate on the question in July 1851; in his capacity as Prime Minister, Aberdeen now gave a foretaste of what was to prove, five years later, a satisfactory solution to the deadlock still then existing as between the Lords and the Commons. Hinting that each House should be allowed to determine its attitude independently of the other he advised the peers that on this question 'which touches so nearly the character of the House of Commons and its composition' they would be wise, despite the latitude of judgement permitted them, to be careful in pressing their perseverance. Advancing reasons in justification of his change of opinion Aberdeen reproached the opponents of Emancipation for forcing precepts upon others which they failed to practise themselves. Although the Lords had not actually 'unchristianized' Parliament they had 'unchristianized' legislative bodies by virtue of approving those very Acts of Parliament responsible for setting up the legislatures of

Canada and Jamaica to which Jews had been admitted. Turning then to another of the arguments against Emancipation, Aberdeen contended that it was for Providence, and not for opponents of the remission of disabilities, to determine how certain biblical prophecies should relate to the Jews. Here it was interesting that Aberdeen's free-will interpretation of the Crucifixion was quite unlike that of Disraeli's, with its stress on the Jews having been little more than God's chosen instruments for the achievement of a divine purpose. He, Aberdeen, could not deny that the Jews might yet be labouring under 'the obloquy of a crime of inconceivable magnitude', that they may indeed have 'imprecated upon their own heads the curse which is to pursue them from that event'; he did however hold to the unshakeable conviction that it would be wrong for men to attempt to usurp God's wrath by presuming to carry into effect the vengeance of the Almighty. And even in respect of mortals the peers must not exceed their jurisdiction; the curbing of the rights of Christian electors to select whom they pleased as their representatives constituted nothing other than an act of injustice towards Parliament itself and inflicted both hardship and injustice on the electors.

This last contention was one which had always been particularly associated with Archbishop Whately; his argument that Emancipation legislation would, primarily, serve the purpose of relieving a Christian electorate had indeed been given such a paradoxical twist when first advanced in the debate of August 1833 as to render it comparatively unconvincing besides the similar argument of Melbourne's; on the present occasion Whately went so far as to tell the House of Lords that the title of the current bill was a misnomer: the measure was not one 'for removing the disabilities of the Jews' but was intended rather 'for the relief of electors'. With professions of principle which might variably be construed as no less ingenious or ingenuous than those of F. D. Maurice, Whately loftily and disinterestedly declared that feeling on both sides of the Emancipation controversy was totally irrespective of the ground on which he took his stand. The question was usually considered as one 'for' or 'against' the admission of the Jews to Parliament: yet he stood neither for admission nor against it. He was not anxious to see the Jews in Parliament but he was anxious to see removed all restriction on the freedom of Christians to elect Jews to Parliament, so that Christians might in future enjoy the liberty to elect whomsoever they chose to serve as their representatives. It was, moreover, wrong of opponents to insist upon a unity of 'Christianity' when so often in the past those professing to such a nominal Christianity had believed in the existence of a fallible, semi-mythical philosopher-legislator Christ. Whately's thought was here interesting for so closely resembling that of Maurice and Gladstone. He observed how pantheistic Christianity sometimes served as a convenient cover for deism or atheism: its adherents, being further removed than the Jews themselves from the precepts of Christianity, found themselves enabled to achieve an unchristianization of the legislature correspondingly greater than that which could ever be brought about by any future admission of the Jews. Although these arguments did not prevail and the Emancipation bill was defeated in the Lords by 164 votes to 115 votes, a majority of 49, as many as eight members of the episcopate divided in favour of the measure.[52]

A month later, in May 1853, Lyndhurst introduced into the Lords an Alteration of Oaths Bill, the purpose of which was to consolidate the three Oaths of Allegiance, Supremacy and Abjuration into one single oath which could be taken by any loyal subject. Because the words 'upon the true faith of a Christian' were retained in the proposed oath, contrary to Lyndhurst's personal desire, the bill could not strictly be regarded as one for the removal of Jewish disabilities. But Lyndhurst does appear to have anticipated that the controversial words would be struck out in the Commons and that, on the occasion of the bill being referred back to the Lords, the peers would not then venture to reject it by reason of such 'a slender and reasonable' amendment. When Lyndhurst ventured to confess that he personally favoured the abolition of the declaration, Lord Derby recorded his objection to any tortuous course which might be adopted for the purpose of thwarting the will of the Lords. He harboured a sneaking suspicion that the Government would connive to pervert the bill, thereby effecting the removal of disabilities by a sidewind. Wilberforce, the Bishop of Oxford, entertained even greater suspicion that the measure was 'a well-contrived second Jew Bill', the introduction of which had been arranged for a date so late in the session as to preclude any opportunity for the peers of reinserting the controversial words of the Abjuration Oath when the bill was finally returned to them from the Commons. Thereupon Lyndhurst's measure was rejected by 84 votes to 69, a majority of 15.[53]

It was to the House of Commons that the next General Oaths Bill was presented; this particular measure, introduced by Russell in May 1854, did however make clear the proposal to omit the controversial declaration in the Abjuration Oath and thus, unlike its predecessor, could not be held to cast doubt on the intentions of its sponsors. Yet, this favourable comparison with Lyndhurst's bill notwithstanding, the measure could not divest itself of those faults appertaining to all such species of comprehensive bill; Members were resigned in the knowledge that not until the bill reached the second reading stage would they be allowed an opportunity of pronouncing judgement on the measure in its various parts.

Russell, so effectively castigated by Disraeli six years earlier for having then been tempted to reintroduce Emancipation legislation a second time during the course of one parliamentary session, now found the same adversary no less keen in the execration of his inability to appreciate the fundamental importance of constitutional niceties. Disraeli conveyed the suspicious mood of the House when he criticised

a Bill which is to substitute one oath for the various oaths that have

hitherto been taken by us when we approach the table of this House. . . .
It has been said that there are three objects that are to be obtained by this
Bill. By the omission of certain words at the end of one oath, a Jew may be
admitted into Parliament; by the alteration of another oath the views of the
Romanising Protestants are to be advanced; and by the change and
reconstruction of a third oath, the objects of the Roman Catholics themselves are to be promoted.

G. F. Muntz, one of the Members for Birmingham, surprised some by
declaring that he too would have to vote against the second reading; he set
this decision against the fact that he had uniformly voted with Russell in his
attempt to remove Jewish disabilities 'and would be always ready to do so
whenever it was attempted in a straightforward manner'. Muntz told Russell
that if he were to bring in a bill to admit the Jews and frame such an oath for
them as would be binding on their conscience he could then count upon his
[Muntz's] support, 'but he could not subscribe to a measure which, like the
present, proposed to alter the oaths agreed to at the settlement of 1829, and
to break the compact then entered into, which was considered satisfactory
by all parties'.

The House concurred in this opinion that a change in the law designed to
meet a particular purpose must necessarily precede any such comprehensive
scheme for a reform of statute law and in the ensuing division Russell's bill
was defeated by 251 votes to 247, a majority of 4.[54] The diarist Greville,
whose political judgement was often unreliable, was at least correct on this
occasion in writing that Russell's bill 'was an ill-advised measure, which
drew down upon itself those who are against the Jews and those who are
against the Catholics'.[55] Indeed, The hostility of Pope Pius IX towards
Italian and other Continental liberals in the aftermath of the 1848–49 revo-
lutions, the exuberantly proclaimed reestablishment of a Roman Catholic
hierarchy in England and the conversions to Catholicism from the Oxford
Movement, all combined to create a climate of suspicion which the Government had sought to assuage by enactment of the Ecclesiastical Titles
legislation; for the present, guarantees upon civil and religious liberties
seemed as important an issue as their extension. Gladstone wrote of 'a
parliament which, were the measure of 1829 not law at this moment, would I
think probably refuse to make it law',[56] and the record of the 1853–54
session, with the rejection of one bill which would have allowed the building
of nunneries and of another bill which would have permitted Catholic
worship in the prisons of Middlesex, confirms the validity of his judgement.
And the Jews themselves, not unaware of the inherent dangers of comprehensive oaths bills, were as anxious that their case for Emancipation
should be judged purely on its own merits as were many Members of
Parliament that Emancipation should not be enacted by one of Russell's
'sidewind' or 'subterfuge' composite oaths measures. Disraeli, in having
criticised Russell's handling of the question, thereby earned himself a

commendation from D. W. Marks, the minister of the London Reform Synagogue: 'You have rendered the most essential service to the Jewish cause, and have neutralized to a considerable extent the mischiefs inflicted upon it by the ill-judged measure of Lord John Russell.'[57]

As one of the latest in a number of legislative setbacks, the cumulative effect of the débâcle of the first Commons defeat for Emancipation in the twenty-two years of that chamber's reformed existence was to make Russell despair of his ability to lead the House and only seven weeks after the debate he asked Aberdeen to accept his resignation. On 14 July Russell wrote:

> The frequent defeats we have sustained, the number of measures we have been forced to withdraw, and the general want of confidence which prevails among the liberal party form a sufficient motive and justification for the step I now take—You have been, on the other hand, successful in the House of Lords. This only makes it more incumbent upon me to be the first to move—The weakness of the government lies in the House of Commons, and a change of leader may remedy the defect.

For the meantime Aberdeen was able to dissuade Russell from leaving his Government;[58] when the resignation did occur six months later it was precipitated not by any sense of personal shortcoming which the Leader of the House may still have felt but by the Cabinet disagreement arising from Russell's insistence upon the setting-up of a committee of enquiry to investigate the setbacks in the Crimea.

Indeed, the 1854–55 session was dominated by events in the Crimea and the heavy load of parliamentary business, coming after years of setbacks to Emancipation bills in the Lords, acted as a disincentive to those supporters of the Jewish cause who might otherwise have introduced a straightforward Emancipation bill. Lord Lyndhurst did contemplate the introduction of a measure but this was as suspect of subterfuge as his 1853 bill. It was drafted with a view to pursuing the familiar tactic of letting the words 'upon the true faith of a Christian' stand as part of the text during the first passage through the Lords, of having these words subsequently struck out by the Commons and of then attempting to persuade the Lords to agree to the measure as amended. Lord Derby warned Lyndhurst as to the commanding Tory majority in the Lords which his advocacy would have to overcome and the bill was consequently withdrawn, professedly on account of the lateness of the session.[59]

What effect developments in the Crimea may have had in determining the eventual outcome of the campaign for Emancipation, apart from causing a brief postponement of any further consideration of the question, is not easy to gauge; it is curious that the one figure who comes closest to providing an answer, Lord Shaftesbury, was himself quite removed from both the conduct of the war and the controversy engendered by its mishandling.

First there were Shaftesbury's hopes for the colonization of the Holy

Land, which millenarian event would provide confirmation that the Jews were 'the sovereign family of the human race'. In 1841 Shaftesbury had been instrumental in persuading Peel's Government to appoint a bishop at Jerusalem in the person of Dr. Alexander, a converted Jew; this innovation of an episcopal mission to the Jews in the Holy Land, for which the Church of England and the Prussian Evangelical Church bore joint responsibility, and which was thus an exercise in Anglican-Lutheran cooperation incurring the predictable opposition of Newman, Pusey and the Tractarians, was acclaimed by Shaftesbury as a project 'deeply rooted in the heart of England . . . [an] incarnation of love for God's people . . . [which would] save the country'.[60] Bishop Alexander died in 1845 but the increased British role in the region, as witnessed by the larger investment of capital and the establishment of a vice-consulate at Jerusalem, caused Shaftesbury to revive some plans of 1840 in which he had proposed to Palmerston the colonization of Syria and Palestine under the guaranteeing auspices of the Great Powers. In May 1854 Shaftesbury recorded one of the most moving entries in his diary concerning the content of a letter which he had written to Sir Moses Montefiore—Shaftesbury felt so united to Montefiore in a common bond of devout religiosity as to later request recommendation of his elevation to the peerage. Shaftesbury recorded that he had addressed Montefiore

> to learn if I could, the sentiments of his nation respecting a plan I have already opened to Clarendon [Foreign Secretary] and Clarendon to Lord Stratford [British ambassador to the Porte] that the Sultan should be moved to issue a firman granting to the Jewish people power to hold land in Syria, or in any part of the Turkish dominions. . . . All the East is stirred; the Turkish Empire is in rapid decay . . . Syria 'is wasted without an inhabitant'; these vast and fertile regions will soon be without a ruler, without a known and acknowledged power to claim dominion. The territory must be assigned to some one or other; can it be given to any European potentate? to any American colony? to any Asiatic sovereign or tribe? Are there aspirants from Africa to fasten a demand on the soil from Hamath to the river of Egypt? No, no, no! There is a country *without a nation;* and God now, in His wisdom and mercy, directs us to *a nation without a country.* His own once loved, nay, still loved people, the sons of Abraham, of Isaac, and of Jacob.[61]

The disasters which so soon afterwards befell the British troops in the Crimea rendered consideration of millenarian schemes more impracticable than ever; subsequently, not merely did the terms of the eventual peace settlement impart so changed an aspect to the Eastern Question as to make any of the Great Powers wary of repeating Russia's intervention in a zone of latent international rivalries but the very reason given for Britain's original participation in the war could not easily justify her in any future repetition of such an intervention.

And at home evangelicalism, of which millenarian convictions could be considered part and parcel, seemed also—albeit temporarily—to be falling into disfavour. The year 1855 saw both repeal of the previous year's legislation for the regulation of the sale of beer on Sundays and withdrawal of a bill for the prohibition of Sunday trading in the metropolis. The inarticulate cry was for plain men and popular measures: of the called-for virile self-help, of standing up for British national interests, Aberdeen's irresolute ministry seemed to be the negation and an alternative, Palmerstonian, conduct of foreign policy the veritable embodiment. After the Commons' defeat sustained by Aberdeen's ministry at the beginning of 1855 on the very issue over which Russell had resigned—the condition of the army and the supply services—Palmerston was invited to form a Government. Shaftesbury was one of those approached with an offer of a seat in Cabinet; his reply gave whatever signification was needed of his inability to meet the mood of the hour. Shaftesbury stated that he could accept Palmerston's offer only on the condition that he be allowed to maintain his positions in respect of Jewish Emancipation, Sunday Observance, restrictions on Catholicism and Irish questions including Maynooth. It so happened that there arose anyway some unexpected difficulties relating to the overall composition of the Cabinet: the suspension of the offer necessitated by the further consultations brought relief equally to Palmerston and to Shaftesbury.[62]

The man of the hour was emphatically Palmerston; insofar as the war had been responsible for propelling him to the premiership and the possible success of Jewish Emancipation might come to depend upon this wartime popularity being carried through to the next general election, then the change of mood wrought by developments in the Crimea may be adjudged to have improved the prospects of Emancipation.

The session of 1855–56 was not however allowed to pass without one further attempt at Emancipation. Early in the new year T. Milner-Gibson, the Manchester Member of Parliament who had risen to political prominence as an orator of the Anti-Corn Law League, sponsored a private member's bill to abrogate the Abjuration Oath and in the second reading debate of 9 April he presented a convincing case for dispensing with a requirement which was full of anomalies. Milner-Gibson referred to the observation made by Baron Alderson, in the Court of Exchequer case of Miller *v* Salomons, that the controversial declaration appended to the Abjuration Oath had been inserted solely for the purpose of foiling the Jesuit interpretation. From opposite sides of the House Russell and Spencer Walpole found themselves in agreement on two matters: that absence of any surviving issue did indeed render unnecessary continued abjuration of the descendants of James II, but that some acknowledgement would instead have to be made by the House of the Protestant character of the constitution.

Disagreement focused rather on Milner-Gibson's choice of tactics. Spencer Walpole, reiterating the opinion of the Commons majority of two years before, declared that 'when measures are brought forward in this

House, they ought to be brought forward for purposes only for which they are professedly intended'. This protestation was effectively stood on its head by the Lord Advocate, Moncrieff, who argued that discrimination was itself being maintained by a sidewind. 'Independently, however, of all questions of an historical character,' he asked, 'was it befitting the character of that House that they do by a side wind that which, if it were to be done at all, should be done openly and directly? If they were not prepared to enact a law by which Jews should be excluded from that House, was it creditable to exclude them by retaining certain words at the fag end of an oath which had nothing whatever to do with the matter?' More commonly accepted, however, was the interpretation of the expression 'sidewind' as offered by Disraeli. While nonetheless affirming that he now found himself able to reverse the vote which he had given against the previous 'sidewind' bill in 1854, Disraeli indicated his preference for a retention of the declaration in the Abjuration Oath so that the case of the Jews might then be met by the introduction of a separate clause.

Milner-Gibson's bill was accorded a second reading by 230 votes to 195, a majority of 35, and subsequent to the third reading an amendment tabled by Thesiger, to restore to the bill the controversial wording of the Abjuration Oath declaration, met defeat by a majority of 49.[63] Salomons, now Lord Mayor of London, was optimistic that with discreet management the bill would be ensured of its passage through the Lords,[64] but the peers refused a second reading by 110 votes to 78, a majority of 32, with the episcopate predictably dividing 14 to 6 against the measure.[65] The supporters of Emancipation could only hope that Palmerston's popularity would soon beget a majority in a newly elected Commons sufficiently impressive as to overcome that resistance for which the Upper House was by now renowned.

NOTES

1. Disraeli, *Hansard*, Third Series, 105, 14 May 1849, 462.
2. W. Dexter (ed.), *The Nonesuch Dickens. The Letters of Charles Dickens*, II, 1847–57, letters from Dickens to the Hon. Richard Watson, pp. 164–65, 21 July 1849, pp. 220–21, 3 July 1850, this last comparing Disraeli with the dead Peel.
3. *Hansard*, Third Series, 104, 7 May 1849, 1396–1449; *Hansard*, Third Series, 105, 11 June 1849, 1373–1434.
4. *Hansard*, Third Series, 106, 26 June 1849, 872–922; Sumner, Archbishop of Canterbury, cols. 888–91; Whately, Archbishop of Dublin, col. 892.
5. The following account of the 1849 by-election in the City of London is based on *The Times* (all issues for 1849), 28 June, p. 8; 29 June, p. 8; 30 June, p. 5; 3 July, p. 7; 4 July, p. 8; 5 July, p. 8.
6. R. E. Leader (ed.) *Life and Letters of John Arthur Roebuck with chapters of autobiography*, p. 233, letter entry for 4 March 1850, and cf. Roebuck, *Hansard*, Third Series, 105, 11 June 1849, 1416–24.
7. *Hansard*, Third Series, 109, 12 March 1850, 809–16; Peel, cols. 813–14.
8. P. H. Emden, *Quakers in Commerce: A Record of Business Achievement*, pp. 53–54.
9. C. Roth, *The Magnificent Rothschilds*, pp. 46–47.
10. *Hansard*, Third Series, 113, 26 July 1850, 297–333.
11. *Hansard*, Third Series, 113, 29 July 1850, 396–453.

12. *Hansard*, Third Series, 113, 30 July 1850, 486–533.
13. *Hansard*, Third Series, 113, 5 August 1850, 769–817; Disraeli, cols. 788–95.
14. U. R. Q. Henriques, *Religious Toleration in England, 1787–1833*, p. 91.
15. T. Pyne, *Judaea Libera: or, the Eligibility of the Jews (the ancient People of God) to Parliament*, p. 14.
16. *Hansard*, Third Series, 116, 1 May 1851, 367–412.
17. *The Times*, 3 May 1851, leading article.
18. The ensuing account of the 1851 by-election at Greenwich is based upon the Greenwich Local History Library collection, poster no. 58 (claim by supporters of D. W. Wire that Salomons's election would entail disenfranchisement), and the following newspaper reports and comments (all issues for 1851): *Kentish Mercury*, 21 June, pp. 1, 2 (leading article); 28 June, pp. 1, 3; *The Kentish Independent*, 21 June, p. 5; 28 June, p. 4; *The Times*, 27 June, p. 8; 28 June, p. 6.
19. L. Loewe (ed.), *The Diaries of Sir Moses and Lady Montefiore*, II, pp. 9–10, 10 April 1848.
20. *Hansard*, Third Series, 118, 3 July 1851, 142–47; Russell, cols. 144–45.
21. J. H. Harris, third Earl of Malmesbury, *Memoirs of an Ex-Minister. An Autobiography*, I, p. 283.
22. Russell Papers, P.R.O. 30/22, 9d, 259–60, 16 July 1851, letter from Sumner, Archbishop of Canterbury, to Russell.
23. *Hansard*, Third Series, 118, 17 July 1851, 859–909; Shaftesbury, cols. 881–87.
24. *Hansard*, Third Series, 118, 18 July 1851, 979–86.
25. Russell Papers, P.R.O. 30/22, 9d, 269–72, 19 July 1851, letter from C. S. Shaw-Lefèvre, Speaker of the House of Commons, to Russell; Russell Papers, P.R.O. 30/22, 9d, 267–68, 19 July 1851, letter from Salomons to Russell. (The numbering of the letters, the order they have been placed in this Russell letter-book, is misleading.)
26. *Hansard*, Third Series, 118, 21 July 1851, 1143–1217.
27. *Hansard*, Third Series, 118, 22 July 1851, 1318–66.
28. *Hansard*, Third Series, 118, 28 July 1851, 1573–1629.
29. F. Pollock, *Essays in Jurisprudence and Ethics*, p. 193.
30. Cf. D. Salomons, *Parliamentary Oaths: Observations on the Law and Practice with regard to the administration of oaths*, pp. 27–31, where this particular abstruse point is developed, and Russell Papers, P.R.O. 30/22, 9d, 267–68, 19 July 1851, letter from Salomons to Russell, cited above, in which Salomons referred Russell to the Catholic relief legislation as an instance of the power given to change the sovereign's name.
31. Cf. D. Salomons, *Parliamentary Oaths*, pp. 7–8, 11–12, 25.
32. A. Goldsmid (ed.), *Report of the Case of Miller versus Salomons, M. P. with a summary of the preliminary proceedings in the House of Commons*, pp. 26–28.
33. F. Pollock, *Essays in Jurisprudence and Ethics*, p. 193.
34. D. Salomons, *Alteration of Oaths considered in a Letter to the Earl of Derby*, p. 5.
35. Derby Papers, Box no. 156/8, correspondence of Spencer Walpole, Home Secretary, with Derby, letter undated; letter from Derby to Salomons, 24 April 1852; letter from Salomons to Derby, 28 April 1852; letter from Lord St. Leonards, Lord Chancellor, to Derby, 1 May 1852; letters from Salomons to Derby and Derby to Salomons, both 3 May 1852; letter from Salomons to Derby, 5 May 1852.
36. John, Lord Campbell, *Lives of the Lord Chancellors and Keepers of the Great Seal of England, from the earliest times to the reign of Queen Victoria*, VIII, pp. 175–76.
37. Minute Books of the Board of Deputies, VII, pp. 97–99, 28 October 1852.
38. Russell Papers, P.R.O. 30/22, 9e, 68–77, 12 August 1851, memorandum of Lord John Russell, tenth proposal, fol. no. 75.
39. Russell Papers, P.R.O. 30/22, 9e, 120–28, 17 August 1851, letter from Prince Albert to Russell.
40. Russell Papers, P.R.O. 30/22, 10c, 66–67, Russell's *Address to the Electors of the City of London*, May 1852.
41. The following account of the 1852 election at Greenwich is based upon *The Kentish Independent* (all issues for 1852), 26 June, p. 4 (leading article); 3 July, p. 4 (leading article); 10 July, pp. 4–5 (including leading article).
42. *Hansard*, Third Series, 124, 24 February 1853, 590–625; Russell, cols. 597–98; Inglis, cols. 605–6; Drumlanrig, cols. 616–17. For Drumlanrig's earlier opposition to Emancipation, cf. *Hansard*, Third Series, 95, 17 December 1847, cols. 1376–77.
43. Aberdeen Papers, B.M.ADD.MSS. 43066, fol. nos. 318–19, 25 February 1853, letter from Russell to Aberdeen.
44. Russell Papers, P.R.O. 30/22, 10h, 105–6, 25 February 1853, letter from Aberdeen to Russell.
45. Gladstone Papers, B.M.ADD.MSS. 44778, fol. nos. 5–20, 12 March 1852, memorandum, referring to Gladstone's visit of the previous day to Lord Aberdeen.

46. Aberdeen Papers, B.M.ADD.MSS. 43066, fol. nos. 322–23, 26 February 1853, letter from Russell to Aberdeen.

47. Aberdeen Papers, B.M.ADD.MSS. 43070, fol. nos. 298–99, 27 February 1853, letter from Gladstone to Aberdeen.

48. *Hansard,* Third Series, 125, 11 March 1853, 71–122; Thesiger, cols. 76–77; Sidney Herbert, cols. 105–6.

49. J. Travis Mills, *John Bright and the Quakers,* I, pp. 97–98.

50. *Hansard,* Third Series, 125, 15 April 1853, 1217–91; Bright, cols. 1255–61. For Bright's previous contributions, cf. *Hansard,* Third Series, 105, 14 May 1849, 446–48; *Hansard,* Third Series, 113, 5 August 1850, 809–10, 814–15; *Hansard,* Third Series, 118, 21 July 1851, 1195–99; *Hansard,* Third Series, 118, 22 July 1851, 1349–52, 1361.

51. J. B. Conacher, *The Aberdeen Coalition, 1852–1855. A study in mid-nineteenth century party politics,* p. 105. For the earlier stance of the Peelites on religious questions, cf. G. I. T. Machin, 'The Maynooth Grant, the Dissenters and Disestablishment, 1845–1847', *English Historical Review,* 82, pp. 61–85.

52. *Hansard,* Third Series, 126, 29 April 1853, 753–95; Aberdeen, cols. 753–59; Whately, Archbishop of Dublin, cols. 772–75. For Whately's two earlier contributions, cf. *Hansard,* Third Series, 20, 1 August 1833, 226–35, and *Hansard,* Third Series, 106, 26 June 1849, 891–94, already cited in this 1849 context.

53. *Hansard,* Third Series, 127, 31 May 1853, 838–62; Campbell, *Lives of the Lord Chancellors,* VIII, p. 180–82; T. Martin, *A Life of Lord Lyndhurst, from letters and papers in possession of his family,* pp. 451–53; R. G. Wilberforce, *The Life of the Rt. Rev. Samuel Wilberforce. D. D. . . . with selections from his diaries and correspondence,* II, p. 188, 13 June 1853.

54. *Hansard,* Third Series, 133, 25 May 1854, 870–974.

55. C. C. F. Greville, *The Greville Memoirs. A Journal of the Reigns of King George IV, King William IV and Queen Victoria* (ed. H. Reeve), VII, pp. 162–63, 28 May 1854.

56. J. Morley, *The Life of William Ewart Gladstone,* I, p. 506.

57. Hughenden Papers, Box 136: B/XXI/M/209, 29 May 1854, letter from Rabbi D. W. Marks to B. Disraeli.

58. Aberdeen Papers, B.M.ADD.MSS. 43068, fol. nos. 116–17, 14 July 1854, letter from Russell to Aberdeen, and 119–20, 14 July 1854, letter from Aberdeen to Russell.

59. J. Campbell, *Lives of the Lord Chancellors,* VIII, p. 192.

60. E. Hodder, *The Life and Work of the Seventh Earl of Shaftesbury, with Extracts from Lord Shaftesbury's Diaries and Journals,* pp. 197–200, diary for 12 October 1841. For other important references concerning Emancipation and the future of the Jews, see ibid., pp. 126–27 (quoting Ashley's observations on a review notice of Lord Lindsay's *Letters on Egypt, Edom, and the Holy Land* in the *Quarterly Review,* 63, January 1839, pp. 166–92); ibid., pp. 166–67, diary for 24 July 1840; ibid., pp. 177–78, diary for 12 March 1841; ibid., pp. 328–29, diary for 15 December 1845. Cf. also the three Parliamentary speeches: Ashley, *Hansard,* Third Series, 95, 16 December 1847, 1272–82; Shaftesbury, *Hansard,* Third Series, 118, 17 July 1851, 881–87; Shaftesbury, *Hansard,* Third Series, 126, 29 April 1853, 759–67. Cf. A. L. Tibawi, *British Interests in Palestine, 1800–1901,* for developments in respect of the Jerusalem Bishopric; pp. 46–47, for the opposition of Pusey and Newman.

61. Ibid., p. 493; diary for 17 May 1854. The Earl of Clarendon was the Foreign Secretary; Stratford Canning, Viscount Stratford, was the British ambassador to the Ottoman Empire. Cf. ibid., pp. 166, diary for 24 July 1840, for the earlier presentation of colonization proposals to Palmerston.

62. Ibid., pp. 500–502; two letters from Palmerston to Shaftesbury, 7 February 1855, and two letters from Shaftesbury to Palmerston, 7 February 1855.

63. *Hansard,* Third Series, 141, 9 April 1856, 703–59; *Hansard,* Third Series, 142, 23 May 1856, 595–605; *Hansard,* Third Series, 142, 9 June 1856, 1165–97.

64. Hughenden Papers, Box 142: B/XXI/S/29, 1 June 1856, letter from D. Salomons to B. Disraeli.

65. *Hansard,* Third Series, 142, 23 June 1856, 1772–1807.

11
Traits Similar and Dissimilar

The gentile response to the Jewish claims could not but be partly determined by the image which the Jewish minority conveyed to the gentile majority and this chapter therefore turns aside—albeit briefly—from tracing the development of the political campaign so as to enquire to what extent the characteristics borne by, or imputed to, the Jewish community were seen to resemble those of the gentile population, that resemblance taking the form of reciprocation of whatever opportunities for integration had been afforded to the Jews by the middle decades of the century.

The posing of this question necessarily precludes two other approaches to the problem of analysing public sentiment. Remembering that it was the Jews who had to meet the expectations of the gentiles, and not vice versa, any approach which amounts to the conducting of a posthumous show-trial on the Victorians, of deciding where they might be placed on a philosemitism/antisemitism scale, seems essentially false. And not merely false, but dangerous too, as one example suffices to make clear. Disraeli's novel *Tancred* was published in 1847; soon after publication the magazine *Punch,* as accompaniment to an article 'The Jewish Champion' which alleged that Disraeli required a Mosaic Parliament sitting in Rag Fair in order to see the object of his mission or 'new crusade' accomplished, printed a cartoon entitled 'The House of Commons according to Mr. Disraeli's views'. The Commons was here turned into an unruly Sanhedrin. Uncouth men in top hats jostled each other for seating room; a Jew involved in the East End clothes trade was usually represented in prints as wearing several hats on his head and in this cartoon such a figure was most conspicuously depicted as the Speaker.[1] The cartoon might seem to some observers rabidly anti-semitic, but what then of another full-page cartoon published by *Punch* little more than two years later entitled 'A Parcel of Old—Frightened at a Nasty! Great! Ugly! Jew Bill'? This full-page cartoon parodied the opponents of Emancipation assembled in the Lords as a panic-stricken bunch of old women; as an elongated, bow-legged, nasty-antennaed caterpillar of an insect marked 'Jewish Disabilities Bill' crawls menacingly towards the coroneted peers they contemplate the creepie-crawlie with dread horror and, holding up their robes as though they were skirts, fretfully prance and scamper panic-stricken about the chamber while one of their number, a particularly obese and old-womanish character, attempts to knock the insect senseless with the mace.[2] Likewise, in another issue of *Punch* of the same year, an article entitled 'Miss Benimble's Tea—and Toast' seemed to accuse the peers of indulging the luxury of resorting to a cynical expediency in their treatment of the Jews, their lordships freed from the anxieties which had been caused them the year before by the Chartist disturbances. A Mr. Lovelace predicts that the Lords will throw out the forthcoming Jews' Bill 'for this reason. It's a bit of bigotry they can enjoy in comfort. That is, they know there won't be much fuss about the matter. There'll be no buttoning up of pockets—no stopping of the supplies—no marching of iron men from Birmingham, and so forth.'[3] Would not an observer be tempted to conclude from this article and second cartoon that *Punch* had by 1849 become as rabidly hostile towards the opponents of the Jews as it had been earlier towards the Jews themselves? The answer, of course, is that *Punch* should not be read with a seriousness it does not merit; the parodying of *both* Jews and peers represents a healthy impudence, a satirical bringing out of the most ridiculous of all worlds.

Having discarded the approach which uses simplistic criteria to make value judgements which anyhow should not be made, it is apposite to point to the perils of a second approach. When, of a sample of respondents representing a cross-section of the adult population of a country, an insignificant 4 per cent is found to agree with the proposition that 'the Jews are the most despicable form of mankind which crawls on this earth', yet a full 84 per cent of the selfsame group concur in the statement that 'the dislike of many people for the Jews is based on prejudice, but is nevertheless not without a certain justification',[4] one becomes conscious of the hazards to be apprehended in defining antisemitism—indeed of how erroneous and misleading it can be, on a question as complex as attitudes towards Jews, to attempt to quantify public opinion. The margin of 80 per cent between the two supposed indices of antisemitism in the above sample reveals the absurdity of such attempts at quantification: the individual minds of all but a rather small minority in this sample must, on the evidence of the 80 per cent disparity alone, be composed of any number of emotions, feelings, gut reactions and considered opinions towards the Jews which defy immediate synthesis. Public sentiment, impossible to measure, can be discerned only by judicious assessment.

It would nevertheless not be absurd to expect that some sort of assessment could be arrived at by striking a balance between the views of that minority most committed to Emancipation and that minority most opposed, on the premise that the biases of one group would be almost certain to cancel out those of the other. And virtues and vices being in the eye of the beholder it is indeed fascinating to note the designations chosen by that tiny minority which in either instance did feel sufficiently committed to submit petitions to Parliament. The petitions submitted to the House of Lords *in favour of*

Emancipation tended to come from those who consciously thought of themselves as burgesses, merchants and manufacturers, financiers and bankers, members of the medical and legal professions, town councillors, other pillars of the urban establishment, Dissenters and the Welsh; the petitions to the Lords *against* Emancipation tended, by the same token of self-designation, to emanate from landholders, magistrates, churchmen, parishioners, countryfolk, Presbyterians and Scots.[5]

Yet interesting though this categorization is, the assessment of Jews which might be arrived at by blending the views of those most disposed to favour the claims of the Jews and those most antipathetic to them would be quite unreliable, for the vehemence common to the two groups would be quite unrepresentative of the mood of the mass of public opinion which lay between them; their observations must, therefore, for the purposes of this survey yield to the information which was gleaned by a small number of especially perceptive contemporary observers, most of whom were familiar with important facets of London life.

Of these the most penetrating were the Reverend John Mills, a Welsh Calvinistic missionary minister, whose lapidary work, *The British Jews*, was published in 1853, and the eminent physician J. H. Stallard, author of a substantial number of works on pauperism, welfare and public health, whose authoritative *London Pauperism amongst Jews and Christians* was published in 1867. Mills was careful to state at the outset of his observations that he could not countenance any theory based upon the idea that the difference of character among nations was founded upon constitutional and unchangeable principles;[6] Stallard simply prefaced his book by remarking on the Jews: 'We find them neither much better nor much worse than other people.'[7] By these comments their respective authors did not however mean to imply that the Jewish community lacked a distinctive character: they found upon it indeed the strongest imprint of the prevailing practical philosophy of self-help, with the Jews possessing almost the whole range of attributes, positive and negative, which are invariably to be associated with those who believe that in self-help lies the solution to most of life's problems.

Mills, Stallard, and that most thorough observer of so many aspects of the mid-century London social scene, Henry Mayhew, were all of one opinion in noting the Jews' love of independence and self-employment. The ambition of a typical humble Jew seemed to be to emulate the successful rise of a Rothschild: perhaps exchanging an itinerant for a propertied status and a retail role for a wholesale-distributive and commercial one he would hope to graduate from wheelbarrow to stall, from shop to mixed trading premises, and from purpose-built warehouse to City bank. The itinerant Jew may have realized that such progression could scarcely hope to be achieved within the space of one generation, but with the educational, social and other advantages which money might obtain, he could assuredly trust that his grandchildren or great-grandchildren would reap the benefits of his initial labours. For most Jews earned their living in business of one description or another: even of that interrelated cousinhood some of whose members were so prominent in the campaign for Emancipation few as yet emulated F. H. Goldsmid in entering the professions, preferring rather to confine themselves to the traditional spheres of banking and finance. Responsible for a greater diffusion of prosperity were the merchants, contractors, shippers and warehousemen with import and export businesses; the only significant incursion of Jews into manufacturing was to be seen in the Manchester textile industry, many of the newcomers here being Sephardim, and in the ready-made clothing trade conducted in particular by the two very large London factories of Moses & Co. and Hyam's, the latter firm in the middle years of the century employing six thousand people and running an annual wage bill of more than £200,000.[8] Sweatshops were already coming into existence; the Jews working in these obviously comprised a less prosperous group along with the tailors and second-hand dealers in slop-clothing who still abounded in Liverpool and other seaports and in certain London districts east of the City. Others not so prosperous included those engaged in the selling of goods to stallkeepers and street vendors or in the commissioning of crockery and jewellery items from small masters and journeymen makers; since the late eighteenth century the fashionable market of a London West End had enabled a number of Jews to open shops as goldsmiths, jewellers, watchmakers and embroiderers.

Contemporary observers were good interpreters of community aspirations when attempting to fathom why so many Jews should have been drawn to engage in businesses which involved merchandise in fruit and additional consumption goods, watches, jewellery and other precious items. This was not merely because commerce, as observed by Gabriel Riesser, the prominent Jewish advocate of Emancipation in the 1848–49 Frankfurt Parliament, requires the many and distant connections with relatives and other co-religionists which the Jews happened to possess;[9] as Mayhew wrote in 1851: 'The trades which the Jews most effect, I was told by one of themselves, are those in which, as they describe it, *there's a chance;* that is, they prefer a trade in such commodity as is not subjected to a fixed price, so that there may be abundant scope for speculation, and something like a gambler's chance for profit or loss. In this way, Sir Walter Scott has said, trade has *all the fascination of gambling, without the moral guilt.*'[10] The attraction of trades which allowed for bartering and high profits was likewise noted by Stallard.[11] Yet the privation, thrift, industriousness and perseverance which were necessary requirements of success in business—and in themselves enviable qualities—seemed, in a curious combination of virtue and indulgence almost incomprehensible to both Mills and Stallard, to be subservient to the ultimate goal of maximising financial gains.[12] With ready money, observed Stallard, the Jew was not very scrupulous as to the character of its investment 'so only that it presents a reasonable chance of a large profit'.[13]

Because the whole community, and not merely a part of it, was imbued with the self-help philosophy, Anglo-Jewry could be thought of, in a very literal sense of the term, as *democratic*. The most prosperous and established of bankers shared with the poorest and most newly-arrived of immigrants the twin ambitions of working for oneself and acquiring wealth; among Anglicans, if not among Dissenters, the attendance of two such socially diverse types of individual at the same place of worship would have been almost inconceivable. One must recall the communal set of values which had come, perforce, over the course of centuries, to inform the Jews' distinctive Diaspora function; here Stallard failed to perceive that the money-making propensities of Jews, originally inculcated by the circumstances of dispersion and ghetto life but now the conditioned defensive reflex to the discrimination which might otherwise be exercised against them, were far more important in defining the Jews' range of occupations than either social ambitions or such constraints of religion as the requirements to be absent from work on Sabbath days and on festivals or to eat only kosher food, an injunction which, as Mayhew knew himself, was sometimes breached.[14]

From the quirk of social, as opposed to economic, classification Mills also was not immune; he estimated that 20 per cent of the Jews of Britain could be considered 'upper class' and an additional 32 per cent as 'middle class'.[15] Even more remarkable were the figures given by *The St. James Medley* of 1855 which, specifying more clearly than Mills how it had arrived at its class criteria, placed seven-twelfths of Britain's Jews in the 'upper' and 'middle' classes.[16] The community, receiving from abroad each year before the 1860s not more than an average of some few hundred immigrants who did not wish to take advantage of the greater opportunities of emigrating to America, and relatively more prosperous than it had been several decades before for reasons which included the lifting of restrictions on retail trading in the City of London, was witnessing the gradual disappearance of indigent Jews. For this improvement the Jewish system of relief, as was noted by both the Handloom Weavers' Commission of 1840 and by Stallard a quarter of a century later, was also responsible. Whereas the treatment of pauperism by the Poor Law Board was characterised by Bumble-thinking which deprived the indigent of any self-respect by, for example, consigning them as distasteful outcasts to workhouses, an approach which worsened rather than alleviated the problem, the treatment which the poor were accorded by Jewish communal institutions was marked by wise and judicious forethought which avoided indiscriminate expenditure. Far from denying or encroaching upon the self-respect of individuals, the Jewish organizations successfully relied upon and encouraged the innate human sense of pride and independence. The Jews' Hospital at Mile End, the Jews' Free School and other welfare and educational institutions had long since undertaken systematic efforts to prepare children for some such useful trade as tailoring, shirt, cap and slipper making, shoe and boot binding and making, upholstering and furniture making. The problems of the indigent were the particular concern of the Jewish Board of Guardians, as reconstituted in the late 1850s, and Stallard commented of one of the Guardians' schemes that the lending out to the poor of large numbers of sewing machines had rescued hundreds of families from misery and degrading pauperism by a project with 'nothing eleemosynary about it. . . . It simply helps the poor to help themselves, which is the most effective form of charity.' The Jews never became a charge upon the general public welfare funds and although there were still in the England of the 1850s about two hundred to two hundred and fifty Jewish hawkers, pedlars, street-vendors and stallholders and five to six hundred Jewish old clothes men, these figures, anyway comprised largely of the less assimilable first generation immigrants, represented a considerable change from the time when Patrick Colquhoun, the Metropolitan police magistrate of the last years of the eighteenth century, had estimated that the Jewish old clothes sellers alone constituted one thousand five hundred men.[17]

Realization of ambition was naturally reflected in choice of home and as soon as they were able many of London's Jews took the opportunity of moving out of the most congested areas of the city. Until the middle decades of the nineteenth century the areas in London of predominant Jewish settlement were the Aldgate and Portsoken wards of David Salomons fame, with the greatest concentration of inhabitants in the triangle bounded by St. Mary Axe, Bevis Marks/Duke Street and Leadenhall Street; a second concentration existed in the Minories, extending southwards from Aldgate to Tower Hill, while outside the City to the east there were the three districts of Houndsditch, the quadrilateral around the Tenter Ground known as Goodman's Fields and the Rosemary Lane area to the south around the Royal Mint which constituted the traditional centre of the old clothes trade. Although in 1850 the majority of the community was still to be found living in the City or in the streets immediately to the east, such areas as Finsbury, Tyburnia (Bayswater) and Barnsbury were attracting substantial numbers of Jewish newcomers; then, as later, the story of Jewish as of non-Jewish migration in a north-west direction out of old London relates directly to all the factors, such as use of the horse-drawn omnibus and the development of the railways and of the underground, which facilitated mobility and the expansion of the metropolis.[18]

Those few who could afford to do so moved to more salubrious suburban or parkland residences where they could breathe unpolluted air; the returns of the 1851 Census of Worship would seem to indicate the newfound favour of Westminster and St. Marylebone. Sir Moses Montefiore moved from St. Swithun's Lane to Park Lane and a number of his relatives also chose to live in Mayfair; the Goldsmids moved to the spacious squares and terraces east of Marble Arch, with I. L. Goldsmid deciding to live further out at Regent's Park; the Mocattas moved to Bloomsbury. One of David Salomons's homes was outside London altogether, a house at Broomhill near Tunbridge Wells in Kent being constructed for him by the renowned architect Decimus Burton. The opulence of others held for many a certain glamour: Countess Frances Waldegrave, the daughter of the singer John Braham and one of the most fashionable ballroom hostesses of the day, found herself after the death of her husband in 1846 in possession of the entire Waldegrave estates and these included Horace Walpole's Gothic Revival house at Strawberry Hill. The Rothschild choice of homes was also of interest: N. M. Rothschild moved from St. Swithun's Lane to Piccadilly while Meyer Amschel Rothschild lived for part of the year at Mentmore House in Buckinghamshire, a house built for him between the years 1852 and 1854 and remarkable for its date in having hot-water heating and artificial ventilation throughout.

The majority of Jews for whom such a standard of living was no more than a fantasy did however evince a concern for physical well-being and the prevention of degeneracy. The Handloom Weavers' Commission of 1840 found the Jews very strong, in fine physical condition, and fond of good eating. The sobriety and abstemiousness, which were considered by Stallard to be the best traits in the Jewish character, meant that the disgusting scenes of intoxication, which disfigured many gentile localities, were rarely evident in the Jewish areas; Mills noted that abstemiousness was characteristic not only of public parties but also of private family life.[19]

The low incidence of criminality among Jews was also commented upon, though it was interesting that Stallard should have seen in his research a need to counteract the general impression that the Jewish crime rate was higher than it actually was; he noted that at the time of writing there were only fifteen male convicts at Portsmouth, to which place all Jewish convicts were sent because the prison there possessed a synagogue at hand for their use; of these prisoners more than half anyway were foreigners. Stallard's search through the prison records could, moreover, reveal no instances of a convicted Jewess.[20] Dickens, although accurately depicting a type when presenting Fagin as a receiver of stolen goods and instructor of pickpockets, was mistaken in representing him as a cruel, vindictive, sanguinary murderer: the existence of more than one or two such characters would have imparted to the whole community a degree of unpopularity from which it had not suffered since the 1770s and 1780s when a notorious murder committed by several Jews in Chelsea had inflamed gentile opinion; the radical tailor Francis Place, who died in his eighties in 1854 and whose knowledge of London life was as extensive as that of Dickens, commented that the change in opinion during his own lifetime, caused not least by a grudging admiration for the Jews' proficiency in learning the art of self-defence, meant that any persons who insulted Jews in the streets of early Victorian London would have been in danger of chastisement from the passers-by and of punishment from the police.[21] One Jewish correspondent took Dickens to task for his casting of Fagin; the author redressed any possible sense of grievance by introducing into *Our Mutual Friend* the benevolent Jewish figure of Mr. Riah, and in 1868, at the request of *The Jewish Chronicle*, Dickens consented to omit the story of the murder in *Oliver Twist* from his future series of public readings.[22]

In no sphere was Jewish self-esteem seen to be more beneficial than in that of housing and health. The provision by which even the poorest of families would each inhabit separate rooms was contrasted by Mills with the practice, commonly found among the London poor and most particularly among the Irish, of a dozen or more persons of both sexes living and sleeping in one dark and filthy room, without any partition whatever.[23] To Stallard were even more evident the advantages of the decency of dwellings and of the lack of the squalid destitution which was so often the result of intemperance. The houses of penurious Jews were, on the whole, noted to be more clean, more tidy and more comfortable than those of gentiles of similar means. The children were better clothed and more cleanly, their 'round and ruddy faces' presenting a strong contrast to the 'pale and scrofulous countenances' of the neighbouring gentile children in the same overcrowded streets; indeed scrofula was almost non-existent among the Jews while the injunction which forbade the giving of alcohol to young Jews until such time as they could be admitted as members of the synagogue meant that children were not dosed with gin and opium, to the destruction of their health. The absence of hereditary syphilis was also commented upon. And good health naturally begot better health: the absence of syphilis and scrofula in one generation would be conducive to survival in the next. The generally healthy condition of prospective Jewish parents, the availability of nurses for even the poorest of expectant mothers and the friendly, practical concern of neighbours which made for a cheerful contemplation of the birth were all factors which were thought by Stallard to be responsible for the relatively smaller proportion of stillborn babies. Insofar as a slightly lower than average communal birthrate was the result of many Jews deferring marriage until such time as they could afford to raise a family, the lower incidence of mortality of both Jewish babies and of Jewish children under five years of age, noted by Stallard to apply also on the Continent and which was attributed by him to the children's generally healthy condition from birth and their upbringing in caring and hygienic households, was a 'compensating' factor which cold statistics cannot bespeak. Stallard found the barest evidence of neglect, with mothers refusing to undertake any work which might take them away from their children, while fatalities attributable to lack of food or the exigencies of poverty seemed, if that were possible, to be even more rare.[24]

It was ironical that whereas Jews still had to fight hard for Emancipation from political disabilities they appeared, by their own efforts, to have achieved, by gentile standards, a relative emancipation from the hazards of physical disease. The primitivism of Victorian medicine, all too often entailing risk of faulty diagnosis of illness and subsequent prescription of remedies which might impair rather than improve the condition of a patient, meant in a quite literal sense that prevention was better than cure. Importance was attached to the setting-up of food kitchens in the sound belief that the nourishment thus provided would stave off a communal problem of indigent illness brought about by exhaustion and debility.[25] Religious injunctions were thought by Mills to be one cause of the cleanliness of the Jews and strict observation of certain alimentary prohibitions, among other factors, was considered by Stallard to be conducive to the Jews' proper hygiene.[26] Certainly, in an age when risk of death through disease was infinitely greater than risk of death at the hands of an enemy in war, strict adherence to the Jewish dietary laws, with their proscription on the preparation and consumption of popular foods derived from swine and shellfish, must have saved countless lives. Again, the sanitation of Jewish homes and the relief work undertaken by such communal organizations as the Jewish Board of Guardians saved all but a few members of the community from the fearsome toll of deaths wrought by the pandemic cholera outbreaks which affected Britain in the early part of the century and recurred in the four middle decades. Mills, noting the findings of the report of the General Board of Health, commented on how the Jews in the years before 1853 had been enabled to emerge relatively unscathed from cholera, with thirteen deaths as against an overall figure of almost thirteen thousand deaths. The spread of cholera was facilitated by revolting sewage and effluent: in 1866 the negligence of the East London Water Company in supplying unfiltered water in breach of the Metropolitan Water Act of 1852, the most horrific result of which could be seen in the breeding of foot-long eels in the water-pipes of houses, contributed to raising the total number of deaths from cholera in London for that year to almost six thousand. Once again the Jewish community escaped with comparative immunity, with only seventeen deaths resulting from cholera and six from diarrhoea. The Jewish Board of Guardians, with the close cooperation of its medical officers and resort to ancillary medical services, won the cooperation of landlords and at small expense undertook inspection and a number of corrective measures to prevent the spread of cholera, typhus and fever: stand-pipes with a constant supply of water in the densest quarters, a system of house-to-house visitation, the cleansing and whitewashing of unsuitable houses, the use of fluid, carbolic and disinfectants, distribution of articles of bedding, the supply of extra meat and rice and of wine, brandy and other most desired stimulants supplied to the order of the medical officers, and the renting of a set of houses as a convalescent home for recuperation.[27]

Many of the virtues of the close-knit Jewish community seemed particularly to apply to family life. Apart from noting the Jews' inoffensiveness and keeping of the public peace, Stallard also commented upon their domestic-

ity, concern for the wellbeing of their own relations, the greater care taken of
both young and old, the fond rearing of orphans, the few cases of concubin-
age, the synagogue encouraging morality by the granting of financial aid to
the newly married, the comparative rarity of instances of desertion, the
exceptionally low incidence of suicide, and how utterly unknown it was in
the community for violence to be inflicted on women and children. The
parents seemed rather to err on the side of indulgence: Stallard could not but
notice that trait of possessiveness in many Jewish parents which assumed
the form of spoiling children and of sometimes making unjustifiable sacrifices
for their benefit.[28] The kind and liberal charitability of Jews not only towards
the poor of their own faith but also towards needy gentiles won the attention
of Mayhew, Mills and Stallard and of a number of politicians who favoured
the Jews' political claims.[29] The hospitality of Jewish families on the
Sabbath and on festivals, which also benefited the poorer members of the
community, was thought by Mills to be not only laudable in itself: the days
free from work provided Jews with an opportunity, more often seized by
them than by gentiles in respect of Sundays, of taking a sabbatarian break in
their routine of toil to 'renovate the body' and 'improve the mind'.[30]

The reclusiveness of the community also attracted comment; the
philosopher-historian Harriet Martineau noted the Jews' lack of proselytizing tendencies and Mills praised Judaism as a religion which, in contrast to
Roman Catholicism, was to be found 'not intermeddling with the civil rights
of other creeds'. The synagogue prayers, containing one for the wellbeing of
the Royal Family, furnished confirmatory evidence of the Jews' patriotism:
extending his comparison which, though invidious, was in keeping with
public sentiment in the aftermath of the 'Papal Aggression', Mills wrote that
the tenets of Judaism, as distinct from certain dogmas of Catholicism, could
be seen to be consistent with perfect loyalty. More positively Mills perceived how the loyalty of the Jews to Britain sprang not merely from
indifference but from love of the country and of its free institutions: he noted
both the pride of English-born Jews in their country and the admiration of
Britain expressed by Jews from all parts of Europe.[31]

For the majority of the Jews wished to reciprocate whatever opportunities
of integration were afforded them. For a long time previously dress had been
the most obvious manifestation of how acclimatized to their environment the
Jews of Britain were. Whereas in almost every European country during the
seventeenth and eighteenth centuries there was a recognized Jewish mode of
dress, in the Dutch, British and North American lands Jews, with the
exception of some first generation immigrants, invariably wore the same
dress as their Christian counterparts: this resemblance extended even to a
Protestant Dissenting style of rabbinical dress and by the close of the
eighteenth century many very orthodox Ashkenazim in Britain had chosen
to discard ragged beards and foreign dress.[32] Yet basic conformity in speech
and dress are, of course, the very minimum required of those wishing to

demonstrate their preparedness for integration, and the willingness to slough off the remnants of autonomy could be seen during the period of Emancipation to extend in particular to the sphere of education:[33] although the denominational character of English education which persisted throughout this period meant that for Jewish, as for other non-Anglican parents, there could be only one happy choice of school, as early as 1807 the educationist Hyman Hurwitz, in discussing the problems of schools in a non-Jewish environment, was to be found expressing some anxiety about the incursion of secular education into that part of the timetable formerly reserved for Hebrew and biblical studies.

It was actually conversionist initiative which prompted the community into reforming its system of educational provision. Between 1807 and 1813 the conversionists established three schools in the traditional Jewish quarters of London. The ban on enrolment by the Chief Rabbi was insufficient to stifle agitation for more provision; many Jews were not merely still illiterate but unable even to understand English and the prospect of choosing between education in the English language at a conversionist school and receiving in Spanish or polyglot pseudodialects of Ladino and Yiddish what amounted to a travesty of proper instruction was not one to commend itself to most parents. Much therefore was expected of the initiative taken by Dr. Joshua Van Oven and others in the years between 1815 and 1818 in transforming the old Ashkenazi Talmud Torah Charity into the Jews' Free School of Bell Lane, Spitalfields, and of the establishment in 1820, in the Westminster-Soho district, of the Western Institute for Educating, Clothing and Apprenticing Indigent Jewish Boys, the future Westminster Jews' Free School.

Rapid thenceforth was the increase in educational instruction. In the earliest days of the Jews' Free School 270 boys had been taught in a general range of subjects by only one master and the Handloom Weavers' Commission of 1840, in finding that only 314 boys and 130 girls attended the school instead of the numbers of 600 and 300 respectively for which there were places, lamented that education was not sufficiently esteemed by many working Jews. By 1850 however the number of boys at the Jews' Free School had risen to 555 and the number of girls to 400 and three years later the corresponding figures had increased to 700 and 460. The Jews' Free School was, moreover, only the largest of the half-dozen or more schools situated in the traditional Jewish quarter of London. Mills noted the existence of other schools in the important provincial centres of Liverpool, Manchester and Birmingham, each containing between sixty and ninety pupils; these numbers would of course have grown by 1867 at a time when Stallard reckoned that more than four thousand Jewish children were to be found attending London schools. Whatever problems the Jewish educational establishments may have had to contend with in respect of the teacher-pupil ratio, this being on average approximately one to thirty, were probably less acute than those which bedevilled most British schools. At the

Jews' Free School in the early 1850s between a third and a half of the staff of thirty-eight appear to have been pupil teachers, particularly among the women, and so the abandonment by this time of the monitorial system was evidence not that Jewish educational institutions had failed to adapt for their own purposes useful aspects of the prevailing Lancaster and Bell systems but that the priority accorded to education had allowed the Jews' Free School to discard such improvisation. The Master of the Jews' Free School reported to the Handloom Weavers' Commission on how those former pupils who had themselves received instruction twenty years before attached more importance to education than had their own parents; Mills noted that in 1844 there had been established for adults the Literary and Scientific Institution of Sussex Hall in Leadenhall Street, which, possessing a library of five thousand volumes and reading rooms amply supplied with English, French and German material of topical interest, offered lectures and instruction in moral, philosophical, historical, scientific and religious subjects and in languages, literature and art. The community, of course, evinced no lack of goodwill for the success of the University of London and particularly for University College, administered as a joint-stock company. Here there existed neither religious tests as qualification for entry nor religious instruction of any description, Hebrew being taught as a linguistic subject in the same manner as Latin or Greek; the influence not of Oxford and Cambridge but of the German and Scottish universities and of Benthamite utilitarianism predominated and so there was a modern bias in the teaching, with emphasis on medicine, engineering, mathematics, the sciences, political economy, law, philosophy and modern languages.

Improvements in the sphere of education were thus to be gauged not merely in a quantitative sense; the conclusion of the Handloom Weavers' Commission of 1840 that no signs could be discerned in the Jewish schools of seeking to maintain 'a middle wall of partition' between the Jews and the rest of the native-born subjects of the Crown attested to the degree of voluntary synchronization of traditional English and Jewish curricular requirements which Jewish educational establishments had by that time attained. Use was made of the Authorized Version of the Bible, of the moral and allegorical material in *A Selection from Instructive Tales* by the popular educationist Mrs. Sarah Trimmer, and of other textbooks in common usage. The staple curriculum was divided between Hebrew and biblical studies and instruction in the subjects invariably taught in all schools: arithmetic, reading, writing, grammar, composition, music, algebra, model-drawing and object and gallery instruction; girls were prepared in laundry and needlework. A very small number of pupils at the Jews' Free School were given a specialized Hebraic and rabbinical training and it was partly to augment the present limited opportunities of such an education that Jews' College was established in the 1850s. The very anxiety to conform with current practice can be seen with reference to one or two subjects. In 1840 the Handloom Weavers'

Commission had commented upon the inadequacy of the history and geography taught in Jewish schools and had criticised too the absence of wallmaps and of works of nature. The observations of Mills thirteen years later reveal the extent to which these defects had been remedied. Although the Jews' Free School still persisted in a splitting up of its history syllabus into parts 'sacred and profane', a pejorative labelling which betrayed how unemancipated some Jews still were in being unable to cast aside religious bias in favour of the dispassionate and disinterested approach to which the discipline of history was entitled in its own right, the schools did now possess an ample supply of maps, pictures, natural and artificial objects, and standard textbooks. These included Miss Mangnall's *A Compendium of Geography,* Dr. Ebenezer Brewer's *A Guide to the Scientific Knowledge of Things Familiar* and Thomas Ewing's *A System of Geography with an account of the Solar System.* Classics and languages appear to have been taught but rarely, although one of the few reputedly efficient private schools, an establishment in Edmonton, did offer tuition in Latin, French, German and Spanish.

Mills, with his perceptive powers of observation and dedication to accuracy in giving a portrayal of Anglo-Jewry, cannot be accused of displaying prejudice when commenting on some of the less desirable traits of many in the community. He apportioned blame for the existence of a number of defects to both Jew and gentile: although the laws of the country and the Anglican complexion of its institutions excluded Jews from all civil and literary posts and so offered them 'Mammon-seeking' as the only vent for the exercising of their tact and talent, Jews made too little effort to counteract the traditional enforced conditions of degradation and debasement. These manifested themselves in excessive preoccupation with affairs of business, the nurturing of a non-literary tradition of *Yidishkayt,* and the pursuit of pleasure. Mills wished that the Jews might devote more time to an edifying pursuit of leisure through the promotion of literature and other civilising studies: in particular he regretted a certain lack of support for the Literary and Scientific Institution of Sussex Hall in Leadenhall Street. Anglo-Jewish literature itself was not only meagre and unimportant, a circumstance for which the smallness of the community could be held to be largely responsible, but whatever writings were published seemed to be characterised by 'a kind of bombastic style, being always the result of imperfect taste and inferior training'.[34] This same defect was to be noted too in a more mundane context. With some exceptions, especially among the Sephardim, Jews were wont to display an unnecessary amount of finery, with rings and chains being worn by flashily-attired men and an excess of real and counterfeit jewellery being worn by women, who in other ways too made themselves conspicuous by a gaudy dressiness.[35] Mills, as was only to be expected from a Calvinist minister of religion, deplored also the card-playing to which so many in the community seemed passionately attached; to displace such activity he wished, with the genuine interests of one who had earlier made great efforts to extend musical culture in Wales, that the Jews' talents for classical music might be encouraged.[36] Mayhew too noted the prevalence of gambling and card-playing among the street Jews.[37] Then there was the liking of many Jews for theatrical performances, popular concerts and balls, forms of amusement likewise considered by Mills to be 'lax schools of education'.[38] That *The Jewish Chronicle* should even more strongly have concurred in this set of strictures affords confirmation of the fairness of Mills's assessment; a leading article in the paper reproached young Jewesses both for their vulgarity, vanity and shabby gentility in wearing the 'second-hand finery of a duchess' and for their frequenting of casinos and low dancing places.[39] Mills observed too the lack of charm and manners of many Jews, their excitable, contentious and intolerant natures finding natural self-expression in incessant clamour, brawls and quarrelling and a lack of charitable behaviour towards one another. Thus there were times and circumstances when assertive individualism, far from deserving commendation as a manifestation of healthy independence, was to be condemned as betraying a perverse sense of self-importance, Jews then conveying the impression of 'every one feeling his own importance, and wishing to be the guide and not the guided'.[40] As the more serious and protracted of these disputes commonly concerned not the problems of the 'have-nots' but those of the 'haves', assuming the form of contests over wills and rival claims to ownership of substantial amounts of property, they were noteworthy more for their sensational value; Mills and Stallard were at one in agreeing that the Jews presented no social problem. Nonetheless Mills as a Christian minister was as entitled as David Salomons to deplore the rabbinical resort to excommunication in cases where there was disagreement only on inessential points, for such factiousness and pettiness was incongruous and ill became Jews at a time when they themselves were so anxious for others to grant them perfect liberty.[41]

Mills attributed the persistence of such faults as narrow-mindedness and assumed superiority to the exclusiveness of the community, for by 'turning almost entirely within the circle of their own community, having little intercourse with their neighbours, and consequently in great ignorance of Gentile and Christian society' the Jews debarred themselves from the improvement they could derive from Christians and Christian literature. The ignorance and superstitiousness which thrived on unenlightenment were not dispelled and, lacking a comparative scale of values by which their own Jewish assumptions could be tested, pride and self-approval were allowed to proceed unchecked. These traits, thought by Mills to be partly based on the Jews' antiquity as a nation, were conducive to a popular, boastful misinterpretation of the phrase by which the Jews had in former times been designated 'the chosen people';[42] Harriet Martineau likewise noted in connection with this exclusiveness that the Jews considered themselves 'the peerage of the human race'.[43]

These were reservations of little substance; the nub of criticism was concerned with the supposed fault of many Jews in seeking to 'commercialize' life. There were a few caricatures such as that entitled 'Repulsed but not Discouraged', printed in the year 1830, which represented the Jew as another non-Anglican claimant to parliamentary Emancipation with Daniel O'Connell depicted as saying 'Agitate friend Moses, Agitate! That's the way I got in.'[44] The majority however of the prints and cartoons somehow contrived to connect the Jews with the power of money or commerce. The most successful of these prints in evoking a response of popular recognition were those which, with Byronic ridicule, caricatured the Rothschilds as bloated capitalists, pillars of the Stock Exchange, upgraded versions of 'the Wandering Jew', the omnipotent sixth power of Europe which could be seen to possess and manipulate the others and so arbitrate at will for global war and peace. One satirical print, commenting on Duncombe's allusion to the Rothschilds as the financial power which could make or break governments, was entitled 'Secret Influence behind the Curtain!!' or 'The Jew and the Doctor' after a farce of that name of 1800; one of the Rothschilds is here to be seen on the extreme left of the engraving, descending on the wing and carrying in each hand a bag of gold. With a use of words parodying the accent and expostulatory idiom of an unassimilated immigrant Rothschild ejaculates 'Si help me Cot! de Sinking Job will go to de bottom of de melting pot if you don't stick out Herry! You bote know dat *I* and only *I* am de Incorporial—never mind. I gave de Don Miggel and all de oder Dons de monish! plesh my hearts.' Another similar caricature took as its subject a meeting of the European powers in Downing Street at which one of the Rothschilds was threatening not to lend any more money to the various governments unless his immediate requests were acceded to.[45] The image of the Jewish financier was not of course the only one which commended itself to portrayers of the Jews; apart from that cartoon in *Punch* which lampooned the views of Disraeli a number of prints exploited the Jews' traditional connection with the old clothes trade and one of these of 1830, entitled 'Knock and ye shall enter', satirised the unsuccessful attempt to achieve Emancipation in that year by depicting an old clothes dealer and a Moroccan Jewish pedlar waiting expectantly at the door of the House of Commons.[46]

The inference to be drawn here was that the benefits of entry to the legislature might almost be reduced to the success of some commercial proposition. The designation of *Jew* had long since passed into the English language as a generic term to describe certain types of activity, irrespective of whether the actual practitioners of these activities were Jews or not. A London crockery and glassware street-seller and barterer recounted to

Mayhew his experiences of ladies who slyly stopped him in the streets asking him to call at their homes at a certain hour. He found on arrival that 'they smuggles you quietly into some room by yourselves, and then sets to work Jewing away as hard as they can, pricing up their own things, and downcrying yourn'. For a particular example of this 'Jewing' Mayhew reported the man's account of a visit to a fashionable part of Pimlico where a lady wanted a complete chamber service, with soap trays and brush trays, together with four breakfast cups, in return for a couple of old washed-out light waistcoats and a pair of light trousers. The woman attempted to persuade the crock that the buttons alone on the waistcoats 'was worth 6d a piece' and in consequence no deal could be made because, as the man told Mayhew, 'at first start off I'm sure they wouldn't have cost 1d each'.[47]

Sometimes the pursuit of such commercial activities not only applied explicitly to the Jews as a clearly-defined group, but could be seen to have a direct bearing on the consideration of their claims to Emancipation. At a public meeting in favour of the remission of disabilities held on 31 January 1848, at the time when the issue was in the political forefront, Mr. John Macgregor, one of the Members of Parliament for Glasgow and a highly respected and distinguished former joint Secretary at the Board of Trade, outlined the position of Jews on the Continent. There is never a need to deny what no one asserts and it was therefore significant that Macgregor should have found it necessary to state that 'with reference to the charge that they [the Jews] were always ready to overreach those with whom they dealt, his experience tended to quite a contrary result'.[48]

Justified as some criticisms of the Jews may have been, there were undoubtedly occasions when unctuous disapproval was little more than a guise for prejudice and jealousy. On occasions the mask slipped. In January 1852, at a time when the Court of Exchequer was preoccupied with examining Salomons's claims to be seated in Parliament, some fictitious theatre posters appeared in the Greenwich constituency which billed a new production entitled *Shylock!* In this the leading role was played by one 'Ikey Salomons', a semi-criminal character, and in the first scene, at a small house in Bevis Marks, Shylock receives his father's advice. 'Get Monish my Poy, Honestly if you can, but get Monish.' When Shylock spends his 'monish' too freely and meets a setback he vows to a confidant 'Never mind my Poy, I'LL JEW-'EM-YET.'[49] In 1859, when Salomons was no longer hampered by disabilities in fighting the Greenwich constituency, there were, as in the contest of 1852, three Liberal candidates competing for election to the two seats. The editor of one small local newspaper accused the editor of the rival *Kentish Mercury,* who happened also to be both chairman of the regional dock company and a friend of Salomons, of a 'Judaistical trick' in alleging that Angerstein, one of Salomons's fellow Liberal candidates, was involved in unbecoming transactions in a joint stock company engaged upon the purpose of forming commercial docks in the Greenwich Marshes.[50]

The Christian Socialist Movement undoubtedly carried undertones of anti-Jewish sentiment; its principals and journalistic sympathisers, though advancing the not unreasonable case that the new industrial order was a perversion of God's order inasmuch as it served to promote rivalry and competition rather than the well-being of human society in its entirety, did tend to focus undue attention upon the comparatively limited role of the Jews. Mayhew, in the simplistic belief that the production of cheap goods in a free and unprotected market must inevitably lead to exploitation of the market in labour at the cheapest possible price, used his connection with the *Morning Chronicle* to attack such Jewish clothes-making firms as Moses & Co. for their use of the slop-system, by which clothes were given out to a middleman intermediary who in turn subdivided the various jobs among a number of small workers. The novelist Charles Kingsley even published a pamphlet with the suggestive title *Cheap Clothes and Nasty*, which contained jibes at Nebuchadnezzar & Co.'s 'Emporium of Fashion', a fictitious firm clearly modelled on such establishments as Moses & Co. and Hyam's. The acquisition of wealth was considered quite reprehensible and particular censure was reserved for one notorious 'sweater' of coats and paletots whose meteoric rise from the position of street sponge seller to that of contractor making a profit of more than three thousand pounds a year had been advertised by the choice of a well-appointed carriage.[51] As for some of the silliest jealousies these were probably to be encountered in the City; some remarkably petty incidents seem to have punctuated a feud between Rothschilds and the very large private City banking house of Jones, Loyd, & Co. and transactions between the two banks had finally to cease.[52]

There can be little doubt that the refusal of Queen Victoria in 1869 to accede to Gladstone's first request to confer a peerage on Lionel Rothschild accorded with the feelings of the majority of her subjects, even if the objections which she articulated on their behalf were all too obviously a reflection of a general nineteenth-century jealousy of the Jews and of English sanctimonious hypocrisy in particular. The Queen wrote to Gladstone:

> It is not only the feeling of which she cannot divest herself, against making a person of the Jewish religion, a Peer; but she cannot think that one who owes his great wealth to contracts with Foreign Governments for Loans, or to successful speculations on the Stock Exchange can fairly claim a British peerage. However high Sir L. Rothschild may stand personally in Public Estimation, this seems to her not the less a species of gambling, because it is on a gigantic scale—and far removed from that legitimate trading which she delights to honour, in which men have raised themselves by patient industry and unswerving probity to positions of wealth and influence.[53]

The image which the Jewish minority conveyed to the gentile majority and of which the various traits of character all seemed to be a part, was preeminently that of ambition. There was the ambition of self-help, the ambition to improve the wellbeing of the whole community, the ambition to reciprocate opportunities of integration. And there were the less commendable traits of ambition, many of them derived from a past of persecution and for the continued existence of which therefore the Jews themselves could be held only partly responsible. In Britain a large measure of tolerance and toleration preceded the removal of legal and political disabilities; there was indeed acceptance but because the removal of prejudice must necessarily always be the last and longest of the processes of Emancipation that acceptance could not be total.

NOTES

1. *Punch*, XII, 10 April 1847, pp. 145, 149.
2. Ibid., XVII, July–December 1849, p. 17.
3. Ibid., XVI, January–July 1849, pp. 193–94, spring 1849.
4. See H. J. Eysenck, *The Psychology of Politics*, pp. 81–82, discussion concerning a study by H. J. Eysenck and S. Brown on antisemitism.
5. *Journals of the House of Lords*, 1828–60: petitions submitted to the Lords concerning Admission of the Jews to Parliament. Cf. also the petitions to Parliament of May 1830 from Liverpool and the City of London, *Hansard*, New Series, 24, 4 May 1830, 375–77, and *Hansard*, New Series, 24, 17 May 1830, 769–74.
6. J. Mills, *The British Jews*, pp. 347–48.
7. J. H. Stallard, *London Pauperism amongst Jews and Christians*, p. 4.
8. V. D. Lipman, *Social History of the Jews in England, 1850–1950*, pp. 27–29, 67, upon which this and the succeeding paragraphs are based.
9. Gabriel Riesser, cited in D. Philipson, *Old European Jewries*, p. 206.
10. *Mayhew's London. Being selections from 'London Labour and the London Poor'* (ed. P. Quennell), p. 285.
11. J. H. Stallard, *London Pauperism amongst Jews and Christians*, p. 9.
12. J. Mills, *The British Jews*, pp. 348–55; J. H. Stallard, *London Pauperism amongst Jews and Christians*, pp. 9–10.
13. J. H. Stallard, *London Pauperism amongst Jews and Christians*, p. 10.
14. Ibid., pp. 8–9; *Mayhew's London*, pp. 289–91, 295.
15. J. Mills, *The British Jews*, p. 258.
16. *The St. James Medley*, I, no. IV, November 1855, pp. 235–36.
17. J. H. Stallard, *London Pauperism amongst Jews and Christians*, pp. 10, 19–22, 43–48, 74–77, 86, 99–100, 153–58, 161–74, 189, 192, 262, 300–302, 305, 308–9; *Parliamentary Papers*, Reports from Commissioners: (8). Handloom Weavers. Session 16 January–11 August 1840, vol. XXIII, 1840. Reports from Assistant Handloom Weavers' Commissioners. 43—Part II, 4 February 1840, pp. 112–14; L. Magnus, *The Jewish Board of Guardians and the Men Who Made It, 1859–1909*, pp. 25–32; V. D. Lipman, pp. 29–31.
18. V. D. Lipman, *Social History of the Jews in England*, pp. 11–17, 27–28, 68–69; V. D. Lipman, 'The Structure of London Jewry in the Mid-Nineteenth Century', in *Essays presented to Chief Rabbi Israel Brodie on the occasion of his seventieth birthday* (ed. H. J. Zimmels, J. Rabbinowitz, I. Finestein), pp. 253–73, particularly pp. 259–60.
19. Handloom Weavers' Commission of 1840, pp. 112, 114; J. H. Stallard, *London Pauperism amongst Jews and Christians*, pp. 10–11; J. Mills, *The British Jews*, pp. 348–49.
20. J. H. Stallard, *London Pauperism amongst Jews and Christians*, p. 17.
21. M. D. George, *London Life in the Eighteenth Century*, p. 132. For eighteenth-century public attitudes towards the Jews, cf. also T. W. Perry, *Public Opinion, Propaganda, and Politics in Eighteenth-Century England. A Study of the Jew Bill of 1753;* R. J. Robson, *The Oxfordshire Election of 1754*.
22. 'Fagin and Riah', *The Dickensian*, vol. XVII, no. 3, July 1921, pp. 144–52 (no author given); *The Jewish Chronicle*, 4 December 1868, p. 3; *The Jewish Chronicle*, 1 January 1869, p. 4.
23. J. Mills, *The British Jews*, p. 349.

24. J. H. Stallard, *London Pauperism amongst Jews and Christians,* pp. 10–15.

25. Ibid., pp. 63–69.

26. Ibid., pp. 13–14; 63–69; J. Mills, *The British Jews,* pp. 347–55.

27. J. Mills, *The British Jews,* pp. 347–55; F. Sheppard, *London, 1808–1870: The Infernal Wen,* p. 295; J. H. Stallard, *London Pauperism amongst Jews and Christians,* pp. 66–69, 74.

28. J. H. Stallard, *London Pauperism amongst Jews and Christians,* pp. 11–20.

29. *The Unknown Mayhew. Selections from the 'Morning Chronicle', 1849–1850* (ed. E. P. Thompson and E. Yeo), pp. 261–62, Mayhew's letter XXXIII, *Morning Chronicle,* 7 February 1850; J. Mills, *The British Jews,* pp. 273–87, 347–55; J. H. Stallard, *London Pauperism amongst Jews and Christians,* pp. 17–20, 86, 302–4. Cf. also the Commons' speeches complimenting Jews for their philanthropy, Lord George Bentinck, *Hansard,* Third Series, 95, 17 December 1847, 1384, and Lord John Russell, *Hansard,* Third Series, 124, 24 February 1853, 599.

30. J. Mills, *The British Jews,* pp. 349–50.

31. Harriet Martineau, *The History of England during the Thirty Years' Peace: 1816–1846,* I, p. 547; J. Mills, *The British Jews,* pp. 340–42.

32. Cf. A. Rubens, *A History of Jewish Costume,* pp. 3, 188–90.

33. The following discussion of education and Anglo-Jewry is based upon: Handloom Weavers' Commission of 1840, pp. 112–14; Sampson Low, *The Charities of London, comprehending the Benevolent, Educational, and Religious Institutions,* p. 323; J. Mills, *The British Jews,* pp. 292–323; J. H. Stallard, *London Pauperism amongst Jews and Christians,* pp. 18, 43–44, 101; S. Stein, *The Beginnings of Hebrew Studies at University College,* a lecture delivered at University College, London, 1 August 1951, pp. 11–12; C. Roth, *Essays and Portraits in Anglo-Jewish History,* pp. 219–31; F. Sheppard, *London, 1808–1870: The Infernal Wen,* pp. 219–20.

34. J. Mills, *The British Jews,* pp. 303–4, 324–25, 352.

35. Ibid., pp. 351–52.

36. Ibid.

37. *Mayhew's London,* pp. 288–89, 291, 293, 296.

38. J. Mills, *The British Jews,* pp. 303–4, 324–25, 352.

39. *The Jewish Chronicle,* 26 June 1857, leading article, 'Purity of Domestic Life Among Our Masses'.

40. J. Mills, *The British Jews,* pp. 303–4, 324–25, 352.

41. Ibid.; J. H. Stallard, *London Pauperism amongst Jews and Christians,* passim.

42. J. Mills, *The British Jews,* pp. 303–4, 324–25, 352.

43. H. Martineau, *The History of England during the Thirty Years' Peace,* I, 547.

44. A. Rubens, *A Jewish Iconography,* p. 29. Rubens's cataloguing no. 1386, caricature 'Repulsed but not Discouraged', 1830.

45. *The Hebrew Talisman!* (no date), a satire on N. M. de Rothschild including a caricature 'A Pillar of the Exchange', this being an adaptation of a caricature of N. M. de Rothschild published in 1829 by F. V. Webster & Co 'at his Histrionic Repository, 11 Broad Court, Long Acre': David Salomons Mementos, Broomhill (Southborough, near Tunbridge Wells, Kent), Scrapbook of Original Drawings and Cards, no. 325, caricature no. 61, 'A Pillar of the Exchange'; A. Rubens, *Anglo-Jewish Portraits,* p. 98 (this same caricature, Rubens's cataloguing no. 240, with explanation of theme from contemporary sources and subsequent exhibition and art catalogue references); pp. 96–97, Rubens's cataloguing no. 238, caricature 'Secret Influence behind the Curtain!!' or 'The Jew and the Doctor', 1828, the caricature (and first of these titles particularly) being a representation of a theme developed by Thomas Duncombe in the Commons, Duncombe, *Hansard,* New Series, 18, 18 February 1828, 540–43. Duncombe was contributing to a debate concerning the reasons for the break-up of the previous Government. (According to *The Times,* 19 February 1828, the particular 'incorporeal being' actually referred to by Duncombe was the Duke of Newcastle, pp. 97–100, caricatures on theme of the Rothschild family as 'powerful moneybags behind the throne', Rubens's cataloguing nos. 239, 242, 245, this last representing Rothschild meeting with the Powers in Downing Street, pp. 126–27, Rubens's cataloguing no. 299, caricature 'A New Court Fire Screen', referring to the formation of the Alliance British and Foreign Life and Fire Assurance Co. and, apart from hostile depiction of Jews, hinting heavily as the 'sixth power of Europe' theme. See in connection with these caricatures of the Rothschilds, Byron's 'The Age of Bronze'.

46. *Punch,* see above, p. 201; A. Rubens, *A Jewish Iconography,* p. 29, Rubens's cataloguing no. 1387, caricature 'Knock and ye shall enter', c. 1830, and passim.

47. *The Street Trader's Lot. A selection from Mayhew's London,* pp. 110–11.

48. *The Illustrated London News,* XII, January–June 1848, no. 301, for week ending 5 February 1848, p. 75. Parliamentary Portraits Series: Mr. Macgregor, M. P.

49. Unnumbered item in the Martin Collection, Greenwich Local History Centre library, playbill dated 14 January 1852.

50. *The Woolwich Advertiser, and Plumstead and Charlton Trade Circular,* no. 14, 10 February 1859, p. 2.

51. *The Unknown Mayhew*, pp. 34–38, including report in *Bell's Weekly Messenger*, 2 November 1850, of a meeting addressed by Mayhew, pp. 221–22, Mayhew's letter XVIII, *Morning Chronicle*, 18 December 1849; C. Kingsley, *Alton Locke*, containing reprint of the tract *Cheap Clothes and Nasty*, first published in the early 1850s under the pseudonym 'Parson Lot'; F. Sheppard, *London, 1808–1870: The Infernal Wen*, pp. 241–42; G. Kendall, *Charles Kingsley and His Ideas*, pp. 61–62; T. Christensen, *Origin and History of Christian Socialism, 1848–54*, pp. 133, 218.

52. F. G. Hilton Price, *A Handbook of London Bankers*, pp. 95–96.

53. A. M. Hyamson, 'The First Jewish Peer', *Transactions of the Jewish Historical Society of England*, XVII pp. 287–90, reprint of letter from Queen Victoria to W. E. Gladstone, 1 November 1869.

12
Constitutional Compromise and Settlement

The change of Ministry brought about by the Crimean War had made the Jews aware of how dependent upon Palmerston's continued political success were their own hopes of achieving Emancipation: insofar as the electorate's estimation of Palmerston's character meant that the Prime Minister would fare best in any contest dominated by a call of endorsement for his conduct of foreign policy, the Jews may reasonably have surmised that an opportunity had been missed when Palmerston decided not to appeal to the country immediately upon the cessation of hostilities in the Crimea. The months after the defeat of Milner-Gibson's bill were, for the Jews, months of frustration: then, as if by chance, the concatenation of favourable circumstance suddenly reappeared. In the House of Commons in March 1857 a bizarre combination of Tories, Peelites and 'peace-party' reformers carried a motion criticising Palmerston's conduct of the second war with China; the Prime Minister, fortunate in that his critics had opted for so unwise a challenge, shrewdly turned the tables on them by the calling of a general election.

Lord John Russell, not a member of the Government, had voted against Palmerston in the critical China division and this factor largely explained why, after an unbroken constituency representation of sixteen years, the City of London Liberal Registration Association did not readopt him as one of the four official 'Liberal and Commercial' candidates.[1] Rothschild, who was renominated, disapproved of this rejection. At one meeting he expressed sorrow at the City Liberals' treatment of Russell and concern lest such factiousness endanger the cohesion of the party. He told the Jewish electors of the City that they would disgrace themselves if they were to vote as a body against Russell and in this personal endorsement he had the enthusiastic support of Salomons, who campaigned assiduously for Russell on the eve of the poll. This was an impressive show of Jewish unanimity which quite overshadowed one minor and rather interesting manifestation of intra-Jewish disagreement. After Rothschild had expressed disapproval of some of Salomons's past tactics, which adoption he understood had given more offence to the peers than anything else and induced them to vote against Emancipation, Salomons was naturally moved at one campaign meeting to disagree with this interpretation of the effect of his past actions.

The result of the City poll was: Sir J. Duke (L) 6,664; L. N. Rothschild (L)

6,398; Lord John Russell (Ind L) 6,308; R.W. Crawford (L) 5,808; and R. Currie (L) 4,519. Whereas the return of Rothschild met with universal acclaim in the Liberal ranks, the failure to secure displacement of Russell by Currie represented a severe blow to the prestige of the City Liberal caucus.

Whatever measure of satisfaction the Jews may have derived from the poll in the City, even more gratifying to them was the overall election result. Although a number of sympathetic radicals and free traders, tainted by accusations of pacifism, found themselves out of favour with the electors—some, including Bright, only temporarily—this loss was more than compensated for by the success, even in some cases in the same constituencies, of an additional number of candidates pledged to support of the Ministry. Campaigners for the Jewish cause, looking first to the new Palmerstonian ascendancy of approximately ninety votes, might reasonably calculate that, in any division on Emancipation taken at a time when almost all the Members of Parliament were present in the House, the support or abstention of a small group of dissentient Tories might lift that majority to a figure nearer to 140 or 150.

The Oaths Bill introduced by the Palmerston Government shortly after the election was a comprehensive one, but differed from some of the earlier measures sponsored by Russell and Lyndhurst in that it enabled Members to consider the Jewish question quite separately from the abrogation of anomalies. When discussion of the bill opened on 15 May, the House listened to an argument from the Prime Minister not unlike one advanced many years before in the Upper House by Archbishop Whately, to the effect that Jews refrained from either proselytization of Christians or interference with Christianity. Palmerston, after first pouring ridicule on the very notion that the admission of a few Jews to Parliament could shake the Christian religion, then gave expression to that distinctively Anglo-Saxon puritan view which neatly associated optimism for the future strength of Christianity with its past debt to the Jews. Observation that Jews had become Christians but Christians had not become Jews, that the preparation of the Old Testament for the New Testament precluded all possibility of the New leading back to the Old, led Palmerston naturally to the evangelical, optimistic conclusion, so typical of the Victorian age, that 'the progress of mankind is governed by laws which admit of no retrogression'.[2]

On 15 June, with the House of Commons once again taking the bill in committee, Thesiger proposed that there should be inserted as part of a new oath the words 'and I do make this promise, renunciation, and declaration, heartily, willingly, and truly, on the true faith of a Christian.' Among the speeches opposing such insertion importance attached to two in particular. First there was the contribution of Sir John Pakington, the former Secretary for War and Colonies in the Derby Cabinet of 1852, whose avowed reversal of a former stance of opposition testified to the small but significant increase in the number of Tories prepared to support—or at least to acquiesce in—remission of disabilities. After rehearsing some of the familiar arguments in favour of Emancipation, for example that Unitarians were enabled to sit in Parliament and that individual Jews, having served as magistrates, aldermen and Lord Mayors of London, had undergone the necessary apprenticeship for the performance of legislative tasks, Pakington referred to the state of the law in other of the Christian nations of Europe. His observation that the laws of several European countries, irrespective of whether they were Catholic or Protestant, all permitted Jews to sit in their respective legislatures, did something to belie as obsolete the entirely one-sided picture presented by Archbishop Howley in the 1830s that the Jews of Britain were free of the legal restrictions of exclusion, direction and prohibition borne by many of their European co-religionists.

A no less interesting contribution to the debate was the speech which, almost immediately afterwards, was forthcoming from the former Chief Secretary for Ireland, Edward Horsman; this, though not his first on the subject, was important on the present occasion for affording confirmation of the unity of outlook which prevailed in the ministerialist ranks. Horsman, who had many years earlier acquired a reputation as an outspoken and uncompromising opponent of the Chartist demands for a sweeping extension of the franchise, was nine years later to be foremost among those Adullamite Whigs responsible for inflicting defeat on the second Russell Government over its proposals for a second reform bill, so bringing about that Administration's demise and subsequent replacement by a Tory Government. Contending that the cause of the Jews was the same as that for which the Protestant Dissenters and Roman Catholics had fought in earlier decades, Horsman admonished the opponents of Emancipation to act in accord with their own precepts; delicately playing on Evangelical sensibilities which might be tempted to interpret recent promulgation of the anti-Josephinian Habsburg-Papal Concordat as betokening a victory for 'Papal Aggression' Horsman asserted that a denial at home of the principle of freedom of conscience in matters of religion ill became those who clamoured for protection of Protestants in the Austrian dominions.

Palmerston wound up the debate: he, of course, as former Canningite and precursor of the Adullamites, enjoyed a preeminence among those of liberal persuasion whose commitment to upholding standards of worth and excellence led them to juxtapose the likely consequences of a broad extension of the franchise with the benefits thought to accrue from adherence to the concept of $\alpha\rho\iota\sigma\tau\text{o}\kappa\rho\alpha\tau\iota\alpha$ (rule of the best). Of these benefits Palmerston averred that civil and religious liberty was the true and vital spirit of the constitution, found, as always, behind free institutions; developing an argument made familiar by Peel and Gladstone, that the House of Commons was not a religious assembly but a political assembly, chosen for political purposes, Palmerston emphasised that a man's religious opinions were relevant only if they influenced and swayed his political conduct.

The vote which followed Palmerston's speech was of great importance for revealing that both an overwhelming and an absolute majority of the Commons now favoured Emancipation: in an exceptionally large turnout of Members Thesiger's amendment was rejected by 341 votes to 201 votes, a majority of 140.[3] Particularly significant was the presence in the Emancipation lobby of no less than four members of the Tory front bench. The most senior was Disraeli who, as the former Chancellor of the Exchequer in the 1852 Government and the present Tory leader in the Commons, was emerging as successor to Derby as overall leader of the Tory party. Then there was Sir John Pakington, also possessing the authority of an ex-Cabinet minister. The third of the dissentients was Sir Fitzroy Kelly, formerly Solicitor-General in 1845–46 and again in 1852; his support for Emancipation must have owed something to the experience which he had gained by acting as Leading Counsel for Salomons in the Court of Exchequer trial of five years before. And finally, as the most junior member of the group, there was the son and heir of Lord Derby himself, Lord Stanley, already well-known as a supporter of the abolition of the Church Rate. Whatever encouragement Disraeli may have derived from the backing of this particular group must have been augmented by the knowledge that the further group of Tories who had recorded votes in favour of Emancipation included the only other surviving dissentients of the December 1847 debate, namely Milnes Gaskell and the financier Tom Baring.

The division figures on third reading were equally clear-cut, the Commons reaffirming its earlier decision by 291 votes to 168, a majority of 123.[4] When the bill passed to the Upper House Lord Lyndhurst, now in his eighty-sixth year, made every attempt to persuade his fellow peers to accede to the measure. As veteran Lord Chancellor of every Tory Government from the construction of Canning's in 1827 until the fall of Peel's in 1846, Lyndhurst had shared responsibility both for the relief legislation of 1828 and 1829 and for the measures outlawing the variety of municipal and obsolete disabilities which had until comparatively recently obstructed straightforward consideration of the Jews' parliamentary claims. On the present occasion Lyndhurst recalled the fears advanced at the time of Catholic Emancipation, which events since had proved to have been greatly exaggerated: that Catholics would betray hostility to a Church which had taken Catholic property, that they would proselytize and that they would avow allegiance to a 'foreign Sovereign' who might at any time declare war on England. Lyndhurst believed the anxieties concerning unchristianization to be equally unjustified. Both the Courts of Justice and the municipal corporations were looked upon as Christian despite the admission of Jews to a share in the functions which they exercised. Lyndhurst adverted to the fact that Salomons had recently headed the Christian Corporation of the City of London and noted too that there existed no impediment to the heading of a Christian tribunal by a Jew. Possibly more effective in palliating the anxiety of opponents on this score were the arguments of Campbell Tait, Bishop of London; his stance of support for Emancipation presented an interesting contrast to the opposition of his immediate predecessor, Blomfield. In an argument not unlike that previously advanced by *The Times* Tait contended that the religious character of the House of Lords and of the legislature in general depended not on the existence of oaths but upon the existence of religious feeling throughout the country; as the Christian character of the country, and thus, by extension, of the legislature, was more strongly marked than it had been in the time of disabilities and had indeed been gradually deepening during the recent quarter-century which had seen additional rights granted to the Jews, opponents must be perverse if they continued to maintain that remission of the one remaining political disability would entail a reversal of this Christianizing trend.

The Jews, after so long, were beginning to attract some vital episcopal support and they could derive encouragement too from that concluding portion of Lyndhurst's address which was devoted to an examination and definition of the constitutional role of the House of Lords. Declared Lyndhurst:

> I have sometimes ventured to state my opinion as to the relative duties of the two Houses of Parliament, the one representing the great mass of the constituencies, the other not representing the people, but rather what may be termed the Conservative influences of the constitution. My Lords, I have always considered the duty of this House to be to mature all plans of sound legislation—to serve as a check against the rash, hasty, and unwise proceedings of the other House, and to give time for consideration, and even for the abandonment of improper measures. I have never thought, however, that this House ought to be a perpetual barrier against sound and progressive legislation. No wise or prudent man can approve such a course. It must lead to a conflict with the other House, and in that conflict, unless we are supported by a great majority of the people, we must succumb.

But Lyndhurst's words went for the moment unheeded. The peers refused to 'succumb' and, with the episcopate dividing sixteen to seven against relief, the bill was rejected by 171 votes to 139 votes, a majority against Emancipation of 32.[5]

The continuing deadlock between the two Houses of Parliament was particularly galling to Russell as a Member for the City and in the Commons he taunted the peers on the question of finding a solution to the dilemma posed by Rothschild's repeated election. Whereas a 25 to 30 majority in the Commons might reasonably have been construed by the peers as representing so even a division of public opinion as to justify them in maintaining their resistance, a majority of 140 on the decisive test with respect to the words 'upon the true faith of a Christian' afforded no such justification for thwarting the wishes of the other House. Russell did however counsel caution, advising Members to discuss further the question of oaths and disabilities and to desist meanwhile from contemplating the possibility of seating Jews in the Commons by a unilateral Resolution of that House;[6] this drastic procedure, urged on him by some Members, was as fiercely resisted by others who feared that such a move might imperil the constitution. F. H. Goldsmid, one of the proponents of the Resolution procedure, pointed out in a letter to Russell that twenty-seven years had elapsed since his father had first brought the question to Parliament's attention and the constitutional impasse which had characterized this long campaign made for a most unfavourable comparison with the Roman Catholic relief bills. Wrote Goldsmid: 'The disabilities of the Roman Catholics are believed to be the subject of the most lasting variance of opinion previously known between the two Houses. But the fourth bill passed by the Commons for the removal of these disabilities became law, and the majorities in the lower house in favour of the three former bills had been under thirty.'[7]

The Chief Justice, Lord Campbell, a known supporter of Emancipation, was among the most influential of those urging Russell not to yield to the entreaties of Goldsmid and the 'Resolution' lobby. He hoped that Russell would 'continue to resist the *coup d'état* of introducing the Jews into the House of Commons by Resolution' and would instead wait for 'a constitutional and legal consummation of our wishes'. The proposal which lay behind the Resolution, of defining as breach of privilege any action which might be taken against a Jew for refusal to swear 'upon the true faith of a Christian', was decried by Campbell as 'a bare-faced attempt by one House to make laws against the will of the other and without the consent of the crown'. In a further letter Campbell again emphasised that the Commons could not do by Resolution that which was forbidden by public Act of Parliament; the case of the Quaker Pease served as no valid precedent because the legislature had previously expressed the clear intention that Quakers might be allowed to affirm in all instances where swearing would otherwise be necessary.[8]

When the Commons resumed on 21 July Russell referred to the dilemma in which Members had been placed by the Lords and expressed the opinion that the Commons was now entitled to proceed by unilateral Resolution. Declaring that his concern was not for the revision of oaths but for the enactment of legislation which would enable Jews to take the oaths as presently constituted, Russell introduced a bill to amend 1 & 2 Vict, c. 105, 'An Act to remove Doubts as to the Validity of certain Oaths'. From the Tory front bench Spencer Walpole deprecated a second discussion of the Jewish question during the same parliamentary session. Maintaining that Russell, and not the House of Lords, was guilty of violating the general practice of Parliament, Spencer Walpole averred that although Russell's bill differed in form from that introduced by Palmerston, in spirit, if not according to the letter, Russell had broken one of the unwritten rules of parliamentary proceedings. It was a somewhat reluctant Commons which, by 246 votes to 154, a majority of 92, granted leave to Russell to introduce the first stage of his Oaths Validity Act Amendment Bill.[9]

Meanwhile, as a result of the Lords' rejection of the Parliamentary Oaths Bill on 10 July, Rothschild had resigned his seat in the City of London so that he might be enabled to fight a by-election on the issue—he had, however, delayed his resignation for a few days in the hope that the Government would support the idea of proceeding by unilateral Resolution of the Commons.[10] Rothschild contended that the issue was now one of Government, people and Commons versus a section of the House of Lords, 'the men who went but very seldom among the people, who knew not the wishes of the people, and who, in fact, attended to very little but their own pleasure and amusement'. When nominations were proposed at the Guildhall on 29 July no other candidates came forward; even more remarkably when the Sheriff called for a show of hands every hand in the hall, according to *The Times*'s reporter, was held up in Rothschild's favour. In his speech of thanks Rothschild compared the encouraging majority of 140 in the Commons with the adverse one of 32 in the Lords; as no rival had been forthcoming in the by-election he felt entitled to assume that none of the citizens of London harboured any strong hostility towards his claims.

In the Commons at the beginning of August Russell, erroneously citing the affirmation of Pease as precedent, moved that a committee of the House be set up for the purpose of examining the oaths as prescribed for Members.[11] The Select Committee was duly constituted, took some days to deliberate and then, by a vote of sixteen to thirteen, arrived at the decision that any unilateral Resolution of the Commons which admitted Jews into the House by allowing them to omit the controversial words of the Abjuration Oath would be both unsound in law and unconstitutional, even if such Resolution were based on 5 & 6 Will IV, c. 62, s. 8, which was legislation concerned with the minor technicalities of oath-taking. Beating a tactful retreat Russell thereupon informed the Commons that as the session was so far advanced he would not proceed with his bill but would introduce a new one early in the next session.

The rejection of the proposal for a unilateral Commons Resolution was of great constitutional importance and the three-vote majority by which the Select Committee of the Commons had arrived at its decision was to be explained by the refusal of a number of its members who, though indubitably to be reckoned among that Emancipation lobby whose preponderance within the committee reflected its overwhelming ascendancy of more than five to three in the House as a whole, refused to condone Russell's argument that in this instance the ends justified the means: those of this group who did not merely absent themselves or abstain from the vote but were to be found among the Resolution's sixteen recorded opponents included Gladstone and Sir George Grey, the Home Secretary.[12]

Erskine May, in writing of the increased power of the House of Commons in the half-century prior to the settlement of the Emancipation question, observed that it was characteristic of the British constitution, and a proof of its freedom from the spirit of democracy, that the more dominant the power of the Commons the greater had become its respect for the law and the more carefully had its acts been restrained within the proper limits of its own jurisdiction. It is an interesting comment on the evolution of the constitution and on the changed meaning of the term *democracy* from Erskine May's day to our own that a century ago he should with such strong approval have discerned proof of the British constitution's character and freedom not, as we might suppose, in some opportune decision taken by the temporary majority in the Commons to exercise an exclusive right of judgement on a constitutional issue, but in the very refusal of that temporary majority to exercise so singular a jurisdiction; Erskine May noted that all the while the authority of the Commons had been 'uncertain and ill-defined,—while it [the Commons] was struggling against the crown,—jealous of the House of Lords,—distrustful of the press,—and irresponsible to the people', it had been tempted to exceed its constitutional powers, but since its political position had become established it had been less provoked to strain its jurisdiction; and deference to public opinion and experience of past errors had taught the Commons wisdom and moderation. In 1851, at the time of Salomons's incursion into the Commons, Members had alluded to the case of Wilkes; now, in 1857, there had been very serious consideration of the idea of a Resolution. Erskine May saw a contrast between the treatment of the Jewish question and the earlier handling of the Wilkes case, in which the Commons' privileges had been strained or abandoned at pleasure, and the laws of the land had been outraged, in order to exclude and persecute an obnoxious member. More recently, however, the House of Commons, though entrusted with exclusive jurisdiction over its own members' seats and with every inducement to accept a broad and liberal interpretation, in the case of the Jews had not defaulted in administering the law strictly, and to the letter. The failures to solve the difficulty by legislation had not tempted the Commons to usurp legislative power under the semblance of judicial interpretation.[13]

Early in the parliamentary session of 1857–58 Russell, with the concurrence of Palmerston, prepared a new oaths bill. Dramatically perceiving in the present deadlock a parallel with earlier struggles against the exercise of arbitrary power, Russell advised the Commons not to feel too alarmed at the prospect of a conflict with the Courts of Law; he conjectured that if the Commons had been satisfied with the opinion of past judges the country might still have been paying Ship Money and been at the mercy of the prerogative of the Crown.[14] Russell's bill, read for a first time, came on for the second reading debate in February. The radical Member for Sheffield, J. A. Roebuck, already known to the House as a vehement critic of the oath qualification, on this occasion lived up to his reputation as scourge of all things established by attacking, not as usual the incompetence of the Ministry or the shortcomings of some institution, but the irrationality which he considered lay behind religious profession: very few men actually having a reason for their particular faith, but the great mass of mankind coming as if by heredity to their religious profession because they were born and educated in it. Their individual religious disposition was thus nothing more than the 'sport of chance'. The Tory benches naturally baulked at this extreme manifestation of secular radicalism but the House as a whole, immersed in examination of the technicalities of the bill, approved a second reading.[15]

The House directed its full attention to the case of the Jews only on 22 March, after Russell had defeated by 345 votes to 66 votes, a majority of 279, an amendment which would have enabled Catholics in the Commons to take the same oaths as their fellow Members of Parliament—this amendment, said Russell, with all the conviction of one who had learned from experience the dangers likely to befall comprehensive oaths bills, would only frustrate his attempt to relieve the Jews. Whereupon Members moved to consider the relevant fifth clause of Russell's bill. From the Tory front bench Spencer Walpole rehearsed an argument of the type advanced many years before by both Blomfield and Inglis, to the effect that although nothing could be found in the statute book specifically excluding non-Christians from the state, the reason for this was quite simply that it had never been contemplated that there would ever be such persons and no provision had therefore been made on the subject; in England from time immemorial the test to any position of power had always been taken upon some Christian relic or symbol, if not upon the Christian volume of the Bible. The admission of the Jews to Parliament, whilst affording gratification to a few, would risk the displeasure of the many. Russell, in reply, spurned the contention that in a political assembly particular agreement was required to certain articles of faith; what mattered was precisely that basis of religious principle which could not be obtained by oaths or tests. Reiterating an argument which he had propounded ten years before with reference to Roman Catholic endowments and the Christian title of Unitarian chapels, but unlike Archbishop Whately sensibly refraining from deducing from it the characteristically paradoxical axiom that the nearer persons had been in religion to one another the greater had been the danger, Russell remarked on the variety of subjects which had in recent years witnessed a split among the Christians who sat together in the legislature: the inter-Christian disagreements over Church Rates, Maynooth and Church Establishment had been productive of bones of contention far greater than any which had arisen as a result of the difference between Christians and Jews.

In a division on this fifth clause of Russell's bill the principle of Emancipation was approved by 297 votes to 144, a majority of 153. Instead however of deriving unqualified encouragement from this result some Jews were inclined to attach overmuch importance to the views put forward during the debate by C. N. Newdegate, that intemperate critic not only of aspirations for political Emancipation but also of the Jewish religion, who had been one of the influential Protectionist whips at the time of Lord George Bentinck's deposition. According to Newdegate the campaign for Emancipation was a Talmudic plot which itself constituted part of an Ultramontane Roman Catholic conspiracy, directed from Rome by the Jesuits with the purpose of destroying Britain's religion, free constitution and prosperity. Ascribing all manner of evil intent to the Talmud, Newdegate appeared to suggest on the basis of a sermon delivered by the Chief Rabbi ten years before that Dr. Adler was bound to view with disfavour the claims of Jews to sit in a Christian legislature.[16] The Chief Rabbi, instead of ignoring Newdegate's misrepresentations, paid great attention to them as providing him with an opportunity for clarifying to a correspondent his own position on Emancipation. In a letter of reply to the enquirer, which was given prominence by *The Jewish Chronicle*, the Chief Rabbi wrote: 'Observing in your report of Mr. Newdegate's speech of last night that, among other hostile and false accusations against the Jews, he mentioned my name as having stated in one of my sermons, "that the introduction of Jews into Parliament would subvert the Jewish law", I feel it my bounden duty to deny utterly ever having made such or a similar statement. *I have, on the contrary, always expressed myself in favour of the measure in question.*'[17]

The very same issue of *The Jewish Chronicle* was rather more interesting for perceiving in current political changes a development likely to prove of great significance. During February Palmerston's Government had been defeated in the Commons and had chosen to resign rather than seek a vote of confidence. The suggestion of *The Jewish Chronicle* that had Palmerston's Ministry lasted longer Emancipation would have had no chance for many years to come and that the dissolution of the Ministry had taken place 'just in the right nick of time' to prevent Emancipation falling between the two stools of a Palmerston Reform Bill and a Russell Oaths Bill[18] may, in view of Palmerston's personal aversion to franchise reform, have been somewhat far-fetched, but undoubtedly the fall of the Ministry without a dissolution being precipitated thereby did open up an unexpectedly promising opportunity for the advocates of Emancipation. The licensed freedom of manoeuvre which any parliamentary opposition enjoys had now for the Tories to yield to the constraints of governmental responsibility: the Derby Administration, until such time as it felt confident of its electoral prospects, would have to govern with the assent of the large Whiggish-liberal majority in the Commons which had recently been tempted to act unilaterally by Resolution. And if the Government could scarcely allow Emancipation, of all issues, to become a subject of contention between itself and the Commons, even less could it afford to expose that division on the question which prevailed within the ministerial ranks. For nothing might jeopardize the

Tories' electoral prospects more than a reminder to the voters that on a crucial matter of policy the Chancellor of the Exchequer and leader of the party in the Commons, Disraeli, and three other senior members of the Government, two of them fellow Cabinet ministers, remained irreconcilably opposed to the party leadership. Compromise might prove not only unavoidable for the Tory leadership but also desirable.

Russell, seeing his bill sent up to the Lords by such a large majority, requested Macaulay, who had recently been made a peer, to employ his oratorical gifts once again on the Jews' behalf: Macaulay, feeling he had nothing new to say, replied that he would give a silent vote.[19] Whether he could have influenced the outcome of the Lords' vote remains doubtful: on 27 April, with the proposed oaths bill in committee, the fifth clause relating to the Jews' admission to Parliament was negatived by 119 votes to 80, a majority of 39.[20] The result of the division seemed to make even more intractable the problem of how to resolve the difference of opinion between the two Houses; Derby, however, far from exulting in a result which he knew might cause the Commons finally to lose patience and so proceed unilaterally, now moved towards adoption of a compromise, though he did not approve of Disraeli giving a hint to Russell as to what form such a compromise might take.[21]

The forebodings of Derby were to prove justified beyond expectation. When, on 10 May, the oaths bill came down from the Lords with the clause relating to the Jews struck out, a motion proposed by Russell that the Commons disagree with this amendment was accepted by 263 votes to 150, a majority of 113; the House then gave favourable consideration to a motion that Rothschild be appointed a member of the Commons committee entrusted with the responsibility for drawing up the 'Reasons' for the Commons' disagreement with the Lords' amendments to the oaths bill. The argument underpinning this astute move, that an unsworn Member was entitled to exercise all the privileges which attached to membership of the Commons except those of voting or sitting in the House, was able to draw upon a respectable precedent of 1715 and given the large majority for Emancipation which existed in the Commons it was not surprising that the motion should have been approved. The voting was 251 in favour of Rothschild's co-option and 196 against, a majority of 55. A number of supporters of Emancipation, including Gladstone, Sir James Graham and Tom Baring, were to be found on this occasion voting with the minority; the fact that the proposer of the motion should have been none other than Tom Duncombe, the radical Member for Finsbury, would for some have provided sufficient deterrent against adoption of such a drastic tactic. Members had reason to question whether the man whose attitude towards the exercise of power by the Rothschilds was now as favourable as once it had been unfavourable was not indeed acting out of populist rather than liberal motives: advancement of the claims of the elected chamber providing the key as to why denigration of foreign-born Government financiers should now have been superseded by denigration of hereditary peers.[22]

In the space of only two days the Commons' committee was able to produce its 'Reasons' for disagreement with the Lords. These were several: that the relevant oath as originally framed had been directed not against the Jews but against the Catholics; that freedom of conscience must be allowed; that no charge of disloyalty could be imputed to the Jews; that Jews were not unfit either for admission to office or for the exercise of legislative power; that disabilities imposed on account of faith amounted to persecution and that these could not be justified in view of the concession of religious liberty to more powerful non-Anglican communities. The Report also referred to the number of bills passed by the Commons to remove disabilities, the increasing majorities in favour of those bills, which the Commons' committee saw as a reflection of public opinion, the support forthcoming from members of all parties for the remission of the disabilities, and the frustration of the electors' rights caused by the inability to admit to the House those (i.e., Rothschild and Salomons) who had been lawfully returned to the Commons as Members. The Report made the final point that the disabilities imposed were really anomalies. Russell, having put these 'Reasons' before the House, then won approval for an important proposal that they be conferred to the House of Lords.[23]

The Lords' endorsement of this motion for the communication of the proposals or 'conference' of Commons with Lords marked a change in the relationship between the two Houses.[24] The question now was who in the Lords would reciprocate the action of the Commons by seizing the initiative for a compromise. When, on 31 May, the peers came to consider the Report of the Conference on the Oaths Bill it was the Earl of Lucan, one of the generals of the Crimean War and a Tory in politics, who appeared to emerge as bridge-builder between the two Houses. He had been one of the 119 opponents of Russell's proposed measure in the division of 27 April. Lucan emphasised that he was not acting in concert with any party in the Lords and that he had even abstained from informing the Prime Minister of his intention. He argued that it should be lawful for either House of Parliament to modify the oath which it required its members to take; though aware that objections would be raised to the admission of Jews to one of the two Houses if the particular House in question were unilaterally to pass a Resolution, he could see no reason why such unilateral Resolution should not be allowed if such proceeding were first legalized by Act of Parliament. Lucan declared that his object was to restore harmony between the two Houses of Parliament, even if 'the provocative conduct' of the Commons in appointing a member of the Jewish persuasion to serve on the committee responsible for drawing up the 'Reasons' for disagreement with the Lords' amendments had constituted an action which 'amounted to something very like an insult' to the Upper House. Lucan's initiative was greeted with relief by many among the peers, and not least by the Tory leadership: before withdrawing his amendment, so that the Lords might have time to consider the matter further, Lucan was asked by Derby to elucidate the purpose and aim of his proposals.[25]

When, however, the Lords next discussed the question, on 7 June 1858, the peers found themselves not with one bill but with two. The first bill was Lucan's, 'to provide for the Relief of Her Majesty's Subjects professing the Jewish Religion'. The other emanated from Lyndhurst who, reverting to a familiar tactic, presented a bill 'to substitute one Oath for the Oaths of Allegiance, Supremacy, and Abjuration, and for relieving the Religious Scruples of certain of Her Majesty's Subjects'.[26] Given the known parliamentary dislike of comprehensive oaths measures Lyndhurst can scarcely have expected that his own bill would be preferred to Lucan's one, and there were anyway other compelling reasons why the Government should have felt unable to adopt his approach. On 13 June Derby told Lyndhurst that independently of objections common to both his bill and Lucan's,

> Yours is farther objected to on the ground that it introduces a second Bill on the same subject during the same parliament, the first having all but gone through both Houses. I also hear that in some quarters there would be less objection to the admission of Jews into the House of Commons by Resolution, if the proposition came from the House of Commons itself— which it might do if our Bill were sent back, insisting on our Amendments, with our Reasons, and the Commons were then to return the Bill with this provision inserted as an Amendment on our Amendment.[27]

Derby sought a solution of the type offered by Lucan because this would not preclude insertion of a caveat: the compromise which the peers were prepared to come to would emphatically not be one admitting of some supposed error on their part in respect of the principle of Emancipation but one conceding nothing more than that it was necessary to break a constitutional deadlock; indeed, to such a 'compromise' there would be appended 'Reasons' for disagreement with the principle of Emancipation. The peers were in fact already working on this assumption and on 22 June a House of Lords Committee presented its six 'Reasons' for disagreeing with the nine 'Reasons' of the Commons.[28]

On 1 July there ensued a full debate in the Lords.[29] This was opened by the Prime Minister who, at the same time as reaffirming his personal opposition to the admission of Jews to a Christian legislature, conceded the need for a compromise. Reverting to the technicality of the choice of bills before the Lords, Derby expressed a clear preference for Lucan's, which he saw as the enabling measure offering the only solution to a difficulty which had existed for a decade: no alternative solution presented itself of bringing into agreement the two Houses of Parliament. This was the overriding consideration in Derby's mind: he declared that Lucan's measure 'maintains the dignity of your Lordships' House with regard to that portion of the question which is more immediately subject to your jurisdiction'. The bill

> maintains the law as it stands at the present moment, but it enables the House of Commons, upon a question that specially relates to persons taking their seats in that House, to dispense with the words which stand in the way of what appears to be the decided wish of that House. . . . I think there is less difficulty and less practical inconvenience and danger arising from giving a limited consent to the views of the House of Commons [as embodied in Lucan's Bill], than in persisting in an opposition which all practical experience proves cannot be pushed beyond a certain limit between the two Houses. . . . I take the course which I have adopted from no other feeling than a desire to see an amicable settlement between the two Houses with regard to a question of grave interest, and with respect to which I see no other solution.

Lucan himself urged compromise on his fellow Tories and outlined the aims of his measure. Jews would be admissible into the Commons by a Resolution of that House. Before such a Resolution could be passed however it would first be necessary for an elected Jew to present himself at the table of the House for the ceremony of swearing-in; only then, if he maintained objection to a subscribing of the Abjuration Oath 'upon the true faith of a Christian', would the House be empowered to direct the omission of those words from the oath. Lucan sought to allay fears that the Resolution procedure might involve infringement of the constitution: although a precedent was being set the Commons would not thereby be encouraged to act independently in the future.

Lucan then offered a most compelling justification for his compromise, declaiming on the theme of public apathy. He observed that while for the past six weeks the country had been well aware that the issue of the Jews might be settled through a compromise, during that period the electors had scarcely raised the question. His belief was that over those past six weeks less than half a dozen petitions on the subject had been presented to the Commons and this presented a very strong contrast to the bill at present before the Lords for the abolition of Church Rates, which had excited 213 petitions in favour of its passage in the space of one day alone. The silence on the Jewish question led him to conclude that the people were perfectly indifferent about it.

These were more than clever debating points. Two of the political figures who had always evinced the keenest interest in the outcome of the Jewish question had not allowed their own involvement to deceive them as to the level of interest to be found among others. Gladstone had in March 1841 been forced to admit that 'the question at present is scarcely before the public mind';[30] Ashley, who in November 1850 observed how the Papal decision to restore a regular Catholic diocesan hierarchy in England was the cause of a 'surprising ferment . . . a storm over the whole ocean',[31] was to remark by contrast in April 1853 that as far as Jewish Emancipation was concerned

> the popular voice, to take it in the full extent of the term, is neither upon one side or the other. There is, upon the whole, a general apathy upon the question. Where any feeling is entertained in its regard, that feeling is deep and serious; but that feeling has not, however, pervaded the whole mass of the community. And I cannot do better to prove that position than by giving the last statement of the returns made by the House of Commons of the petitions for and against this measure. . . . It appears from these returns that the number of petitions for the removal of Jewish disabilities was 39, and the number of signatures 1,734; while against the removal there were four petitions, and 329 signatures. Again, for the alteration of Parliamentary oaths the petitions were only one, the signatures being 198; while against the alteration the petitions were 846, and the signatures 42,289—clearly showing that, so far as the national expression is concerned, there has been no national expression of opinion on one side or the other.[32]

This apathy had persisted. Although ever since the session of 1847–48, when the Commons had first approved the principle of Emancipation by substantial majorities in a comparatively full House, the number of petitions to the Lords against Emancipation had exceeded those in favour—a reversal of a previous ratio perhaps symptomatic of a change in prospects concerning the final outcome—the petitions considered as a total were so few as to deprive them of any significance.[33] The 'Jew Bill' of a hundred years before had attracted far greater attention. Salomons had, of course, interpreted public indifference as conducive to, indeed almost indistinguishable from, the languid tolerance which even the law connived at; *The Saturday Review*, which favoured Emancipation, presented perhaps a more nearly accurate assessment when it declared in May 1858 that 'public opinion acquiesces in the justice of the Jewish claims, but it can hardly be said to be enthusiastic in their favour'.[34] Shaftesbury offered confirmation both of his earlier impressions and of Lucan's similar reasoning, when he recorded in his diary for 1 July:

> This evening Jew Bill in Lords. Had signified my intention, to many, of offering no further resistance. It is in vain, and altogether useless, nor is it wanting in a tinge of peril, to deny, pertinaciously and hopelessly (for the country is, and ever has been, quite indifferent) the yearly demands of the Commons—I yield to force, not to reason. I think my responsibility satisfied on this side; and, by prolonged refusal, I should begin responsibility on the other.—See how the question stands. Commons, for many years, have sent up Bills with vastly-increasing majorities. Country quite apathetic, though numerous elections have occurred during that time. The Commons have decided that a Jew can sit on their committees, manage a conference with the Lords, take part in debate, and use every influence, but from the vote he is excluded. This, added to the actual state of the

question, leaves the House of Lords scarcely anything, and certainly nothing of value, to refuse. More opposition is therefore futile.[35]

And so, their decision determined by criteria similar to those advanced by Lyndhurst in the debate of almost exactly a year before, some of the most influential of the peers were now prepared to abandon their opposition to Emancipation. No 'great majority of the people' was to be found calling for continued resistance; on asking whether the conflict between the two Houses was to drag on indefinitely Lucan averred that after twenty-five years it could not: the need now was for compromise.

Whereupon Lucan's bill was given a second reading by 143 votes to 97 votes, a majority of 46. The Archbishop of Canterbury and ten bishops voted against the measure, while seven bishops voted in its favour; although a reversal of these figures would indeed have been remarkable those advocating the Lucan compromise had seemed almost to confirm the good sense of Lord Holland's earlier dictum that 'one bishop is worth five laymen' by not failing to point out during the debates on the legislation that the episcopate had long since lost all semblance of uniformity on the question. Of the most senior Tory Cabinet ministers, Lords Derby, Salisbury, Hardwicke and Malmesbury all voted for the compromise; Lord Chelmsford, however, the former Sir Frederic Thesiger, who was now Lord Chancellor, voted against it. As for Lord Shaftesbury, he, not surprisingly, had concluded that absence from either voting lobby would constitute the better part of valour.

When the Lords again discussed the question on 5 July Derby commended Lucan's proposals. Any Resolution to seat Jewish Members of Parliament would be good and valid only for the duration of the particular parliament which had passed the Resolution and therefore if public opinion subsequently turned hostile to Emancipation the Commons would be able to rescind it.[36] The majority in the Lords was anxious to demonstrate how qualified was the present assent: when the peers a week later debated the third reading they also revised their 'Reasons' for disagreement with the principle of Emancipation. The fourth 'Reason', which had severely stigmatized as a 'mockery' any Jewish participation in a legislature where prayers were offered for Christ's guidance, was now toned down. But Derby insisted on proposing the following amendment:

> Without imputing any Disloyalty or Disaffection to Her Majesty's Subjects of the Jewish Persuasion, the Lords consider that the Denial and Rejection of that Saviour in whose Name each House of Parliament daily offers up its collective Prayers for the Divine Blessing on its Counsels, constitutes a moral Unfitness to take Part in the Legislation of a professedly Christian community.

Lord Granville, leader of the Liberals in the Lords, condemned this 'Reason', arguing that it would offend the Commons, insult the Jews, and indelibly brand Jews as different from other Members. Derby retorted that the House of Lords was still opposed to the principle of Emancipation and that remission of disabilities had only been agreed to as a conciliatory measure. Indeed, continued Derby, had the Lords wished to change its mind on the principle of Emancipation it would earlier have accepted one of the bills sent up by the Commons. The Foreign Secretary, Lord Malmesbury, whose stand on the question was identical to that assumed by Lord Derby, likewise expressed himself 'anxious that no mistake whatever, now or hereafter, should attach to the Government with respect to their opinions and views on this question, and that it should be known that if a concession had been made, it had been made to a political necessity and not from moral conviction'. It was necessary to reply to the 'Reasons' of the Commons, said Malmesbury, and the 'Reasons' of the Lords must be those of the majority of the peers who were in principle opposed to the admission of the Jews to Parliament. Hardwicke, the Lord Privy Seal, was another Cabinet minister who rejected the charge that simultaneous adoption of Lucan's compromise and of Derby's 'Reasons' implied inconsistency.

In two divisions the Lords first accepted Derby's 'Reasons' by 50 votes to 42 votes, a majority of eight, and then granted a third reading to Lucan's bill by 33 votes to 12, a majority of 21.[37] On the following day, 13 July, 'An Act for the Relief of Her Majesty's Subjects professing the Jewish Religion' was brought from the Lords and ordered by the Commons to be printed. The important first clause of the bill stated that either House of Parliament might be enabled to modify the form of the Oaths to be taken by a Jew, and thus to procure for the said individual a seat and vote in such House; this arrangement would, however, endure only for the lifetime of the Resolution. The Lords' 'Reasons', including the amended fourth one, were appended to the bill so that they too might receive the consideration of the Commons.[38]

In the Commons on 16 July Russell moved the second reading of Lucan's bill. Palmerston articulated a feeling widespread in the House when he said that the Lords had not resolved 'fairly and handsomely' to settle the question; though finding it indeed incredible that a bill 'so objectionable in principle, upon constitutional grounds, would be allowed to remain permanently on the statute book' Palmerston stated that he would support the legislation in the hope that it might lead to a more complete measure. The Commons then passed to a division and the bill received a second reading by the margin of 156 votes to 65, a majority of 91.[39]

On 21 July the House of Lords was informed that Lucan's bill had been returned from the Lower House 'agreed to' and that the Commons had also returned the Oaths Bill with a message that 'they do *not insist* upon this disagreement to the Amendment made by the Lords upon which the Lords insist'[40]—the Amendment here referred to by the Commons was that which had embraced Lord Derby's 'Reasons' and then been passed through the Lords by a majority of eight. The Commons, approving the third reading of

Lucan's measure by 129 votes to 55, a majority of 74, agreed, in a spirit of conciliation, that it was not necessary to question the Lords' 'Reasons' for insisting on the exclusion of the Jews from Parliament, because the peers, by supporting the Lucan bill, had at last *provided means* for resolving the controversy.[41]

On Friday 23 July 'An Act to substitute One Oath for the Oaths of Allegiance, Supremacy and Abjuration; and for the Relief of Her Majesty's Subjects professing the Jewish Religion' (21 & 22 Vict, c. 48), and 'An Act to provide for the Relief of Her Majesty's Subjects professing the Jewish Religion' (21 & 22 Vict, c. 49) received the Royal Assent in the House of Lords.[42] The draftsmen had evidently considered that Lucan's proposals could best be enacted in two separate pieces of legislation. 21 & 22 Vict, c. 48, now simply and conveniently, but with no alterations of substance, compounded as one oath the three former Oaths of Allegiance, Supremacy and Abjuration; it extended the benefits of Lyndhurst's 1845 measure in respect of municipal offices (8 & 9 Vict, c. 52) to all other offices and employments entry to which had hitherto normally required subscription to the declaration imposed by the act 9 Geo IV, c. 17. Act 21 & 22 Vict, c. 49 enabled Jews, if so permitted by the body to which they sought admission, specifically to omit the words 'upon the true faith of a Christian' when subscribing the new oath. Henceforth all Crown offices, with a few exceptions, were open to Jews; the only important disability remaining, relating to the appointment of a Jewish Lord Chancellor, was removed by the Promissory Oaths Act of 1871.

Three days later, on Monday 26 July, Rothschild appeared in the Commons to take his seat. The motion that any Jew in taking the Oath might omit the words 'and I make this declaration upon the true faith of a Christian' was approved by 69 votes to 37, a majority of 32. Using the Old Testament Rothschild was then sworn in as a Member. Two Members in particular were overcome with emotion. Lord John Russell, acting as one of the sponsors for his City colleague, exclaimed: 'I rejoice at the success which has attended our efforts this question, and believe that the principle of religious liberty has made great progress.' Disraeli, who as Leader of the House had been responsible for finding the time and negotiating the passage of Lucan's measure through the Commons, shook hands with Rothschild as the new Member was about to take his seat on the opposition benches.[43]

Sir Frederick Pollock, with his unrivalled knowledge of the history of the law, was to adjudge the Emancipation legislation, 21 & 22 Vict, c. 48 and c. 49, as having been a 'peculiarly English compromise'.[44] At no time during the settlement of the dispute between Lords and Commons had either House been prepared to admit openly that it was having to make concessions; Parliament, by invoking usage of the expedient Resolution procedure, had conferred autonomy on each of its own two chambers to decide whether or not to admit Jews. The legislation inevitably bore a temporary appearance and it was theoretically conceivable, though very unlikely, not least in view of the composition of the party leadership, that in the event of the Tories winning an overall majority at the next general election they might refuse to renew the necessary Commons Resolution at the start of a new session.

On 3 March 1859, Duncombe, the Finsbury Member, attempted to convert the Resolution into a Standing Order, but Disraeli, as Leader of the House, arguing that the *status quo* should not be rashly disturbed, persuaded the Commons to set up a Select Committee to examine and report on the act 21 & 22 Vict, c. 49.[45] The decision to set up a Select Committee was necessary. Many Members of Parliament, including some ministers, were confused as to the correct usage of Resolutions and Standing Orders. At a number of meetings held at roughly twice-weekly intervals during March and the first half of April, Erskine May, the officer of the Commons most conversant with parliamentary rules, procedure and practice, was summoned to appear before the Select Committee. The authoritative standing of Erskine May explained the unusual circumstance by which he was the sole witness called to give evidence at some of the meetings; Spencer Walpole, the Home Secretary, did however also possess a sound knowledge of constitutional matters and as chairman of the committee he was well able to guide the other members in interpreting the technicalities. The members particularly wished to know if Resolutions could have a binding effect not merely in future sessions but in future parliaments. Erskine May answered that Resolutions must necessarily lapse and expire at the end of the particular session during which they had been agreed; only Standing Orders could be of permanent operation. They remained in force until rescinded and thus if a Standing Order were approved as replacement for the Resolution of 1858 no new Resolution would have to be passed at the beginning of every session, as happened at present. Erskine May was able to reassure the committee that should the Commons ever desire that such Standing Order be rescinded the House would encounter no impediment, though obviously this repeal could not be undertaken at the beginning of a new parliament until the great mass of Members had been sworn in by the Speaker. In that event, however, Christian Members would obviously be unable to rescind the Standing Order if Jewish Members had cleverly anticipated their move by having themselves rapidly sworn in. Erskine May was asked at what stage of the swearing-in a new House could be considered quorate and the committee deduced from his answers as to the number of Members sworn in on each day that the Commons could be considered quorate on the fourth day. On 11 April the committee members agreed therefore to a Report which recommended a Standing Order with a proviso inserted that Jews could not be sworn in before the fourth day.[46] On 14 April the Report of the Select Committee was presented to the Commons. Ironically the very acceptance of Spencer Walpole's suggestion that Parliament should abide by the *status quo* now involved the Commons in passing, for the purpose of preserving the Resolution procedure of 1858, yet another Resolution, which was itself made into a Standing Order.[47]

The general election of the late spring, which saw the return of the Whig-liberal majority and the subsequent replacement of Derby's Government by one led by Palmerston, betokened further change. On 20 March 1860 Duncombe reintroduced his proposals of the 1859 session to amend 21 & 22 Vict, c. 49.[48] His bill could be construed as emphasising that Emancipation involved recognition of the positive assertion of individual rights under the law: that any elected Jew was entitled to present himself before the Commons and then to subscribe the declaration in accordance with the legislative requirements.[49] From the Tory front bench the point was made that in the event of Duncombe's bill becoming law it would be possible for a Jewish Member of Parliament to subscribe the oaths in the usual manner, whereas if the Crown conferred a peerage on a Jew he would be enabled to take his seat in the Lords only after passage of a special Resolution. As however the Commons did not accept that Duncombe's bill would be 'placing this House in an inferior position' a second reading was granted by 117 votes to 75, a majority of 42.[50]

On 12 July this Jews' Act Amendment Bill was brought on for discussion in the Lords by Lyndhurst, who pointed out that only with the assent of the House of Lords could a Resolution of the House of Commons be converted into a Standing Order; the arrangement by which each House was allowed to exercise discretion as to whether to admit Jews among its number was cumbersome, as the summoning of every separate parliament incurred the necessity of passing a Resolution whenever Jewish Members presented themselves to take their seats. Indeed, despite Erskine May's earlier clarification, there still existed some confusion as to whether a single Resolution remained valid for the duration of a whole parliament or required renewal at the beginning of each succeeding session of that parliament. Lord Eversley, the former Charles Shaw-Lefèvre, Speaker of the House of Commons from 1839 to 1857, confirmed that whereas a Resolution of the House would not be valid beyond the session during which it was passed, a Standing Order would remain valid in each succeeding session until such time as it was repealed. Lord Chelmsford then agreed that there could be no objection in principle to the Jews' Act Amendment Bill.[51]

The wording of Duncombe's bill was, however, too radical for the majority of peers. Though prepared to modify any requirements which might seem to suggest that an elected Jewish representative of a constituency was compelled to plead almost *in forma pauperis* for leave to take the oaths, they wished to retain that wording of the compromise which implied that the rights of the electors were to some extent circumscribed, with Parliament jealously preserving its own right to rescind the legislation. The Lords revised the measure and when the amended bill was published it was found to have the opposite verbal effect to Duncombe's bill. For the bill now emphasised that Emancipation flowed from Parliament's constitutional prerogative, being a concession strictly defined by the legal provisions enacted in 1858 and 1859. An elected Jew was not entitled to claim rights—the word 'entitled' was indeed now deleted—but must passively submit to the prevailing will of Parliament 'pursuant' to the legislative concessions of 1858, 1859 and, now, 1860 for as long as Parliament should allow these to continue.[52] The amended bill was sent back to the Commons which, though dissatisfied that the spirit of Duncombe's original measure had not been honoured, decided to accept in its present form and without further alteration a bill which achieved Duncombe's desired purpose; on 6 August the Royal Assent was duly conferred upon the Jews' Act Amendment Bill (23 & 24 Vict, c. 63).[53] In the Commons on 15 August Duncombe first moved that the Resolution which allowed elected Jews to omit the words 'upon the true faith of a Christian' be made into a Standing Order of the House; upon this motion being agreed to he then proposed that the Standing Order of 14 April 1859, which contained 'the fourth day' proviso, be repealed and this motion too was accepted.[54]

This further, characteristically British, modification of existing law imparted not merely a permanence to the Emancipation legislation which it had hitherto lacked; by reconciling the substantive will of the House of Commons with the definitive interpretation of the House of Lords the settlement of 1860 consummated the constitutionality of that legislation. Parliament in future could afford to concern itself exclusively with impartial law revision. The Parliamentary Oaths Acts of 1866 (29 & 30 Vict, c. 19) repealed the former legislation relating to the parliamentary oaths and in their stead prescribed for all Members, with the exception of those such as Quakers who were as before allowed to affirm, a new and shortened form of oath which concluded with the words 'so help me God'. The words 'upon the true faith of a Christian' were thus swept away forever. The memory of past struggles could not, however, so quickly die: Lionel Rothschild continued to sit as one of the Liberal Members for the City, with but one break of a few months, until the general election of 1874; Salomons sat as a Liberal Member for Greenwich from February 1859 until his death in July 1873, heading the poll in that constituency in the 1859, 1865 and 1868 general elections; F. H. Goldsmid, whose father died in April 1859 in the happy knowledge that Emancipation had been achieved, sat as a Liberal Member for Reading from January 1860 until his own death in 1878. When in 1869 Gladstone, by then Prime Minister and, interestingly, Salomons's fellow Member for Greenwich, compiled a private *List of Dissenting Members of the House of Commons,* a significant choice of appellation, he placed six Jews, including Salomons, F. H. Goldsmid, Lionel Rothschild and two other Rothschilds, in the middle of a ninety-five Member list which began with fifty-three Protestant Dissenters, including nine Unitarians, and concluded with thirty-six Roman Catholics.[55]

NOTES

1. The following account of the 1857 general election campaign in the City of London is based on *The Times* (all issues for 1857), 20 March, p. 7; 26 March, p. 7; 27 March, p. 5; 30 March, p. 6; 31 March, p. 7.
2. *Hansard*, Third Series, 145, 15 May 1857, 318–338. Palmerston, col. 324. Cf. Whately, Archbishop of Dublin, *Hansard*, Third Series, 20, 1 August 1833, 228–29.
3. *Hansard*, Third Series, 145, 15 June 1857, 1759–1868. Pakington, cols. 1817–23, and cf. Howley, Archbishop of Canterbury, *Hansard*, Third Series, 24, 23 June 1834, 724–28. Horsman, cols. 1828–33 and cf. *Hansard*, Third Series, 96, 11 February 1848, 486–93, for Horsman's earlier speech. Palmerston, cols. 1854–57.
4. *Hansard*, Third Series, 146, 25 June 1857, 347–69.
5. *Hansard*, Third Series, 146, 10 July 1857, 1209–78. Lyndhurst, cols. 1236–48; Campbell Tait, Bishop of London, cols. 1257–59.
6. *Hansard*, Third Series, 146, 17 July 1857, 1699–1704.
7. Russell Papers, P.R.O. 30/22, 13d, 21–22, 20 July 1857, letter from F. H. Goldsmid to Russell.
8. Russell Papers, P.R.O. 30/22, 13d, 23–27, 20 July 1857, 39–42, 27 July 1857, letters from Lord Campbell to Russell.
9. *Hansard*, Third Series, 147, 21 July 1857, 134–95.
10. The following account of the 1857 by-election in the City of London is based on *The Times* (both issues for 1857), 24 July, p. 11; 29 July, p. 11.
11. *Hansard*, Third Series, 147, 3 August 1857, 933–60; *Hansard*, Third Series, 147, 4 August 1857, 1010–20.
12. *Parliamentary Papers, Reports from Committees*, 1857, session 2 [253], vol. IX, 477–84, 10 August 1857; *Journals of the House of Commons*, 112, 10 August 1857, 390; *Hansard*, Third Series, 147, 10 August 1857, 1287–88.
13. T. Erskine May, *The Constitutional History of England since the Accession of George the Third, 1760–1860*, II, pp. 83–85.
14. Russell Papers, P.R.O. 30/22, 13d, 264–65, 26 November 1857; *Hansard*, Third Series, 148, 10 December 1857, 469–99. Russell, col. 495.
15. *Hansard*, Third Series, 148, 10 February 1858, 1084–1118. Roebuck, cols. 1095–1101. For Roebuck's other contributions to parliamentary debates on Emancipation, cf. *Hansard*, Third Series, 105, 11 June 1849, 1416–24; *Hansard*, Third Series, 116, 1 May 1851, 382–87; *Hansard*, Third Series, 142, 23 May 1856, 601, 602, 603; *Hansard*, Third Series, 149, 22 March 1858, 533–36.
16. *Hansard*, Third Series, 149, 22 March 1858, 465–550. Russell, cols. 468–70, 541–46; cf. Russell, *Hansard*, Third Series, 98, 4 May 1848, 664–66, and Whately, Archbishop of Dublin, *Hansard*, Third Series, 1 August 1833, 229–35. Spencer Walpole, cols. 519–28; cf. Blomfield, Bishop of London, *Hansard*, Third Series, 20, 1 August 1833, 237; Inglis, *Hansard*, New Series, 23, 5 April 1830, 1304, and Inglis, *Hansard*, Third Series, 95, 16 December 1847, 1258–61. Newdegate, cols. 490–506.
17. *The Jewish Chronicle*, 26 March 1858, p. 117, 'Dr. Adler and Mr. Newdegate'.
18. *The Jewish Chronicle*, 26 March 1858, p. 116, leading article.
19. Russell Papers, P.R.O. 30/22, 13f, 23, 6 April 1858, letter from Lord Macaulay to Russell.
20. *Hansard*, Third Series, 149, 27 April 1858, 1749–97.
21. Russell Papers, P.R.O. 30/22, 13f, 70, 6 May 1858, letter from B. Disraeli to Russell; Papers of the fourteenth Earl of Derby, Letter Books of the fourteenth Earl of Derby [referred to hereinafter simply as the Derby Letter Books], Box no. 184/1, 31 December 1857–17 December 1858, pp. 145–46, letter from Derby to B. Disraeli, 9 May 1858, marked 'Confidential'.
22. *Hansard*, Third Series, 150, 10 May 1858, 336–54, including contributions by Duncombe; see also, p. 215 in the preceding chapter, *Traits Similar and Dissimilar*, where Duncombe's opinions are considered in a different context. *Hansard*, Third Series, 150, 11 May 1858, 430–43.
23. *Hansard*, Third Series, 150, 13 May 1858, 529–30.

24. *Hansard,* Third Series, 150, 17 May 1858, 763–64; *Hansard,* Third Series, 150, 18 May 1858, 858, 859.

25. Derby Letter Books, Box no. 184/2, 25 February 1858–6 August 1858, p. 127, letter from Derby to Lucan (bearing no date, but from its placement in this letter book most probably written not earlier than 24 May 1858 and not later than 28 May 1858).

26. *Hansard,* Third Series, 150, 7 June 1858, 1600–1601.

27. Derby Letter Books, Box no. 184/1, 31 December 1857–17th December 1858, pp. 192–94, letter from Derby to Lyndhurst, 13 June 1858, marked 'Confidential'.

28. *Hansard,* Third Series, 151, 22 June 1858, 154–56.

29. *Hansard,* Third Series, 151, 1 July 1858, 693–730, for all the following references to this debate and the ensuing division.

30. Gladstone Papers, DLXV, B.M.ADD.MSS. 44650, ff. 74–75. Notes, in preparation for speech, on the Jews' Municipal Bill, dated 31 March 1841. Two drafts. Gladstone, it will be remembered, saw at this time an intimate connection between the outlawing of municipal disabilities and the eventuality of parliamentary Emancipation.

31. Ashley, in E. Hodder, *The Life and Work of the Seventh Earl of Shaftesbury,* p. 431, diary for 25 November 1850.

32. Shaftesbury, *Hansard,* Third Series, 126, 29 April 1853, 760.

33. *Journals of the House of Lords.*

34. *The Saturday Review,* no. 132, vol. 5, 8 May 1858, p. 467, article entitled 'Jewish Disabilities'.

35. Shaftesbury, in E. Hodder, *The Life and Work of the Seventh Earl of Shaftesbury,* p. 553, diary for 1 July 1858.

36. *Hansard,* Third Series, 151, 5 July 1858, 916–30.

37. *Hansard,* Third Series, 151, 12 July 1858, 1243–66.

38. *Parliamentary Papers, Public Bills,* Session 3 December 1857–2 August 1858, II, pp. 591–94, bill no. 210.

39. *Hansard,* Third Series, 151, 16 July 1858, 1633–36.

40. *Hansard,* Third Series, 151, 21 July 1858, 1866.

41. *Hansard,* Third Series, 151, 21 July 1858, 1879–1906.

42. *Hansard,* Third Series, 151, 23 July 1858, 1967.

43. *Hansard,* Third Series, 151, 26 July 1858, 2105–15; *The Times,* 27 July 1858, p. 7; W. F. Monypenny and G. E. Buckle, *The Life of Benjamin Disraeli,* I, pp. 1568–69, letter from Disraeli to Mrs. Brydges Williams, 26 July 1858.

44. F. Pollock, *Essays in Jurisprudence and Ethics,* pp. 194–95.

45. *Hansard,* Third Series, 152, 3 March 1859, 1175–89.

46. *Parliamentary Papers, Reports from Committees,* Session 3 February–19 April 1859 [205], vol. I, bk. III, pp. 35–66. Report from the Select Committee on the Jews Act, together with the Proceedings of the Committee and Minutes of Evidence, ordered by the House of Commons to be printed, 11 April 1859.

47. *Hansard,* Third Series, 153, 14 April 1859, 1766–71.

48. *Hansard,* Third Series, 157, 20 March 1860, 960–63.

49. *Parliamentary Papers, Public Bills,* Session 24 January–28 August 1860, III, pp. 779–82, bill no. 80.

50. *Hansard,* Third Series, 157, 18 April 1860, 1916–19.

51. *Hansard,* Third Series, 159, 12 July 1860, 1745–50.

52. *Parliamentary Papers, Public Bills,* Session 24 January–28 August 1860, III, pp. 783–86, bill no. 280.

53. *Hansard,* Third Series, 160, 6 August 1860, 687.

54. *Hansard,* Third Series, 160, 15 August 1860, 1346–47.

55. Gladstone Papers, B.M.ADD.MSS. 44612, ff. 138–39, private note, December 1869.

Conclusion

The Emancipation of the Jews in Britain is a story which belongs essentially to that phase in the evolution of modern Western societies which may be characterised as representing a struggle as between doctrinal and undenominational concepts in national life. Building upon claims to be considered as the third branch of non-Anglican religious dissent and gradually detaching itself from the sterility of ideological debate as to the merits or demerits of Emancipation, Anglo-Jewry learned how to apply libertarian concepts in the conduct of its own internal affairs while at the same time remaining loyal to the traditional demands of Judaism and to the interests of Jews elsewhere.[1]

And if this was one of the two great achievements of David Salomons the other was in evolving a precisely compatible strategy for the participation of Jews in public affairs. Not arguing, *qua* Jew, simply that disabilities should be removed, but, as an individual of the Jewish faith, standing for a particular office, fighting to remove any obstacles of ineligibility to filling that office, and ultimately, serving in that office with distinction.[2]

Lord John Russell, as heir to the Foxite cause of civil and religious liberty, led that reforming bloc in Parliament which was foremost in championing the Jews' claims; with the Reform of Parliament and the barriers to the Jews' advancement gradually removed, Emancipation came to commend itself to those outside this group who had originally been opposed. The worth of the Jews invalidated earlier fears of incivism; the realization that any threat to the influence of the Church came now, not as in the past from other churches and religions, but from the civil power itself, strengthened, rather than weakened, those innumerable claims to Emancipation which rested upon non-Anglican precedent. And the exigencies of the constitution too demanded a settlement: the election and continued re-election of a Jew to Parliament transformed the question of Emancipation, hitherto an abstract and hypothetical one, into a constitutional issue as to how to resolve the variance of opinion as between the two Houses of Parliament and between constituency and constitution.

The Emancipation of the Jews was therefore a triumph for undenominational concepts. But if the legacy of the centuries from the seventeenth to the nineteenth had been to wean men away from the belief that the differences between faiths transcended their common truths, the anxiety for the twentieth was whether the process of secularisation would be carried so far as to sever both Jew and gentile from the shared theistic, the shared spiritual roots which underlay their respective identities. Gladstone, more than any of his contemporaries, was acutely aware of the danger: while Salomons, Russell and many of the other campaigners for Emancipation fought the Whig-Erastian battles of the past (just as most opponents fought the Tory Church-State battles of the past), Gladstone was almost alone in perceiving that the consequence of Liberalism and religion failing to reach an accommodation with each other would be the destruction of both. 'It is not by the State that man can be regenerated,'[3] wrote Gladstone in 1894; perhaps his was the presentiment that the modern secular state Leviathan could pose as deadly a threat to liberty and religion as once bigotry and tyranny had posed to civil and religious liberty.

NOTES

1. And thus unlike the German Jews who were confronted with the demands of *ein theologisches Volk,* as the historian Heinrich Graetz noted with envy. 'You [the English Jews] had not to give solemn assurance that you are good patriots, that you love your native country as much as your fellow-citizens.' 'The honours you have received have been granted to you *sans phrase* as the descendants of Jacob, as the guardians of your ancient birthright.' H. Graetz, *Historic Parallels in Jewish History,* p. 18, and quotation from talk delivered before English Jews, in I. Abrahams, *Jewish Life under Emancipation,* p. 9.

2. James Picciotto and Elim d'Avigdor, among later Victorian observers of Anglo-Jewry, attributed overmuch importance to the early campaigning zeal of the Goldsmids. Picciotto was however justified in denouncing the role of the Board of Deputies, whose members collectively he criticised for their 'timidity' and 'dread of responsibility', and one may at least adjudge Elim d'Avigdor, on behalf of the Goldsmid family, as more sinned against than sinning when correcting the assertion of Lucien Wolf, author of the 1884 centennial biography of Montefiore, and of other adulatory writers, that the removal of disabilities could in large measure be attributed to Montefiore and the Deputies. Only in 1939 was Salomons's role given due appreciation, by his nephew Albert Hyamson. J. Picciotto, *Sketches of Anglo-Jewish History,* pp. 119–20, 247; L. Wolf, *Sir Moses Montefiore,* pp. 49, 61; Lucien Wolf Papers, Mocatta Library, fol. mark B.20.GOL, Elim d'Avigdor to Lucien Wolf, 9 August 1885, notes for Mr. Wolf; A. M. Hyamson, *David Salomons.*

3. Gladstone, quoted in J. Morley, *The Life of William Ewart Gladstone,* I, p. 375. It cannot be emphasised too strongly, lest there be any danger of misinterpreting this quotation, that Gladstone addresses himself as churchman rather than as proponent of a Cobdenite individualism.

Bibliography

SEVENTEENTH-, EIGHTEENTH- AND EARLY-NINETEENTH-CENTURY SOURCES

(a) Law Report

Cases argued and determined in the Court of Common Pleas. Reports of Chief Justice Willes, 1737–60, ed. C. Durnford, 1799, Hilary 18 Geo II [Omichund *v* Barker, 23 February in Chancery], pp. 538–54.

(b) Printed Works

Addison, Joseph, *The Spectator*, essay no. 495, 27 September 1712, in *The Spectator*, ed. D. F. Bond, 1965, IV, pp. 255–58.

Basnage, Jacques, *The History of the Jews*, trans. T. Taylor, 1708.

Colquhoun, P., *A Treatise on the Police of the Metropolis*, first edn. 1796, sixth edn. 1800.

Defoe, Daniel, *The Complete English Tradesman*, 2 vols. first published 1725–27, fourth and revised edn. 1738.

Herder, Johann Gottfried, 'Über die politische Bekehrung der Juden' in *Adrastea und das 18 Jahrhundert, 1801–03*.

Locke, John, *Epistola de Tolerantia: A Letter on Toleration* (first edn. published at Gouda, 1689), trans. J. W. Gough, ed. R. Klibansky (1968).

Montagu, Lady Mary Wortley, *The Complete Letters of Lady Mary Wortley Montagu*, ed. R. Halsband, 3 vols. 1965–67.

Montesquieu, Charles de Secondat, Baron de, *De l'esprit des lois*.

St. Constant, J. L. Ferri de, *Londres et Les Anglais*, Paris, 1804 or year 12 of the Republican Era, IV.

Tovey, D'Blossiers, *'Anglia Judaica'; or, the History and Antiquities of the Jews in England*, 1738.

Voltaire [François-Marie Arouet], *Lettres philosophiques*, ed. G. Lanson, 2 vols. 1909.

PRIMARY SOURCES

(a) Manuscript Sources and Memento Collections

Aberdeen MSS, The British Library.

N. M. Adler Letter Books, United Synagogue Archives, Office of the Chief Rabbinate, Woburn House, Woburn Square, London W.C.1. No letter books before 1851 extant. Letter Books 2–7 (and 83, 84 for indexes).

Bentinck MSS, Nottingham University Library. One relevant item.

Louis Cohen–Moses Montefiore Correspondence, 1837–74, Mocatta Library, University College, London.

Board of Deputies of the British Jews, Minute Books I–IX, 1760–1864, Woburn House.

Derby MSS, Queen's College, Oxford.

Gladstone MSS, The British Library.

I. L. Goldsmid Letter Books, Watson Library, University College, London.

The Greenwich Local History Library Collection, Greenwich Local History Centre, Mycenae Road, London, S.E.3.

Guildhall Records, Corporation of the City of London. Repertories of the Court of Aldermen, Guildhall Records Repository, City of London.

Hughenden MSS, Hughenden Manor, Hughenden, near High Wycombe, Buckinghamshire.

Jewish Museum Papers, Jewish Central Library, Woburn House.

The Martin Collection, Greenwich Local History Centre.

Mocatta Miscellaneous MSS, Mocatta Library.

Moses Montefiore–Louis Loewe Collection of Montefiore Autograph Letters, in possession of Raphael Loewe Esq.

Extant Letter Books of Sir Moses Montefiore, Mocatta Library, nos. 712, 718, 719, 720.

Peel MSS, The British Library.

Russell MSS, Public Record Office.

David Salomons Mementos, Wall Certificates, etc., Broomhill, Southborough, near Tunbridge Wells, Kent.

Whately MSS, Lambeth Palace Library, London.

Whittaker MSS, Jewish Central Library.

Lucien Wolf Papers, Mocatta Library.

(b) Government Publications, in Addition to Statutes of the Realm

Journals of the House of Commons.

Journals of the House of Lords.

The Parliamentary History of England, from the earliest period to the year 1803 [printed and published by T. C. Hansard, 1813], XIV, 1747–53, pp. 1365–1432, debate in House of Commons on the Jews' Naturalization Bill; XV, 1753–65, pp. 91–163, debates in House of Lords and House of Commons on Repeal of the Jews' Naturalization Act.

Parliamentary Debates, Hansard, New Series until accession of William IV, Third Series thereafter.

Parliamentary Papers:

Reports from Commissioners: (8) Handloom Weavers. Session 16 January–11 August 1840. Vol. XXIII, 1840. Reports from Assistant Handloom Weavers' Commissioners. 43–Part II, 4 February 1840.

1845, February–August, XIV [631], pp. 1–160, 30 May 1845. First Report of Her Majesty's Commissioners for Revising and Consolidating the Criminal Law.

Reports from Commissioners: twenty vols. Vol. 8—Corporation of London. Session, 31 January 1854–12 August 1854. Volume XXVI [1772]—Report of the

Commissioners appointed to enquire into the existing state of the Corporation of the City of London, and to collect information respecting its constitution, order and government, etc. together with the Minutes of Evidence, and appendix, 1854, pp. xiv–xv.

Public Bills, December 1854–August 1855, II, pp. 25–64. Drafts of bills to amend the Dissenters' Marriage Acts.

Public Bills, January–July 1856, III, 'A Bill to amend the Provisions of the Marriage Act relating to Dissenters', 7 February 1856, pp. 11–12.

Public Bills, 30 April–28 August 1857, I, A Bill entitled An Act to amend the Law relating to Divorce and Matrimonial Causes in England, 25 June 1857, pp. 541–56, bill no. 86.

Reports from Committees, 1857, Session 2 [253], vol. IX, pp. 477–84, 10 August 1857. Proceedings of a Select Committee of the House of Commons to examine the oaths to be taken by Members.

Public Bills, 1857, 30 April–28 August 1857, I, A Bill [as amended in Committee] entitled An Act to amend the Law relating to Divorce and Matrimonial Causes in England, 19 August 1857, pp. 557–74, bill no. 197.

Public Bills, December 1857–August 1858, II, pp. 591–94, bill no. 210. 'An Act for the Relief of Her Majesty's Subjects professing the Jewish Religion'.

1859, session February–April [205], Vol. I, Book III, pp. 35–66, 11 April 1859. Report from the Select Committee on the Jews Act, together with the Proceedings of the Committee and Minutes of Evidence.

Public Bills, January–August 1860, III, pp. 779–82, bill no. 80. 'The Jews' Act Amendment Bill'.

Public Bills, January–August 1860, III, pp. 783–86, bill no. 280. 'The Jews' Act Amendment Bill'.

(c) Newspapers and Contemporary Journals

Edinburgh Review.
The Illustrated London News.
The Illustrated Times.
*The Jewish Chronicle.**
John Bull.
The Kentish Independent.
Kentish Mercury.
Manchester Guardian.
The Morning Advertiser.
Morning Chronicle.
Morning Herald.
The Morning Post.
Punch.
Quarterly Review.
The St. James's Medley.
The Saturday Review.
The Spectator.
The Standard.
The Times.
The Voice of Jacob.
Westminster Review.
The Woolwich Advertiser, and Plumstead and Charlton Trade Circular.

*The full title of *The Jewish Chronicle* was subject to constant revision in the years after its foundation in 1841. Throughout this book therefore the newspaper is referred to simply as *The Jewish Chronicle*.

(d) Contemporary Books, Pamphlets, Memoirs, Diaries, Letters, Reports, Review Articles, etc. [(P) = *Pro-Emancipation literature;* (A) = *Anti-Emancipation literature*]

Adler, N. M., *The Bonds of Brotherhood. A Sermon,* 1849.

Anichini, P., *A Few Remarks on the Expediency and Justice of Emancipating the Jews, addressed to His Grace the Duke of Wellington, K. G.,* 1829 (P).

——, *A Word or Two to the 228 Members who voted against the Second Reading of the Jews' Relief Bill, on the 17th May, 1830, by an Ausonian,* 1830 (P).

Anonymous, 'Jewish Disabilities' and 'Parliamentary Prospects', *Quarterly Review,* 81, September 1847, pp. 526–40, 541–78.

——, 'Religious Disabilities', reviews of (i) Cobbett. W., *Good Friday; or, the Murder of Jesus Christ by the Jews;* (ii) Cobbett's weekly *Political Register,* 5 June 1830; Goldsmid, F. H., *Two Letters in Answer to the Objections urged against Mr. Grant's Bill for the Relief of the Jews, Westminster Review,* XXV, July 1830, pp. 188–97.

——, *An Appeal to the Public in Behalf of the Jews with considerations on the policy of removing their civil disabilities . . . comprehending a brief historical sketch of their residence in this country, from their first settlement to the present time,* 1834 (P).

Ashley, Lord (later seventh Earl of Shaftesbury), review notice of Lord Lindsay's *Letters on Egypt, Edom, and the Holy Land, Quarterly Review,* 63, January 1839, pp. 166–92.

A Barrister, *An Answer to the Speech of the Rt. Hon. Sir Robert Peel, M. P. in the House of Commons on February 11th, 1848,* 1848 (A).

A Believing Jew, *Jews' Disabilities Bill. Protest by a believing Jew* (A).

Benisch, A., *The Principal Charges of Dr. M'Caul's Old Paths . . . as stated by Mr. Newdegate in the House of Commons, considered and answered,* 1858.

Bird, C. S., *The Vicar of Gainsborough to his parishioners on the question of the Removal of the Jewish Disabilities,* 1847 (A).

Birks, T. R., *A Letter to the Rt. Hon. Lord John Russell, M. P. on The Admission of the Jews to Parliament,* 1848 (A).

Blunt, J. E., *A History of the Establishment and Residence of the Jews in England with an Enquiry into their Civil Disabilities,* 1830.

The British Jew to His Fellow Countryman, 1833 (P).

Bulwer, E. Lytton, *England and the English,* first published in 2 vols., 1833.

Byron, Lord, 'The Age of Bronze'.

Campbell, W. F., *A Short Statement of the Grounds which justify the House of Lords in repeating their decision of last year upon the Jewish question; being the substance of a speech in the House of Commons, May 4th, 1848; together with a prefatory letter to Spencer Walpole, Esq. M. P.,* 1849.

——, *Letters on the Oath of Abjuration,* 1856.

Che Sarà, Sarà or Lord John Russell and the Jews, 1848 (A).

A Christian, *Emancipation of the Jews,* undated (P).

A Clergyman's Apology for favouring the Removal of Jewish Disabilities as bearing on the position, prospects, and policy of the Church of England, 1847 (P).

A Clergyman of the Church of England, *England's Duty to Israel's Sons,* being a candid inquiry into the policy of admitting the Jewish People . . ., 1849 (P).

Cobbett, J. M. and J. P., (eds.), Selections from Cobbett's Political Works: being a complete abridgement of the 100 volumes which comprise the writings of "Porcupine" and the "Weekly Political Register". With notes, historical and explanatory, 1835.

Cobbett, W., *Paper against Gold or, the History and mystery of the Bank of England, of the Debt, of the Stocks, of the Sinking Fund, and of all the other tricks and contrivances carried on by the means of Paper Money*, 1828.

———, *Good Friday; or, the Murder of Jesus Christ by the Jews*, 1830.

———, *A History of the Protestant Reformation in England and Ireland; showing how that event has impoverished the main body of the people in those countries; and containing a list of the abbeys, priories, nunneries . . . confiscated by the Protestant "Reformation" sovereigns, and parliaments . . . In a series of letters, etc.*, 1850 edn.; first published 1824–26; edn. with notes and preface by F. A. Gasquet, 1896.

———, *Rural Rides*, 1853 edn.; first published 1830.

Cohen, A., *The Lords and the Jews*, 1853 (P).

Coles, J., *Observations on the Civil Disabilities of British Jews*, 1834 (P).

A Conservative, *Remarks on the Civil Disabilities of the Jews*, undated (P).

Cookesley, W. G., *Thoughts on the Admission of Jews to Parliament, and on the Separation of the Church from the State, suggested by the late election of representatives for the University of Oxford*, 1852 (A).

Cosmopolite, *A Letter to the Rt. Hon. Sir Robert Peel. Bart. on the Civil Disabilities of the Jews*, 1844 (P).

A Country Vicar, *Jewish Emancipation. A Christian Duty*, 1853 (P).

Croly, G., *The Claims of the Jews incompatible with the National Profession of Christianity*, 1848 (A).

Crooll, R. Joseph, *The Restoration of Israel*, 1812 (A).

———, *The Fifth Empire, delivered in a discourse by thirty-six men; every one made a speech, and when the one had finished another began; and it is decided among them that the Fifth Empire is to be the inheritance of the people of Israel*, 1819 (A).

———, *The Last Generation*, 1829 (A).

Dexter, W. (ed.), *The Nonesuch Dickens. The Letters of Charles Dickens*, 3 vols., 1938.

Digamma, *The Exclusion of Baron Lionel de Rothschild from Parliament*, 1850 (P).

Disraeli, B., *Coningsby or The New Generation*, first published 1844; Dent, Everyman Library edn. 1959.

———, *Sybil or The Two Nations*, first published 1845; Longmans edn. 1880.

———, *Tancred or The New Crusade*, first published 1847; Longmans edn., 1880; 1914 edn. published at Munich and Berlin, trans. and a postscript by Oscar Levy.

———, *Lord George Bentinck: A Political Biography*, first published 1852; eighth and revised edn. 1872; 1905 edn. with an introduction by C. Whibley.

Disraeli, R. (ed.), *Lord Beaconsfield's Letters, 1830–1852*, 1887.

Egan, C., *The status of the Jews in England from the time of the Normans to the reign of Queen Victoria, impartially considered . . . including a synopsis, with comments, of the debates on the Jewish Disabilities Bill*, 1848.

Emerson, Ralph Waldo, *English Traits*, first published 1856; in *The Complete Essays and other Writings of Ralph Waldo Emerson*, edited, with a biographical introduction by Brooks Atkinson, New York, 1940, pp. 521–690.

Faudel, H., *A few words on the Jewish disabilities addressed to Sir R. H. Inglis [in reply to his speech on the Jewish Disabilities Bill]*, 1848 (P).

Forty Reasons for resisting the removal of the Jewish Disabilities. Shewing Good Cause—Why, in this matter, the Commons should agree with the Lords, rather than the Lords be coerced by the Commons, undated (A).

Gawler, G., *The Emancipation of the Jews indispensable for the maintenance of the Protestant profession of the Empire; and in other respects most entitled to the support of the British Nation. In extracts from a correspondence recently addressed to the Morning Herald* and now corrected and enlarged, 1847 (P).

Gillmor, Clotworthy, *Jewish Legislators: A Word in Season on the General Subject of Jewish Disabilities*, 1847 (P).

Gladstone, William Ewart, *Substance of a Speech on the Motion of Lord John Russell for a Committee of the whole House, with a view to the removal of the remaining Jewish disabilities; delivered in the House of Commons, on Thursday, December 16th 1847*, together with a Preface, 1848.

Goldsmid, A. (ed.), *Report of the Case of Miller versus Salomons, M. P. with a summary of the preliminary proceedings in the House of Commons*, 1852.

Goldsmid, F. H., *Remarks on the Civil Disabilities of British Jews*, 1830 (P).

————, *Two Letters, in Answer to the Objections urged against Mr. Grant's Bill for the Relief of the Jews*, 1830 (P).

————, *The Arguments advanced against the Enfranchisement of the Jews, considered in a series of letters*, first edn. 1831; second edn. 1833 (P).

————, *Reply to the Arguments advanced against the removal of the remaining disabilities of the Jews*, 1848 (P).

Goldsmid, I. L., *Address from I. L. Goldsmid to the Jewish Electors of the City of London*, 18 June 1841.

A Graduate of the University of Cambridge: *A Few Words on the Proposed Admission of Jews into Parliament*, 1848 (A).

To the Great Jewish People, whether they dwell in the silence of the vast city, upon the once loved banks of the Jordan, or as citizens here at home, to the People of God, I dedicate this my first defence of their ancient faith. Two pamphlets, 1841 (P).

Green, A. L., *Dr. Croly. LL. D. versus Civil and Religious Liberty*, 1850 (P).

Hawkes, H., *A Sermon, preached to a congregation of Christians at Portsmouth on the occasion of the death of Solomon Herschel*, 1843 (P).

Haynes, M. P., *The Position of the Jews as indicated and affected by the return to Parliament of Baron Lionel de Rothschild with considerations whether he can take his seat*, 1847 (P).

Hazlitt, William, 'Emancipation of the Jews', first published in *The Tatler*, 28 March 1831; in *The Complete Works of William Hazlitt*, ed. P. P. Howe, 1930–34, 19, 1933, pp. 320–24.

The Hebrew Talisman!, undated (A), with caricature of N. M. de Rothschild: 'A Pillar of the Exchange', 1829 or later.

Heine, Heinrich, *Sämmtliche Werke*, Leipzig, 1828.

Higginson, F., *A Free Inquiry into the Policy of Admitting the Jews into Parliament, and Full Participation in the Advantages, Honours and Privileges of British Denizens, viewed as regards Religion, Justice and Expediency*, 1848 (P).

Holland, Lord (Henry Richard Vassall Fox, Baron Holland), *The opinions of Lord*

Holland, as recorded in the Journals of the House of Lords, from 1797 to 1841. Collected and edited by D. C. Moylan, 1841.

Hurwitz, H., *A Letter to Isaac L. Goldsmid . . . on certain recent mis-statements respecting the Jewish Religion*, 1833 (P).

An Israelite, *Jewish Emancipation*, 1845 (P).

Israelite, *To the Rev. Henry Mackenzie, Minister of the parish of Great Yarmouth. 'Let not your own, but the Public wishes actuate you.'* 1847 (P).

The Jew. Our Lawgiver, 1853 (A).

Landon, J. T. B., *Eureka, a sequel to Lord John Russell's Post-Bag, etc.*, 1851.

————, *Eureka, a sequel to Lord John Russell's Post-Bag, etc.* no. 2, 1853

Lettis, J. W., *The Right of a Jew to sit in Parliament*, 1851 (P).

Levason, L., *Jewish Disabilities. To young Mr. Pope*, 1847 (P).

Loewe. L. (ed.), *The Diaries of Sir Moses and Lady Montefiore*, 2 vols. 1890.

Low, S., *The Charities of London, comprehending the Benevolent, Educational, and Religious Institutions*, 1850.

Lupton, J., *A Sermon—Should Jews be admitted to Civil Offices among their Christian subjects?* 1857 (P).

Macaulay, T. B., 'Civil Disabilities of the Jews', *Edinburgh Review*, 52, January 1831, pp. 363–74.

Malmesbury, J. H. Harris, third Earl of, *Memoirs of an Ex-Minister. An Autobiography*, 2 vols., 1884.

Marks, D. W., *Discourse delivered in the West London Synagogue of British Jews . . . on the day of its consecration. 27th January 1842*, 1842.

Martineau, Harriet, *The History of England during the Thirty Years' Peace, 1816–1846*, 3 vols., 1849–51.

Marx, Karl, 'On the Jewish Question', 1843–44; in *Writings of the Young Marx on Philosophy and Society*, trans. and ed. L. D. Easton and K. H. Guddat, New York, 1967, pp. 216–48.

Maurice, F. D., 'Thoughts on Jewish Disabilities', *Fraser's Magazine for Town and Country*, vol. XXXVI, July–December 1847, no. CCXV, November 1847, pp. 623–30.

Mayhew, H., *The Unknown Mayhew. Selections from the 'Morning Chronicle', 1849–1850*, edited and introduced by E. P. Thompson and E. Yeo, 1971.

————, *Mayhew's London*, ed. P. Quennell. *Being selections from 'London Labour and the London Poor'*, first published in 1851, 1969 edn.

————, *The Street Trader's Lot. A selection from Mayhew's 'London Labour and the London Poor'*, ed. S. Rubinstein, introduction by M. D. George, 1947.

A Member of the late Parliament, *Thoughts on the Oath of Abjuration in a letter to the Earl of Aberdeen*, 1853 (A).

Mendelssohn, Moses, *Jerusalem. A Treatise on Ecclesiastical Authority and Judaism*, trans. M. Samuels, 2 vols., 1838.

Michelet, Jules, *Le Peuple*, first published 1845; trans. C. Cocks, third edn. 1846.

Mills, J., *The British Jews*, 1853.

Milman, H. H., *The History of the Jews*, 1829 and 1866 editions.

Montagu, B., *A Letter to Henry Warburton, Esq., M.P. upon the Emancipation of the Jews*, 1833 (P).

——, *A Letter to the Rt. Revd. the Lord Bishop of Chichester, upon the Emancipation of the Jews*, 1834 (P).

National Club: by order of the committee, *Address of the Committee of the National Club on the Oaths Bill, for admitting Jews to legislate for Christians*, 15 January 1858 (A).

A New Song to an Old Tune, 1841, on Lord John Russell's election as Member for the City of London.

Observations addressed to the English Jews, undated (P).

One of the People, *A Word with the Earl of Winchelsea*, 1848 (P).

——, *The Admission of Jews into Parliament, a violation of the British Constitution*, 1854 (A).

——, *Second Letter to the Rt. Hon. the Earl of Derby, on the Jews Bill, commonly called "The Oaths Bill". Its Religious Bearings*, 1858 (A).

Padley, A., *An Answer to some of the opinions and statements respecting the Jews made by B. Disraeli, Esq. M.P. in the twenty-fourth chapter of his biographical memoir of Lord George Bentinck*, 1852 (A).

Pellatt, A., *Brief Memoir of the Jews, in relation to their civil and municipal disabilities*, 1829 (P).

Perceval, D. M., *Maynooth and the Jew Bill: further illustrations of the Speech of the Rt. Hon. Spencer Perceval on the Roman Catholic Question in May 1805*, 1845 (A).

Reports of the Philo-Judean Society, 1827–29.

Phoenix, *Scriptural Reasonings in support of the Jewish claims to sit in the Commons House of Parliament, addressed to the conscience of the Christian people of the British Empire*, 1850 (P).

A Protectionist, *Some Arguments against the Admission of Jews into Parliament*, 1852 (A).

Pyne, T., *Judaea Libera: or, the Eligibility of the Jews (the ancient People of God) to Parliament*, 1850 (P).

D. R., *A Christmas Appeal to the British People: An Imaginary Speech in Parliament against the Jewish Disabilities Bill*, 1847–48 (A).

Raphall, M. J. and Newdegate, C. N., *Jewish Dogmas. A Correspondence between Dr. Raphall. M.A. and C. N. Newdegate. M. P.*, 1849.

Robertson, J., *The Macaulay Election of 1846, containing comments on the Macaulay Rejection of 1847*, 1847 (A).

Robinson, J. Travers, *Remarks deprecating the proposed admission of Her Majesty's Jewish subjects to seats in the House of Commons* 1848 (A).

Russell, Lord John, *These are my sentiments!*, 1841, two election addresses of 1841.

Russellas: a political poem for "the People" etc., 1865, a satire on the political career of Earl Russell.

Salomons, D., *A Short Statement on behalf of His Majesty's Subjects professing the Jewish Religion*, 1835.

——, *Further Observations on behalf of His Majesty's Subjects professing the Jewish Religion*, 1836.

——, (under pseudonym of Britannicus), *The Case of Mr. Salomons, alderman elect of the ward of Aldgate*, 1836.

——, *An Account of the recent persecution of the Jews at Damascus*, 1840.

——, *The Case of David Salomons, Esq., being His Address to the Court of Aldermen, on applying for admission as Alderman of the Ward of Portsoken, on Tuesday, October 15th, 1844*, 1844.

——, *Parliamentary Oaths: Observations on the Law and Practice with regard to the administration of oaths. Dedicated to the House of Commons*, 1850.

——, *Alteration of Oaths considered in a Letter to the Earl of Derby*, 1853.

——, *Notes on the History of the Oaths of Allegiance, Supremacy and Abjuration*, 1857.

Samuel, M., *An Address on the Position of the Jews in Britain with reference to their literary, political, civil, and religious condition*, undated (P).

Stallard, J. H., *London Pauperism amongst Jews and Christians. An Inquiry into the Principles and Practice of Out-Door Relief in the Metropolis and the Result upon the Moral and Physical Condition of the Pauper Class*, 1867.

Stanley, A. P., *The Life and Correspondence of Thomas Arnold. D.D.*, 1844 and 1881 editions.

Stepney, *An Appeal to the subjects of this professedly Protestant Christian Country*, undated (A).

Sumner, J. B., 'The Jewish Nation, a sermon on Isa. xliii.21', *Thirty-Seventh Report of the London Society for Promoting Christianity amongst the Jews*, sermon preached at the Episcopal Jews' Chapel, Cambridge-Heath, 8 May 1845.

Thornborrow, W., *Advocacy of Jewish Freedom*, 1848.

Tocqueville, Alexis de, *Journeys to England and Ireland*, trans. G. Lawrence and K. P. Mayer, ed. J. P. Mayer, 1958, reference to some observations recorded in 1835.

——, *Democracy in America*, trans. G. Lawrence, ed. J. P. Mayer, first edn., 1840; New York, 1969.

Van Oven, B., *An Appeal to the British Nation on behalf of the Jews*, 1829 (P).

——, *Ought Baron de Rothschild to sit in Parliament? An imaginary conversation between JUDAEUS and AMICUS NOBILIS*, 1847 (P).

Veritas, *The Jew Question considered in a letter addressed to Sir Robert H. Inglis. Bart. M. P.*, 1851 (A).

SECONDARY SOURCES

Abrahams, I., *Jewish Life in the Middle Ages*, first published, 1896; 1932 edn., revised by C. Roth.

——, *Jewish Life under Emancipation*, 1917.

Abrahams, L., 'Sir I. L. Goldsmid and the Admission of the Jews of England to Parliament', *Transactions of the Jewish Historical Society of England*. IV (1903), pp. 116–29, Appendix, pp. 130–76.

Achad-Ha-Am (Asher Ginzberg), *Ten Essays on Zionism and Judaism*, trans. L. Simon, 1922.

Anderson, O., *A Liberal State At War: English Politics and Economics during the Crimean War*, New York, 1967.

Arendt, H., *The Origins of Totalitarianism*, 1958.

Ashton, T. S., *Iron and Steel in the Industrial Revolution*, 1924.

Bagehot, Walter, *The Collected Works of Walter Bagehot*, ed. N. St. J. Stevas, 1965.

Barnett, R. D., 'Anglo-Jewry in the Eighteenth Century', in *Three Centuries of Anglo-Jewish History*, ed. V. D. Lipman, 1961, pp. 45–68.

——, (ed.), *The Sephardi Heritage. Essays on the history and cultural contribution of the Jews of Spain and Portugal*, vol. I, 1971.

Baron, S. W., *The Dynamics of Emancipation: Great Ages and Ideas of the Jewish People*, 1956.

Beaven, A. B., *The Aldermen of the City of London*, 2 vols. 1908 and 1913.

Bergman, S. H., 'Israel and the Oikoumenē', *Studies in Rationalism, Judaism and Universalism. In memory of Leon Roth*, ed. R. Loewe, 1966, pp. 47–65.

Best, G. F. A., 'The Religious Difficulties of National Education in England, 1800–1870', *The Cambridge Historical Journal*, vol. XII, no. 2, 1956, pp. 155–73.

Birnbaum, S. A., 'The Jewries of Eastern Europe', *The Slavonic and East European Review*, vol. 29, 1950–51, pp. 420–43.

Blake, R., *Disraeli, 1966*.

Bloom, H. I., *The Economic Activities of the Jews of Amsterdam in the Seventeenth and Eighteenth Centuries*, Williamsport, 1937.

Bossy, J., *The English Catholic Community, 1570–1850*, 1976.

Briggs, A., *Victorian People. Some reassessments of people, institutions, ideas and events, 1851–1867*, 1954.

Brose, O. J., *Church and Parliament. The Reshaping of the Church of England, 1828–1860*, Stanford, 1959.

Brown, M. D., *David Salomons House, Catalogue of Mementos*, 1968.

——, *David Salomons House, Catalogue of Medals*, 1968.

——, *David Salomons House, Catalogue of Ballooniana*, 1971.

Buckley, J. H., *The Victorian Temper*, first published 1952; 1966 edn.

Burn, W. L., *The Age of Equipoise: a study of the mid-Victorian generation*, 1964.

Burrow, J. W., *Evolution and Society: a study in Victorian social theory*, first published 1966; 1970 edn.

Campbell, John Lord, *Lives of the Lord Chancellors and Keepers of the Great Seal of England, from the earliest times to the reign of Queen Victoria*, 8 vols., 1845–69, VIII, 1869.

Carsten, F. L., 'The Court Jews: A Prelude to Emancipation,' *Leo Baeck Year Book*, III, 1958, pp. 140–56.

Chadwick, W. O., *The Victorian Church*, 2 vols., 1970 edn.

Christensen, T., *Origin and History of Christian Socialism, 1848–1854*, 1962.

Kitson Clark, G. S. R., *Peel and the Conservative Party. A Study in Party Politics, 1832–41*, 1929.

Conacher, J. B., *The Aberdeen Coalition, 1852–1855. A study in mid-nineteenth century party politics*, 1968.

——, *The Peelites and the Party System, 1846–1852*, 1972.

The Dickensian, vol. XVII, July 1921, no. 3, pp. 144–52. 'Fagin and Riah', no author given.

Domnitz, M., *Immigration and Integration. Experiences of the Anglo-Jewish Community*, 1971.

Dubnow, S. M., *History of the Jews*, 3 vols., trans. M. Spiegel, New Brunswick, 1967.

Emanuel, C. H. L., *A Century and a Half of Jewish History*, 1910.

Emden, P. H., *Quakers in Commerce: a record of business achievement*, 1940.

Endelman, T. M., *The Jews of Georgian England, 1714–1830*, 1979.

Epstein, I., *Judaism*, 1945.

Eysenck, H. J., *The Psychology of Politics*, first published 1954; second impression 1957.

Feiling, K. G., *The Second Tory Party, 1714–1832*, 1938.

Finestein, I., *A Short History of Anglo-Jewry*, 1957.

———, 'Anglo-Jewry and the Law of Divorce', *The Jewish Chronicle*, 19 April 1957.

———, 'Forcing the Pace of the Law', *The Jewish Chronicle*, 8 November 1957. (I. L. Goldsmid's election campaign at Beverley, Yorks.)

———, 'Anglo-Jewish Opinion during the Struggle for Emancipation, 1828–1858', *Transactions of the Jewish Historical Society of England*, XX, 1959–61, pp. 113–43.

———, 'An Aspect of the Jews and English Marriage Law during the Emancipation: The Prohibited Degrees', *The Jewish Journal of Sociology*, VII, no. 1, June 1965, pp. 3–21.

———, 'The Anglo-Jewish Revolt of 1853', *The Jewish Quarterly*, XXVI, 3–4 (97/98), autumn–winter 1978–79, pp. 103–13.

———, *Post-Emancipation Jewry: The Anglo-Jewish Experience*, 1980.

Foot, M. R. D. and Matthew, H. C. G. (eds.), *The Gladstone Diaries*, vol. III, 1840–47, 1974.

Fraser, D., 'The Agitation for Parliamentary Reform', in *Popular Movements, c. 1830–1850*, ed. J. T. Ward, pp. 31–53.

Gash, N., *Reaction and Reconstruction in English Politics, 1832–1852*, 1965.

Gaster, M., *History of the Ancient Synagogue of the Spanish and Portuguese Jews*, 1901.

George, M. D., *London Life in the Eighteenth Century*, first edn. 1925, third edn. 1951.

Gibb, H. A. R. and Bowen, H., *Islamic Society and the West*, 2 vols., 1950 and 1957.

Graetz, H., *Historic Parallels in Jewish History*, 1887.

———, *History of the Jews* . . . edited and in part translated by B. Löwy, 1891–92.

———, *A Popular History of the Jews*, first published, 1919; fourth edn. in 5 vols., New York, 1930.

Green, J. R., *A Short History of the English People*, illustrated edn., ed. Mrs. J. R. Green and K. Norgate, 4 vols., 1892–94.

Greville, C. C. F., *The Greville Memoirs. A Journal of the Reigns of King George IV, King William IV and Queen Victoria*, ed. H. Reeve, 1888 edn.

Guttman, J., *The History of Jewish Philosophy from Biblical Times to Franz Rosenzweig*, 1964.

Hennessy, J. Pope, *Monckton Milnes*, 2 vols., 1949–52, vol. I, *The Years of Promise, 1809–51*; vol. II, *The Flight of Youth, 1851–85*.

Henriques, H. S. Q., *The Law of Aliens and Naturalization, including the text of the 1905 Aliens Act*, 1906.

———, *The Jews and the English Law*, 1908.

———, *Jewish Marriages and the English Law*, 1909.

Henriques, U. R. Q., *Religious Toleration in England, 1787–1833*, 1961.

——, 'The Jewish Emancipation Controversy in Nineteenth-Century Britain', *Past and Present*, 40, July 1968, pp. 126–46.

Herzl, Theodor, *The Jewish State. An Attempt at a Modern Solution of the Jewish Question*, first published 1896, trans. S. D'Avigdor and revised by I. Cohen, 1946.

Hill, C., *Society and Puritanism in Pre-Revolutionary England*, 1964.

Hodder, E., *The Life and Work of the Seventh Earl of Shaftesbury, with Extracts from Lord Shaftesbury's Diaries and Journals*, 1892.

Houghton, W. E., *The Victorian Frame of Mind, 1830–1870*, New Haven, 1957.

Hyamson, A. M., *A History of the Jews in England*, 1908.

——, *David Salomons*, 1939.

——, *The Sephardim of England. A History of the Spanish and Portuguese Jewish Community, 1492–1951*, 1951.

——, 'The First Jewish Peer', *Transactions of the Jewish Historical Society of England*, XVII, 1951–52, pp. 287–90.

——, *Jews' College, London, 1855–1955*, 1955.

Hyman, L., *The Jews of Ireland: from earliest times to the year 1910*, 1972.

The Jewish Encyclopaedia, New York, 1925.

Jennings, L. J. (ed.), *The Croker Papers. The Correspondence and Diaries of the late Rt. Hon. John Wilson Croker*, second revised edn. 1885.

Jones, W. D. and Erickson, A. B., *The Peelites, 1846–57*, Ohio State University Press, 1972.

Jordan, W. K., *The Development of Religious Toleration in England*, 4 vols., 1932–40.

Jost, I. M., *Geschichte des Judenthums und seiner Sekten*, Leipzig, 1857–59.

Katz, J., *Tradition and Crisis. Jewish Society at the End of the Middle Ages*, 1961.

——, *Exclusiveness and Tolerance. Studies in Jewish-Gentile Relations in Mediaeval and Modern Times*, 1961.

——, *Emancipation and Assimilation: Studies in Modern Jewish History*, 1972. Includes the article 'The term "Jewish Emancipation": Its Origin and Historical Impact', first published in 1964.

——, *Out of the Ghetto. The Social Background of Jewish Emancipation, 1770–1870*, Harvard, 1973.

Kendall, G., *Charles Kingsley and His Ideas*, 1946.

Kingsley, Charles, *Alton Locke*, 1900 edn., containing reprint of the tract *Cheap Clothes and Nasty*, first published in the early 1850s under the pseudonym 'Parson Lot'.

Kohn, H., *The Age of Nationalism. The First Era of Global History*, New York, 1962.

Krause, J. T., 'Changes in English Fertility and Mortality, 1781–1850', in *The Economic History Review*, second series, vol. XI, no. 1 1958, pp. 52–70.

Landsberger, F., *Rembrandt, the Jews and the Bible*, translated from the German by F. N. Gerson, The Jewish Publication Society of America, Philadelphia, 1945–46.

Laqueur, W. Z., *A History of Zionism*, 1972.

Lathbury, D. C., *Correspondence on Church and Religion of William Ewart Gladstone*, 2 vols., 1910.

Leader, R. E. (ed.), *Life and Letters of John Arthur Roebuck with chapters of autobiography*, 1897.

Lipman, V. D., 'A Survey of Anglo-Jewry in 1851', *Transactions of the Jewish Historical Society of England*, XVII, 1951–52, pp. 171–88.

———, *Social History of the Jews in England, 1850–1950*, 1954.

———, 'The Age of Emancipation, 1815–1880', in *Three Centuries of Anglo-Jewish History*, ed. V. D. Lipman, 1961, pp. 69–106.

———, 'The Structure of London Jewry in the Mid-Nineteenth Century', in *Essays presented to Chief Rabbi Israel Brodie on the occasion of his seventieth birthday*, ed. H. J. Zimmels, J. Rabbinowitz and I. Finestein, 1967. Jews' College Publications; New Series, no. 3.

Machin, G. I. T., *The Catholic Question in English Politics, 1820 to 1830*, 1964.

———, 'The Maynooth Grant, the Dissenters and Disestablishment, 1845–1847', *The English Historical Review*, 82, 1967, pp. 61–85.

———, 'Gladstone and Nonconformity in the 1860's: the formation of an alliance', *The Historical Journal*, XVII, 2, 1974, pp. 347–64.

———, *Politics and the Churches in Great Britain, 1832 to 1868*, 1977.

Magnus, L., *The Jewish Board of Guardians and the Men Who Made it, 1859–1909*, 1909.

Manning, B. L., *The Protestant Dissenting Deputies*, ed. O. Greenwood, 1952.

Margoliouth, M., *The History of the Jews in Great Britain*, 3 vols., 1851.

Marks, D. W. and Löwy, A., *Memoir of Sir F. H. Goldsmid. Q.C., M.P.*, second edn., 1882.

Martin, T., *A Life of Lord Lyndhurst, from letters and papers in possession of his family*, second edn., 1884.

May, T. Erskine, *The Constitutional History of England since the Accession of George the Third, 1760–1860*, sixth edn., 1878.

Melville, L., *The Life and Letters of William Cobbett in England and America*, 1913.

Mills, J. Travis, *John Bright and the Quakers*, 2 vols., 1935.

Milman, H. H., *The History of the Jews*, 1829 and 1866 editions.

Mitchell, B. R. and Deane, P., *Abstract of British Historical Statistics*, 1962.

Monypenny, W. F. and Buckle, G. E., *The Life of Benjamin Disraeli, Earl of Beaconsfield*, 2 vol. edn., 1929.

Morley, J., *The Life of William Ewart Gladstone*, 3 vols. in the year of first publication, 1903.

Ogden, J., *Isaac D'Israeli*, 1969.

Parker, C. S. (ed.), *Life and Letters of Sir James Graham, 1792–1861*, 2 vols., 1907.

Parkes, J. W., *The story of three David Salomons at Broomhill*, 1953.

Perry, T. W., *Public Opinion, Propaganda, and Politics in Eighteenth Century England. A Study of the Jew Bill of 1753*. Harvard Historical Monographs no. 51, Harvard, 1962.

Pevsner, N. et al., *The Buildings of England*, continuing series.

Philipson, D., *Old European Jewries*, Philadelphia, 1894.

———, *The Reform Movement in Judaism*, 1907.

Picciotto, J., *Sketches of Anglo-Jewish History*, first published, 1875; 1956 edn., ed. I. Finestein.

Pollock, F., *Essays in Jurisprudence and Ethics*, 1882.

Price, F. G. Hilton, *A Handbook of London Bankers*, 1890–91.

Pulzer, P. G. J., *The Rise of Political Antisemitism in Germany and Austria*, 1964.

Raisin, M., *A History of the Jews in Modern Times*, New York, 1930. Sixth and companion volume to H. Graetz, *A Popular History of the Jews*, 5 vols., New York, 1930.

Read, D., *Press and People, 1790–1850. Opinion in three English cities*, 1961.

Robson, R. J., *The Oxfordshire Election of 1754*, 1949.

Rosenberg, E., *From Shylock to Svengali*, 1961.

Rosenblum, B., *'Punch* and the Jews, 1841–1858', *Transactions of the Jewish Historical Society of England*, XXIV, 1975, pp. 205–10.

Roth, C., *History of the Jews in Venice*, 1930.

———, *A History of the Marranos*, 1932.

———, *Anglo-Jewish Letters, 1158–1917*, 1938.

———, *The Magnificent Rothschilds*, 1939.

———, *The History of the Jews in Italy*, Philadelphia, 1946.

———, 'The Rise of Provincial Jewry. The early history of the Jewish communities in the English countryside, 1740–1840', *Jewish Monthly*, 1950.

———, *Benjamin Disraeli, Earl of Beaconsfield*, New York, 1952.

———, *Essays and Portraits in Anglo-Jewish History*, Philadelphia, 1962.

———, *A History of the Jews in England*, third edn., 1964.

Roth, L., *Judaism. A Portrait*, 1960.

Rubens, A., *Anglo-Jewish Portraits*, 1935.

———, *A Jewish Iconography*, 1954.

———, *Portrait of Anglo-Jewry, 1656–1836*, 1959.

———, *A History of Jewish Costume*, 1967 edn., and new, enlarged and revised edn. 1973.

Sachar, H. M., *The Course of Modern Jewish History*, 1958.

Salbstein, M. C. N., *The Emancipation of the Jews in Britain: An Essay on the Preconditions*, 1977.

Schapiro, J. S., 'Thomas Carlyle, Prophet of Fascism', *The Journal of Modern History*, XVII, June 1945, no. 2, pp. 97–115.

Sheppard, F., *London, 1808–1870: The Infernal Wen*, 1971.

Shillman, B. J., *A Short History of the Jews in Ireland*, 1945.

Sombart, W., *The Jews and Modern Capitalism*, trans. M. Epstein, 1918.

Stanley, A. P., *The Life and Correspondence of Thomas Arnold. D.D.*, twelfth edn., 1881, in 2 vols.

———, *Essays chiefly on Questions of Church and State. From 1850 to 1870*, 1884 edn.

Steed, H. Wickham, *The Hapsburg Monarchy*, fourth edn., 1919.

Stein, S., *The Beginnings of Hebrew Studies at University College*, 1952.

———, *Some Ashkenazi Charities in London at the End of the Eighteenth and the Beginning of the Nineteenth Centuries*, 1964, reprinted from *Transactions of the Jewish Historical Society of England*, XX.

Stern, S., *The Court Jew. A Contribution to the History of the Period of Absolutism in Central Europe*, 1950.

Stevenson, T. H. C., 'The Fertility of Various Social Classes in England and Wales from the middle of the nineteenth century to 1911', *Journal of the Royal Statistical Society*, 83, May 1920, pp. 401–32.

Stewart, R., *The Politics of Protection: Lord Derby and the Protectionist Party, 1841–1852*, 1971.

Stone, L., *The Causes of the English Revolution, 1529–1642*, 1972.

Stromberg, R. N., *Religious Liberalism in Eighteenth-Century England*, 1954.

Sugar, P. F. and Lederer, I. J. (eds.), *Nationalism in Eastern Europe*, 1969.

Sykes, N., *Church and State in England since the Reformation*, 1929.

——, *Church and State in England in the Eighteenth Century*, 1931–33 Birkbeck lectures in ecclesiastical history, 1934.

——, *The English Religious Tradition. Sketches of its influence on church, state and society*, 1961.

Talmon, J. L., *Romanticism and Revolt, 1815–1848*, 1967.

Tawney, R. H., *Religion and the Rise of Capitalism*, 1936.

Tibawi, A. L., *British Interests in Palestine, 1800–1901*, 1961.

Toynbee, Arnold, *A Study of History*, 1934–54.

Vereté, M., *The Restoration of the Jews in English Protestant Thought, 1790–1840*, 1972.

Ward, J. T. (ed.), *Popular Movements, c. 1830–1850*, 1970.

Watts, M. R., *The Dissenters from the Reformation to the French Revolution*, 1978.

Weber, Max, *The Sociology of Religion*, first published 1922; introduction by Talcott Parsons; fourth and revised edition 1956; English trans. E. Fischoff from the fourth edition 1963; first published in Britain 1965.

——, *The Protestant Ethic and the Spirit of Capitalism*, 1930.

Weinreich, M., *"Yidishkayt" and Yiddish. On the Impact of Religion on Language in Ashkenazic Jewry*, New York, 1953.

Whately, E. J., *Life and Correspondence of Richard Whately. D. D. Late Archbishop of Dublin*, 2 vols., 1866.

Whibley, C., *Lord John Manners and His Friends*, 2 vols., 1925 edn.

Wilberforce, R. G., *The Life of the Rt. Rev. Samuel Wilberforce. D. D. . . . with selections from his diaries and correspondence*, 3 vols., 1881.

Williams, E., *Capitalism and Slavery*, first published 1943–44; 1964 edn.

Wistrich, R. S., *Revolutionary Jews from Marx to Trotsky*, 1976.

Wolf, L., *Sir Moses Montefiore. A Centennial Biography. With extracts from letters and journals*, 1884.

——, *Essays in Jewish History*, 1934.

Zangwill, I., *Dreamers of the Ghetto*, 1898.

Zimmels, H. J., *Ashkenazim and Sephardim. Their relations, differences, and problems as reflected in the Rabbinical Responsa, etc.*, 1958.

Index